Understanding the Social Dimension of Sustainability

Routledge Studies in Development and Society

17. Understanding the Social Dimension of Sustainability
Edited by Jesse Dillard,
Veronica Dujon, and Mary C. King

Understanding the Social Dimension of Sustainability

Edited by Jesse Dillard,
Veronica Dujon, and Mary C. King

Routledge
Taylor & Francis Group
New York   London

First published 2009
by Routledge
711 Third Avenue, New York, NY 10017

Simultaneously published in the UK
by Routledge
2 Park Square, Milton Park, Abingdon, Oxon OX14 4RN

Routledge is an imprint of the Taylor & Francis Group, an informa business

First issued in paperback 2012

Typeset in Sabon by IBT Global.

Library of Congress Cataloging in Publication Data
    Understanding the social dimension of sustainability / edited by Jesse Dillard, Veronica Dujon and Mary C. King.
        p. cm. — (Routledge studies in development and society ; 17)
    Includes index.
    1. Social capital (Sociology)   2. Environmental policy—Social aspects.   3. Sustainable development—Social aspects.   I. Dillard, Jesse F.   II. Dujon, Veronica.   III. King, Mary C.
    HM708.U535 2008
    304.2 — dc22
    2008004542

ISBN13: 978-0-415-96465-4 (hbk)
ISBN13: 978-0-415-53667-7 (pbk)
ISBN13: 978-0-203-89297-8 (ebk)

To Rebecca, Cathy, Alice and James
To Ismael Antonio and Alejandra Sofia
To Rosa Aiyana and Rio Valentine
With the hope that we've played some small part in making
the world a better place for them.

Contents

Figures

Tables

Acknowledgments

We have received a great deal of help and support as we worked on this project, for which we are most grateful. First, of course, our thanks go to the authors of each of the chapters, for their hard work on their own contributions and for their support of each other as members of the Portland State University Social Sustainability Colloquia series. Second, we would like to thank the other members of the Colloquia series, particularly Marion Sharp, our coordinator. Third, for support of the Colloquia series, and wider efforts to advance the thinking on the social aspect of sustainability, we thank Provost Roy Koch, David Ervin, and Jennifer Allen of Portland State University's Center for Sustainable Processes and Practices; the Portland State University Center for Professional Integrity and Accountability; and, especially, Mary Kay Tetreault, whose early support as Provost was critical. Finally, we thank our editors and reviewers at Routledge for their assistance in making this a better, more readable book.

1 Introduction

Jesse Dillard, Veronica Dujon,
and Mary C. King

At this moment, we humans are caught between the twin imperatives to raise the living standards of the world's poor, partially captured in the Millenium Development Goals, and to live within environmental limits, exemplified by the current concern over global warming. The challenge of sustainability is to limit the environmental harm created by human activity while reducing the deprivation and suffering resulting from poverty as well as excess.

Recent years have witnessed increasing international attention to sustainability issues and, in response, a substantial upsurge in business, governmental, and nongovernmental organization engagement in social responsibility initiatives, programs, and policies. What was often regarded as a largely peripheral issue has now become a mainstream concern for many in practical affairs and within the academy. The necessity of community involvement in environmental efforts reflects the dawning realization that social sustainability is the only bedrock on which meaningful environmental sustainability can be grounded. It is within the social sphere that people design institutions that not only facilitate relationally based needs, but also construct their understanding of the natural world.

This expansion and mainstreaming of civic, governmental, and managerial interest in social sustainability has been reflected in a growing number of undergraduate and postgraduate business and management courses, which now include elements of social sustainability in their curriculum, although the area has not yet crystallized to the point that it is so labeled. This process takes place as disciplines such as economics, sociology, public administration, and business begin to consider the interrelatedness of the social with the environmental. Also, the traditional environmental disciplines such as engineering, applied sciences, and agriculture are beginning to recognize the relevance of the social aspect of sustainability.

One important aspect of social sustainability is the manner in which governments, organizations, and citizens address and discharge duties of accountability to a range of stakeholders regarding the social and environmental impact of individuals and institutions. In line with the growing interest in social sustainability in general, there has been a substantial increase in research, teaching, and practitioner engagement with related issues and mechanisms.

Sustainability is often thought of as comprised of three overlapping, mutually dependent goals: (a) to live in a way that is environmentally sustainable or viable over the long term; (b) to live in a way that is economically sustainable, maintaining living standards over the long-term; and (c) to live in a way that is socially sustainable, now and in the future.

Many might argue that economic life should properly be thought of as an element of social sustainability because the economy is clearly a social construction rather than a natural phenomenon such as the weather. Indeed, the perhaps exaggerated place of economic concerns—reflected in its customary distinction from other social issues in this conception of sustainability—may be part of the challenge faced by advocates of greater sustainability. Further, the overemphasis on the economic leads to a too-exclusive focus on the production and consumption of marketed goods and services. The role of households, communities, and the public sector in providing supports that are difficult to value in economic terms are neglected, although critical to the accomplishment of well-being and sustainability.

As of today, concerns with environmental and economic sustainability have eclipsed efforts to understand the social aspects of sustainability. As noted by several of the authors of chapters in this volume, thinking on the social aspect of sustainability has been relatively neglected and is by far the least developed. Yet an increasing number of people are attempting to integrate social concerns into their work on sustainability, both theoretically and in practice. This anthology provides guidance for a developing field of thought from a variety of perspectives.

At present, consensus does not exist even on a definition of *social sustainability*. Polese and Stren (2000), writing up the findings of a UNESCO project on the "social sustainability of cities," identify social sustainability as "policies and institutions that have the overall effect of integrating diverse groups and cultural practices in a just and equitable fashion" (p. 229).

Many analysts have followed Robert Putnam (2000) in an exploration of "social capital," asserted by the World Bank (2007) among others, to consist of "the norms and networks that enable collective action." Researchers working in this vein have understood social capital to result from participation in civic institutions. Creation of the term *social capital* is an attempt to use the analogy of capital to understand the role of social institutions and processes in the economy, much as environmental economists have used the term *natural capital* to describe natural resources and amenities. Presumably social sustainability would require that social capital be maintained at sustainable levels for future generations, perhaps requiring social support of effective civic institutions to this end.

Most business sustainability efforts appear to construe social sustainability as charity, performed as an act of public relations. These are "policies that encourage community involvement, volunteering, [and] development of local communities" (Taylor, 2003). According to a recent PricewaterhouseCoopers (2002) survey of large U.S. businesses, three quarters of the firms that responded to the survey were implementing some sustainable business practices, although relatively few are pursuing the social leg of the "triple bottom line"—corporate language for meeting financial, environmental, and social objectives as an organization. Where businesses are attending to the social aspect of sustainability, they are interpreting it as corporate philanthropy and sometimes as policies to help employees achieve work/family balance or to avoid burnout. Businesses do not seem to be weighing these projects in balance with initiatives generated elsewhere in the firm that impact social health, such as corporate support for tax-cutting measures that reduce funding for local schools or policies that limit part-time work or parental leave.

In urban planning circles, the tripartite understanding of sustainability is sometimes referred to as the three Es: environment, economy, and equity. Social sustainability is conceived of as equity, without much thought as to what that might require or whether equity alone is sufficient for social sustainability.

A more thought-out and satisfactory definition of social sustainability is provided by Harris and Goodwin (2001): "a socially sustainable system must achieve fairness in distribution and opportunity, adequate provision of social services, including health and education, gender equity, and political accountability and participation" (p. xxix).

Although more solid, this definition still misses the social process required to achieve economic and environmental sustainability that concern many. For instance, initiatives taken by the U.S. Forest Service under the leadership of one of our chapter authors, Gary Larsen, now include community involvement with the understanding that community engagement is necessary for successful implementation of environmental policies. Environmental economists have focused substantial attention on the issue of property rights, with the idea that clear ownership facilitates better environmental management.

However, social institutions conducive to better environmental outcomes may have adverse social consequences. This concern in highlighted in Randall Bluffstone's chapter (Chapter 7), which examines the impact of particular systems of forest property rights on child labor in Bolivia. Often these social considerations are overlooked, as in the case of ecologists pointing out the ecological advantages of collective management of group resources without noting that the group governance is not democratic, but empowers only a small portion of the community (e.g., Alcorn & Toledo, 1998).

Consequently, several contributors to this volume use a working definition of the social aspect of sustainability developed over time in our workshops and graduate seminars:

that social aspect of sustainability should be understood as both

(a) the processes that generate social health and well-being now and in the future, and
(b) those social institutions that facilitate environmental and economic sustainability now and for the future.

The processes are both a means to, and an end of, social sustainability. Indeed, for the social aspect of sustainability in particular, processes may often be more important than outcomes. For instance, high rates of literacy achieved by a citizenry engaged in a democratic planning process, as in Kerala, India, may be far more socially sustainable than even higher rates of literacy accomplished in an authoritarian fashion (Thomas Isaac & Franke, 2002).

However, an adequate working definition of the social aspect of sustainability represents only the first step in developing an understanding of the concept. A number of faculty and graduate students at Portland State University have been working together over the last few years on the Social Sustainability Project of the Center for Professional Integrity and Accountability in an attempt to gain an analytical grasp of the social aspect of sustainability. One of the activities in which we engaged was an ongoing, interdisciplinary seminar series. This volume is largely the result of that seminar series.

As demonstrated by the following chapters, we employ a multidisciplinary perspective to explore a diverse range of topics along different geographical scales within varying locations to better understand the social aspect of sustainability. Rather than grapple with one particular facet of the social aspect of sustainability, we have chosen to each pursue that angle for which our expertise best suits us. Our hope is to provide spots of illumination in the large, multidimensional arena of social sustainability to serve as building blocks for further efforts.

Several general questions guided our investigations:

- How can the social aspect of sustainability be most usefully identified to facilitate measurement or movement toward progress?
- Is there any value to the codification of the social aspect of sustainability whether in legislation, business codes, or otherwise? If there is, how and at what level should they be codified?
- In which spheres of activity is the voluntary pursuit of social sustainability effective and in which spheres are regulation and enforcement more effective and appropriate? What are the dynamics between voluntary and mandated actions?

- What are the appropriate roles of small and large businesses, states and international organizations, and civil society and nongovernmental organizations in the pursuit of social sustainability?
- Is social sustainability compatible with a market-driven economy as we know it, or do markets require greater social accountability via state intervention in the economy?
- What is the role of democracy in the pursuit of social sustainability?
- What are the connections between the pursuit of social sustainability at the local and global levels, and how do these affect the success of outcomes at either level?
- Can and should social sustainability be accomplished in developing nations, or is it a "luxury" of greater affluence? Might Third World nations accomplish sustainability more easily than the First World by applying lessons for the history of the wealthy nations without the vast numbers already accustomed to mass consumption?

We do not claim to have answered all of these questions or even to have directly taken on each of them. A great deal remains to be done. Following from our working definition specified earlier, we explore the meaning and application of the social aspect of sustainability from a number of angles and perspectives, including theoretical development, empirical measurement issues, and policy applications in both First and Third Worlds. The discussion ranges from macro-issues, such as the role for democracy in the international governance and the ability of Third World nations to balance an interest in sustainability with an imperative to grow, to micro-studies, such as the impact of changing property rights regimes in the Andes and the practices of small business owners anxious to operate as sustainably as possible.

The contributions of each of the chapters are reviewed in the next section.

PART I: OVERVIEWS OF THE FIELD

Part I comprises three chapters that view the field broadly at a high level of abstraction. It is in this section that we most directly confront questions of our theoretical understanding of the concept of the social aspect of sustainability, the importance of democracy, the necessity of "thinking globally," and actionable measures for social sustainability.

In Chapter 2, "Emergent Principles of Social Sustainability," Kristen Magis and Craig Shinn review the literature on the social aspect of sustainability to identify and explore what they find are the four emergent principles of social sustainability: human well-being, equality, democratic government, and democratic society. Three traditional perspectives—

human-oriented development, sustainability, and community well-being—are reviewed and synthesized, resulting in the identification and substantiation of the four principles of social sustainability. The authors argue that these four principles of social sustainability create a self-reinforcing *virtuous* cycle that facilitates progress toward environmental sustainability, provides guidelines for economic policies, and affords resilience to the requisite institutional framework.

In Chapter 3, "An Inquiry into the Theoretical Basis of Sustainability: Ten Propositions," Gary L. Larsen builds on sociological theory, finding a Habermasian grounded theoretical context particularly useful. He offers ten propositions articulating the dimensions of sustainable development and providing a basis for developing a prototypal general theory of sustainability. Sustainability and sustainable development are fundamentally about people, the choices they make, associated consequences, and the human learning that takes place. Larsen develops a typology of sustainability discourses, explores basic constructs in the human quest for sustainability, and suggests that sustainability is both a human cognitive structure and a mediating structure located in civil society.

A case is made to expand our understanding of the economics of sustainability in Chapter 4, "An Antidote to a Partial Economics of Sustainability" by Mary C. King. The author argues that the present conception of the economics of sustainability—currently limited to a focus on private-sector, market interactions—appears particularly inadequate when considering the social aspect of sustainability. Several powerful developments in economic thinking over the last 30 years need to be incorporated into economists' thinking about sustainability, in development economics, in feminist economics, and in public-sector economics. King proposes measures for the social aspect of sustainability to underpin future research efforts geared toward developing a more holistic and useful economics of sustainability.

PART II: INTERNATIONAL PERSPECTIVES

Part II is comprised of three chapters that consider social sustainability from an international perspective. Authors in this section speak to the questions of the roles of different governmental entities, nonprofit organizations, and civil society, as well as the possibility of leadership on issues of social sustainability from the developing world and the need for a sophisticated understanding of the role of particular institutions in mediating the social impact of market dynamics.

Kristen Magis explores the nature and impact of a global (international) civil society in Chapter 5, "Global Civil Society: Architect and Agent of International Democracy and Sustainability," considering the influences of international civil society on international government organizations and the relationship between social capital and social sustainability. Civil society, democracy, and sustainability are interrelated and complementary, and, according to Magis, none can be sustained without the others. Global civil society is a powerful force for norms related to democracy and sustainability. It has been a primary architect and champion of virtually all international regimes related to human and environmental protection and has promoted democratic governance at all levels. However, because there is no formal or institutional venue that protects its voice and parlays its intent into international governance, global civil society's advocacy efforts will continue to be hindered by hostile and unreceptive political and economic forces that are accorded legal legitimacy and guaranteed access to international policymaking venues. Magis calls for global civil society to be accorded a legally legitimated voice in international governance.

In Chapter 6, "In the Absence of Affluence: The Struggle for Social Sustainability in the Third World," Veronica Dujon discusses perspectives on sustainability efforts in the Third World, with an emphasis on the social aspect of sustainability. Dujon states that within the context of increasing ecological scarcity, neoliberal market-oriented economic systems have failed to foster sustainable, healthy, and productive societies for the majority of people in the contexts of either affluence or deprivation. Key cases, including Brazil, Bolivia, Venezuela, Ecuador, and Mexico, are considered. She provides convincing evidence that people living in economically and politically oppressive conditions have been able to advance more socially sustainable societies and economies despite the odds against them. The urgency and motivation for citizens to pursue structural economic change are driven by different social, material, and political conditions in First and Third World countries. In situations where people are most deprived, both economically and politically, they may have a clearer grasp of their basic needs for social reproduction and be most highly motivated to effect change. The ability to do so successfully is enhanced by the vigor of democratic civil society and its ability to influence the state. The author points to the recent rise of social movements in Latin America that challenge neoliberal market policies, such as the privatization of basic needs such as water, health care, and education, to illustrate the key role of a civil society that incorporates both the environmental and economic consciousness of a new era in the struggle for social sustainability. In some of the most successful cases, grassroots associations are engaged in developing local solutions and making social demands on the state to hold it accountable, illustrating a viable alternative to the dominant neoliberal prescriptions for development.

An environmental economist, Randall Bluffstone examines the social impact of environmentally driven policy changes in Chapter 7, "Child

Labor and Improved Common Forest Management in Bolivia." He assesses the social and environmental impacts of different community property rights regimes in rural Bolivia, with a particular focus on the impact of different structures for the use of child labor in peasant households. Environmental economists are interested in the ways in which the incentives embedded in different structures of property rights in communal assets such as forests affect environmental outcomes. Using household data collected in the Bolivian Altiplano, Bluffstone shows that policymakers need to be attentive as well to the way in which economic incentives are changed that may result in the increasing use of child labor, reducing children's ability to attend school.

PART III: THE ROLE OF BUSINESS

Part III considers the measurement and reporting issues that have evolved with respect to the social aspects of sustainability as they relate to business enterprises operating within First World economies. The four chapters that comprise this section illustrate the struggle that society and business organizations face as the economic sector is being called on to be accountable for the social aspects of sustainability. It is here that chapter authors investigate the appropriate role of businesses in advancing the social aspect of sustainability, the limits of voluntary action, and the potential interaction among voluntary efforts, business codes, and regulation.

Chapter 8, "Social Sustainability: An Organizational-Level Analysis," by Jan Bebbington and Jesse Dillard explores the utility of accounting and accountability concepts for social sustainability and analyzes current corporate reporting thereon. Four factors contribute to the relative neglect of the social aspects of sustainability. First, given the dominant economic aims, most commonly expressed as maximizing shareholder wealth, business organizations are not always cognizant of the wide-ranging social impact of their behavior; as a result, social impacts have not always been given visibility. Second, social sustainability has its modern origins in environmental sustainability issues. Thus, social issues have sometimes been seen to be of secondary importance or as relating solely to developing world issues, such as access to water, education, and health care. Third, aspects of social sustainability (e.g., social cohesion, flourishing communities, or the maintenance of human rights) are often seen to be the responsibility of the state and/or civil society, rather than business. Finally, social sustainability appears to present different and more severe challenges in specification, understanding, and communication than environmental sustainability because there is no widely accepted scientific basis for analysis, unlike the ability to debate population ecology, acceptable levels of toxicity, or acceptable concentrations of greenhouse gases in the atmosphere. Nor is there a common unit of measure, such as monetary units, with the economic dimension of sustainability. A two-dimensional analysis of social sustainability is undertaken, concluding that awareness of the implications of organizational actions is a necessary, but not sufficient, condition for change. Institutional change also is required, and possibilities for such change are considered.

Chapter 9, "Social Sustainability: One Company's Story," by Jesse Dillard and David Layzell describes how a large, progressive, multinational corporation (Intel, a Fortune 100 firm) operationalizes and reports on the social aspects of sustainability, and why it does so. First, the authors consider how the company defines social sustainability and analyze the conceptual frames used when referring to related constructs, practices, and procedures. The term *social sustainability* is not explicitly used, but *social responsibility* and *sustainability* are. The two phrases generally coalesce around the term *corporate social responsibility*. The meaning and operationalization of these terms are followed through their application in the areas of governance, ethics, compliance, risks, and controls. In this way, the company's emergent programs and procedures associated with social sustainability are identified, and the underlying motivations are considered. Four sources of motivation for socially related action are identified. The authors consider the implications that follow from the descriptive analysis of Intel for prescriptive insights helpful in moving the social sustainability agenda forward.

Realizing that small business owners interested in sustainability appeared to be operating with relatively high social standards, Kathryn Thomsen and Mary C. King interviewed several for Chapter 10, "Working out Social Sustainability on the Ground." Given the lack of attention accorded to the social aspect of sustainability, practitioners have been left to their own devices in its specification and implementation. The authors find that, although each of the organizations set standards for labor practices and community engagement substantially higher than the conventional business model, they are not working with a clear idea of social sustainability, nor of how social goals connect with progress toward environmental sustainability. Nevertheless, several of their practices not only fit within our working definition of the social aspect of sustainability, but are perceived by the business owners as making good business sense. An analysis and synthesis of their practices may provide the building blocks of a potential code for the social aspect of sustainability, similar to the guidelines found in green building standards for environmental sustainability.

In Chapter 11 "Triple Bottom Line: A Business Metaphor for a Social Construct," Darrell Brown, Jesse Dillard, and Scott Marshall describe what currently constitutes triple bottom line reporting, evaluates it application, and propose an alternative perspective. The *triple bottom line* is a popular term in the corporate responsibility world. Businesses use triple bottom line reporting to convey an image of concern and sensitivity to economic, environmental, and social sustainability. The authors trace the development of the triple bottom line concept and draw analogies with the development of financial accounting measures and their use. Then the authors discuss the fundamental differences among the three components of the triple bottom line, asking whether a common metaphor for understanding these components is feasible. Alternative frameworks are considered that might yield more meaningful representations of a business organization's contributions, positive and negative, to social sustainability.

PART IV: LOCAL APPLICATIONS

Part IV contains three chapters and describes recent local implementations of the social aspect of sustainability. The importance of place, community connections, and activated citizenship within an urban context are discussed in these chapters as critical elements in promoting social sustainability across diverse groups of people who find themselves sharing limited space and resources and are motivated to work on more socially healthy ways of doing so. The learning that takes place as they pursue these objectives enhances the potential for further progress

Leslie McBride considers the components of community food systems and their potential as indicators of social sustainability in Chapter 12, "Exploring Common Ground: Community Food Systems and Social Sustainability." The author focuses on three questions: Can a community's food system serve as an indicator of social sustainability for that region? Are there initiatives and programs within the community food system movement that contribute in essential ways to social sustainability? If so, and if we examine the nature of their contributions, will we increase our understanding about how social sustainability is developed and strengthened? Three program innovations are considered in terms of their relationship to social sustainability: farmers markets, community gardens, and food policy councils. The chapter's ending discussion concludes that community food systems impact social sustainability indicators, although some more than others, and that these indicators provide the best opportunity for exploring common ground.

In Chapter 13, "Social Capital and Community: University Partnerships," W. Barry Messer and Kevin Kecskes examine the possibilities for higher education in promoting social sustainability through community–university partnerships, considering necessary infrastructure as well as the means for specifying and measuring the effects of such partnerships. The authors begin by posing this question: How do we operationalize social sustainability to inform community development policy? Messer and Kecskes offer social sustainability as a valuable construct for shaping community-enhancing programs in higher education institutions. The authors map social sustainability principles onto actionable social capital constructs.

An agenda is proposed for framing social sustainability in terms of community–university partnerships, focusing on the innovative programs undertaken at Portland State University. The Community Watershed Stewardship Program is presented as an "actionable" example of how the learning and community engagement can be joined in formulating and implementing an active and successful social sustainability agenda. The diverse outcomes from this project illustrate the benefits that can accrue to both the university and the community through implementation of this agenda, and the mechanisms employed represent identifiable dimensions along which both "hard" (resource utilization, cost-effectiveness, capacity utilization and expansion) and "soft" (voluntarism, diversity, aesthetic appeal) community outcomes can be specified and monitored. Well-designed and effectively delivered community–university partnerships can facilitate social sustainability in local and regional communities, can help address entrenched public issues, and can provide direction for university–community initiatives.

In Chapter 14, "Advancing Social Sustainability: An Intervention Approach," Jan C. Semenza reports how a specific community development project promoted social sustainability within an urban Portland neighborhood. The principles on which the project was based include honoring the community as the expert, creating an accessible and inclusive participatory process, and integrating local community values, history, and geography. The chapter describes and empirically assesses the effect of an intersection repair project undertaken and carried out by a neighborhood group. The project not only improved the physical appearance of the community, but also actively engaged the residents in a process of creating, developing, permitting, and constructing interactive urban features. In the process, localized, bridging, and linking social capital were created and developed. Through collaboration and cooperation between city official and residents, the author claims that local-level democratic process can be revived and social transformation brought about. By employing quantitative and qualitative methodologies, both the positive and negative implications and outcomes of the project are specified and assessed.

PART V: INTEGRATION AND CONCLUSION

In Part V, we provide an overview of the ideas presented, relate them to each other and our overarching questions, and project future directions for research and application in the social aspects of sustainability. To adequately address social sustainability requires a significant interdisciplinary effort that includes expertise from the varied fields of social science. The key question is the extent to which a market-driven economy is compatible with the pursuit of social sustainability and is reflected in the debate concerning the role of state intervention in compliance with socially responsible behavior. Undergirding this debate is the emergence from a democratic civil society of the rights and responsibilities of societal actors and how they are to be articulated, implemented, and enforced. The work reported herein emphasizes the iterative process in understanding and defining sustainability and the role of people and social institutions in making progress toward achieving it.

REFERENCES

Alcorn, Janis B., and Victor M. Toledo. 1998. "Resilient Resource Management in Mexico's Forest Ecosystems: The Contribution of Property Rights." In *Linking Social and Ecological Systems: Management Practices and Social Mechanisms for Building Resilience*, edited by Fikret Berkes and Carl Folke. Cambridge, UK: Cambridge University Press.

Harris, Jonathan M., and Neva R. Goodwin. 2001. "Volume Introduction." In *A Survey of Sustainable Development: Social and Economic Dimensions*, edited by Jonathan M. Harris, Timothy A. Wise, Kevin P. Gallagher, and Neva R. Goodwin. Washington, DC: Island Press.

Polese, Mario, and Richard Stren. 2000. *The Social Sustainability of Cities: Diversity and the Management of Change*. Toronto: University of Toronto Press.

PricewaterhouseCoopers LLP. 2002. *2002 Social Sustainability Survey Report*. Available at http://www.pwcglobal.com/fas/pdfs/sustainability%20survey%20 report.pdf

Putnam, Robert D. 2000. *Bowling Alone: The Collapse and Revival of American Community*. New York: Simon & Schuster.

Taylor, Sully. 2003, Feb. 10. "The Human Resource Side of Sustainability." Presentation at Portland State University.

Thomas Isaac, T. M., and Richard W. Franke. 2002. *Local Democracy and Development: The Kerala People's Campaign for Decentralized Planning*. Lanham, MD: Rowman & Littlefield.

World Bank. 2007. *Program on Social Capital*. Accessed on October 9, 2007, from http://www1.worldbank.org/prem/poverty/scapital/home.htm.

Part I
Overviews of the Field

2 Emergent Principles of Social Sustainability

Kristen Magis and Craig Shinn

Social sustainability gained formal and international repute following the World Commission on Environment and Development (WCED) report to the United Nations (UN), which stipulated that sustainable development required concerted attention to social, ecological, and economic conditions (World Commission on Environment and Development , 1987). Social sustainability is the least developed of the three constructs and often is posited in relation to ecological or economic sustainability (Stephen McKenzie, 2004).

Ecologically focused renditions of sustainability typically posit social sustainability in relation to the environment, focusing primarily on society's threat to natural resources and its ecological stewardship function (Wollenberg and Colfer, 1997; Beckley, 2000; Constanza, Low, Ostrom, and Wilson, 2001). For example, Fikret Berkes and Carl Folke (1998) explore social mechanisms and management practices utilized to deal with local ecosystems. From the vast array of components within the social system, only those relevant to the environment are elicited (e.g., property rights, land and resource tenure, and environmental knowledge and ethics).

Economic renditions of sustainability embed society within the construct of economics. In this perspective, people are equated with input into the economy. For example, social capital, an essential constituent of social sustainability, is accorded import because it reduces economic transaction costs (Elkington, 1998; Fukuyama, 1995). Likewise, meeting basic human needs is assigned value because it ensures a healthy, well-fed, and skilled labor force, which is essential for the production of goods and services (World Bank, 1980). Although important, studies subordinating social systems to economics or the environment fail to delve into the factors that sustain a community of people.

Society must be sustained in its own right. Mahbub ul Haq (1999) asserts that the pursuit of human development dates to antiquity. Aristotle (384–322 B.C.) (1996) stipulated that political institutions be judged by their contribution to people's ability to lead flourishing lives. Immanuel Kant (1724–1804) (2002) asserted, "So act as to treat humanity, whether in their own person or in that of any other, in every case as an end withal, never as means only" (p. 13). The necessity of maintaining society confers social sustainability with intrinsic value. Social sustainability also is critical from a sustainability perspective. Sustainability is premised on systems theory, stipulating that society, the environment, and the economy are interrelated constituents of a larger system. The system can only remain viable to the extent that each of the constituents functions properly (Harris, 2000). To adequately identify and employ the contributions of social sustainability, it needs to be understood as a phenomenon distinct from, albeit interrelated with, ecological and economic sustainability.

Although the construct of social sustainability is in formative stages within the sustainability dialogue, it is informed by a rich and mature tradition of research on social well-being. Robert Prescott-Allen (2001) describes social well-being as the fulfillment of basic needs and the exercise of political, economic, and social freedoms. Three traditions of research and practice add definition to the concept of social well-being and, hence, social sustainability: Human-Centered Development, Sustainability, and Community Well-Being.

Although the traditions are unique, they arise from the same foundation, have developed over the same time period, and have grown in strikingly similar directions. From these traditions, four universal principles emerge: human well-being, equity, democratic government, and democratic civil society. The emergence and precedence of the four principles across these traditions creates the basis for the primary premise of this chapter: Human well-being, equity, democratic government, and democratic civil society are central constituents of social sustainability.

The purpose of this chapter is to illustrate the primacy of the four principles in each of the traditions. The chapter opens with an overview of the critique of growth-oriented development, the practice of which galvanized significant opposition and motivated the conception of two alternative paradigms. The alternative paradigms—Human-Centered Development and Sustainability—are then introduced. The chapter then turns to a review of social principles paramount in the traditions of Human-Centered Development, Sustainability and Community Well-Being. These social principles were designed to define and facilitate social well-being and, as such, provide a rich foundation for the construct of social sustainability. The chapter concludes with the explication of these four emergent themes and the assertion that they are principle constituents of social sustainability.

REORIENTING DEVELOPMENT

The goals of economic growth and income expansion have long been central to development policy. Critiques of this growth paradigm, however, have emerged from multiple realms. The critiques have to do with the growth model and its primary indicator of success, the Gross Domestic Product (GDP).

GROWTH-ORIENTED DEVELOPMENT

Critiques of the growth model stress that growth is not synonymous with development. Herman Daly (1996) differentiates growth from development, asserting that growth is a quantitative increase, whereas development is a qualitative change. Growth increases size via assimilation of resources, whereas development transitions to a better state. Karl Polanyi's (2001) study of British economic history provides a case in point. Polanyi documented the devastating effects of market liberalization and the elimination of a basic system of social security. The combined force of these two interventions undermined values important to society's well-being (e.g., civic participation, reciprocity, and redistribution) and led to the decline of civil society.

In contemporary society, the institution of the growth model has resulted in extremely disparate development. Wealth is expanding for an extremely small portion of the world's people, causing excess and inequitable consumption and deterioration of democratic institutions (United Nations Development Programme, 2002). Meanwhile, a rising number of people are becoming permanently superfluous to the world's economy, adding to the persistently high numbers of extremely poor and malnourished people. The result of these twin dynamics is extreme wealth accompanied by widespread and abject poverty (Chakravarty, 1991; Galbraith, 1998; Chomsky, 1999; Douthwaite, 1999; Harris, 2000; Wise, 2001; International Forum on Globalization, 2002).

This extreme inequity " . . . distorts the allocation of economic resources, excludes all but the very rich from meaningful democratic participation, undermines institutional legitimacy and creates social instability" (International Forum on Globalization, 2002, p. 75). This inequity and its associated maladies buttress Haq's (1999) declaration that the use of income is as important as its generation. Wealth distribution, he states, is not handled equitably by the marketplace. Rather, it needs to be a political determination made by people through democratic governance.

Two critiques present serious challenges to the growth model's indicator of success, GDP. The first criticism is that GDP is a partial and inaccurate measure of economic well-being. GDP is a gross tally of economic transactions, all of which are presumed to add to well-being. It does not discriminate between transactions that result in social or environmental *bads*, and those that contribute to social or economic well-being, *goods*. Tyler Norris Associates (1997) provide a case in point, explaining that urban sprawl, pollution, and decimated inner cities exist concurrently with job growth, new housing, and road improvements. The GDP obfuscates these societal bads and counts them as contributions, creating the fallacious impression of a stronger economy and improved well-being (Organisation for Economic Cooperation and Development, 2001; Redefining Progress, nd).

A second criticism of GDP concerns its relation to human well-being. Human well-being is multidimensional, with economic well-being and its associated measure, GDP, constituting just one dimension (Harris, 2000; Organisation for Economic Cooperation and Development, 2001). Furthermore, growth in GDP is only weakly correlated to improvements in basic needs and, hence, human well-being (Morawetz, 1977; Harris, 2000). Significant and mounting data corroborate these claims.

The Index of Social Health, a standard measure of inequality, measures the gap between the rich and the poor in the United States (Miringoff and Miringoff, 1999). From 1970–1996, the inequality gap increased by 19%. Although the GDP grew by 158%, social health worsened by 38%. Growth, the Miringoffs concluded, is not related to social health in the United States. World Bank (2000) data illustrate that, although the total world income increased by 2.5% annually in the 1990s, the number of people in poverty rose by 100 million. United Nations Development Programme (2002) data reveal that the annual income of 1% of the world's people equals that of the poorest 57%.

Data such as these reinforced a widespread belief that the GDP fails to illustrate well-being, further prompting the development of more accurate measures, such as the Genuine Progress Indicator (Atkinson, et al., 1997; Venetoulis and Cobb, 2004). Moreover, the data substantiated the claim that the means—growth—is being confused with the ends—human development (van Dieren, 1995; Haq, 1999). The appropriate end is human development, not growth.

Even as the discussion of Human-Centered Development unfolded, concern over environmental destruction resulting from unbridled growth and extreme poverty gained worldwide precedence. The mounting alarm prompted the UN to appoint the World Commission on Environment and Development (WCED) to propose strategies to improve human well-being without threatening the global environment (Brundtland,1991). The WCED concluded that ecological degradation could not be halted without addressing its root causes, namely, poverty, uneven development, and population growth. The WCED further legitimized sustainable development as an organizing principle for worldwide development (World Commission on Environment and Development, 1987). Organisation for Economic Cooperation and Development (2001) characterizes sustainable development as quality economic growth and improvement of human well-being. The WCED offered recommendations that set in motion multilevel endeavors—international, national, and local—to understand and move toward sustainable development.

RECALIBRATING THE COMPASS

Sustainability does not dictate the end of human progress. However, it does require rejection of the myth that equates growth with human progress

(Korten, 1992). This paradigmatic change compels fundamental transformations. It requires refocusing the goal of development, revalidating the role of governance, restructuring the development process, and redefining indicators of success.

First, the goal of development needs to be rearticulated. Aristotle argued, "wealth is evidently not the good we are seeking, for it is merely useful and for the sake of something else" (Haq, 1999, p. 13). That something else, asserts Haq, is the betterment of people's lives. Development must first be reoriented toward human development. Principle 1 of the 1992 Rio Declaration on Environment and Development[1] places people directly at the center of sustainable development. Moreover, in the pursuit of human development, the environment must be protected and sustained (Harris, 2000).

Second, governance needs to be revalidated. A primary tenet of the growth-oriented development model is the elimination of government influence on the market (Williamson, 1994). Operationalizing this principle led to what Haq (1999) calls a "garage sale of public enterprises" (p. 140) and the inevitable weakening of government's ability to protect social and environmental goals (Streeten, 2001). Democratic governance, however, is required to direct economic development, protect society from the vagaries of the international market, enforce accountability, and ensure that growth is sustainable and equitable (Polese and Stren, 2000; Annan, in United Nations Development Programme, 2002; International Forum on Globalization , 2002; Stiglitz, 2002).

Third, development needs to be restructured to include human-centered processes and eliminate destructive processes. Human-centered development processes will sustain: (a) basic human needs such as nutrition and shelter (Streeten, Burki, Haq, Hicks, and Stewart, 1981); (b) human freedoms including political rights, economic facilities, social opportunities, transparency guarantees, and protective security (Sen, 1999); and (c) human development, which expands social, economic, cultural, and political choices and leads to equity, sustainability, productivity, and empowerment (Haq, 1999). Human-centered development also promotes "pro-poor growth strategies," simultaneously facilitating sustainable growth and poverty reduction (Stiglitz, 2002). Destructive processes that need be eliminated include: (a) the unsustainable perpetuation of inequitable lifestyles (Harris, 2000), (b) consumption patterns that exploit and appropriate resources critically needed by those in poverty and that severely tax the global ecosystem (Agenda 21, 7.1; Daily and Ehrlich, 1996), and (c) development that compromises the integrity of critically important ecosystems (Daly, 1996; Harris, 2000).

Finally, indicators of success need to be redefined to focus on Human-Centered Development and sustainability. Generating desired future visions and goals is a critical, but insufficient, step toward actualizing those visions. Decisions and actions need to be aligned with the vision. Social indicators, statistics designed to measure and provide information on specified system conditions, need to be utilized to highlight the effects of the decisions and actions in relation to the vision of Human-Centered Development and sustainability. The information they provide then needs to be utilized to inform policy analysis and align decision making more closely with the vision (Machlis and Force, 1997; Bossel, 1999; Miringoff and Miringoff, 1999; Wright, Alward, Hoekstra, Tegler, and Turner, 2002; Pepperdine, 2005).

The consequences of growth-oriented development reoriented the world toward alternative goals—Human-Centered Development and sustainability—which accord social and environmental systems equal import to economic systems. Endeavors to raise the import of social and environmental well-being, and subsequent efforts to operationalize them, have given definition to social sustainability. Three such traditions are explored herein—Human-Centered Development, Sustainability, and Community Well-Being. Four primary principles of social well-being—human well-being, equity, democratic government, and democratic civil society—emerge in each of the traditions. These principles are advanced herein as central constituents of social sustainability.

WELLSPRING OF SOCIAL SUSTAINABILITY

In this section, an overview of the three traditions is provided, and then characteristics central to each are described. Finally, the relation of the characteristics to the four primary principles of social well-being is presented. Figure 2.1 portrays the characteristics from each of the traditions as they relate to the four principles.

HUMAN-CENTERED DEVELOPMENT

Human-Centered Development is defined by three primary constructs—the Basic Needs Approach, the Human Development Approach, and the Freedoms Approach.

Basic Needs

The first endeavor to reorient development toward human well-being is the Basic Needs Approach (Streeten et al., 1981), which designates the world's poor as the primary beneficiaries of development. People's full physical, mental, and social development is accorded import. Although nonmaterial needs such as self-determination, self-reliance, security, participation in decision making, national and cultural identity, sense of purpose in life, and work are considered important, the focus of the Basic Needs Approach is on fulfillment of basic physiological needs: nutrition, water, shelter, and sanitation. These minimum sustenance requirements are justified on

	Human-Centered Development			Sustainability		Community Well-Being 1990
	Basic Needs 1976	**Human Development** 1990	**Freedom** 1999	**Agenda 21 Rio Declaration Forests Principles** 1992	**Montreal Process LUCID** 1998 **Mt. Hood** 1998	
Human Well-Being	Objective 1: Basic Sustenance - Nutrition; Education; Health; Sanitation; Water Supply; Housing	Productivity Empowerment	Protective Security Social Opportunities	A21 – Sec. I: Social & Economic Dimensions; Rio – Healthy, Productive Life; Eradicate Poverty; Forest – Social, Economic, Ecological, Cultural & Spiritual Needs	MP – C6: Cultural & Spiritual Needs & Values; Employment & Community Needs; LUCID – Institutional & Community Capacity; Social & Cultural Values; Mt. Hood - Community Livability	Livable Communities - education and health care; access to public goods and services; employment; transportation; housing
Equity	Equitable Economic Opportunity	Economic Equity Political Equity	Economic Opportunities	A21 – Sec. I: Social & Economic Dimensions; Rio – Reduce Living Standard Disparities	LUCID – Social Equity; Social & Cultural Values; Mt. Hood - Social & Cultural Values	Equal Access Social Justice
Democratic Government	Objective 2: Social Infrastructure Producer, Rule of Law, Financer	Political Freedom	Transparency Guarantees Civil Rights Political Freedom	A21 - Sec. IV: Governance, Rule of Law; Rio – Environmental Laws; Forests – Policy Inclusive and Protective of People	MP – C7: Institutional Framework; LUCID – Institutional Capacity; Collaborative Stewardship; Mt. Hood – Institutional Adequacy	Community Inclusion in Public Policy; Democratic, Efficient & Equitable; Complement & Facilitate Communities
Democratic Civil Society	Objective 3: Democratic Participation Self Determination, Participation National and Cultural Identity	Empowerment Political Freedom	Civil Rights Political Freedoms	A21 - Sec. III: Democratic Participation; Rio - Citizen Participation; Indigenous, Women, Youth; Forests- Wide Participation	MP – C7: Public Participation; LUCID – Community Capacity; Collaborative Stewardship; Mt. Hood - Collaborative Stewardship; Community Resilience	Informed Public Dialogue & Decision-Making Collaboration; Social Integration and Inclusion

Figure 2.1 Emergent principles of social sustainability.

instrumental grounds—that is, they are requirements for a minimally acceptable level of well-being, and they are basic human rights (Paul Streeten & Burki, 1978; Atkinson et al., 1997). The World Commission on Environment and Development (1987) perceived fulfillment of basic needs as so important that it designated poverty alleviation as one of the two prime objectives of sustainable development.

Streeten et al. (1981) outlined the primary objectives of the Basic Needs Approach as: (a) remunerative livelihoods that accord people a primary claim on the fruits of their labor, as well as income adequate to purchase basic sustenance; (b) a social infrastructure capable of delivering public services, including education, health care, water, and sanitation; and (c) people's democratic participation in the policies and projects relevant to their lives. The categories of basic needs are nutrition, primary education, health, sanitation, water supply, and housing.

The three objectives and six basic needs are further defined in Figure 2.1. Objective 1: Basic Sustenance contributes directly to human well-being, as do all the basic needs. Equitable economic opportunity, another primary tenet of this approach, embraces the notion of equity. Objective 2: Social Infrastructure defines democratic government. Objective 3: Democratic Participation delineates democratic civil society.

Human Development

The second endeavor to reorient development, the Human Development Approach, was championed by Haq (1999) and the UNDP. This approach embraces and transcends the Basic Needs Approach. Its objective is to create an enabling environment in which people can enjoy long, healthy, and creative lives. Its purpose is to continually enlarge people's choices in all of life's spheres: economic, social, cultural, and political (United Nations Development Programme, 1990). The Human Development Approach conceives of economic growth as a process designed to enhance the well-being of the majority, so prioritizes its quality and distributional aspects. It further recognizes democratic governance as necessary to direct economic activity toward desired societal ends (Harris, Wise, Gallagher, and Goodwin, 2001; United Nations Development Programme, 2003). The Human Development Approach includes four components: equity, sustainability, productivity, and empowerment (Haq, 1999).

Equity refers to access to political and economic opportunities. Based on the premise that equitable distribution of wealth is critical to human development, equity requires a restructuring of power through wealth redistribution; elimination of social, economic, and legal barriers; and the removal of excessive political powers from the minority.

Sustainability gives precedence to maintenance of worthwhile life opportunities and elimination of human deprivation. Inter- and intragenerational equity is central to sustainability. "In the last analysis, it is human life that must be sustained" (Haq, 1999, p. 18). Sustainability also dictates that the disparities within and across nations be eliminated.

Productivity refers to the contribution that people make to economic development. Haq (1999) contends that, although human productivity is important, it is critical that people not be seen as an input into the production process. Rather, they are the primary beneficiaries and their well-being the purpose for economic development. He further asserts that for people to achieve their maximum potential, they must be supported by an enabling macroeconomic environment.

Empowerment refers to people's active and legitimized engagement in the policies and practices that influence their lives (i.e., political democracy). Empowerment requires investment in people through education, health care, and access to credit and productive assets.

The Human Development Index[2] was developed to track progress toward equity, sustainability, productivity, and empowerment (United Nations Development Programme, 2004). The Index is published annually as the Human Development Report (HDR). However, it only provides a partial measure of the social dimensions of human development (United Nations Development Programme, 2002). Conspicuously missing are indicators of political freedom, absent primarily due to the opposition of some authoritarian governments, but also because of the difficulty of developing associated indicators (Haq, 1999).

In the 2004 HDR (United Nations Development Programme, 2004), Haq laments the fact that the selection of indicators has contributed to a popular misperception that political freedom and participation are not crucial to human development. This quandary highlights serious issues with social indicators. First, it is difficult to design and measure indicators of some conditions essential to human development. Second, and more important, it is dangerous and all too easy to assume that indicators reflect the full array of important values related to human well-being when, in fact, they may really represent the limitations in data availability and collection.

Although the HDR does not track indicators related to political freedom, UNDP attempts to address the dilemma in two ways. First, a framework for a Political Freedom Index was developed, including indicators related to legislatures, civil society participation in governance, the judiciary, rule of law, freedom of expression, and nondiscrimination. Second, the HDR reports on the endeavors of other institutions that track political freedoms. The Polity Score[3] tracks the competitiveness and openness of chief executive recruitment. Freedom House[4] tracks civil liberties (e.g., the freedom of expression and association), as well as human and economic rights and the rule of law. It tracks political rights (e.g., free and fair elections, political organization, significant opposition, freedom from domination of powerful groups, inclusion of minorities, and freedom of the press). The World Bank Governance Indicators Dataset[5] tracks voice and accountability (e.g., elections, press, civil liberties, political rights, transparency), political stability and lack of violence (e.g., perceptions of likelihood of destabilization), rule of law (e.g., enforceability of contracts, corruption, and crime), government effectiveness (e.g., bureaucratic quality, transaction costs, quality of public health care, and government stability), and graft. Transparency International[6] tracks corruption, and the International Country Risk Guide[7] tracks law and order (e.g., legal impartiality and popular observance of law).

The four components of the Human Development Approach align precisely with the four principles of social well-being (see Fig. 2.1). Productivity and Empowerment are critical for human well-being, Economic and Political Equity are central to equity, Political Freedom is characteristic of democratic government, and Empowerment and Political Freedom are paramount to a democratic civil society.

Freedoms

As the sustainable development dialogue unfolded, the exploration of human well-being gathered momentum. Sen (1999) extended the conception of human well-being to include human freedoms, stating that freedoms are of intrinsic and paramount importance. He maintained that expansion of freedoms and elimination of unfreedoms are both the primary ends and the principle means of development.

Freedoms are directly related to people's ability to sustain themselves and to their ability to influence the world around them. Freedoms enable personal agency—the capacity to effect change. Freedom is facilitated by the processes that enable decision making and by the availability of opportunities for decision making. Sen (1999) outlines five critical freedoms: economic facilities, protective security, political and civil rights, transparency guarantees, and social opportunities.

Economic facility refers to opportunities to engage in remunerative activities. People are entitled economically to the degree that they have access to resources (e.g., finance, land, skills, and materials), which can be put to use for production or exchange. Because engagement in the economy enables people to fend for themselves, the freedom to participate competitively is critical. Unfreedoms associated with economic facility include denial of access to labor and product markets. Forced separation from the market leads to unemployment, which compromises people's ability to sustain themselves and results in social exclusion. Moreover, it threatens physical health. Economic unfreedom, states Sen (1999), manifests as extreme poverty and leads to " . . . premature mortality, significant undernourishment, persistent morbidity, widespread illiteracy" (p. 20).

Because of the extreme dangers threatening those disaffected by the market, Sen asserts that protective security is another basic human freedom. Protective security provides a formal social safety net designed to prevent people from falling into abject poverty. It provides protections such as income supplements and ad hoc measures to cover emergencies.

Political and civil freedoms refer to the opportunities people have to participate in governance. They include political entitlements such as freedom of dialogue and dissent, assembly, choice of political affiliation, voting, and holding political figures accountable. Political and civil freedoms have intrinsic value. They are important in their own right because deprivation of people's right to participate in crucial governance issues restricts their social, political, and economic lives. Political and civil freedoms also have instrumental value in that they directly contribute to the development process.

Closely related to political and civil freedoms are transparency guarantees. Transparency guarantees are evidenced in a society that ensures openness and full disclosure and that promotes an environment of trust. Transparency guarantees are critical to enable transactions between people and to mitigate corruption.

The final freedom is social opportunity, which includes public assurance of services vital to enabling people's ability to access the other freedoms. These include, for example, education and health care.

Although each freedom is vital, Sen (1999) maintains that their greater power lies in their extensive interrelations. The freedoms facilitate and are dependent on each other. Some examples demonstrate this interconnectedness: (a) basic education—a social freedom—is requisite for engaging in economic activity; (b) an open atmosphere—transparency guarantee—empowers people with information that they can then use to engage in political activities—political and civic freedom; (b) medical care and education—social freedoms—prepare people to successfully address significant personal and community stressors—political and economic freedoms; and (d) the right to gather and voice concerns—political freedom—empowers people to effectively combat egregious and illegal behaviors and to demand transparency and accountability—transparency guarantees.

The freedoms also align with the emergent principles of social well-being. Protective security and social opportunities are essential for human well-being. Economic opportunities and release from economic unfreedoms are fundamental to the principle of equity. Transparency guarantees, civil rights, and political freedoms are essential components of democratic government, and civil rights and political freedom are indispensable for a democratic civil society.

SUSTAINABILITY

The tradition of sustainability influences many facets of contemporary society, from individual lifestyles to design and management of urban centers to management of natural resources. For the purposes of this chapter, sustainability is explored from two perspectives: its original conception as articulated through internationally recognized agreements, and its integration into forest management.

Sustainability: An International Conceived Vision

As part of its endeavors to reorient development dialogue to Human-Centered Development and sustainability, the WCED created the UN Commission on Sustainable Development (CSD) and directed it to monitor and report on the implementation of the international agreements reached at the Earth Summits held in Rio de Janeiro (1992) and Johannesburg (2002).[8] Three primary international agreements were reached at the Earth Summits, all of which addressed the social aspects of sustainability. The agreements included *Agenda 21*, the *Rio Declaration on Environment and Development*, and the Statement of Principles for the Sustainable Management of Forests.[9]

Agenda 21 provided a design to move toward social, economic, and environmental sustainability. Agenda 21 referenced social sustainability in three sections (see Fig. 2.1). Section 1: Social and Economic Dimensions includes indicators related to poverty, consumption patterns, human health, and sustainable development, providing definition to both human well-being and equity. Section 3: Strengthening the Role of Major Groups addresses democratic participation of all groups, a direct articulation of democratic civil society. Section 4: Means of Implementation addresses governance and the rule of law, stipulating important principles of democratic governance.

The Rio Declaration defined the rights and responsibilities of nations in the pursuit of human development and well-being. Five of its primary principles address the emergent principles of social sustainability (see Fig. 2.1): (a) People are entitled to a healthy and productive life in harmony with nature—human well-being; (b) eradicating poverty and reducing disparities in living standards throughout the world are essential—equity; (c) citizen participation in environmental issues shall be facilitated and encouraged by states—democratic civil society; (d) States shall enact effective environmental laws to protect victims of environmental damage—democratic government; (e) States should recognize and support the identity, culture, and interests of indigenous people and facilitate the full inclusion of women and youth—democratic civil society.

The Sustainable Forests document stated principles to guide the management, conservation, and sustainable development of forests.[10] Several of the principles addressed social sustainability (see Fig. 2.1): (a) Forests should be managed to meet the social, economic, ecological, cultural; and spiritual needs of present and future generations—human well-being; (b) women, forest dwellers, indigenous people, industries, workers, and nongovernment organizations need to participate in forest management—democratic civil society; and (c) forest policies should support indigenous people and forest dwellers, incorporate their knowledge and offer economic activity and land tenure that encourage sustainable forest use, and provide them with an adequate livelihood and level of well-being—democratic government.

Forest Sustainability

In 1994, the Working Group on Criteria and Indicators for the Conservation and Sustainable Management of Temperate and Boreal Forests convened to develop the Montréal Process Criteria and Indicators (MPC&I).[11] Subsequently, the Montréal Process countries issued the Santiago Declaration, which indicated their commitment to utilize the MPC&I to guide the sustainable management of forests. Criteria 6 and 7 relate to social sustainability (see Fig. 2.1). Criterion 6, *Maintenance and Enhancement of Long-Term Multiple Socio-Economic Benefits to Meet the Needs of Society*, includes indicators related to employment and wages; subsistence; community resilience; value of the forest to people; and cultural, social, and spiritual needs. All are indicators of human well-being. Criterion 7, *Legal, Institutional, and Economic Framework for Forest Conservation and Sustainable Management*, includes indicators related to public involvement—democratic civil society—and the institutional framework for government—democratic government.

In 1998, USDA Forest Service Chief, Mike Dombeck, chartered the Local Unit Criteria and Indicator Development (LUCID) project to customize the Montreal Process Criteria and Indicators for sustainable management of local forest units. Carol J. Pierce Colfer et al. (1995) define sustainable forest management in relation to the Brundtland definition, stating that sustainable forest management aims to meet the needs of the present generation without compromising the ability of future generations to meet their needs. It further requires the maintenance of both ecosystem integrity and the well-being of people. The LUCID project, based on these tenets, endeavored to develop a monitoring instrument that would identify critical aspects of all three domains of sustainability:social, ecological, and economic (Wright et al., 2002).

The discussion of social sustainability elicited debate regarding the relevancy of broad concepts of social well-being to forest management. Historically, the forest management conception of social sustainability was limited to communities and people as both a threat and a means to sustainable forests (Beckley, 2000). The LUCID research into social sustainability, however, transcended the traditional focus to advocate a comprehensive definition of social well-being (see Fig. 2.1). The LUCID social sustainability criteria and indicators include: collaborative stewardship, social and cultural values, social equity, and institutional and community capacity.

Collaborative stewardship is " . . . the opportunity to have one's values, attitudes and beliefs heard and considered in national forests decision-making, and the ability to participate in consultative and stewardship actions" (Wright et al., 2002, p. 102). It is based on the notion that respect for and integration of public values into forest management activities are central to sustainability. Collaborative planning " . . . is not merely a case of the public being offered an opportunity to contribute to the planning process per se, but one of plans becoming central to a forum of debate and communication which is essential for sustainable development" (Selman, 1996, p. 124). Collaborative stewardship embraces both democratic government and democratic civil society.

Social and cultural values refer to values people explicitly express in policy, as well as those that are implicitly embedded in the fabric of social life. The values are contextualized in a sense of place. *Place* is both a geographical and a social term. It is rooted both in the tangible—visual and tactile—and the intangible—ideas and imagination (Electronic Journals of the U.S. Information Agency, 1996). This criterion includes values related to consumption and cultural gathering/harvesting, aesthetics and solitude, education and research, cultural values and historic features, spiritual values and places, access and use rights, recreation and tourism, value of the forest to people, and customs and culture. Social and cultural values address both human well-being and equity.

Social equity refers to the inter- and intragenerational distribution of costs and benefits of sustainability. Particular attention is paid to the needs of minority, disenfranchised, or nonmainstream groups. Equity issues include worker and public health and safety, accessibility, environmental justice, and civil rights.

Institutional and community capacity measures communities' resilience or capacity.

> Community resilience is the existence, development and engagement of community resources to thrive in a dynamic environment characterized by change, uncertainty, unpredictability and surprise. Resilient communities intentionally develop and engage personal and collective capacity to respond to and influence change, to sustain and renew the community and to develop new trajectories for the communities' future. (Magis, 2007, p. 10)

Institutions are presumed conventions of social life that provide the deep structure for social processes. Institutions are constituted and enforced both formally, through rules and laws, and informally, through norms, conventions, and codes of conduct (Berkes & Folke, 1998). Institutions guide how people interact and provide the means for problem resolution. Institutional capacity is improved through adaptable, complex, flexible, and multidirectional policy and information flows. Institutional capacity provides definition to democratic government, and community capacity explicates democratic civil society.

The Mt. Hood LUCID team divided institutional and community capacity three ways—community livability, community resilience, and institutional adequacy—to enable further elaboration on these important features of sustainability (see Fig. 2.1). Community livability addresses basic needs—human well-being, community resilience focuses on physical and social capital—democratic civil society, and institutional adequacy deals with legal frameworks, authority structures, and tenure—democratic government.

COMMUNITY WELL-BEING

In 1993, the President's Council on Sustainable Development drafted a plan for national sustainability.[12] Goal 6 states, "Americans should encourage people to work together to create healthy communities where natural and historic resources are preserved, jobs are available, sprawl is contained, neighborhoods are secure, education is lifelong, transportation and health care are accessible, and all citizens have opportunities to improve the quality of their lives." Pursuit of this vision, however, was already well underway in America's communities.

The Community Well-Being Movement is not an integrated and singularly directed movement. Rather, it is comprised of multiple self-organizing movements focused on Community Well-Being and quality of life. Included in the ranks are Healthy Communities, Livable Communities, Civic Democracy, Safe Communities, Quality of Life, Social Well-Being and Sustainable Communities. John T. Kesler, Drew O'Connor, and Tyler Norris (2001) define the *American Community Movement* as " . . . the modern face of de Tocqueville's view of our democracy . . . " (p. 304). Although these grassroots endeavors cover a variety of interests, they share many commonalities. Furthermore, their principles, frameworks, conventions, models, and declarations do not conflict, which, according to Paul Hawkin (2000), is historically unprecedented. The American Community Movement, states Kesler, is maturing into a vibrant civic sector, characterized by sophisticated organizational capabilities, stable processes and structures, and space for deliberation of critical community issues.

Polese and Stren (2000) posit a definition of sustainable communities that concisely addresses the principles and goals shared by these movements. Social sustainability is " . . . development that is compatible with the harmonious evolution of civil society, fostering an environment conducive to the compatible cohabitation of culturally and socially diverse groups while at the same time encouraging social integration, with improvements in the quality of life for all segments of the population" (pp. 15–16).

Among the commonalities shared by the Community Well-Being Movement is a predilection to utilize customized indicators, which empower citizens and enable their effective involvement in public policy. The indicators monitor community progress toward specific goals, identify issues, inform deliberation and decisions, and guide specific initiatives and policies (Hart, 1999; Kesler, 2001; Norris et al., 1997). Indicators utilized by groups within the Community Well-Being Movement are strikingly similar. They focus broadly on the four emergent principles of social sustainability: livable communities, equity, democratic civil society, and democratic governance (see Fig. 2.1).

Livable communities—a direct reflection of human well-being—address basic needs such as education and health care, access to public goods and services, employment, transportation, and housing (Mitchell, 2005; Polese & Stren, 2000; Porter, Platt, Leinberger, Blakely, and Maxman, 2000). Equity addresses equal access and social justice for all economic and social groups, as well as future generations (Beatley and Manning, 1997; Polese and Stren, 2000; Kesler, 2001; Molnar and Jorgan, 2001).

Democratic governance refers to government that promotes community participation in public discourse and the design, implementation, and evaluation of public policy (Mitchelle, 2005; Polese &and Stren, 2000; Serageldin and Grootaert, 2000; Kesler, 2001). Governance has a direct effect on community endeavors, enhancing or debilitating them via its policies, structures, and processes. Democratic governance, at all levels, complements and facilitates community movements.

Finally, democratic civil society addresses informed public dialogue and decision making (Kesler, 2001; Miringoff and Miringoff, 1999; Molnar and Jorgan, 2001), collaboration in building desired community outcomes (Kesler, 2001; Mitchell, 2005; Molnar and Jorgan, 2001), and intentional social integration of the full diversity of the communities' residents (Kesler, 2001; Mitchell, 2005; Molnar and Jorgan, 2001; Polese and Stren, 2000).

Of particular note is the virtuous cycle created by this highly democratic process. The informed, collaborative, inclusive, and participatory practices of the Community Well-Being Movement result in enhanced skills and knowledge, strengthened relationships, improved communication, greater community initiative, and increased community adaptability. These are outcomes associated with community success (Flora et al., 1999). They also are critical input into the further development of social capital (i.e., the ability of the community to engage constructively in endeavors considered important to its well-being).

EMERGENT PRINCIPLES OF SOCIAL SUSTAINABILITY

In this section, human well-being, equity, democratic government, and democratic civil society are posited as primary constituents of social sustainability. Then lessons from Human-Centered Development, Sustainability, and Community Well-Being are synthesized to offer a broad portrayal of each.

The 2002 HDR states that public policy is about selecting priorities from the multitude of competing interests and issues. It delineates two criteria to select ideas that will take precedence over others. First, the idea must be universally accepted by people throughout the world, and, second, it must be so fundamental that its absence would close off many life options.

The evidence presented in this chapter fulfills these two criteria, thereby substantiating the assertion that human well-being, equity, democratic government, and democratic civil society are primary constituents of social sustainability.

Examination of Human-Centered Development, Sustainability, and the Community Well-Being Movement reveals shared perceptions of essential principles of social well-being, and, hence, social sustainability. Human well-being, equity, democratic government, and democratic civil society emerge as principles shared by citizens and local communities around the world, as well as by regional, national, and international governments. The principles, furthermore, are characterized as fundamental to life options for all people.

The proposal that human well-being, equity, democratic government, and democratic civil society are primary constituents of social sustainability is corroborated in the following definitions, mined from community development, sustainable development, the World Bank, the OECD, and the Australian regional government. Social sustainability requires equity within and between generations, cultural integration, widespread political participation, community ownership, and self-determination (McKenzie, 2004). Democratic participation (i.e., empowering and engaging citizens to direct their own future) is critical to Community Well-Being (Gahin and Patterson, 2001). A socially sustainable system must achieve adequate provision of social services, distributional and gender equity, participatory and pluralistic democracy, and political accountability (Harris, 2000). Development requires participatory democracy, decentralization, and social capital represented by strong local organization, as well as involvement of local and state government and nongovernmental organizations (World Bank, 1997). Social sustainability requires safety nets, high employment, equity, and democratic, participatory decision making (Organization for Economic Cooperation and Development, 2001). Socially sustainable communities are equitable, diverse, connected, and democratic, and they provide a good quality of life (Western Australian Council of Social Services, 2000).

Human Well-Being

Prescott-Allen (2001) maintains that social well-being is achieved through the fulfillment of basic needs, as well as through political, economic, and social freedoms. Haq (1999) adds that social well-being is realized when people enjoy long, healthy, and creative lives and continually enlarge their choices in all of life's affairs.

Social well-being needs to be decoupled from economism (Robinson and Tinker, 1997). Social well-being perceives economic development as a means to make qualitative improvements in human well-being. Economism, in contrast, perceives economic development as the end, and it distinguishes attainment of prosperity as society's ultimate goal. As so eloquently stated by Haq (1999), "We have finally begun to accept the axiom that human welfare—not GNP—is the true end of development" (p. 4). The importance of decoupling is multiplied when consideration is given to the fact that income expansion does not automatically improve social well-being and often degrades it. In fact, human poverty and mass consumption societies are implicated as the prime culprits of environmental degradation (British Columbia Round Table, 1993; Nigel Richardson, 1994). Accordingly, the Organization for Economic Cooperation and Development (2001) declared that sustainable development is concerned with the quality, as well as the quantity, of economic growth and with human well-being alongside economic growth.

Social and human well-being are differentiated in that social well-being refers to the community of people and addresses all four constituents of social sustainability, whereas human well-being refers to the individual and focuses on the fulfillment of basic needs. Social sustainability assumes that basic needs are met for all members of the community (Western Australian Council of Social Services, 2000). Prescott-Allen (2001) defines *human well-being* as including the ability to meet one's needs, the opportunity to be creative and productive, security against crime and violence, and guaranteed human rights. Streeten et al. (1981) claim that the first objective of development is remunerative livelihoods that accord people a primary claim of the fruits of their labor and income adequate to purchase basic sustenance. These items include food, water, and shelter, as well as the capacity and opportunity to engage in economic endeavors through which those necessities can be purchased for oneself.

The Human-Centered Development model, the Freedom model, the Sustainability model, and the Community Well-Being Movement all accept and incorporate Streeten's (1981) conception of basic needs and transcend it to include social and political freedoms. They further assert that the fulfillment of these needs and freedoms is a basic human right, and they stress that economic development must not imperil human well-being.

Equity

Advocating for equity and suggesting alternative indicators to measure it dates back to Streeten et al. (1981) and the Basic Needs approach. It winds its way through all the Human-Centered Development, Sustainability, and Community Well-Being literature. Within the Communities movement, social sustainability is equated with the degree to which inequalities are reduced (Polese and Stren, 2000). Communities and government are seen as agents of the provision of equitable rights, opportunities and outcomes for all (Hart, 1999; Western Australian Council of Social Services, 2000).

Within the sustainability community, it is commonly accepted that inequity is the basic cause of environmental damage and that sustainability absolutely requires a concerted focus on eradication of inequities (World Commission on Environment and Development, 1987). Within the Human-Centered Development community, there is resounding concurrence that equity in political and economic opportunities is a basic human right, and that income inequality is a significant malady. Inequalities exacerbate the effects of market and policy failures, which then further hinder poverty alleviation. The problem is magnified in poor countries, which are subject to imperfect markets and institutional failures (United Nations Development Programme, 2002). The World Commission on Environment and Development (1987) holds that development is a " . . . progressive transformation of economy and society. . . . Physical sustainability cannot be secured unless development policies pay attention to such considerations as changes in access to resources and in the distribution of costs and benefits" (p. 43). Sustainable development, then, requires economic growth to be redefined (Harris, 2000).

Stanley R. Euston and William E. Gibson (1995) advance the notion of *Sufficiency of Sustenance*, which creates a standard of enough for all without excess and wastefulness. The basic needs of all people would be met in an equitable fashion. Concurrently, conspicuous and wasteful consumption would be halted, and the gross gap between wealth and income would be eliminated. Alan Durning (1992) adds the third leg to this strategy, asserting the requirement for strong social institutions and a healthy environment.

DEMOCRATIC GOVERNANCE

The 1990s witnessed a momentous worldwide expansion in democratic governance. This movement was informed by Human-Centered Development projects, initiated and demanded by people, facilitated by increasing worldwide interdependencies, and promoted by the UN. The World Social Forum Charter of Principles[13] explicitly states that human rights rest on democratic international systems, which serve to promote social justice, equality, and the sovereignty of the people. The United Nations Millennium Declaration (2000) states, "We will spare no effort to promote democracy and strengthen the rule of law, as well as respect for all internationally recognized human rights and fundamental freedoms."[14]

Democracy is valuable in its own right and because it is the cornerstone to the advancement of human development. The political and civil rights afforded people in a democracy endow them with information and skills critical to make choices; a voice, the freedom, and the opportunity to actively participate in governing their lives; and the authority to hold their government accountable (Sen, 1999; The United Nations General Assembly, 2001; United Nations Development Programme, 2002).

Democracy also is invaluable to sustainable development. Living sustainably requires that people continually monitor and improve social, economic, and environmental conditions, and, further, that they make associated decisions regarding policy formulation and implementation. Hence, living sustainably requires access to information, full inclusion, participation, and collaboration. Additionally, it requires government institutions that are open, transparent, accountable, and supportive of community action (Brundtland, 1991; Skcopol, 1996; President's Council on Sustainable Development, 1996; Western Australian Council of Social Services, 2000; United Nations Development Programme, 2002; Johannesburg Declaration on Sustainable Development[15]; World Summit on Sustainable Development[16]).

The link between democracy and human development, however, is not automatic. Further, it can be subverted in a number of ways. Social injustice, discrimination, and inequities are widespread in democracies. Economic growth is not guaranteed by democracy (United Nations Development Programme, 2002; Sen, 1999). People, who are victims of the electoralism fallacy, assume that free elections are synonymous with deep democracy and disclaim further responsibility for upholding democratic practices (Schmitter and Karl, 1991). Nationless transnational corporations use their unmatched economic power to capture and turn international institutions to their advantage (Anderson, 2000; Oxfam, 2002; Wallach, Woodall, and Nader, 2004; Wesselius, 2002). Excesses of wealth threaten democracy as the wealthy pursue private interests at the expense of the public good and abuse their economic and political power (de Tocqueville, 1969; Boesche, 1987). This tyranny of the minority robs the majority of its voice and its claims. Finally, corrupt government officials and deficient public institutions impede proper democratic processes and structures (United Nations Development Programme, 2002).

Democracy can promote human development. However, it must be a conscious choice, facilitated by deliberate and strategic decisions, strong governing institutions, and democratic politics. Democracy, in its essence, is the rule of the people, by the people, and for all the people. The Inter-Parliamentary Union's (IPU) Universal Declaration of Democracy[17] declares that human rights are inseparable from democracy (Inter-Parliamentary Union, 1997). Preserving those rights is crucial for people's well-being, for a humane society, and for enabling an active and engaged civil society.

Democracy takes many forms because it is integrated into the multitude of cultures around the world (Schmitter and Karl, 1991). However, there are core principles that distinguish it from other forms of governance and that guide its development. Two core principles identified by the IPU are participation and accountability. Effective public participation in governance requires civil and political rights, including freedom of association and assembly, freedom of expression and conscience, and freedom of the press (Gran, 1983; United Nations Development Programme, 2002). Governing bodies must represent and be held accountable to the people. Accountability is institutionalized through popularly controlled legislative bodies, an independent judiciary bound to the rule of law and democratic political parties (Gran, 1983; Sen, 1999; United Nations Development Programme, 2002). Of note, at the 2004 World Social Forum, a survey of participants revealed that the majority want UN General Assembly representatives directly elected by citizens. Further, that majority wants the creation of a popularly elected UN Parliament (GlobalScan, 2004).

People share a "social contract" with their governments (Stiglitz, 2002), an essential trust that all will share in the burdens and benefits of society, and that civil society and governments will collaboratively govern that society (Evans, 1996; World Summit on Sustainable Development[18]). So, democracy is activated by democratic governing institutions and by an engaged and democratic civil society. This shared responsibility for the governing of a society is called *governance* (Salamon, 2002) and is differentiated from government, which addresses only government organizations. Both democratic government and democratic civil society were widely and prominently evident throughout the literature on Human-Centered Development, Sustainability, and Community Well-Being.

Democratic Government

Government fulfills critical and irreplaceable roles in democratic governance. It must consistently ensure that governance is oriented to the people, it must provide a stabilizing force within society, and it must uphold and advance the democratic cause.

Government needs to orient governance to the people. Because of its significant impact on people's lives, government is the holder of the public trust (United Nations Development Programme, 2002) and, as such, must be responsive to the people and accountable for its decisions. This most fundamental of principles is true for all levels of government. One example is Walden Bello (2000), who challenged the United Nations Conference on Trade and Development (UNCTAD) to pursue a paradigm that establishes social equity and environmental integrity as paramount objectives of government. This call for equity is widespread and includes, for example, equity for women (UN General Assembly, 2001), future generations (Agenda 21), and tolerance for difference (Inter-Parliamentary Union, 1997). It also is widely understood that ungoverned markets and growth-oriented development do not protect human rights or preserve equity. Rather, equity requires collective (i.e., political) actions to ensure that all people share in the benefits and costs of society. Moreover, that decision must be enforced by government institutions (Harrison, 2000) through democratizing and directing the market (Ehrenberg, 2002) and ensuring reforms and redistributive measures are consistently and effectively implemented (Bello, 1994).

Government also is a stabilizing force in society, protecting basic needs and rights as well as the space for the contestation so critical to democracies.

The most recognizable protection regards government's role in ensuring public goods are provided when externalities prevent their distribution through the market (Streeten et al., 1981). Government's protective role, however, extends beyond a narrow market focus to encompass protection of human rights and fundamental freedoms, protection from discrimination, elimination of poverty, expansion of choices in all realms of life, and protection from economic, physical, and political catastrophes (UN General Assembly, 2001). Government also plays a stabilizing role by creating open space for political opposition and ensuring peaceful power transfers (UN General Assembly, 2001; Inter-Parliamentary Union, 1997). David Truman (1971) describes government decisions as the product of the contest among interests. Ensuring that entry to the deliberation is not obstructed and mediating tensions among society's competing forces are two critical roles of government.

Finally, government plays a vital role in cultivating the democratic polity by facilitating civil society's engagement and being responsive to the people. Sustaining democracy means nurturing and reinforcing a democratic culture (i.e., civil society) (Inter-Parliamentary Union, 1997). Through its roles, rules, and procedures (Krishna, 2000), government operates a political system that secures and empowers effective citizen participation (Sharp, 1992; World Commission on Environment and Development, 1987) and makes democratic rule a good in itself (United Nations Development Programme, 2002). Responsive governments are accountable to the people, ensuring economic and social policies address people's needs and aspirations, ensuring the vote to those who bear the costs, limiting the rights and powers of absentee owners, and holding decision makers liable for the harm of their actions (International Forum on Globalization, 2004; Inter-Parliamentary Union, 1997; United Nations Development Programme, 2002). Finally, responsive governments are responsible for institution building to deepen democratic governance (World Summit on Sustainable Development[19]). These institutions include a system of representation, an electoral system, and the rule of law.

Democratic Civil Society

The 2002 HDR refers to the promotion of civil society participation in democratic governance as the " . . . third pillar of 21st century human development strategy" (United Nations Development Programme, 2002, p. 53). Collective action by civil society is, it states, an emerging consensus among the nations. The HDR notes the growth of civil society groups from 1,083 in 1914 to 37,000 in 2,000. Civil society made a remarkable appearance in national and world governance in the 1990s, with nearly one fifth of its growth occurring in just that decade.

This expansion of civic activism has had historic influence on both national and international governments. Through volunteerism, whistle-blowing, norms development, oversight, contentious politics, and collaboration in decision making, civil society has forced its presence into governance, broadened democratic space, strengthened democratic institutions, and promoted social change (Kaldor, Anheier, and Glasius, 2003; Salamon, 2004). In fact, global civil society theorists provide substantial evidence of civil society's active agency in numerous significant social changes (i.e., human rights, international corruption, democratic governance, development, peace, and environmental conservation) (Clark, 1995; Florini, 2000; Keck and Sikkink, 1998; Khagram, Riker, and Sikkink, 2002; Lipschutz, 1992; Weiss and Gordenker, 1996; Willetts, 1996).

Civil society provides both generative and countervailing forces in society. It is generative in that it creates and nurtures civic space and empowers people to utilize that space for deepening democratic practices and building democratic governance. de Tocqueville (1969) emphasized the importance of this civic space, stating that, through association, people interact, find common ground, and empower and inspire each other to engage in activities to promote the common good. Civil society is embedded in community, whether it is the place-based community so important to sustainability and the Community Well-Being Movement, or the interest-based community propelling international civic endeavors (Gahin and Patterson, 2001; IUCN, UNEP & WWF, 1996). Former Secretary General Boutros Boutros Ghali states that, although nongovernmental organizations have no standing in the UN, they are, in fact, "full participants in international life" and are "a basic form of popular participation and representation" (Weiss and Gordenker, 1996, pp. 7, 18).

Civil society also plays a countervailing role in society. Civil society's ever-present diligence compels government to work democratically (Gahin and Patterson, 2001). Through the exercise of political rights, civil society educates and builds consensus about its needs and its responsibility to play an active political role in ensuring that those needs are met (Sen, 1999). The relationship between government and civil society in a democracy will always have some level of contention. It is the primary role of civil society to ensure that government is functioning according to the will of its people. However, government may deviate from the course prescribed by the people, requiring consequent civil society intervention to redirect and hold government accountable. Further, civil society will always be divided among itself, especially in a democracy wherein diversity is celebrated and nurtured. In a representative democracy, a full 49% of the population could be disaffected by the workings of a government representing the other 51%. Because of the inherent discord between civil society and government, civil society must be institutionalized to prevent government abuse of citizens' rights (Bello, 1994) and to protect the voice of the people in democratic governance. Civic engagement in the polity is paramount to the survival and achievements of democracy (Sen, 1999).

CONCLUSION

Social sustainability concerns the ability of human beings of every generation to not merely survive, but to thrive. It is reflected in Aristotle's notion
of flourishing and Jefferson's notion of the informed and engaged polity.
Social sustainability is of value in its own right. Furthermore, it plays a
paramount role in the continuous journey toward sustainability because,
ultimately, it is human beings, individually and in collectives, that will
determine economic and environmental well-being.

Lessons from three traditions—Human-Centered Development, Sustainability, and Community Well-Being—provide the foundation for the
conclusions drawn in this chapter. Although unique and separate, the traditions have evolved over the same period, requiring each to respond to
similar environmental, social, economic, and political conditions. Their
responses overwhelmingly support four conditions critical to social well-
being and, hence, social sustainability: human well-being, equity, democratic government, and democratic civil society. These four principles are
posited herein as primary constituents of social sustainability.

The constituents create a self-reinforcing virtuous cycle that enables
movement toward environmental sustainability, balances multiple and
divergent interests, guides sustainable economic policies, and develops
resilience to manage the changes, reversals, and surprises inherent in
systems. Human well-being ensures the protections of basic needs and
security and the continuous development of human potential through
expansion of choices in all facets of life, political, economic, social, and so
on. Equity ensures protections against conditions that would enrich some
at the expense of others, and it creates mechanisms to guarantee equitable
sharing of society's benefits and costs. Democratic government ensures
that governance is oriented to people, provides a stabilizing force within
society, and upholds and advances the democratic cause. Civil society creates and nurtures civic space and empowers people to utilize that space
for deepening democratic practices and building democratic governance.
Moreover, it compels government to work democratically through ever-
present diligence. Social sustainability, thus defined, is of absolute importance to sustainability.

NOTES

1. www.un.org/documents/ga/conf151/aconf15126–1annex1.htm
2. www.undp.org/hdr
3. Polity IV dataset, University of Maryland
4. www.freedomhouse.org/ratings/
5. www.worldbank.org/wbi/governance/data.html
6. www.globalcorruptionreport.org/
7. www.icrgonline.com/
8. www.iisd.ca/wssd/portal.html
9. http://www.iisd.org/rio+5/agenda/riodocs.htm

10. www.un.org/documents/ga/conf151/aconf15126-3annex3.htm
11. www.mpci.org/home_e.html
12. http://clinton2.nara.gov/PCSD/Publications/TF_Reports/amer-top.html
13. www.forumsocialmundial.org.br/main.php?id_menu=4&cd_language=2
14. www.un.org/millennium/
15. www.A/CONF.199/L.6/Rev.1
16. www.johannesburgsummit.org/html/documents/summit_docs/aconf199_17_add1.pdf
17. www.ipu.org/english/strcture/cnldocs/161-dem.htm
18. www.johannesburgsummit.org/html/documents/summit_docs/aconf199_17_add1.pdf
19. www.johannesburgsummit.org/html/documents/summit_docs/aconf199_17_add1.pdf

REFERENCES

Anderson, Sarah, ed. 2000. *Views From the South: The Effects of Globalization and the WTO on the Third World Countries*. Chicago, IL: Food First Books & The International Forum on Globalization.

Aristotle. 1996. "The Politics." In *Princeton Readings in Political Thought*, edited by M. Cohen and N. Fermon. Princeton, NJ: Princeton University Press.

Atkinson, Giles, Richard Dubourg, Kirk Hamilton, Mohan Munasinghe, David Pearce, and Carlos Young. 1997. *Measuring Sustainable Development: Macroeconomics and the Environment*. Cheltenham, UK: Edward Elgar Publishing Limited.

Beatley, Timothy, and Kristy Manning. 1997. *The Ecology of Place*. Washington, DC: Island Press.

Beckley, Thomas. 2000. *Sustainability for Whom? Social Indicators for Forest-Dependent Communities in Canada*. Edmonton, Alberta: Sustainable Forest Management Network, University of Alberta.

Bello, Walden. 1994. "Equitable and Sustainable Growth in the Philippines in the 1990s." In *Beyond Brettonwoods: Alternatives to the Global Economic Order*, edited by John Cavanagh, Daphne Wysham, and Marcos Arruda. London, Englad: Pluto Press.

———. 2000. *Civil Society as Global Actor: Promise and Pitfalls. Focus on the Global South 2000*. Available at *www.focusweb.org/publications/2000/*: Focus on the Global South.

Berkes, Fikret, and Carl Folke. 1998. *Linking Social and Ecological Systems: Management Practices and Social Mechanisms for Building Resilience*. Cambridge, UK: Cambridge University Press.

Boesche, Roger. 1987. *The Strange Liberalism of Alexis de Tocqueville*. Ithaca, NY: Cornell University Press.

Bossell, Hartmut, ed. 1999. *Indicators for Sustainable Development: Theory, Method, Applications, A Report to the Balaton Group*. Winnipeg, Canada: International Institute for Sustainable Development.

British Columbia Round Table on the Environment and the Economy. 1993. *Strategic Directions for Community Sustainability*. Victoria, BC: Author.

Brundtland, Gro Harlem. 1991. "Sustainable Development: The Challenges Ahead." In *Sustainable Development*, edited by Olav Stokke. London, England: Frank Class and Company Limited.

Chakravarty, Sukhamoy. 1991. "Sustainable Development." In *Sustainable Development*, edited by Olav Stokke. London, England: Frank Class and Company Limited.

Chomsky, Noam. 1999. *Profit Over People: Neoliberalism and Global Order.* New York: Seven Stories Press.

Clark, Ann Marie. 1995. "Non-Governmental Organizations and Their Influence on International Society." *Journal of International Affairs* 48 (Winter 2): 507–526.

Colfer, Carol J. Pierce, Ravi Prabhu, Mario Gunter, Cynthia McDougall, Noemi Miyasaka Porro, and Roberto Porro. 1995. "Who Counts Most? Assessing Human Well-Being in Sustainable Forest Management." In *Criteria and Indicators Toolbox Series No. 8.* Bogor, Indonesia: Center for International Forestry Research.

Constanza, Robert, Bobbi Low, Lin Ostrom, and James Wilson. 2001. *Institutions, Ecosystems, and Sustainability.* Boca Raton, FL: CRC Press LLC.

Daily, Gretchen, and Paul Ehrlich. 1996. "Socioeconomic Equity, Sustainability, and Earth's Carrying Capacity." *Ecological Applications* 6 (November 4): 991–1001.

Daly, Herman. 1996. "From Adjustment to Sustainable Development: The Obstacle of Free Trade." In *Beyond Growth: The Economics of Sustainable Development.* Boston, MA: Beacon Press.

de Tocqueville, Alexis. 1969. *Democracy in America*, edited by J. P. Mayer. Garden City, NY: Doubleday.

Dieren, Wouter van, ed. 1995. *Taking Nature into Account, A Report to the Club of Rome: Toward a Sustainable National Income.* New York: Copernicus, an imprint of Springer-Verlag.

Douthwaite, Richard. 1999. *The Growth Illusion: How Economic Growth has Enriched the Few, Impoverished the Many and Endangered the Planet.* Devon, UK: Lilliput Press.

Durning, Alan. 1992. "How Much is Enough? The Consumer Society and the Future of Earth." In *Worldwatch Environmental Alert Series*, edited by L. Starke. New York: W.W. Norton.

Ehrenberg, John. 2002. "Equality, Democracy, and Community from Tocqueville to Putnam." In *Social Capital: Historical and Theoretical Perspectives on Civil Society*, edited by Scott McLean, David Schultz, and Manfred B. Steger. New York: New York University Press.

Electronic Journals of the U.S. Information Agency. 1996, August 1. Washington, DC: USIA Office of Thematic Programs.

Elkington, John. 1998. *Cannibals With Forks: The Triple Bottom Line of 21st Century Business.* Gabriola Island, Canada: New Society Publishers.

Euston, Stanley R., and William E. Gibson. 1995. "The Ethic of Sustainability" *Earth Ethics* 6 (Summer): 5–7.

Evans, Peter. 1996. "Government Action, Social Capital, and Development: Reviewing the Evidence on Synergy." *World Development* 24 (6): 1119–1132.

Flora, Cornelia, Michael Kinsley, Vicki Luther, Milan Wall, Susan Odell, Shanna Ratner, and Janet Topolsky. 1999. *Measuring Community Success and Sustainability.* Ames, IA: North Central Regional Center for Rural Development.

Florini, Ann, ed. 2000. *The Third Force: The Rise of Transnational Civil Society.* Washington, DC: Carnegie Endowment for International Peace.

Fukuyama, Francis. 1995. *Trust: The Social Virtues and the Creation of Prosperity.* New York: Free Press.

Gahin, Randa, and Chris Paterson. 2001. "Community Indicators: Past, Present, and Future." *National Civic Review* 90 (4, Winter): 347–363.

Galbraith, John. 1998. *The Affluent Society.* New York: Houghton Mifflin Company.

GlobalScan. 2004. *Public Opinion on Governance.* Survey conducted for International Secretariat of the World Social Forum: Global Issues Monitor.

Gran, Guy. 1983. *Development by People: Citizen Construction of a Just World.* New York: Praeger.

Haq, Mahbub ul. 1999. *Reflections on Human Development.* Oxford, UK: Oxford University Press.

Harris, Jonathan. 2000. *Basic Principles of Sustainable Development.* Global Development and Environment Institute, Tufts University.

———, Timothy Wise, Kevin Gallagher, and Neva Goodwin, eds. 2001. *A Survey of Sustainable Development: Social and Economic Dimensions.* Washington, DC: Island Press.

Harrison, Neil. 2000. *Constructing Sustainable Development.* Albany, NY: State University of New York Press.

Hart, Maureen. 1999. *Guide to Sustainable Community Indicators.* North Andover, MA: Sustainable Measures.

Hawkin, Paul. 2000. "Five Signs of the Coming Revolutions." *Utne Reader* (November–December).

Inter-Parliamentary Union. 1997. *The Inter-Parliamentary Union Universal Declaration of Democracy* [Electronic Version], 2005. Available at http://www.ipu.org/cnl-e/161-dem.htm.

International Forum on Globalization. 2002. *Alternatives to Economic Globalization: A Better World is Possible.* San Francisco: CA: Berrett-Koehler Publishers, Inc.

Kaldor, Mary, Helmut Anheier, and Marlies Glasius, eds. 2003. *Global Civil Society.* Oxford, UK: Oxford University Press.

Kant, Immanuel. 2002. *Groundwork of the Metaphysic of Morals*, edited by A. Wood. New Haven, CT: Yale University Press. Original edition, 1785.

Keck, Margarate, and Kathryn Sikkink. 1998. *Activists Beyond Borders: Advocacy Networks in International Politics.* Ithaca, NY: Cornell University Press.

Kesler, John T., Drew O'Connor, and Tyler Norris. 2001. "The American Communities Movement." *National Civic Review* 90 (4, Winter): 295–319.

Khagram, Sanjeev, James Riker, and Kathryn Sikkink, eds. 2002. *Restructuring World Politics: Transnational Social Movements, Networks, and Norms.* Vol. 14. Minneapolis, MN: University of Minnesota Press.

Korten, David. 1992. "Sustainable Development." *World Policy Journal* XX: Vol IX, No. 1 157–190.

Krishna, Anirudh. 2000. "Creating and Harnessing Social Capital." In *Social Capital: A Multifaceted Perspective*, edited by P. S. Dasgupta Ismail. Washington, DC: The World Bank.

Lipschutz, Ronnie. 1992. "Reconstructing World Politics: The Emergence of Global Civil Society." *Millennium: Journal of International Studies* 21 (3): 389–420.

Machlis, Gary and Jo Ellen Force. 1997. "The Human Ecosystem Part II: Social Indicators in Ecosystem Management." *Society and Natural Resources* 10 (4): 347–368.

Magis, Kristen. 2007. *Indicator 38: Community Resilience Literature and Practice Review.* U.S. Roundtable on Sustainable Forests 2007 [cited September 2007]. Available at http://www.sustainableforests.net/index.php.

Manning, Robert D. 1998. "Multicultural Washington, DC: The Changing Social and Economic Landscape of a Post-Industrial Metropolis." *Ethnic and Racial Studies* 21 (2): 328–355.

McKenzie, Stephen. 2004. "Social Sustainability: Towards Some Definitions." In *Hawke Research Institute Working Paper Series, No 27.* Magill, South Australia: Hawke Research Institute, University of South Australia.

Miringoff, Marc, and Marque-Luisa Miringoff. 1999. *The Social Health of the Nation: How America Is Really Doing.* Oxford, UK: Oxford University Press.

Mitchell, Gordon. 2005. *Components that Contribute to Quality of Life.* Environment Centre, University of Leeds nd [cited September 2005]. Available at www.sustainablefutures.org/quality.htm.

Molnar, Daniella, and Jorgan, Alexis J. 2001. *Defining Sustainability, Sustainable Development and Sustainable Communities.* Toronto, ON: A working paper for the Sustainable Toronto Project.

Morawetz, David. 1977. "Twenty-Five Years of Economic Development, 1950 to 1975." In *Socio-Economic Performance Criteria for Development.* Washington, DC: U.S. Agency for International Development, United Nations.

Organisation for Economic Cooperation and Development. 2001. *Sustainable Development: Critical Issues.* Paris, France: Author.

Oxfam. 2002. *Rigged rules and double standards: Make trade fair* 2002 [cited February 13 2003]. Available at http://www.maketradefair.com/stylesheet.

Pepperdine, Sharon. 2005. *Social Indicators of Rural Community Sustainability: An Example from the Woady Yaloak Catchment.* Department of Geography & Environmental Studies, The University of Melbourne 2005 [cited March 2005]. Available at www.regional.org.au/au/countrytowns/strategies/pepperdine.htm.

Polanyi, Karl. 2001. *The Great Transformation: The Political and Economic Origins of Our Lives.* Boston, MA: Beacon Press. Original edition, 1945.

Polese, Mario, and Richard Stren, eds. 2000. *The Social Sustainability of Cities: Diversity and the Management of Change.* Toronto, CA: University of Toronto Press.

Porter, Douglas R., Rutherford H. Platt, Christopher Leinberger, Edward J. Blakely, and Susan Maxman. 2000. *The Practice of Sustainable Development.* Washington, DC: Urban Land Institute.

Prescott-Allen, Robert. 2001. *The Wellbeing of Nations: A Country-by-Country Index of Quality of Life and the Environment.* Washington, DC: Island Press.

President's Council on Sustainable Development. 1996. *Sustainable America: A New Consensus.* Washington, DC: Author.

Redefining Progress. nd. *Genuine Progress Indicator: What's Wrong With the GDP as a Measure of Progress* [Electronic Version]. Available at www.redefiningprogress.org/projects/gpi/whatswrong.html.

Richardson, Nigel. 1994. *Making Our Communities Sustainable: The Central Issue is Will.* Toronto, CA: Ontario Round Table on Environment and Economy.

Robinson, John Bridger, and J. Tinker. 1997. "Reconciling Ecological, Economic and Social Imperatives: A New Conceptual Framework." In *Surviving Globalism: The Social and Environmental Challenges,* edited by Ted Schrecker. London, UK: Macmillan.

Salamon, Lester, ed. 2002. *The Tools of Government: A Guide to the New Governance.* Oxford, UK: Oxford University Press.

———, ed. 2004. *Global Civil Society: Dimensions of the Nonprofit Sector.* Vol. II. Bloomfield, CT: Kumarian Press.

Schmitter, Peter, and Thomas Karl. 1991. "What Democracy Is . . . and Is Not." *Journal of Democracy* II (3, Summer): 75–88.

Selman, Paul. 1996. *Local Sustainability: Managing and Planning Ecologically Sound Places.* New York: St. Martin's Press.

Sen, Amartya. 1999. *Development as Freedom.* New York: Alfred A. Knopf.

Serageldin, Ismail, and Christiaan Grootaert. 2000. "Defining Social Capital: An Integrating View." In *Social Capital: A Multifaceted Perspective,* edited by Partha Dasgupta and Ismail Serageldin. Washington, DC: The World Bank.

Skcopol, Theda. 1996. "Unravelling From Above." *The American Prospect* 25 (March–April): 20–25.

Stiglitz, Joseph. 2002. *Globalization and Its Discontents.* New York: W.W. Norton.

Streeten, Paul. 2001. "Globalization: Threat or Salvation?" In *A Survey of Sustainable Development: Social and Economic Dimensions,* edited by Jonathan Harris, Timothy Wise, Kevin Gallagher, and Neva Goodwin. Washington, DC: Island Press.

———, and Shahid Javed Burki. 1978. "Basic Needs: Some Issues." *World Development* 6: 411–421.

———, Shahid Javed Burki, Mahbubul Haq, Norman Hicks, and Frances Stewart. 1981. *First Things First: Meeting Basic Human Needs in the Developing Countries* New York: Oxford University Press.

The Inter-Parliamentary Union. 1997. *The Inter-Parliamentary Union Universal Declaration of Democracy.* XXXX: Author.

Truman, David. 1971. *The Governmental Process: Political Interests and Public Opinion.* New York: Knopf.

Tyler Norris Associates. 1997. *Redefining Progress & Sustainable Seattle: The Community Indicators Handbook.* San Francisco, CA: Redefining Progress.

United Nations. 2000. United Nations Millennium Declaration: Resolution adopted by the General Assembly (A/55/L.2). New York: United Nations.

United Nations Development Programme. 1990. *Human Development Report.* New York: United Nations.

———. 2002. *Human Development Report.* New York: United Nations.

———. 2003. *Human Development Report.* New York: United Nations.

———. 2004. *Human Development Report.* New York: United Nations.

United Nations General Assembly. 2001. Road Map Towards the Implementation of the United Nations Millennium Declaration. Report of the Secretary-General. 56th Session.

Venetoulis, Jason, and Cliff Cobb. 2004. *The Genuine Progress Indicator: 1950– 2002* (2004 Update) [Electronic Version]. Available at http://www.rprogress. org/publications/2004/gpi_march2004update.pdf.

Wallach, Lori, Patrick Woodall, and Ralph Nader. 2004. *Whose Trade Organization? A Comprehensive Guide to the WTO.* New York: The New Press.

Weiss, Thomas, and Leon Gordenker, eds. 1996. *NGOs, the UN, and Global Governance.* Boulder, CO: Lynne Rienner Publishers.

Wesselius, Erik. 2002. "Behind GATS 2000: Corporate Power at Work." In *TNI Briefing Series, No.6.* Amsterdam, The Netherlands: Transnational Institute.

Western Australian Council of Social Services. 2000. *Model of Social Sustainability* 2000 [cited September 2005]. Available at www.wacoss.org.au/socialpolicy/ sustainability & http://www.sustainability.dpc.wa.gov.au/index.htm.

Willetts, Peter. 1996. *The Conscience of the World: The Influence of Non-Governmental Organizations in the UN System.* Washington, DC: The Brookings Institution.

Williamson, John, ed. 1994. *The Political Economy of Policy Reform.* Washington, DC: Institute for International Economics.

Wise, Timothy. 2001. "Economics of Sustainability: The Social Dimension." In *A Survey of Sustainable Development: Social and Economic Dimensions,* edited by Jonathan Harris, Timothy Wise, Kevin Gallagher, and Neva Goodwin. Washington, DC: Island Press.

Wollenberg, Eva, and Carol Colfer. 1997. "Social Sustainability." In *Beyond Fences: Seeking Social Sustainability in Conservation,* edited by Grazia Borrini-Feyerabend and Dianne Buchan. Gland, Switzerland: IUCN.

World Bank. 1980. *World Development Report*. Chapters 4–5. New York: Oxford University Press.

———. 1997. *World Development Report: The State in a Changing World*. New York: Oxford University Press.

———. 2000. *Global Economic Prospects and the Developing Countries 2000*. Washington, DC: Author.

World Commission on Environment and Development. 1987. *Our Common Future*. Oxford, UK: Oxford University Press.

Wright, Pamela, Gregory Alward, Thomas Hoekstra, Brent Tegler, and Matt Turner. 2002. "Monitoring for Forest Management Unit Scale Sustainability: The Local Unit Criteria andIndicators Development (LUCID) Test" (tech.l ed.). USDA Forest Service Inventory and Monitoring Report No. 4. Fort Collins, CO.

3   An Inquiry Into the Theoretical Basis of Sustainability
Ten Propositions

Gary L. Larsen

Sustainability is fundamentally about the choices that people[1] make and the associated consequences. Ismail Serageldin (1993) notes, "People are the instruments and beneficiaries, as well as the victims, of all development activities"(p. 2). Sustainability and sustainable development are many things to many people and are viewed variously as a rubric, vision, philosophy, mission, goal, mandate, principle, marketing ploy, constraint, criteria, and movement. The Global Development Research Center reports more than 100 definitions of sustainability and sustainable development (Srinivas, 2004). In a recent Oregonian article, Amy Wang (2004) proclaimed that "sustainability should not be a rigid doctrine that we impose at any cost, but instead a liquid concept that we pour down the path of least resistance" (p. 26). In a more scholarly approach, Carlos Castro (2004) declares that the notion of sustainable development "has become one of the most ubiquitous, contested, and indispensable concepts of our time . . . [and] has been defined primarily by the mainstream tradition of economic analysis, which tends to marginalize the issue of ecological sustainability" (p. 195). William Clark, Robert Kates, Alan McGowan, and Timothy O'Riordan (2005) declare that "science and policy for sustainable development analyzes the problems, places, and people where environment and development come together, illuminating concerns from the local to the global" (p. 2).

Despite its complexity and proliferation of ideas, sustainability is a concept that elicits passion and commitment. The journal *Environment* (Clark et al., 2005), for example, just recently dedicated itself to "promote and facilitate dialogues among the increasing numbers of scientists, politicians, corporate employees, and civic activists around the world who are committed to sustainable development" (p. 2). Sustainability, from my perspective, is in its beginnings as a science, as a set of societal goals, as a set of values, and as an approach to dealing with problems in the real world. I believe its defining task is no less than (a) harnessing global capitalism to human needs; (b) securing human dignity in the world order; and (c) mediating the impacts of a world economy, population growth, and human settlement patterns on an Earth that we find suddenly finite.

Sorting out the quest for sustainability is no small task. It needs an approach marked by the kind of thoughtfulness and tentativeness necessary when building theory in an uncharted milieu where there is no common worldview, no common language, and no common agreements or understanding. My first question is, what are its moving parts? For this task, I form a beginning typology. Second, I wonder how the parts operate and how they are connected. This second question is the domain of theory, which in its most rudimentary form is a set of constructs with explanatory linkages. Although many authors note there is no overall comprehensive theory of sustainability (Cabezas and Fath, 2002; Walck, 2004), there is a proliferation of constructs and linkages—think about them as strands of DNA in primordial soup—that occur throughout the many discourses of sustainability and sustainable development (henceforth referred to collectively as *sustainability*). My aim in this chapter is to offer a set of notions aimed at sorting out and better understanding the many different aspects of sustainability. To that end, I have organized this chapter around the following questions. Although the state of the science and the art of sustainability is not far enough along to answer most of these questions definitively, I provide a useful foundation for each.

1. What is the genesis and what are the basic dimensions of sustainability?
2. From what worldview does the idea of sustainability arise?
3. What is the nature of discourses around sustainability?
4. What are the basic constructs in the human quest for sustainability?
5. As a social structure, how does sustainability operate, where is it located, and to what end does it aim?
6. How can we best understand what sustainability is about and how it operates in society?
7. What is a good starting point for social sustainability?

Before we take up the first question, I want to turn to the question of methodology. I use analytic grounded theory method to develop both the questions and propositions presented in this chapter. The purpose of my inquiry is to examine the theoretical basis of sustainability and sustainable development. The field I immerse myself in is the field of existing literature and recursive reflections on my background and experience in the practice of sustainability. I bring an informant's view to this endeavor. I have spent most of my career as a government official in, around, or at the edges of sustainability. Seconded to the State Department, I was the lead U.S. negotiator for four chapters of Agenda 21, the most comprehensive of the outputs of the 1992 Earth Summit in Rio de Janeiro—more properly known as the United Nations Conference on Environment and Development. I have been active throughout my career working with others in the development of criteria and indicators for measuring sustainability—particularly in the arena of forestry and natural resources. I served as a senior policy advisor on natural resources for President Clinton's Commission on Sustainable Development.

I first started this present inquiry with the intent of discovering what was known or speculated about the theoretical basis of sustainability. I found little formal work has been done in this arena and was thus forced to dig a little deeper. My framing question then led me to look outside the immediate field of sustainability to discover what theoretical work has been done that can inform development of theory pertaining to sustainability. By dint of the fact that there is no commonly accepted theory of sustainability as a starting point, the inquiry in this chapter is eclectic in nature, drawing from diverse fields. The science of sustainability, as I have experienced it, emerges from many different corners. For my inquiry, I brought no a priori conditioning other than (a) the basic question itself, allowing the question to re-form as I proceeded; (b) a desire to be open in inquiry and rigorous in drawing out meaning and conclusion; and (c) my own familiarity with sustainability borne of my participation in its birth at Rio de Janeiro and practice from my own corner of forestry and natural resources. The underlying motive that drives my study of the whole field in the first place is the fact that people are rarely dealt with explicitly in the science of natural resources and that people are by and large problematic in policy that deals with natural resources—they are either a problem that needs to be dealt with (as in public notice and comment processes of policy formulation or in lawsuits on agency actions deriving from policy) or its intended beneficiaries. Only recently are agencies beginning to involve people in collaborative fashion in policy development or project planning and implementation. As the result of my inquiry thus far, I have come to a profound recognition that not only are people at the center of development by virtue of their actions—sustainable or not—but people are the very *raison d'etre* of the quest for sustainability in the first place. You will discover that this notion is contested, but it forms, nonetheless, the prime motive for my beginnings here of theory development around sustainability. It is my aim to give voice to and place people in the center of their own development as agents and beneficiaries.

WHAT IS THE GENESIS AND WHAT ARE THE BASIC DIMENSIONS OF SUSTAINABILITY?

The basic concept of sustainable development is generally viewed as having been conceived by the Brundtland Commission report "Our Common Future" (World Commission on Environment and Development, 1987), which defined *sustainable development* in its most enduring formulation as "development that meets the needs of the present without compromising the ability of future generations to meet their own needs" (p. 43). After a difficult 2-year-long incubation of preparatory negotiations, 184 nations participated in the 1992 birth of sustainable development at the Earth Summit in Rio de Janeiro—more properly known as the United Nations Conference on Environment and Development (UNCED). Although UNCED proclaimed the primacy of sustainability, it also proclaimed that sustainability needs to be considered fully from its social, economic, and environmental dimensions (Larsen, 1994). So, from the debate among nations, one of the foundational constructs of sustainability arose—namely, that sustainability occurs in three fundamental dimensions: social, economic, and environmental. Thinking about beginning to build a theory of sustainability, the first foundational explanatory linkage that arose from the negotiations is the deep connection between the three dimensions—namely, that for sustainability to occur, it must occur simultaneously in each of the three dimensions as shown in Fig. 3.1.

> *Proposition 1*: Sustainability occurs in three fundamental dimensions—social, economic, and environmental. For sustainability to occur, it must occur simultaneously in each of the three dimensions.

Region 4 in the Venn diagram is the only area where this simultaneity takes place. The other areas of intersection—regions 1 through 3—illustrate areas of intersection where one of the basic dimensions is missing and, thus, mutual sustainability is not attained.

From this simple foundational construct of sustainability, several interesting notions arise. First, if sustainability requires consideration of all three dimensions, then environmental sustainability, for example, is not a proposition that can stand alone without reference to social and economic dimensions, just like economic sustainability (more intuitively) cannot stand without reference to its social and environmental impacts (dimensions).

A second point of consideration is the nature of the "game." Is sustainability a zero-sum game of competing interests? Or is it a game of converging interests where collaboration can yield synergistic benefits? In fact, there arose from the UNCED negotiations an oft-commonly shared sense that sustainability was about finding converging interests. It was, many proclaimed, not about jobs versus the environment, but more about how a path can be found where both employment and environmental protection can proceed hand in hand. This second point then raises the question of whether the area of convergent sustainability (area 4 in Fig. 3.1) is static or dynamic. If

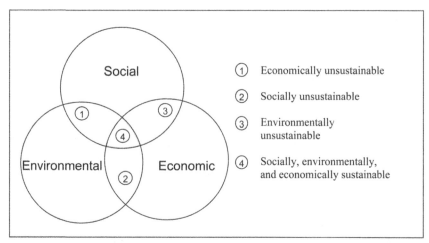

Figure 3.1 Dimensions of sustainability (from Larsen, 1994).

it is dynamic, can it be purposefully grown? The last point I raise here is the subtle implication that if the area of convergence can be grown, it can only happen through cross-disciplinary connections created by people reaching beyond their own immediate goals, interests, or training to other, perhaps unfamiliar, territory.

FROM WHAT WORLDVIEW DOES THE IDEA OF SUSTAINABILITY ARISE?

The quest for sustainability has both human and material dimensions. Writ big, sustainability is a set of emergent discourses and actions arising, in large measure, from civil society. These discourses and actions, like many social phenomena, are played out variously at many levels of human endeavor—from individual to global. According to Pamela Wright et al. (2002) "The quest ultimately requires decisions about what to sustain, for whom, for how long, at what cost, and how" (p. 1). Left unsaid in her work are the following important questions: (a) who gets to decide, (b) who pays, and (c) who is responsible for delivering it? There is yet another dimension of sustainability in that it also is a dynamic. This fact then raises an entirely different set of questions, which include (a) what is the motive power, (b) how does movement take place, (c) who or what are the agents, (d) to what purpose is the movement aimed, (e) what elements are enjoined in the dynamics, and (f) did the dynamic actually reach its intended outcomes?

Discourses about sustainability take place within many different worldviews, each with its own unique set of precepts, values, and assumptions. The answers to sustainability's most important questions importantly depend on one's view of the world. Paul Heppner, Dennis Kivlighan, and Bruce Wampold (1999) observe that worldviews "are the philosophical foundations that guide understanding of the world and how inquiries are made to further that understanding" (p. 236). They posit four worldviews:

1. *Positivism* employs the scientific method. It holds that the nature of the universe can be known, and the scientist's goal is to discover the natural laws that govern the universe.
2. *Postpositivism* also employs the scientific method, but recognizes truth cannot be fully known. We must therefore make probabilistic rather than absolute statements about truth. Methods include peer review and scientific community arbitration.
3. *Constructivism* holds that ideas about the world are constructed in people's minds. Reality is created by the participants of any system, the investigator, and the object under consideration, which cannot be conceived of separately. General methods are hermeneutics and dialectics. There are no truths to be discovered. Methods are recursive rather than linear, and results and method influence each other.

4. *Critical Theory* holds that people's social constructions are shaped by their environment. Investigation involves investigator/subject dialogue, and the dialectic should lead to the participant's understanding that social action is needed to change the social order.

Heppner et al. believe that awareness of the paradigm at hand is crucial to match appropriate methods to belief systems and to create research that is relevant for the associated body of knowledge. They distinguish qualitative research and methods from quantitative, noting the general affiliation of quantitative research with positivist and postpositivist enquiry and qualitative research with constructivist and critical theory research.

Sustainability and sustainable development are concerned with both the material world (e.g., net present value or environmental impacts) and the social world (e.g., environmental justice or equity or politics). This juxtaposition sets up a potential clash of worldviews because the material world is often most appropriately explored within a positivist and postpositivist worldview typically employing quantitative methods, whereas the social world is often most appropriately explored within a constructivist or critical worldview typically employing qualitative methods. Much of the confusion and many of disagreements surrounding sustainability can be traced to differences in worldview. The propositions set forth in this chapter aim at finding ways to bridge worldviews to better inform the quest for sustainability. A first question, then, in sorting out the quest for sustainability provides a grounding that facilitates appropriate purposeful inquiry, debate, and problem solving:

> *Proposition 2*: Worldview matters when investigating the various constructs, linkages, claims, causes, and effects of sustainability, and the method of investigation should be appropriate for the worldview from which it arises.

A claim that a particular set of sustainable forestry practices do not adversely affect the environment, for example, is a claim in a positivist or postpositivist world and can appropriately be supported or refuted by scientific methods. Whether such forestry practices are appropriate for a particular forest in question, however, can have both normative and positive aspects. The question of how to best maintain forest health is a positivist or postpositivist question. However, the question of whether a particular forest in question should be actively managed and, if so, to what purpose is a question best dealt with in a constructivist or critical theory worldview and methods. Continuing with the forest in question, presume for a moment that it is part of the last remaining old-growth stand in the Northwest. Presume further that the manager of the stand in question makes the postpositivist claim that the greatest net value to society occurs when it is actively managed using the latest green-certified silvicultural practices. Others might claim that protecting rare and endangered species is more important. Such counterclaims might be difficult to support or refute in a positivist or postpositivist world. However, they may be fully considered with methods more appropriate to their origin—the constructivist question of what the law says or the critical theory question of biocentric versus anthropocentric rights and values. We see, then, that dialectic inquiry can yield great information about important questions at hand.

Corollary to Proposition 2: When weighing the merits of a particular claim or construct about sustainability, alternative worldviews provide a rich source of insight into both its strengths and shortcomings.

WHAT IS THE NATURE OF DISCOURSES AROUND SUSTAINABILITY?

Discourse about sustainability and sustainable development occurs in several mainstreams, as well as eclectically in a myriad of forums. Castro's (2004) characterization of sustainability being ubiquitous applies particularly to its supporting literature. Clark et al. (2005), in reflecting on sustainability, recognize that

> The concept of sustainable development carries many meanings and attracts many reactions. But this much seems clear: Over the last two decades, the idea of sustainable development has provided space for an amazingly diverse set of interest groups and institutions from around the world that have projected upon it their own fears, hopes, and aspirations for a better life. (p. 3)

Discourses about sustainability occur at many levels and groupings of society, including at the international, national, state, and local levels, as well as in academia and the private sector. I examine two aspects of sustainability discourses in the following discussion. First, I take up the question and give examples of where sustainability discourses take place. Second, I examine the purposes of discourse. In summary, I offer a typology of sustainability discourses arrayed in these two dimensions. Because of the proliferation of entities involved in the discourse, I create only a loosely defined institutional approach to categorize where discourses take place considering both the level and goal orientation. Purposes and underlying intent for discourses and actions taken in the name of sustainability similarly occupy a wide spectrum. Turning to my own managerial roots, I enlist principles put forward by Peter Drucker (1954) in beginning with a managerial approach to unravel the complex purposes surrounding sustainability.

Discourses in Institutions

Most discourses around sustainability take place within and among organizations. Although the basic elements of organizations have remained relatively unchanged through history, there has been and continues to be great variety in form, structure, function, processes, and outcomes. Theories and schools of theories of organizations abound (Shafritz and Ott, 2001). Graham Astley and Andrew Van de Ven (1983) add structure to the various schools through their four views of organization shown in Fig. 3.2. They contrast level of organization (from individual organizations to populations and communities of organizations) with purposes arrayed along a continuum of autonomy (from determinism to volunteerism). They characterize four views of organizations to be natural selection, system structural, collective action, and strategic choice. The utility of this approach is to discriminate among the various views to find isomorphisms within views and contrast differences among views to learn about the nature of organizations. For our purposes here of framing, it informs our needs to segregate the divergence of views surrounding sustainability. From this approach, we recognize utility in arraying both level and purpose.

According to Shafritz and Ott (2001), the various theories of organization date from at least 1491 B.C. and deal with everything from power to chaos, including the organized anarchies of the garbage can model of organizational choice put forward by Michael Cohen, James March, and Johan Olsen (1972 p. 1). The point is that organizations and their elements and aggregations, theories, purposes, and applications span a diverse field of disciplines, logic, worldviews, and language. Although a rigorous sorting out of the various institutions involved in discourses of sustainability would undoubtedly yield great insights, for the purposes of this chapter, I loosely array institutions according to level, with international organizations at one end and individuals and groups in civil society at the other end. To this continuum, I add academia, which I locate at the broadest level because it concerns itself with human endeavor at all scales. I do not rigorously derive the institutional categories used here, but rather choose them

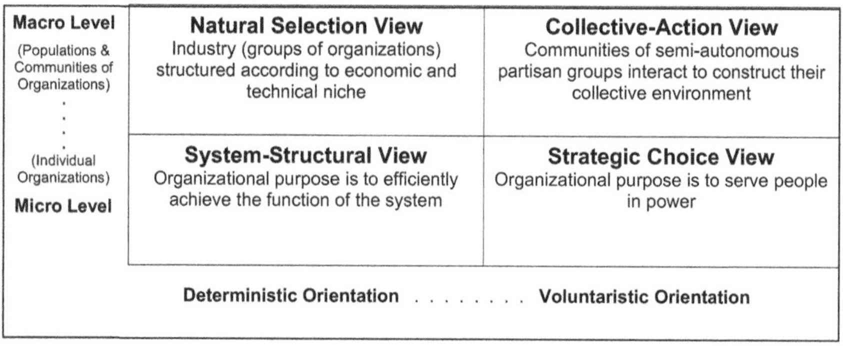

Macro Level (Populations & Communities of Organizations)	Natural Selection View Industry (groups of organizations) structured according to economic and technical niche	Collective-Action View Communities of semi-autonomous partisan groups interact to construct their collective environment
(Individual Organizations) Micro Level	System-Structural View Organizational purpose is to efficiently achieve the function of the system	Strategic Choice View Organizational purpose is to serve people in power

Deterministic Orientation . . . . Voluntaristic Orientation

Figure 3.2 Four views of organization and management (from Astley and Van de Ven, 1983).

inductively for convenience with the aim of bringing at least some order to a diffuse and ubiquitous literature. The institutional discourses I consider here are (a) UN organizations; (b) multilateral international organizations; (c) national, state, and local governments; (d) corporations; (e) civil society, which spans from individuals to nongovernmental organizations; and (f) academia. I take up the question of purposes of discourse after examining some representative discourses.

UN *and Derivative Organizations.*

The founding discourse for sustainability and sustainable development occurred under the aegis of the UN. Many derivative discourses continue. First among these discourses are agreements among nations. Several agreements came out of the Earth Summit (Larsen, 1994), including a consensus among all countries declared in two sets of principles—one entitled the "Rio Declaration on Environment and Development" (United Nations, 1992c) and the other a set of "Forest Principles" (United Nations, 1992b)—and an extensive global action plan for sustainable development "Agenda 21" (United Nations, 1992a). Many subsequent conferences, notably the Johannesburg Summit 2002 (United Nations World Summit on Sustainable Development), have produced numerous pertinent international agreements and accords. Closely allied discourse arises from many of the various organizations of the UN created by international agreement. Examples include the Brundtland Commission report "Our Common Future" (World Commission on Environment and Development, 1987) and various publications by the World Commission on Sustainable Development. This category also includes all the predominantly internal reports generated by secretariats of various conferences to inform negotiations. One example of this type of document is the report on the state of the world's forests, "Conservation and Development of Forests" (United Nations, 1991), a report prepared by the Secretary General of the Conference for Preparatory Committee for the UNCED, for the third session, working group 1, Conches, Switzerland.

Multilateral Organizations

Another significant body of literature lies in the policies, missions, regulations, analyses, and reports of multilateral international institutions outside of the UN family of organizations. Multilateral organizations are distinguished from UN organizations in that their scope, mission, and authority derive from member countries. Conferences of Parties and derivative supporting organizations for various treaties such as Climate Change and Biodiversity are considered multilateral organizations because their authority is derived from countries signing the treaties, rather than from the UN. In some cases, such as the World Trade Organization, considerable power is delegated by member countries, sufficient sometimes to force constitutional amendments for member countries. Thus, the literature produced by multilateral organizations has particular relevance for sustainability and sustainable development. The Santiago Declaration by 10 temperate and boreal forest non-European nations, including the United States and Canada, resulted in the development of a comprehensive set of criteria and indicators for forest conservation and sustainable management known as the Montreal Process Criteria and Indicators (Montréal Process Working Group, 2004). Europe has similar agreements, working groups, and publications. Countries suffering from desertification, particularly African countries, have an international treaty and Commission to Combat Desertification that also adds to the literature. Thirty countries, including the United States, are parties to the Convention on the Organization for Economic Cooperation and Development (OECD), which was signed in 1960. OECD does extensive work in sustainable development, listing more than 1,000 documents and publications pertaining to sustainability—for example, the OECD framework for environmental indicators (Linster and Fletcher, 2004) and the Pressure-State-Response Model (Organization for Economic Cooperation and Development, 2003). The World Bank and the International Monetary Fund are active in sustainable development. A report published by Serageldin (1993) in the journal, *Finance & Development*, outlines the World Bank's philosophy and strategy for sustainable development.

Governments

A variety of countries have produced national reports or undertaken national efforts to promote, measure, and take stock of national efforts of sustainable development. The United States, for example, created the President's Council on Sustainable Development under President Clinton, for which the author served as a natural resource policy advisor and primary writer and editor for the natural resource portions of the Council's first report, "Sustainable America, A New Consensus for the Prosperity, Opportunity and a Healthy Environment for the Future" (President's Council on Sustainable Development, 1996). The report articulates philosophies, values, principles, national goals and objectives, as well as best practices. At the state level, governments have undertaken a variety of programs and initiatives around sustainability, including, for example, Oregon's Board of Forestry's (2003) recently issued strategic plan embracing sustainable development, the "Forestry Program for Oregon." The Oregon Department of Forestry created a companion strategic plan to implement the Board of Forestry's Plan (Oregon Department of Forestry, 2004). The State of Oregon also prepared, working with Portland State University, an assessment of Oregon's sustainability. The Oregon State government has embraced sustainability, as shown in Fig. 3.3 from the Oregon Progress Board. As another example of government activity, the U.S. Department of Agriculture (USDA) Forest Service has regulations, policy, research, and programs in the arena of sustainable development. A recent Forest Service publication documented ground-breaking research in the area of criteria and indicators for sustainability (Wright et al., 2002).

Corporations

Industries working through associations, as well as individual companies also have undertaken significant efforts with regard to sustainable development, thereby creating discourses and an accompanying literature. Members of the American Forest and Paper Association, for example, created a Sustainable Forestry Initiative and agreed in concert with the Earth Summit

> To adhere to a set of forestry principles that would meet the needs of the present without compromising the ability of future generations to meet their own needs. These principles call for a land stewardship ethic that integrates the reforestation, nurturing, and harvesting of trees for useful products with the conservation of soil, air and water resources, wildlife and fish habitat, and forest aesthetics. (American Forest & Paper Association, 1994, p. 1)

The American Institute of Architects (2004), as another example, recently published a set of metrics for measuring sustainability and performance. Norm Thompson, an Oregon corporation, is an example of a corporation with a commitment to sustainability. It has added to the body of literature by adopting and documenting (a) an environmental policy and sustainability objectives; (b) sustainability in the products they use and sell; (c) sustainability in community, interest group, and associate involvement; (d) sustainability awards and recognition; and (e) a green headquarters building (Norm Thompson Inc., 2004).

Civil Society

Organizations and groups within civil society at both the local and international levels make most significant contributions to the understanding, practice, and literature of sustainability and sustainable development. I take up the question of what constitutes civil society in the context of sustainability later in the chapter. Three examples illustrate the point. The first example, Sustainable Northwest, is a nonprofit organization that promotes environmentally sound economic development. It operates on the donations of and through partnerships with private foundations, corporations, government agencies, and private citizens (Sustainable Northwest, 2004). It has four well-documented partnership programs.

A variety of national and international nongovernmental organizations (NGOs) are involved in green or sustainability certification programs. Leadership in Energy and Environmental Design (LEED), for the second

Figure 3.3 Oregon Progress Board Web page.

example, is a voluntary green building rating system created by the U.S. Green Building Council (2004) that represents all segments of the building industry. They publish a set of consensus-based national standards for assessing buildings.

The third example is an international nongovernmental organization, RIOD, which emerged around the Conference of Parties' implementation of the International Treaty to Combat Desertification, an outgrowth of the Earth Summit in Rio. RIOD (after the Earth Summit in *Rio* and the Treaty on Combating *D*esertification) is a network to "strengthen the participation of civil society, particularly women and youth, in the Convention implementation" (Secretariat International RIOD, 2004a). RIOD describes itself as having a flexible and decentralized structure organized at the regional and national levels. They maintain an active website (Secretariat International RIOD, 2004b) which serves as both a directory of organizations, a framework for organizations to communicate, and a repository of information. They also connect together the field operations of many participating NGOs. Their objectives are remarkable for an NGO in both scope and depth. They are to (a) facilitate networking among civil society,

(b) strengthen the capacity for RIOD members to assist in implementation of the Convention, (c) develop and promote partnerships, (d) promote a consultation and lobbying framework to foster on-the-ground engagement of civil society, (e) develop strategies and methods to combat desertification, and (f) implement pilot projects for propagation of the Convention's ideas. While remarkable, this NGO is representative of many other NGOs active in sustainable development and well illustrates the contribution this sector makes to the literature.

Academia

The foremost academic literature around sustainable development is in economics. David Pearce and Edward Barbier (2000) capture the main theme of environmental economics in the "now widely-accepted observation that most environmental problems have their origins in the misworkings of the economic system, and that their solutions therefore lie in the correction of those misworkings" (p. xi). Of course, still within the economics literature, others argue that the system is the problem either from an ecological perspective (Goodland and Daly, 1996) or from a Marxist perspective (Castro, 2004). Another prolific literature topic is that of international development; for example, a recent article examines the implications of the Johannesburg Summit on Sustainable Development on energy (Spalking-Fecher, Winkler, and Mwakasonda, 2005). The natural science literature around ecology and biology also discusses sustainability at length, as in a recent article that proffers ecological sustainability as a conservation concept (Callicott and Mumford, 1997). There is a fledging literature around social sustainability. As a case in point, Markku Lehtonen (2004) observes that the

> *social* dimension has commonly been recognized as the weakest "pillar" of sustainable development, notably when it comes to its analytical and theoretical underpinnings. While increasing attention has lately been paid to **social sustainability**, the interaction between the "environmental" and the **"social"** still remains a largely uncharted terrain. (p. 199; bold italics original)

Although operations research, systems analysis, and systems theory literature are scattered through many literatures, a systems view provides much research and many insights into sustainability and sustainable development. A brief review of this literature shows many applications of a systems analysis approach to studying sustainability in the fields of energy, water resources, life cycle assessments, and transportation, among others. Urban studies, geography, and environmental planning also have a large literature revolving around sustainability and sustainable development. As a testament to the eclectic nature of much of the sustainability literature, I discovered a remarkable article on theory of sustainable systems in a little known journal, *Fluid Phase Equilibria* (Cabezas and Fath, 2002) that the Portland State University reference librarian reports is only physically on the shelves in two universities in the entire United States.

As an acknowledgment to academia and the academic literature, universities also take up the cause of sustainability and produce a variety of publications pertaining to sustainability. Portland State University (2005, p. 1), for example, embraces sustainability in many ways. "Our vision is to be an internationally recognized urban university known for excellence in student learning, innovative research, and community engagement that contributes to the economic vitality, environmental sustainability, and quality of life in the Portland region and beyond" (p. X). Among other things, the university offers a new professional certificate program launched in 2003, "Implementing Sustainability: Building Human Capacity for Implementing Best Practices," and a minor in sustainable urban development. The university sponsors lecture series, publications, workshops, and community partnerships centered on sustainability, including the Millennium Speakers Series, cosponsored with community partners that featured leading sustainability thinkers; the School of Business Administration Sustainability Conversations series in 2002–2003; and the Institute for Portland Metropolitan Studies' Forum on Sustainability and the Economy series. University of Oregon, as another example, published an assessment of their own sustainability (Good Company, 2002). Oregon State University convened and facilitated a landmark assessment of Oregon's forest sustainability in partnership with Oregon Department of Forestry (2001).

Purposes of Discourse

Yosef Jabareen (2004, p. 23) characterizes the discourses around sustainability and sustainable development as fragmented and multidisciplinary. He reports seven metaphors and domains around which the literature is assembled: (a) the *"metaphor of ethical paradox* signifies the ethical domain (italics added)," (b) the *metaphor of natural capital* for the material domain, (c) the *metaphor of fairness* for the social domain, (d) the *metaphor of eco-form* for the spatial domain, (e) the *metaphor of global discourse* for the political domain, (f) the *metaphor of integrative management* for the management domain, and (g) the *utopian metaphor* for the visionary domain. Colin Williams and Andrew Millington (2004) undertake an overview of the diverse meanings of sustainable development and find dialectically opposing views depending on one's beliefs about the relationship between people and nature. One set of definitions is anthropocentric, and the other is biocentric defending nature's biotic rights—a discussion that is taken up later in this chapter. When the meaning of sustainable development is as diverse and contested as reported by Williams and Millington and as dependent on frame as suggested by Jabareen, it is clear that much work remains to be done in sorting out and understanding the various views. To help organize the chaos in sorting out purposes, I first turn to Peter Drucker (1986), who often has been called the father of modern management. His classic managerial structure of planning, organizing, implementing, and monitoring/controlling is a time-honored way for sorting out the chaos facing managers and, thus, provides a good starting point here. Planning can be considered in this context to include discourses about sustainability from the perspective of governance. It is useful to expand the notion of planning to explicitly include policy and goals, thus taking in the process of policy formulation as it pertains to sustainability as well as its resultant goals. Including goal formulation in planning has the additional advantage of including within its realm the purposeful nature of the many individuals, groups, and organizations rising to the quest for sustainability. Organizing in this context corresponds to both the organization of existing institutional settings in which discourses about sustainability take place and the discourses about how to best organize to achieve sustainability. Implementing in the context of sustainability captures discussions about sustainable practices that occur in many of the discourses, as well as the actual implementation of sustainability initiatives. Reflecting on the practical orientation of many individuals and corporations involved in the sustainability movement, Drucker's category of implementation is broadened here to include best practices—a notion often discussed in the context of sustainability. Drucker included both performance monitoring and taking actions to correct deviances in the last managerial action of monitoring/ controlling. Monitoring, of course, can pertain to both measuring natural conditions and conditions altered as the result of man's (and women's) activities, including success and efficacy of sustainability ventures. The controlling aspect pertains here particularly to sustainability cast in a regulatory framework.

Reflecting further on what additional kinds of purposes might exist for sustainability, the institution of academia reminds us of the importance of theory (constructs and their linkages). Considering governance and its often political dimension, it might prove useful to extract ideology as a separate additional purpose for sustainability discourse. Taken together, this brief discussion of the nature of discourses around sustainability suggests the following elements as a starting point for the second dimension of the typology regarding the nature of discourse: (a) theory; (b) ideology; (c) policy, plans, and goals; (d) organizing, (e) implementation and best practices; and (f) monitoring/controlling.

A Typology for Discourses About Sustainability

Having considered the level where sustainability discourses take place and the purposes to which they are aimed, I propose a first typology of sustainability that arrays the discourse around these two dimensions: (a) the institutional location of the discourse, and (b) the nature of the discourse.

The resultant typology is displayed in Table 3.1. Thus, a simple systematic method is proposed for examining various constructs of sustainability. Although this typology falls short of being a comprehensive theory, it can be used to explicate and locate various pieces of the discourses that have imbedded within them individual constructs of sustainability. This typology gives rise to the third proposition about sustainability:

> *Proposition 3:* Discourses around sustainability occur (a) in particular institutional settings, and (b) for a particular purpose.

Understanding these two dimensions is crucial for explicating and understanding particular claims and constructs and for reliably communicating to others.

WHAT ARE THE BASIC CONSTRUCTS IN THE HUMAN QUEST FOR SUSTAINABILITY?

A theory is a series of constructs and their explanatory linkages set within a particular scope, including boundary conditions and assumptions (Bacharach, 1989). Various formulations and constructs of sustainability and their explanatory linkages are scattered throughout many discourses. Although only a comprehensive theory of sustainability could provide a framework to weave together and link all the various constructs, creating such a comprehensive theory is beyond the scope of this chapter. However, it is instructive to explore some prototypal constructs as a precursor to such a task. Max Weber (1978) creates sociology's methodological foundation to include (a) social actions and their consequences imbedded in their meanings, be they individual, plural, or of a theoretically constructed ideal type; (b) establishment of meaning as the basis of intention; and (c) motive as comprising a complex of subjective meaning. Through an examination

Table 3.1 A Typology for Discourses About Sustainability

Institutional Setting	Nature of Discourse
Academia	Theory
UN organizations	Ideology
Multilateral organizations	Policy, plans, and goals
Governments—national, state, and local	Organizing
Corporations	Implementation and best practices
Civil society	Monitoring/controlling

of sustainability as a sociological phenomenon, I claim that sustainable development is a uniquely human quest, whereby societal development closely parallels individual development.

Starting with a Weberian approach, we can begin the task of exploring some of the fundamental propositions of sustainability. First, sustainability is about choices, the consequences of those choices, and the associated motives and meanings. Choices are made by people as individuals or in groups. Choices are informed by people's cognition of the material and social world around them and by their own motives. Choices take place in the context of previous choices and are therefore informed by the social and material effects of previous choices and by the discourses that take place within society about them. The process of considering previous and expected future effects in the social and material world is the process of learning. Learning involves changes in internal maps of the world, internal theories about how its social and material aspects work, and speculation about how internal intent can be affected on the external world, which is parallel to Jean Piaget's (1952) formal operations stage of individual cognitive development discussed later in the chapter. The questions that arise from these beginning propositions about the quest for sustainability are clearly in the domain of social science, particularly human cognitive development. From this simple reduction of sustainability into some of its constituent parts, it becomes apparent that understanding sustainability involves understanding four fundamental dynamics: (a) discourses in society—where and how they take place and to what end, (b) social actions, (c) consequences imbedded in their meanings, and (d) human development—how people learn and adapt.

Proposition 4: The quest for sustainability is comprised of four fundamental dynamics: (a) discourses in society, (b) social actions, (c) their consequences, and (d) the associated learning and adaptation.

Civil Society as a Mediating Structure

We can learn more about discourses by taking a closer look at civil society from which they arise and the symbolism embedded in such discourse. For this task, we first turn to Michael Burawoy (2003), who outlines the convergence of Antonio Gramsci and Karl Polanyi in their critique and extension of classical Marxism. Although his aim was to create a new sociological Marxism to provide a modern critique of today's capitalism, he creates a map of civil society that informs an understanding of where discourses about sustainability take place. His thesis is "the dynamism of 'society,' primarily located between state and economy, is a key to the durability and transcendence of advanced capitalism" (p. 194). Although Marx finds elements of society in communism, Burawoy argues that the need for sociological Marxism arises from the failure of Marx to examine society under capitalism. In keeping with the tradition of the historical materialist conception of history, both Gramsci and Polanyi, who Burawoy cites, describe society in historically specific terms. Gramsci observes trade unions, political parties, public education, and interest groups as civil society mediating the state by either collaborating with the state to contain class struggle or fomenting class struggle in opposition to the state. Polanyi sees trade unions, cooperatives, and other movements mediating the market, a phenomenon Burawoy refers to as *active society* (see Fig. 3.4). For both, Burawoy (2003) describes socialism as "the subordination of market and state to the self-regulating society" (p. 198).

He distinguishes sociological Marxism from sociology in three ways that are useful in informing our understanding of discourses in civil society: (a) society has no coherency of its own—it is merely the institutional space that various entities occupy; (b) society has a duality that provides space for stabilizing the market and the state, but it also provides the same space for subordinating the state and the economy to a self-regulating community; and (c) the sociological mechanisms that are employed to explain and mediate the market and the state are employed in sociological Marxism as critiques of the market and state. Thus, Burwaoy creates civil society as a mediating structure between the market and the state.

The Private and the Public

Burawoy (2003) briefly considers past and modern colonialism as well as feminism to consider the fragmentation of civil society, recognizing that there is much texture and differentiation and many cleavages, levels, and linkages within society today. From the consideration of feminism, he elicits two significant points: (a) the bifurcation of society into public and private spheres, and (b) how women's exploitation in the private sphere can "bleed out" into the public sphere in a way parallel to the way "that needs issue from the economic realm into the social where they are interpreted and contested as class interests . . . whereupon they become claims upon the state" (Burawoy, 2003, p. 249). From a discussion of feminism, he draws the importance of the boundaries between the state, civil society,

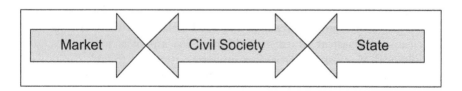

Figure. 3.4 Civil society according to Burawoy (from Polanyi and Gramsci; cited in Burawoy, 2003).

and private spheres, and the importance of intellectuals to illuminating their edges. Last, he shines a light on political participation through discourse in the public sphere, thus setting the stage for the next discussion on the polarizing discourse of civil society.

The Polarizing Discourse of Civil Society

Jeffrey Alexander (1992) picks up where Burawoy leaves off. He talks about solidarity and its fragmentation—its construction, destruction, and deconstruction. Placing himself clearly in the same universe as Burawoy, he defines *civil society* as "a sphere or subsystem of society that is analytically and, to various degrees, empirically separated from the spheres of political, economic, and religious life. Civil society is a sphere of solidarity in which abstract universalism and particularistic versions of community are tensely intertwined" (Alexander, 1992, p. 289). He notes that civil society is connected to the other spheres by requiring their input. Alexander suggests that *moral society* can be defined as "socially established consciousness" of which civil society is a realm. He defines socially established consciousness as "a network of understandings that operates beneath and above explicit institutions and the self-conscious interests of elites" (Alexander, 1992, p. 290). He asserts that symbolic codes are the essence of this subjective dimension of civil society, and these codes constitute the basic engram of two ideal types—pure and impure—into which we place every member of civil society.

Civil Codes of Exclusion and Inclusion

From these ideal types, he draws out a primal human conceptualization of the world in terms of inclusion or exclusion, thus creating civil codes of inclusion and exclusion. Acknowledging that such distinction has no objective reality, he observes that when we make distinctions about who does or does not belong in civil society, we entrain a "systematic, highly elaborated symbolic code" (Alexander, 1992,, p. 291) whose structure was already imbedded the first Greek philosophical conceptualization of democratic societies. Although the symbolic structure takes different variegated forms in different nations based on various historical social, philosophical, and cultural residues, according to Alexander, they all have the common feature of separating civic virtue from civic vice. Thus, he believes that the "language that forms the cultural core of civil society can be isolated as a general structure and studied as a relatively autonomous symbolic form" (Alexander, 1992, p. 291), and that the basic elements follow semiotic patterns—patterns of likenesses. He asserts that members of democratic societies believe the positive and negative symbols sets are good descriptors of real individual and social life and thus, by implication, concrete. The relevance here for the discourses on sustainability is that when conflicts arise as the result of strongly differing world views, a moral indignation often accompanies the evaluation of a differing view of what constitutes sustainability.

Three Sets of Binary Discourses.

Alexander (1992) finds that "binary discourse occurs at three levels: motives, relations, and institutions" (p. 292). The discursive structure at each level splits into a democratic code and a counterdemocratic code. From motives, which judge the person, arise representation of social relationships. From individuals and social relationships arise institutional attributions. Table 3.2 (Alexander, 1992) gives representative examples of qualities associated with each discourse. The discourses are tied together by analogical similarity to any element in another set on the same side. Although simple in their binary forms, according to Alexander (1992), these discourses "reveal the skeletal structures on which social communities build the familiar stories, the rich narrative forms, which guide their everyday, taken-for-granted political life" (p. 294). They thus become the "discourse of liberty."

Discourse Creates Objective Reality

Alexander (1992) submits that, taken together, his propositions create a "general discursive structure . . . used to legitimate friends and delegitimate opponents in the course of real historical time" (p. 299). He makes the argument that, over time, the discourse of repression inevitably comes into play and vilifies opponents as being of the most threatening type. Alexander's arguments and propositions make interesting and useful constructions that shine a light on some of the dynamics and reasons that social and political discourse unfolds the way it does. For discourses in the quest for sustainability, his

Table 3.2 Representative Qualities Associated With Discursive Structures According to Alexander (1992)

Discursive Structure	Democratic Code	Counterdemocratic Code
Social motives	Activism	Passivity
	Autonomy	Dependence
	Rationality	Irrationality
Social relations	Open	Secret
	Trusting	Suspicious
	Straightforward	Calculating
Social institutions	Rule-regulated	Arbitrary
	Law	Power
	Inclusive	Exclusive

insights into the binary nature of public discourses, with their implicit symbolic inclusion or exclusion, point to the importance of searching for meaning and content in differing views of sustainability, rather than rushing to the conclusion of rightness or wrongness.

> *Proposition 5:* The quest for sustainability is best informed by searching for meaning and content in differing views of sustainability, rather than rushing to the conclusion of rightness or wrongness from a particular worldview.

Social Actions

From a Weberian (1978) view, questions about individual choices and motivations are exactly within sociology, which he defines to be the science of "interpretive understanding of social action and . . . causal explanation of its course and consequences" (p. 4). Thus, a Weberian approach to the various constructs related to sustainability might explore the constructs through (a) ideal types, (b) a model of individual choice, and (c) subsequent case studies. A Durkheimian approach, in contrast, would focus on the broader societal constructs from which individual choices are circumscribed (Collins, 1994). Although Weberian analysis is typically case based and leads to historical explanations for observed phenomena, a Durkheimian approach is typically variable based and leads to explanations based on patterns of relationships among variables (Ragin and Zaret, 1983). In this chapter, I rely on Weberian ideal types and theory of rational choice, and I use a Durkheimian approach to build the typology for sustainability discourses outlined earlier.

Two Seminal Ideal Types

With regard to ideal types, there are two seminal precursors to the notion of sustainable development. One is "The Limits to Growth" (Meadows and Club of Rome, 1972) based on the work of Jay Forrester (1971)—the "Club of Rome" report that was sometimes referred to as the "doomsday" report. It proclaimed that (a) without major change, the world will run out of nonrenewable resources, resulting in collapse of society; (b) piecemeal solutions will not solve the problem; and (c) the only answer is immediate limit on population and pollution, as well as cessation of economic growth. According to the study, growth will cease one way or the other—either by our purposeful actions or by our inactions. A second precursor is "The Next 200 Years" (Kahn, Brown, Martel, and Hudson Institute, 1976). It is the "antidote" to the catastrophism of the "Limits of Growth." It was the model for optimism, asserting that " . . . 200 years ago almost everywhere human beings were comparatively few, poor and at the mercy of the forces of nature, and 200 years from now, we expect, almost everywhere they will be numerous, rich and in control of the forces of nature" (p. 1). The study was a series of plausible scenarios based on human ingenuity and technological progress to overcome limits. So here we have the beginnings of Weber's two ideal types: (a) a biocentric view typified by Meadows where people are the problem, and (b) an anthropocentric view typified by Kahn where people are the solution. Thus, we have set the stage with thesis and antithesis for the first part of a Hegelian[2] transform that will be consummated later in this chapter. However, before we take the anthropocentric and biocentric ideal types to a conclusion, we must first firmly situate people in their own development, whether sustainable or not.

Rational Individual Choice

Peter Hedstrom and Richard Swedberg (1996) suggest that rational choice theory includes Weberian approaches and plays an important role in unifying theoretical and empirical work in sociology. According to the authors, rational choice theory is "a simple action theory that is deemed useful because it allows us to understand how aspects of a social situation can influence the choices ad actions of individuals" (p. 128). In its simplest formulation, interests and opportunities guide actions that are best from the individual's standpoint. Because sociology concerns itself with social systems and change, the authors situate individual choice in relation to macrolevel events or states. Figure 3.5 shows how individual action is informed by the current state of affairs and the change in affairs as affected by individual action.

Human Development

Setting the one-step rational choice model in its own historical context of the results of previous choices opens the question of how people learn and adapt. On the topic of learning and adapting, Piaget (1952) describes

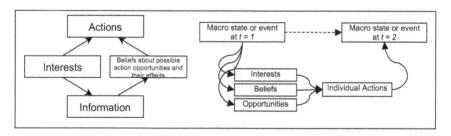

Figure 3.5 Rational choice theory (from Hedstrom and Swedberg, 1996).

cognitive development as occurring in four stages: (a) exploring the world and forming symbolic thought about it (sensorimotor); (b) use of symbolic thought to develop language and solve problems, but without the capacity to escape egocentricity to perceive other people's perspectives (preoperational); (c) acquisition of logical operations to act on concrete objects within one's own head and deal with the real world in a trial-and-error approach (concrete operations); and (d) thinking about abstract concepts and hypothetical possibilities and potential long-term consequences of possible actions, evolving to forming and testing hypothesis through the scientific method (formal operations). There seems to be a remarkable similarity between individual cognitive development and the cognitive development associated with society's understanding of and the quest for sustainable development.

Bronfenbrenner Builds a Bridge to Sustainability

Urie Bronfenbrenner (1979, 1989; Bronfenbrenner and Ceci, 1994;Moen, Elder, Lèuscher, and Bronfenbrenner, 1995), as described by Carol Sigelman (1999), created an ecological systems theory of individual human development that embedded

> The developing person . . . in a series of environmental systems that interact with one another and with the individual to influence development. In Bronfenbrenner's view, people are not just lumps of clay molded by outside forces. They shape their physical and social environments and are, in turn, shaped by the environments they have helped create. In other words, the relationship between person and environment is one of *reciprocal influence*; person and environment form a dynamic, ever-changing system. (p. 44; italics original)

Although Bronfenbrenner explicates the individual human dimension of development, his approach offers a way of placing people not only in the center of their own personal development, but also at the center of the societal quest for sustainable development. Building on Sigelman (1999), Fig. 3.6 overlays the dimensions of sustainability on Bronfenbrenner's model.

Taking the last two points together, this suggests to me that the quest for sustainability may be a cognitive structure or heuristic that people use to explore, learn about, change, and adapt to their environments, which leads to the following proposition:

> *Proposition 6*: Sustainability and sustainable development is a cognitive structure that people—as single agents and agents in groups—use to explore, learn about, change, and adapt to the broader world in which they exist.

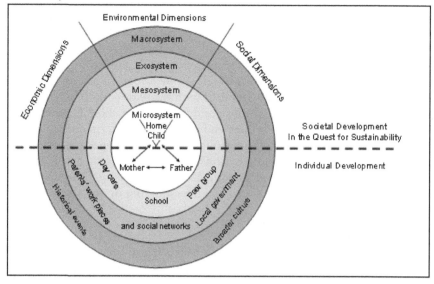

Figure 3.6 Bronfenbrenner's ecological model of development overlain with three dimensions of sustainability.

A Closer Look at the Quest for Sustainability

Considering the basic constructs outlined previously, I apply them to take a closer look at the quest for sustainability. In her recent article on "Healing the Divided Mind: Land as an Integrating Concept for Organizations and the Natural Environment" Walck (2004) also brings sociology into the discussion of sustainability. She first explores the dialectical tension between opposing views of development. She then offers a tantalizing view of repositioning the classic environment versus economy debate in a mediating structure—the land. In so doing, she reflects on the underlying paradigms, the structure of the various arguments, and the implications for society. If one listens closely, one can hear familiar echoes from sociological Marxism and discourses based on semiotic structures. The ensuing discussion (a) captures the main organizing structures, linkages, and propositions put forward by Walck; (b) explores them using concepts from Burawoy and Alexander; and (c) extends them with alternative conceptualizations.

Semiotic Ecological and Economic Discourses

Walck (2004) explores the structures of the economy and ecology paradigms and finds that many authors describe the two paradigms in oppositional terms. She offers her own "set of paired phrases and concepts—binary oppositions—aligned with each paradigm that reflects the work of many of these theorists and writers" (Walck, 2004, p. 171). Table 3.3 shows a representative sample. These terms look remarkably similar to Alexander's discursive structures. Walck (2004), like Alexander, finds that the terms connect together:

> Caught in one paradigm, we cannot engage the other without releasing the grip of the first paradigm from our mind. Such a paradigm shift is tantamount to a conversion, which may explain why environmentalists . . . are often portrayed by those hewing to the economy paradigm as zealots who have left reason behind. (p. 172)

Her logic strengthens both cases. Most interesting, and also strengthening Alexander's case, she finds that

> the strength of the divergence between the economy and ecology paradigms appears to be growing, not diminishing, as conflict, war, and environmental disasters engulf our world. Our political leaders often present us with the demand that we choose between them—jobs or wilderness, economic growth or environmental protection. . . . (Walck, 2004, p. 172)

Completing the Hegelian Transform to the Quest for Sustainability

Walck (2004) cites John Foster (1997), who "believed a forward-looking ecological vision must include a theory of ecological crisis, suggesting that awareness of crisis is a precondition for developing a sustainable society" (p. 173). She notes that, despite two decades of Earth Days and two world summits, the world has not rushed toward sustainability. She offers three alternative reasons: (a) the "ecology paradigm offers no practical solutions" (p. 173), (b) the morass of definitions of sustainable development and lack of tools are not adequate to rise to the vision, or (c) "it is extraordinarily difficult, if not impossible, to engage two mutually exclusive paradigms"

Table 3.3 Representative Oppositional Terms for Economy and Ecology Paradigms (after Walck, 2004)

Economy Paradigm	Ecology Paradigm
Economic growth	Balance, limits
Exploitation of nature	Harmony with nature
Land as asset (real estate)	Land as life
Anthropocentric/egocentric	Ecocentric or biocentric
Rationality	Harmony
Hierarchy	Democracy

(p. 173). This viewpoint is reminiscent of Gramsci and Polanyi striving to explain Marxism's failure to deliver socialism out of capitalism. I believe that the real explanation and limiting factor for sustainability is, extending Walck's (2004) prior second choice, a lack of a unifying theory that (a) brings together motive power to catalyze fundamental change (supplied by biocentrism and socially motivated movements), (b) predisposition to action and continuity (supplied by economic anthropocentrism), (c) sustainable outcomes (supplied and measured by the visions of sustainability), and (d) evaluating the results (measured by the metrics of sustainability). Transforming the thesis of ecocentrism and antithesis of anthropocentrism might, following Hegel, give way to a new synthesis—a unifying theory of sustainability explainable and understandable across worldviews that embraces and explicates competing formulations.

> *Proposition 7:* A unifying theory of sustainability is comprised of at least the following four elements: (a) motive power, which often arises from a critical theory worldview, (b) predisposition and capacity for action, which often arises from a constructivist world view, (c) taking material actions, and (d) evaluating the results—such evaluation having both a positivist aspect of what actually happened and a normative aspect about what should have happened.

Thus, we have created a construction that embraces, describes, and explains particular actions taken in the quest for sustainability—a vector of change. In the next section, we explore where this vector might be located.

AS A SOCIAL STRUCTURE, HOW DOES SUSTAINABILITY OPERATE, WHERE IS IT LOCATED, AND TO WHAT END DOES IT AIM?

Walck (2004) suggests that the current ecological crisis (from a biocentric view of sustainability) arises from the divided (human) mind—the "gap between awareness and action [which] seems both irrational and depressing" (p. 173). She, as does Elisabeth Ryland (2000), whom she cites, invokes Carl Jung in asserting that "healing the divided mind requires an integrating response that leads to a comprehension of a larger unity or whole. . . . Jung called [this integrative process] individuation" (Walck, 2004, p. 174). Ryland invokes *Gaia*, the theory that life processes regulate environmental conditions on Earth, to solve the conflict by positioning the economy in the ecosystem. Walck seeks the "middle way: sustainability" and solves the conflict by placing both the economy and the ecosystem in the *land*— "Land is a compelling mental image with mythic qualities—indigenous cultures see people and land as one indivisible whole, immigrants yearn for lost homelands, and children vividly remember childhood landscapes"

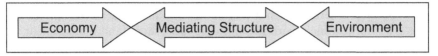

Figure 3.7 Mediating the environment and the economy.

(p. 176). Generalizing Burawoy after the sociological Marxism shown in Fig. 3.2, a model of the environment and economy can be generated as shown in Fig. 3.7.

The market remains in this model, and civil society, from Fig. 3.1, becomes a presently undefined mediating structure between the economy and the ecosystem. In Ryland's solution, the ecosystem subsumes the economy. Walck (2004) places the economy and the ecosystem literally in terrain— the land—a solution that has resonance with Marxist historical materialism. Gramsci observes that in both Fascism and socialism, the boundary between state and civil society dissolve. Although in Fascism the state completely engulfs civil society, in socialism freedom expands and coercion gives way to a self-regulating society. Walck, in looking to others who strive to find a middle way for dealing with the economy and the environment, finds two additional possibilities: (a) sustainability characterized as "green and competitive" for those who want to escape the strict economic view but not surrender to ecocentrism, and (b) stewardship arising from environmentalists and conservationists who are seeking a middle way.

I seek neither to heal the divided mind nor to solve the conflict. I seek instead another way, wherein biocentrism and anthropocentrism can dialectically coexist in the terrain of a yet-to-be-formulated mediating structure of sustainability. Taking the previous raw material, several interesting possibilities present themselves for mediation between the economy and the environment, including (a) the state and civil society joining hands to mediate between the economy and the environment, (b) democratic processes and institutions becoming the mediating structure (three branches of governments and their limitation of power through checks and balances, along with the media), (c) reintroducing the state as a third sphere with all being mediated on the terrain of civil society, and (d) reintroducing the state not as a third sphere, but as the terrain of the mediating mechanism being operated on by civil society as a third sphere. See Fig. 3.8 for the four alternative formulations of mediating structures.

In analyzing the four choices for location and description of the mediating structure of sustainability, each sharpens the focus in one area, whereas other considerations fade to the background. For alternative A, joint action between the state and civil society is highlighted. Examples would include civil action leading to laws that regulate economic activity— both the National Environmental Protection Act and the Clean Air Act illustrate such joint action. What fades into the background in alternative

A is the area where state and private or civil interests are in opposition (e.g., the burgeoning environmental case law where land management or regulatory agencies are taken to task for not sufficiently protecting the environment). Alternative A therefore misses important mediation between the state and civil society. Alternative B is similar to alternative A, but mediation between the economy and ecosystem is centered on processes where citizens exercise their influence on governance, which, in turn, is exercised by the state. In this alternative, the main actors of the state and its citizens fade somewhat into the background, whereas the processes and institutions (institutions in the sociological sense as norms and behaviors) are highlighted. Although this scheme would shed light on many of the processes by which mediation occurs, it would miss those mediations that occur outside of governance through voluntary association (e.g., standards arising from professional associations for certifying particular practices or products as green or neighbors banding together to improve riparian habitat for a stream flowing through their backyards). Alternatives C and

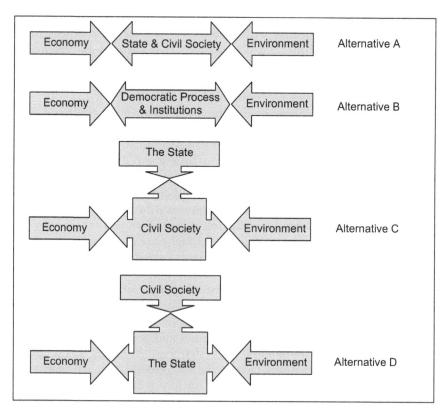

Figure 3.8 Alternatives for mediating structures between the economy and the environment.

D both separate civil society from the state. In the case of alternative D, the state becomes the mediating structure; although mediations by the state would be highlighted, like alternative B, mediation that occurs outside of governance would fade into the background. Alternative C highlights the mediating actions that take place or originate from civil society. Alternative C is the only formulation that puts people at the center of society's quest for sustainable development.

Locating sustainability as a mediating structure in civil society has the advantage of building on an already substantial body of thought, literature, scholarship, and research about the workings of people expressing their interests in the terrain of civil society. In this formulation, sustainability can be well explored from a Durkheimian approach, where the concept of sustainability is the subject of inquiry with people; institutions, the economy, and the environment being variables of interest; and a Weberian approach, where the actions of people or organizations are the central focus with constructs of sustainability being the explanatory variables. Although the foregoing analysis is far from conclusive, it does suggest that placing the mediating structure of sustainability in civil society yields benefits for subsequent analysis.

From the preceding discussion, civil society can be seen as a mediating structure located, according to Burawoy (2003), between the market and the state. Both Burawoy and Alexander suggest that mediation happens through discourse. Alexander shows how discourse in civil society is structured and polarized based on primal civil codes of inclusion and exclusion. From Heppner, Kivlighan, and Wampold (1999), Jabareen (2004), Williams and Millington (2004), and others, we find that worldviews impart the meaning on which discourses are built. We find that sustainability can be viewed instrumentally through the lens of individual choice or rational collective choice or empirically through analysis of societal patterns of relationships. In addition, we find individual or collective rational action to be informed by the process of learning, thus making a link between individual development and societal development learning from the results of its collective action in the human quest for sustainability. We find that, rather than solving the problem of environment versus the economy, the ideal types of anthropocentric versus biocentric perspectives are useful for fostering discourse and shedding light on various claims for sustainability. Last, we have located the quest for sustainability in civil society situated among the economy, the state, and the environment and found it to be a mediating structure. Then, according to the earlier formulation, the following proposition arises for sustainability:

Proposition 8: Sustainability is a quest undertaken by people and organizations who (a) engage in discourse and take actions in the terrain of civil society with (b) the intent of mediating impacts and securing a positive future (c) for today's and tomorrow's generations (d) from social, economic, and environmental perspectives.

HOW CAN WE BEST UNDERSTAND
WHAT SUSTAINABILITY IS ABOUT AND
HOW IT OPERATES IN SOCIETY?

I propose a systems approach, more specifically, a vector of change systems model, as a prototypal theory of sustainability and a tool to describe and explicate the many constructs of sustainability. The model incorporates the basic constructs discussed previously and is oriented around action as described in the rational choice model and along the lines described by Richard Scott (2003), who identifies that, "From the rational system perspective, organizations are instruments designed to attain specified goals" (p. 33). The vector of change systems model blends management and public administration perspectives, as well as the human development and rational choice perspectives outlined above. The vector of change systems model animates a simple classic closed system by setting it in its boundary conditions (see Fig. 3.9). My hypothesis, as a first step in building a comprehensive unifying theory of sustainability and sustainable development, is that this model, taken along with the two proto-ideal types of ecocentrism and anthropocentrism and the typology of streams of discourse and institutional settings described earlier, provide a framework sufficient to describe and explicate the major constructs and associated explanatory relationships of the quest for sustainability and sustainable development. Simply stated, the vector of change systems model serves as a prototypal theory in that it portrays humans as agents of change in their social and material worlds trying to make a better future for themselves and their progeny. According to this model, just as Bronfenbrenner places individuals at the center of their own cognitive development, my prototypal theory of sustainability places humans squarely in the center of the societal quest for development that is sustainable in the long term. At this stage of development, although the model resides and is formed in a worldview somewhere between postpositivist and constructivist, it can be used along with the typology and ideal types as an exploratory and explicatory tool for translating and bridging between world views and disciplines. In the end, it is aimed at fostering discourse.

Vector of Change Systems Model

The vector of change systems model is created from a worldview best characterized by Jurgen Habermas (1972, 1974, 1979), who suggested that there are two fundamental conditions underpinning human society and culture: work and interaction. The work here is the simple input/process/output system associated with taking actions in line with choices made, and the interaction is the process of learning—forming intent and observing and reflecting on the second order effects, as well as their effects on the greater world, that arise from the accomplishment of work. Habermas'

(1972) theory (Taylor and Williams 1993) of knowledge-constitutive interests further argues that we both create and *discover* the world, and knowledge arises from this relation of people to their world. His theory suggests that human cognitive interests arise from the need of humans to survive and reproduce, and to control and manage their environment. Forming intent is the contemplation of work to initiate change as shown in Fig. 3.5 and corresponds to Piaget's cognition. The existing situation corresponds to boundary conditions, social milieu, or social and material worlds relevant to the input/process/change system under consideration. The new situation corresponds to the (desired) change in state of the existing situation caused, in part, by operation of the system under consideration and, in part, by exogenous factors. Forming intent is the linkage between the existing situation and the initiation of a change sequence. It provides a mechanism to capture the beginnings of the dynamism leading ultimately to a purposeful attempt to cause change. Second-order effects emanate from first-order system outputs and are the linkages between the first-order outputs and any change in the greater outside world. A way is thus provided to systematically describe the linkages between primary first-order outputs and the new situation. Three feedback loops are described[3] that, along with forming intent, correspond to Bronfenbrenner's reciprocal influence between people and their environment.

The function of the feedback loops is as follows: (a) negative feedback provides course correction information, (b) positive feedback provides destination correction information, and (c) meta-feedback provides information that alters the system. The main units of analysis are the existing situation; the new or desired situation; the vector of change; the process of forming intent; the process of learning arising from the feedback loops; and the process of causality between output, second-order effects, and the new situation. Subunits of analysis are: (a) input, process, and output of the vector of change; and (b) linkages between second-order effects and forming intent, between output and input, and between output and process.

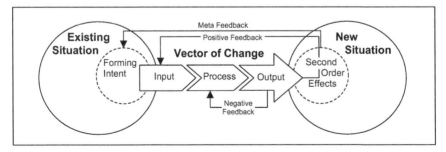

Figure 3.9 Vector of change systems model.

SUMMARY

I believe that the debate between the economy and the environment, between biocentric and anthropocentric views, has obscured a deeper proposition— that sustainability and sustainable development is first about people, how they make choices, and the consequences. I seek here not to solve the conflict, but instead to seek another way wherein ecocentrism and anthropocentrism can dialectically coexist. I look to Piaget's cognitive structures for understanding how people, the economy, and the environment might fit together. My purpose is to place people, the economy, and the environment together in a common terrain in the quest for sustainability and sustainable development. Although notions about sustainability abound, I believe the challenge at hand is to find ways to enrich one's own understanding of our collective quest for sustainability by becoming informed about what other people are thinking. To that end, I offer a typology that points the direction to mainstreams of discourses about sustainability and provides a series of questions to ask about the substance of any particular discourse. I elevate the classic economy versus the environment debate to ideal types that serve a dual function of acknowledging the dialectic nature of debates about sustainability and of providing a warning about the importance of searching for meaning and content in differing views of sustainability, rather than rushing to conclusion of rightness or wrongness. Last, I suggest that the best way to understand all the various strands, constructs, and discourses about sustainability is to employ a systems approach for tracking people, their motivations, and the consequences of their actions in the quest for sustainability.

To bring the discussion in this chapter to a conclusion, I draw from two sources: (a) from Aldo Leopold with regard to the nature of the task before the collective us, and (b) from Polèse and Stren with a provocative and compelling view of what constitutes social sustainability in cities. The earliest formulation I have found of the anthropocentric versus the biocentric view of the world is a quote from Leopold found in an unpublished 1935 paper cited in Jeffrey Sayer and Bruce Campbell (2004):

> One of the anomalies of modern ecology is that it is the creation of two groups, each of which seems barely aware of the existence of the other. The one studies the human community almost as if it were a separate entity, and calls its findings sociology, economics and history. The other studies the plant and animal community and comfortably relegates the hodge-podge of politics to the liberal arts. The inevitable fusion of the two lines of thought will, perhaps, constitute the outstanding advance of the present century. (p. 3)

This fusion, in my judgment, is our quest to integrate the social, economic, and environmental dimensions of sustainability.

Understanding the quest for sustainability thus requires a theoretical approach that is capable of (a) taking a look at the parts of sustainability, including individual constructs and linkages, agent-based actions, the social milieu in which people and their actions are situated, changes thereby wrought on the world, and the associated human learning; (b) synthesizing and integrating the parts into a broader more abstract view; and (c) providing a basis for discourse across a wide range of disciplines and worldviews. Although there are undoubtedly other possibilities, it seems to me that a cybernetic systems-based approach is capable of and particularly well suited to accomplishing such a job, which leads me to my penultimate proposition.

> *Proposition 9*: The human quest for sustainability is best understood using a cybernetic systems analysis approach. Such an approach can be envisioned as a series of agent-based vectors of change emanating from the social, economic, and environmental milieu. Such changes, in this view, have short-term objectives, long-range goals, and strategic intent for changed outcomes in the outside world. Agents evaluate the short-range, long-range, and strategic outcomes by means of feedback loops and learning, which, in turn, form the basis of new intent for change in the world expressed in terms of objectives, goals, or strategy.

WHAT IS A GOOD STARTING POINT FOR SOCIAL SUSTAINABILITY?

Mario Polèse and Richard Stren (2000) focus on integration of a different nature. They assert that "The cities of the twenty-first century must place the citizen at the center of public policy, reinvent the concept of the city, and realize the many ways of sharing in urban life" (p. vii). They offer a definition of *social sustainability* that calls for *"policies and institutions that have the overall effect of integrating diverse groups and cultural practices in a just and equitable fashion"* (p. 3; italics original). They see this notion as the antidote to the observation of social scientists that cities across the world face increases in (a) the rural–urban divide, (b) social inequality, (c) conflicts between cultures, and (d) political fragmentation. They attribute these difficulties to "increasing international migration, public-sector cutbacks, and labour-market restructuring arising from technological change and international economic integration" (p. 9). They believe that, "Without social policy, there can be no effective environmental policy" (p. 15). They offer a second definition of social sustainability for cities of

> development (and/or growth) that is compatible with the harmonious evolution of civil society, fostering an environment conducive to the

compatible cohabitation of culturally and socially diverse groups while at the same time encouraging social integration, with improvements in the quality of life for all segments of the population. (pp. 15–16; italics in original).

Interestingly, they cast social sustainability as the polar opposite of exclusion suggesting

Urban policies conducive to social sustainability must, among other things, seek to bring people together, to weave the various parts of the city into a cohesive whole, and to increase accessibility (spatial and otherwise) to public services and employment, with the framework, ideally, of a local governance structure which is democratic, efficient, and equitable. (p. 16; italics original)

After Polèse and Stren (2000), I believe that truly understanding the human quest for sustainable development requires an approach that brings together the various constructs of sustainability and weaves them into a comprehensible whole, thus increasing accessibility for all those who are interested in pursuing the quest within a framework of governance that is democratic, efficacious, and equitable. I close with a final beginning proposition about social sustainability drawing on earlier points and the work of Polèse and Stren:

Proposition 10:

The quest for social sustainability cannot take place in isolation from the environmental and economic milieu in which people find themselves. Social sustainability must, as a beginning point of departure, (a) build inclusion at the level of the individual, groups, and society; (b) provide for basic human dignity, which includes at least basic human sustenance, freedom from tyranny, freedom of association, and basic human liberty; (c) provide a means for people to influence their governance; and (d) create the capacity for learning at the level of individuals, groups, collectives, governments, corporations, and society.

NOTES TO CHAPTER 3

1. *People* in this context includes people as individuals, groups, organizations, and governments.
2. Hegel argues that history progresses through the interaction of binary oppositions, which, in turn, form new syntheses (cited in Mueller, 1958).
3. Negative and positive feedback loops are used here in the general systems theory approach of characterizing feedback. Feedback is negative when information is supplied back to the system that it is off course, as in an autopilot.

Positive feedback means that, although you might be on the right course, your destination may not be right (i.e., the destination airport might be fogged in and an alternative landing spot needs to be found). Both feedback loops are internal to and part of the system under consideration. Meta-feedback loops are related to but outside the system under consideration and function to change the system.

REFERENCES

Alexander, Jeffrey C. 1992. "Citizen and Enemy as Symbolic Classification: On the Polarizing Discourse of Civil Society." In *Cultivating Differences: Symbolic Boundaries and the Making*, edited by M. Lamont and M. Fournier. Chicago: University of Chicago Press.

American Forest & Paper Association. 1994. *Sustainable Forestry Initiative*. Washington, DC: Author.

American Institute of Architects. 2004. *Defining Sustainable Design: Measure of Sustainability and Performance Metrics*. Washington, DC: American Institute of Architects.

Astley, W. Graham, and Andrew H. Van de Ven. 1983. "Central Perspectives and Debates in Organization Theory." *Administrative Science Quarterly* 28 (2): 245–273.

Bacharach, Samuel B. 1989. "Organizational Theories: Some Criteria for Evaluation." *Academy of Management Review* 14 (4): 496–515.

Bronfenbrenner, Urie. 1979. *The Ecology of Human dDevelopment: Experiments by Nature and Design*. Cambridge, MA: Harvard University Press.

———. 1989. "Ecological Systems Theory." In *Annals of Child Development*, edited by R. Vasta. Greenwich, CT: JAI Press.

———, and Stephen J. Ceci. 1994. "Nature-Nurture Reconceptualized in Developmental Perspective: A Bioecological Model." *Psychological Review* 101 (4): 568–586.

Burawoy, Michael. 2003. "For a Sociological Marxism: The Complementary Convergence of Antonio Gramsci and Karl Polanyi." *Politics & Society* 31 (2): 193–261.

Cabezas, Herberto, and Brian D. Fath. 2002. "Towards a theory of sustainable systems." *Fluid Phase Equilibria* 194–197 (2): 3–15.

Callicott, J. Baird, and Karen Mumford. 1997. "Ecological Sustainability as a Conservation Concept." *Conservation Biology* 11 (1): 32–40.

Castro, Carlos J. 2004. "Sustainable Development." *Organization & Environment* 17 (2): 195–225.

Clark, William C., Robert W. Kates, Alan H. McGowan, and Timothy O'Riordan. 2005. "Science and Policy for Sustainable Development." *Environment* 47 (1): 3.

Cohen, Michael D., James G. March, and Johan P. Olsen. 1972. "A Garbage Can Model of Organization Choice." *Administrative Science Quarterly* 17 (1–25).

Collins, Randall. 1994. *Four Sociological Traditions*. New York, Oxford: Oxford University Press.

Drucker, Peter Ferdinand. 1954. *The Practice of Management*. 1st ed. New York: Harper.

———. 1986. *The Practice of Management*. 1st Perennial Library ed. New York: Perennial Library.

Forrester, Jay Wright. 1971. *World Dynamics*. Cambridge, MA: Wright-Allen Press.

Foster, John B. 1997. "The Crisis of the Earth: Marx's Theory of Ecological Sustainability as a Nature-Imposed Necessity for Human Production." *Organization & Environment* 10 (3): 278–295.

Good Company. 2002. *Sustainability Assessment of the University of Oregon.* Eugene, OR: University of Oregon Press.

Goodland, Robert, and Herman Daly. 1996. "Environmental Sustainability: Universal and Non-Negotiable." *Ecological Applications* 6 (4): 1002–1017.

Habermas, Jurgen. 1972. *Knowledge and Human Interests.* London: Heinemann Educational.

———. 1974. *Theory and Practice.* London: Heinemann.

———. 1979. *Communication and the Evolution of Society.* Boston: Beacon Press.

Hedstrom, Peter, and Richard Swedberg. 1996. "Rational Choice, Empirical Research, and the Sociological Tradition." *European Sociological Review* 12 (2): 127–146.

Heppner, P. Paul, Dennis M. Kivlighan, and Bruce E. Wampold. 1999. *Research Design in Counseling.* 2nd ed. Belmont, CA: Brooks/Cole Wadsworth.

Jabareen, Yosef Rafeq. 2004. "A Knowledge Map for Describing Variegated and Conflict Domains of Sustainable Development." *Journal of Environmental Planning & Management* 47 (4): 623–643.

Jung, Carl G., Herbert Edward Read, Michael Fordham, and Gerhard Adler. 1953. *The Collected Works of C. G. Jung, Bollingen series.* New York: Pantheon Books.

Kahn, Herman, William Morle Brown, Leon Martel, and Hudson Institute. 1976. *The Next 200 Years: A Scenario for America and the World.* New York: Morrow.

Larsen, Gary L. 1994. "Forests at UNCED: An Emerging Global Consensus Toward Sustainability." In *Expanding Horizons of Forest Ecosystem M anagement: Proceedings of the Third Habitat Futures Workshop, October 1992, Vernon, BC,* edited by M. H. Huff, L. K. Norris, J. B. Nyberg, and N. L. Wilkin. Portland, OR: U.S. Department of Agriculture, Forest Service, Pacific Northwest Research Station.

Lehtonen, Markku. 2004. "The Environmental-Social Interface of Sustainable Development: Capabilities, Social Capital, Institutions." *Ecological Economics* 49 (2): 199–215.

Linster, Myriam, and Jill Fletcher. 2004. *Using the Pressure-State-Response Model to Develop Indicators of Sustainability.* OECD Environment Division report.

Meadows, Donella H., and Club of Rome. 1972. *The Limits to Growth; A Report for the Club of Rome's Project on the Predicament of Mankind.* New York: Universe Books.

Moen, Phyllis, Glen H. Elder, Kurt Lèuscher, and Urie Bronfenbrenner. 1995. *Examining Lives in Context: Perspectives on the Ecology of Human Development.* 1st ed. *APA Science Volumes.* Washington, DC: American Psychological Association.

Montréal Process Working Group. 2004. *The Montréal Process Working Group 1998–2004.* Retrieved December 4, 2004, from http://www.mpci.org/home_e.html

Mueller, Gustav E. 1958. "The Hegel Legend of 'Thesis-Antithesis-Synthesis'." *Journal of the History of Ideas* 19 (3): 411–414.

Norm Thompson Inc. (2004). *Our Commitment to Sustainability.* Available at http://www.normthompson.com/content/commitmentmain.jsp

OrganizationOregon Board of Forestry. 2003. *Forestry Program for Oregon.* Salem, OR: Author.

Oregon Department of Forestry. 2004a. *A Landmark Assessment of Oregon's Forest Sustainability.* Oregon Department of Forestry 2001. RetrievedDecember 5, 2004, from http://www.oregonforestry.org/sustainability/symposium/.

―――. 2004b. Oregon Department of Forestry Strategic Plan 2004–2011.
Organization for Economic Cooperation and Development. 2003. *OECD Environmental Indicators: Development, Measurement and Use.* Paris, France: Author.
Pearce, David W., and Edward Barbier. 2000. *Blueprint for a Sustainable Economy.* London: Earthscan.
Piaget, Jean. 1952. *The Origins of Intelligence in Children.* New York: International Universities Press.
Polèse, Mario, and Richard E. Stren. 2000. *The Social Sustainability of Cities: Diversity and the Management of Change.* Toronto: University of Toronto Press.
Portland State University. 2005. *Our Mission, Vision & Values.* Retrieved November 19, 2005, from http://www.pdx.edu/mission.html.
President's Council on Sustainable Development. 1996. *Sustainable America, A New Consensus for the Prosperity, Opportunity and a Healthy Environment for the Future.* Washington, DC: The White House.
Ragin, Charles, and David Zaret. 1983. "Theory and Method in Comparative Research: Two Strategies." *Social Forces* 61 (3): 731–755.
Ryland, Elisabeth 2000. "Gaia Rising: A Jungian Look at Environmental Consciousness and Sustainable Organization." *Organization & Environment* 13 (4): 381–402.
Sayer, Jeffrey, and Bruce M. Campbell. 2004. *The Science of Sustainable Development: Local Livelihoods and the Global Environment.* Cambridge, UK: New York: Cambridge University Press.
Scott, W. Richard. 2003. *Organizations: Rational, Natural, and Open Systems.* 5th ed. Upper Saddle River, NJ: Prentice-Hall.
Secretariat International RIOD. (2004a). *International NGOs Network on Desertification and Drought.* Mission. Retrieved June 3, 2004a, from http://www.riodccd.org/eng/index.html
―――. (2004b). *International NGOs Network on Desertification and Drought.* RIOD Website. Retrieved June 3, 2004c, from http://www.riodccd.org
Serageldin, Ismail. 1993. "Making Development Sustainable." *Finance & Development* 30 (4): 6–11.
Shafritz, Jay M., and J. Steven Ott. 2001. *Classics of organization theory.* 5th ed. Fort Worth, TX: Harcourt College Publishers.
Sigelman, Carol K. 1999. *Life-Span Human Development.* 3rd ed. Pacific Grove, CA: Brooks/Cole.
Spalking-Fecher, Randall, Harald Winkler, and Stanford Mwakasonda. 2005. "Energy and the World Summit on Sustainable Development: What Next?" *Energy Policy* 33 (1): 99–113.
Srinivas, Hari. 2004. *The Environment Sphere: Sustainable Development.* Global Development Research Center 2004. Retrieved December 4, 2004, from http://www.gdrc.org/sustdev/index.html
Sustainable Northwest. 2004. *Sustainable Northwest.* Retrieved December 5, 2004, from http://www.sustainablenorthwest.org/index.php
Taylor, Peter Charles, and Mark Cambell Williams. 1993. "A Critical Constructivist View on Reforming the Traditional Teaching/Learning Process." In *Annual Conference of the Australian Association for Educational Research,* edited by P. Jeffery. Fremantle, WA: Australian Association for Research in Education.
U.S. Green Building Council. 2004. *Leadership in Energy & Environmental Design.* Washington, DC: Author.
United Nations. 1991. *Conservation and Development of Forests.* New York: Author.
―――. 1992a. "Agenda 21: Programme of Action for Sustainable Development." In *Earth Summit Agenda 21, the United Nations' Programme of Action from Rio:*

Final Text of Agreements Negotiated by Governments at the United Nations' Conference on Environment and Development (UNCED); June 3–14, 1992, Rio de Janeiro, Brazil. New York: United Nations, Department of Public Information, United Nations Publication Sales.

————. 1992b. "Forest Principles, Non-legally Binding Authoritative Statement of Principles for a Global Consensus on the Management, Conservation and Sustainable Development of All Types of Forests." In *Earth Summit Agenda 21, the United Nations' Programme of Action From Rio: Final Text of Agreements Negotiated by Governments at the United Nations' Conference on Environment and Development (UNCED); June 3–14, 1992, Rio de Janeiro, Brazil.* New York: United Nations, Department of Public Information, United Nations Publication Sales.

————. 1992c. "Rio Declaration on Environment and Development." In *Earth Summit Agenda 21, the United Nations' Programme of Action from Rio: Final Text of Agreements Negotiated by Governments at the United Nations Conference on Environment and Development (UNCED); June 3–14, 1992, Rio de Janeiro, Brazil.* New York: United Nations, Department of Public Information, United Nations Publication Sales.

Walck, Christa. 2004. "Healing the Divided Mind." *Organization & Environment* 17 (2): 170–193.

Wang, Amy. 2004, November 26. "Expanding the Notion of Sustainability." *The Oregonian*, p. D7.

Weber, Max. 1978. *Economy and Society*, edited by G. Roth. Berkeley and Los Angeles, CA: University of California Press.

Williams, Colin C., and Andrew C. Millington. 2004. "The Diverse and Contested Meanings of Sustainable Development." *Geographic Journal* 170 (2): 99–105.

World Commission on Environment and Development. 1987. *Our Common Future.* Oxford, New York: Oxford University Press.

Wright, Pamela A., Jennifer L. Colby, Gregory Alward, Thomas W. Hoekstra, Brent Tegler, and Matt Turner. 2002. *Monitoring for Forest Management Unit Scale Sustainability: The Local Unit Criteria and Indicators Development (LUCID) Test, Management Edition.* Fort Collins, CO: USDA Forest Service Inventory and Monitoring Institute.

4 An Antidote to a Partial Economics of Sustainability[1]

Mary C. King

The challenge of articulating an economics of the social aspect of sustainability brings into sharp relief the inadequacy of the economics of sustainability as currently conceived. Somehow the economics of sustainability has come to be narrowly defined, inexplicably limited to the consideration of the environmental impact of individual market interactions in the private sector. The project of creating an economic understanding of the social aspect of sustainability—and sustainability more generally—will benefit tremendously from incorporating work in three areas of economics that have made substantial progress in recent decades. Thus far largely overlooked by scholars working out the economics of sustainability, but absolutely critical, are (a) development economics work on human development as the proper aim of development efforts, (b) feminist economics incorporating paid and unpaid caring labor into our theory and analyses, and (c) recent research on the key contributions of the public sector to human well-being.

Sustainability is generally understood to comprise three interlocking goals: environmental, economic, and social sustainability (e.g., Harris, Wise, Gallagher, and Goodwin, 2001). Achieving sustainability requires that we meet all three goals because failures in any one realm are perceived to threaten the others. This perspective has been clearly stated by the Organization for Economic Cooperation and Development (OECD) Project on Sustainable Development. Focused largely on global warming and other environmental challenges, the OECD (2001) report, *Sustainable Development: Critical Issues*, notes that

> [D]isparities in economic conditions and unmet social needs in many parts of the world may make it more difficult to establish strong coalitions of countries who can respond to these [environmental] challenges. Countries characterized by pressing social problems are likely to pay less attention to environmental problems and to be less willing to accept the structural adjustment associated with shifts towards more environmentally sound patterns of production and consumption. (p. 27)

The social aspect of sustainability is being framed as the difficulty of implementing environmentally oriented policies that might reduce growth, given the social imperative to meet urgent human needs resulting from poverty and inequality. The social aspect of sustainability being addressed is a concern for equity. At its root, the issue is the social difficulty of reducing and even reversing the environmental impact of economic growth when a sizeable proportion of the world's population has yet to benefit from economic growth and the legitimacy of their aspirations to do so cannot be denied.

The economics of sustainability must be far more broadly understood to meet the challenge posed by the need to raise the standards of living of a large number of people while reducing the negative environmental consequences of economic activity. We must reorient our fundamental understanding of our goal, from the achievement of economic growth to the achievement of human development and well-being, recognizing the key contributions and challenges for sustainability posed by the activities of government, business, families, and communities.

In particular, the economics of sustainability must be expanded beyond the consideration of private-sector market activity to be of use in analyzing the problems posed by achieving social sustainability. Such a narrow focus cannot encompass efforts to achieve social sustainability as we are defining it as both (a) the processes that generate social health and well-being now and in the future and (b) those social institutions facilitate environmental and economic sustainability now and for the future. Clearly these processes and social institutions are not limited to market transactions in the private sector, the apparent preoccupation of the economics of sustainability.

This chapter is conceived as the first steps toward expanding and reshaping the economics of sustainability as currently understood, so as to serve us more effectively in our quest for sustainability. To that end, we first review economists' understanding of sustainability, including key concepts from early environmental economists who were thinking much more broadly. Next we review the developments in different fields of economics that can be incorporated into an expanded economics of sustainability, capable of analyzing the social aspect of sustainability in particular and the objective of sustainability as a whole. This survey reveals several measures and strategies that can be used to underpin a research agenda investigating the economics of the social aspect of sustainability particularly.

SUSTAINABILITY AND EARLY INSIGHTS
FROM ENVIRONMENTAL ECONOMICS

Over the last 20 years, social scientists have been working to develop analytical clarity for the concept of sustainability and have made some progress. The first and overriding point of agreement is that conceptions of sustainability must prioritize the future, as is captured in the often-cited formulation of the 1987 (Brundtlandt) World Commission on Environment and Development (WCED) that "sustainable development seeks to meet the needs and aspirations of the present without compromising the ability to meet those of the future" (Chapter 1, paragraph 49).

Second, it is now commonplace to assert that sustainable development includes three components: environmental, economic, and social. Of these three, however, by far the least developed component is social sustainability, vaguely formulated as "equity" and largely ignored.

Economists Pearce and Barbier (2000) define *economic sustainability* as "ensuring that future generations have at least the same potential economic opportunities to achieve welfare as the current generation" (p. 21). Effectively they narrow the WCED Brundtlandt definition to focus on economic activities, and they raise the expectation that future generations will have at least what we have today.

Important scholars in the field of the economics of sustainability, Pearce and Barbier can be looked to to represent it. In their widely read *Blueprint for a Sustainable Economy*, Pearce and Barbier (2000) share with other economists interested in sustainability an almost exclusive focus on the private-sector and market outcomes. The big questions are whether natural resources are well understood as a form of capital and, if so, whether "natural capital" is fungible with other forms of capital; how best to internalize environmental impacts into market transactions; and the potential of correctly specified property rights for reducing environmental damage.

We do not see incorporated the work of economists that has transformed the efforts of development bodies, including the United Nations Development Program, from a tight focus on Gross Domestic Product (GDP) per capita to the much more nuanced understanding of the purpose of economic development as human development. We do not see incorporated the work of feminist economists—and environmentalists—who have studied the value of human well-being provided by nonmarket actors, particularly in households and community groups. We do not see the work of economists such as Peter Lindert and Timothy Smeeding, who have clearly demonstrated the contribution to human well-being of the public sector particularly.

We do not see much attention to anything that could be called the social aspect of sustainability. In *Blueprint for a Sustainable Economy*, several substantive chapters are devoted to economic and environmental sustainability, whereas only two pages are devoted to a discussion of social capital and none to any other conceptualization of social sustainability.

The constriction of vision in sustainability economics is ironic; much of the impetus to the development of environmental economics stemmed from the fact that environmental concerns were ignored because they were outside the market calculus. That environmental resources and the environment itself were not valued in economic analyses, other than as potential commodities, is the wellspring of the thinking that has become environmental economics, mutated now also into ecological economics and the economics of sustainability.

The understanding that GDP per capita did *not* define even economic welfare, never mind the quality of life or human well-being, was a fundamental insight of the first environmental economists. Early work by environmental economists called for what amounts to a focus on human well-being as the goal of economic activity, and for including both the value of the environment and the contributions to human well-being made by nonmarket actors. E. F. Schumacher, writing in 1974, proposed "a study of economics as if people mattered." Herman Daly and John Cobb (1989) were reaching for "an economics for community," first to replace the consideration of homo economicus as an oddly isolated individual with "the viewpoint of a person in community" (p. 18) and, second, to expand the notion of community. They advocated that we understand community as that sustained by Wendell Barry's Great Economy, which "sustains the total web of life and everything that depends on the land" (p. 8).

The result has been ongoing work to modify national income accounting, the framework that underlies the construction of the concept of GDP. Scholars hope to replace the ubiquitous use of GDP with a measure along the lines of Daly and Cobb's (1989) Index of Sustainable Economic Welfare, which incorporates the value created by households and takes note of the depletion of natural resources. Only if we change the measure we use to better reflect our understanding of our goals will we be able to judge whether our policies and strategies are moving us closer or farther from greater and more sustainable levels of human well-being.

The OECD's concern that the process of economic growth as generally understood is not sustainable and cannot be relied on to eradicate poverty worldwide was another key insight of the original environmental economists. In the early 1970s, Hermann Daly (1973) was calling for a "steady-state economy" (p. 19), in which "the important issue will be distribution, not production" because "in a finite world continual growth is impossible" (p. 5).

Attention to the importance of the distribution of income, wealth, resources, and well-being has been lacking in much of the economics of sustainability, but must increase. That economists concerned with sustainability have evaded the central issue of distribution is frustrating, but not perhaps surprising. Concerns about distribution have been marginalized for decades in economics. An unthinking reliance on Pareto Optimality—the idea that economists can only be sure that economic welfare is increased by policies that leave everyone at least as well off as they were—has shackled economic analysis. Refusing to admit the possibility of interpersonal comparisons, economists trained in the Anglo-American tradition cannot say that economic welfare is improved by taking the price of breakfast from one of the world's richest people, Bill Gates or Carlos Slim, and giving it to a starving child, although the truth of this assertion would be obvious to most other people.

When faced, then, with the central economic question—how to reduce poverty—economists for decades have been able to advocate nothing but growth. We need to have more, if some are to have any, because we cannot contemplate any having less.

That growth alone cannot eliminate poverty is partially demonstrated by the fact that economists have long since claimed that we were near the point when we could stop growing at or near the point where we would produce enough for everyone. Heilbroner (1996) quotes John Stuart Mill, writing in the 1840s, as saying that, "It is only in the backward countries of the world that increased production is still an important object; in those most advanced, what is economically needed is a better distribution . . ." (p. 145).

Even Marx thought that the most developed nations had grown enough, although he asserted that it was imperative for economies to evolve through the stage of capitalism to develop the preconditions for socialism, including the development of productive capacity. As put by Engels after Marx' death:

> But if . . . division into classes has a certain historical justification, it has this only for a given period, only under given social conditions. It was based upon the insufficiency of production. It will be swept away by the complete development of modern productive forces. . . . .This point is now reached . . . .The possibility of securing for every member of society, by means of socialised production, an existence not only fully sufficient materially, and becoming day by day more full, but an existence guaranteeing to all the free development and exercise of their physical and mental faculties—this possibility is now for the first time here, but *it is here.* (cited in Tucker, 1972, pp. 636–637; italics original)

Juliet Schor (1991) pointed out that Americans could be working half the hours we were in 1990 if we had maintained our consumption at the level of 1948. Certainly we can imagine having "spent" part of our increased output on redistribution and leisure, rather than entirely on rising material standards of living, now increasingly concentrated at the top.

Now, 35 years after Hermann Daly told us that continual growth is impossible, global warming and other environmental concerns make it obvious that we can no longer rely on growth to reduce the world's poverty, if we ever could.[2] The challenge remains, as Daly expressed it, to accomplish development without growth or at least without unsupportable strain on the environment. It is the same quest expressed in our working definition of social sustainability, toward greater social health and human well-being and the development of social institutions that will facilitate environmental and economic sustainability.

For an economics of sustainability up to the task of guiding development without growth, we need to incorporate the work of economists focused on human development, the nonmarket economy, and the public sector.

HUMAN DEVELOPMENT, UNPAID WORK, THE PUBLIC SECTOR, AND HUMAN WELL-BEING

During the same years that economists have been building an economics of sustainability, development economists were grappling with perhaps an even more fundamental flaw of simple growth policies; they did not work, particularly from the perspective of raising living standards at the bottom. Confronted with the inability of top-down, capital-intensive development efforts that targeted the growth of GDP per capita to alter the incidence of poverty and deprivation in the Third World, development economists shifted to a focus on human development, led by economists such as Amartya Sen and Mahbub ul Haq.

Amartya Sen's (1999) work has been extremely influential, advocating a shift from defining development in terms of the growth of GDP, incomes, or the level of industrialization to viewing development as "a process of expanding the real freedoms that people enjoy" (p. 3). Sen argues that greater freedoms and human development are "both (1) the *primary end* and (2) the *principal means* of development" (p. 36; italics in the original).

According to Sen (1999), five kinds of freedoms reinforce each other and work together instrumentally to facilitate both human and economic development: (a) political freedoms; (b) economic facilities; (c) social opportunities, by which he means services such as education and health care; (d) transparency guarantees, which give people the ability to trust; and (e) protective security, referring to an effective social safety net. Sen argues that these freedoms underpin an individual's capabilities, which must be real as well as legal or theoretical. In other words, the legal right to an education does not create a true capability if sexist social norms or extreme poverty preclude school attendance. People's functionings are the outcomes of their choices and actions, given their capabilities, and reflect in part, but not perfectly, their capabilities.

The goal of development policies should then be expanding freedoms and increasing human development. Often greater human development coincides with higher incomes, but not always and not necessarily because wealthier nations can "afford" greater social amenities. As Sen (1999) points out, some relatively low-income nations and regions have achieved a relatively high level of human development. In other cases, investment in human development appears to have been the foundation for later, rapid economic growth.

Under the leadership of Mahbub ul Haq, the United Nations Development Program (UNDP) adopted human development as the goal of international development initiatives. Since 1990, the UNDP has published an annual Human Development Report (HDR), taking on a different topical focus each year, most recently climate change. The HDR consistently includes measures of the Human Development Index (HDI) for each nation. Designed as a practical measure of human development for low-income countries, the HDI comprises measures of purchasing power, literacy and school enrollment, and health as revealed in life expectancy. Hence, the HDI is a good measure for social sustainability in poor countries, where little data are available.

Clearly, the elements of the HDI—purchasing power, literacy, and health—do not flow exclusively from private-sector entities engaged in market transactions. The public sector is a crucial source of education and health care. Subsistence agriculture and other efforts of unpaid members of household and communities are critical, if as generally omitted from economic accounting as environmental "amenities" such as clean water, as has been pointed out forcefully by Marilyn Waring (1988).

The contribution of subsistence agriculture to human well-being, and of the unpaid efforts of women particularly, worldwide has been neglected in economics in general and in the economics of sustainability in particular. This omission is not logical. As Sir Richard Stone (1997) has pointed out, unpaid work in the household was left out of national income accounting based on convenience, not principle. Over the past decades, the work of Luisella Goldschmidt-Clermont (1982), Duncan Ironmonger (1996), and others has demonstrated that the value of unpaid work is most likely the equal of GDP annually, even in the "developed world." It makes no sense to attribute the entire value of human capital to education, of health to commercially provided health care, or of social capital to civic organizations while ignoring the critical role of the family in creating these assets and making a large, valuable contribution to human well-being (National Research Council, 2005). Daly and Cobb's (1989) Index of Sustainable Economic Welfare includes household contributions, but the economics of sustainability does not.

Although common definitions of economics found in introductory textbooks have been biased toward marketized aspects of the economy by focusing on "goods and services," some are moving toward more comprehensive definitions, such as the one found in Case and Fair (1996): "economics is the study of how individuals and societies choose to use the scarce resources that nature and previous generations have provided" (p. 2) or the one found in Goodwin, Nelson, Ackerman, and Weisskopf (2005): "economics is the study of the way people organize themselves to sustain life and enhance its quality" (p. 2). These more wholistic definitions emphasize provisioning for human needs and wants, rather than the production and distribution of commodities. Fernand Braudel's definition of economic life, interpreted by Robert Heilbroner and Aaron Singer (1984), is "the routines of daily work, the everyday round of the tasks by which we sustain ourselves" (p. 6). Julie Nelson

(1993) proposed that economics should be understood as focusing "on the provisioning of human life, that is, on the commodities and processes necessary to human survival . . ." (p. 32). An emphasis on provisioning has become one of the central tenets in the emerging body of work distinguished as feminist economics (Power, 2004).

The importance of recognizing the value created by unpaid labor should not be underestimated, particularly with respect to the social aspect of sustainability. Policies designed to increase human well-being through greater efficiency or growth can backfire badly if created without thought for their negative impact on the invisible economy of unpaid work. For instance, cutting public health expenditures may appear to save resources for other purposes, but only by shifting the cost of care for the sick from the public sector to women working without pay in the household. In extreme situations, such as in poor countries experiencing structural adjustment programs, the demands on household labor can be unsustainable. Diane Elson (1995) reports families disintegrating under the load placed on women and children pulled out of school to help at home.

Development efforts have focused increasingly on the unpaid work done by women, recognizing that reducing the unpaid time spent obtaining water and fuel is critical for increasing the time and effort available for income-earning activities. Increasing female literacy is the most powerful mechanism for reducing child mortality (Sen, 1999). Indeed, the UNDP has created a gender-sensitive HDI largely because it has become clear that investment in women's capabilities, easing women's disproportionately large work burdens, and putting resources in the hands of women, who have their minds focused on children's needs, are absolutely key to development.

The UNDP measures, such as the HDI, although useful for capturing social sustainability in the developing world, are not sensitive to the distinctions among affluent nations. However, as Sen and others have asserted, human development issues are as relevant for the wealthy nations as the less affluent, especially for particular populations and regions. Further, the prosperous countries vary considerably in their success at fostering human development. These variations are captured in the Human Well-Being Index (HWI) developed by Robert Prescott-Allen (2001), who has built a companion Ecosystem Well-Being Index. This index could underpin research into the social sustainability of policies and practices in the developed economies.

Prescott-Allen's (2001) HWI is complex; it comprises five dimensions that each includes 10 elements. The five dimensions are (a) health and population, (b) wealth (household and national), (c) knowledge and culture, (d) community (including freedom, governance, peace, and order), and (e) equity. What variations in the HWI highlight are the benefits of economic arrangements that support the two elements of economies overlooked by economists of sustainability: unpaid work in families and communities and collective provision of public goods.

The well-being indices are highest for Scandinavian countries primarily because of low rates of poverty and the ills of poverty, including low educational attainment, poor health, high likelihood of incarceration, and so on. In other words, the Scandinavian nations have done the best job of facilitating the private provision of family care with policies such as parental leaves supplemented by the public provision of social services (Christopher, 2002; Smeeding, 2006).

One way to view these effective welfare state policies is as minimizing social exclusion, or social marginalization owing to the lack of ability to contribute to society due to low educational attainment, unemployment, incarceration, substance abuse, and so on. There is no better indicator of future social exclusion or marginalization than child poverty (Esping-Andersen, 2002). Indeed, child poverty rates might serve as a simple measure in empirical work on human development and the social aspect of sustainability, in lieu of the more comprehensive HWI.

It appears that investment in social programs is as valuable for promoting both human development and economic growth in the First World, as Sen has argued, as it is in the Third World. Peter Lindert (2004) has shown that the Scandinavian welfare state has facilitated economic growth and productivity there. Recognizing that this finding flies in the face of the dearly held beliefs of many economists, Lindert devotes two volumes to a historical and empirical demonstration of the role of social spending for economic growth. In the case of Sweden in particular, Lindert credits efforts to keep women working and their wages up with high Swedish growth and productivity rates.

It may be that inclusion in general pays off for both economic productivity and social sustainability. Minimizing social exclusion lowers the public bill for prisons, police, emergency room health care, and a host of other defensive responses to social ills. There is a cold economic rationale for social spending that minimizes child poverty, keeps kids in school and their families housed, provides child and health care, and, in the end, produces employed tax payers who parent their children well and can look after their elderly parents.

The public sector has a role to play in the economics of sustainability that is not limited to regulation and the administration of property rights for private actors in the market sector of the economy. The public sector is our best mechanism for providing for many of our collective wants, such as security; it is particularly efficient at providing universal goods and services such as health care and education; and it is the only effective arena in which to accomplish redistribution, so as to reduce the need for growth to eradicate poverty.

TOWARD A MORE COMPREHENSIVE ECONOMICS OF SUSTAINABILITY

In short, it appears that the development of an economics of sustainability capable of meeting the challenge posed 35 years ago by Herman Daly and currently by the OECD Project on Sustainable Development, to achieve development without growth, requires attention to the economics of the social aspect of sustainability. We need to figure out how to accomplish social health and human well-being for all of the world's people, as well as which social institutions will facilitate the accomplishment of environmental and economic sustainability—our working definition of social sustainability.

Clearly, an improved economics of sustainability needs to (a) focus on human development, rather than economic growth, as captured by rising levels of gross domestic product; (b) include in its purview the critical allocation of resources to the creation of human well-being in the nonmarket segments of the economy, particularly the household; and (c) be cognizant of the key role played by the public sector in the provision of human well-being.

Measures of the social aspect of sustainability are available to us for both rich and poor nations in the form of the human development and human well-being indices. The child poverty rate may serve as good proxy for more elaborate measures of social sustainability because it is highly indicative of future social exclusion. Another source of social measures may be the goals included in the human rights treaties ratified by the preponderance of the world's nations, as advocated by economist Radhika Balakrishnan (2005). These documents represent a high degree of international consensus on the elements that constitute the foundation of human well-being.

These measures could underpin an empirical research agenda investigating which policies and practices best increase human well-being while reducing and reversing the unsupportable environmental consequences of our current economic activities, providing a solid, scientific basis for an economics of sustainability capable of incorporating the social aspect of sustainability.

NOTES TO CHAPTER 4

1. Adapted from "What Sustainability Should Mean." CHALLENGE, vol. 51, no. 2 (March–April 2008). Used by permission of M.E. Sharpe, Inc.
2. Many analysts would tell us that market-based economic growth cannot end poverty without significant intervention by the state to redistribute income. Skepticism about the prospects for poverty reduction of market-centered globalization based on the Washington Consensus is expressed in the recent International Labour Organization report by the World Commission on the Social Dimension of Globalization (2004).

REFERENCES

Balakrishnan, Radhika. 2005. "Why MES With Human Rights? Integrating Macro Economic Strategies with Human Rights." Available at http://www.policyinnovations.org/ideas/policy_library/data/01189

Case, Karl E., and Ray C. Fair. 1996. *Principles of Economics* (4th ed.). Upper Saddle River, NJ: Prentice-Hall.

Christopher, Karen. 2002. "Welfare State Regimes and Mothers' Poverty." *Social Politics* 9 (1): 60–86.

Daly, Herman E. 1973. *Toward a Steady-State Economy.* San Francisco: W.H. Freeman.

———., and John B. Cobb, Jr., with contributions by Clifford W. Cobb. 1989. *For the Common Good: Redirecting the Economy Toward Community, the Environment, and a Sustainable Future.* Boston: Beacon Press.

Elson, Diane. 1995. *Male Bias in the Development Process.* Manchester, UK: Manchester University Press.

Esping-Andersen, Gosta. 2002. *Why We Need a New Welfare State.* Oxford, UK: Oxford University Press.

Goldschmidt-Clermont. 1982. *Unpaid Work in the Household: A Review of Economic Evaluation Methods.* Women, Work and Development Series, No. 1. Geneva: International Labour Office.

Goodwin, Neva R., Julie A. Nelson, Frank Ackerman, and Thomas Weisskopf. 2005. *Microeconomics in Context.* Boston: Houghton Mifflin.

Harris, Jonathan M., Timothy A. Wise, Kevin P. Gallagher, and Neva R. Goodwin, eds. 2001. *A Survey of Sustainable Development: Social and Economic Dimensions.* Washington, DC: Island Press.

Heilbroner, Robert. 1996. *Teachings for the Worldly Philosophy.* New York: W.W. Norton.

———., and Aaron Singer. 1984. *The Economic Transformation of America: 1600 to the Present.* San Diego, CA: Harcourt Brace Jovanovich.

Ironmonger, Duncan. 1996. "Counting Outputs, Capital Inputs and Caring Labor: Estimating Gross Household Product." *Feminist Economics* 2 (3): 37–64.

Lindert, Peter. 2004. *Growing Public: Social Spending and Economic Growth Since the Eighteenth Century.* Cambridge, UK: Cambridge University Press.

National Research Council. 2005. *Beyond the Market: Designing Nonmarket Accounts for the United States.* Panel to Study the Design on Nonmarket Accounts, K.G. Abraham and C. Mackie, eds. Committee on National Statistics, Division of Behavioral and Social Sciences and Education. Washington, DC: The National Academy Press.

Nelson, Julie A. 1993. "The Study of Choice or the Study of Provisioning?" In *Beyond Economic Man: Feminist Theory and Economics,* edited by Marianne A. Ferber and Julie A. Nelson. Chicago: University of Chicago Press.

Organization for Economic Cooperation and Development. 2001. *Sustainable Development: Critical Issues.* Paris: Author.

Pearce, David, and Edward B. Barbier. 2000. *Blueprint for a Sustainable Economy.* London: Earthscan Publications.

Power, Marilyn. 2004. "Social Provisioning as a Starting Point for Feminist Economics." *Feminist Economics* 10 (3): 3–19.

Prescott-Allen, Robert. 2001. *The Wellbeing of Nations: A Country-by-Country Index of Quality of Life and the Environment.* Washington, DC: Island Press.

Schor, Juliet B. 1991. *The Overworked American: The Unexpected Decline of Leisure.* New York: Basic Books.

Schumacher, E. F. 1974. *Small Is Beautiful: A Study of Economics as if People Mattered.* London: Abacus.

Sen, Amartya Kumar. 1999. *Development as Freedom.* New York: Knopf.

Smeeding, Timothy. 2006. "Government Programs and Social Outcomes: Comparison of the United States with Other Rich Nations." In *Poverty, the Distribution of Income and Public Policy,* edited by A. J. Auerbach, D. Card, and J. M. Quigley (pp. 149–218). New York: Russell Sage Foundation.

Stone, Richard. 1997. "The Accounts of Society: Nobel Memorial Lecture, 8 December 1984." *American Economic Review* 87 (6): 17–29.

Tucker, Robert C., ed. 1972. *The Marx-Engels Reader.* New York: W.W. Norton.

Waring, Marilyn. 1988. *If Women Counted: A New Feminist Economics.* San Francisco: Harper & Row.

World Commission on Environment and Development. 1987. *Our Common Future.* www.un-documents.net/ocf-01.htm.

World Commission on the Social Dimension of Globalization. 2004. *A Fair Globalization: Creating Opportunities for All.* Geneva: International Labour Organisation.

Part II

International Perspectives

5 Global Civil Society
Architect and Agent of International Democracy and Sustainability

Kristen Magis

Civil society is of paramount import to both democracy and sustainability. It is the foundation on which democratic governance rests and without which democracy cannot survive. Civil society has toppled governments from the Philippines and Panama to South Africa and Czechoslovakia, and it has advocated democratic governance from the United States to Estonia (Mbogori and Chigudu, 1999). Civil society, moreover, transcends nation-states and geographic borders to converge internationally as a force for democracy and sustainability.

Civil society acting internationally has been variously referenced (e.g., international civil society, global social movements, global civil society, and transnational civil society). The term *Global Civil Society* (GCS) is used herein. The definition of GCS is a much-debated topic. GCS is an amorphous, rich, and dynamic concept that raises questions of space and process, historical precedence and contemporary uniqueness, its constitution, and its relationship with the state and the market (Magis, 2007). Reducing GCS to a simplistic definition is dangerous because, in its reduction, there is a necessary loss of richness and complexity that are inherent to its character (Keane, 2003; Anheier, Glasius, and Kaldor, 2005). Rather than attempt to describe GCS, the term can be used as a heuristic devise to understand important matters of social life (Ehrenberg, 1999). GCS is used herein as an ideal type to describe and explain the endeavours of people engaged internationally to promote the public good. It includes agents acting outside both the state and the market and excludes agents of uncivil society.

GCS is recognized as one of the most spectacular developments in global governance during the 20th century (Non-Governmental Liaison Service, 2005). The active involvement of GCS in international endeavours dates back to 1864, when the Geneva Conventions were initiated at the behest of Dr. Henri Dunant, founder of the Red Cross. GCS, however, significantly increased its involvement during the last two decades of the 20th century. In what has been described as a "global associational revolution" (Salamon, 2004), the number of nongovernmental organizations (NGOs) active internationally exploded from 1,300 in 1960 to more than 40,000 at the turn of the century (Edwards and Zadek, 2003). Its growing prominence is further portrayed through changes in language (e.g., its designation as the "third pillar of modern society" Galtung, 2000), and through its formal recognition by both world leaders (e.g., Boutros-Ghali's [1996] recognition of it as a full participant in international life; Weiss and Gordenker, 1996) and IGOs (e.g., the United Nation's reference to it as a social partner, signifying equality of status with governments; Willetts, 2000).

GCS in the 21st century is galvanized by concerns regarding globalization and demands for just and equitable social and economic policies, democratic governance, and democratically guided markets. Theorists provide incontrovertible evidence of the active force of civil society in historic progress on international regimes from human rights, international corruption, democratic governance, development, and peace to environmental conservation (Rosenau, 1990; Wapner and Ruiz, 2000; Clark, 2001; Khagram, Riker, and Sikkink, 2002). GCS championed and led efforts to establish the Ottawa Treaty on Landmines, the International Criminal Court, and the Kyoto Protocol on climate change, as well as to stop the Multilateral Agreement on Investments (Paul, 2005b). These are just a few of its many accomplishments.

GCS is a world champion for democracy and sustainability. Yet it is not accorded a legally and politically legitimated role in international governance. Rather, it must gain access through informal and backdoor strategies that are not protected by democratic rule of law. This structural deficit makes GCS vulnerable, exposing it to the capricious and powerful forces of governments and the market and threatening to silence the voice of the people. Therefore, the principle assertion of this chapter is: GCS must be afforded an institutionally legitimated place at the table of international governance.

The purpose of this chapter is to substantiate this claim through examination of the democratic deficit extant in global governance and the presentation of GCS's critical role as champion of international democracy and sustainability. First, the interrelation and complementarity among GCS, democracy, and sustainability is described. Then the case for international democratic governance is substantiated via a description of the international democratic deficit. Then GCS's role as a champion of democracy and sustainability is explored via its relationships with nation-states and the market and its unique contribution in a context otherwise defined by power and wealth. Finally, although it is the contention of this chapter that GCS needs to be legitimated in international governance, there also is a clear recognition of the challenges GCS must address as a significant player in the international polity. Hence, the final section presents the challenges GCS faces in its bid for international legitimacy. Together these arguments build the rationale for the primary assertion of this chapter—that GCS must be afforded an institutionally legitimated place at the table of international governance.

GLOBAL CIVIL SOCIETY, DEMOCRACY, AND
SUSTAINABILITY: AN INTERRELATED WHOLE

Civil society, democracy, and sustainability are interrelated and complementary. The Outcome Document presented to the 2005 UN World summit
states: "We reaffirm that democracy is a universal value based on the freely
expressed will of people to determine their own political, economic, social
and cultural systems and their full participation in all aspects of their lives"
(United Nations, 2005). Jan Aart Scholte (2002) operationalizes democracy to include self-determination, equal opportunity for participation in
public decisions, and freedom to debate. Democracy is an ongoing political
project created through the active engagement of people to determine the
course of their lives. Hence, democratic politics must engage people in dialogue, respect divergent interests, and anticipate conflict. Through deliberation and civic education, private interests are informed, public interest is
developed, conflict is transformed into cooperation toward mutual benefit,
and the voice of the people is integrated into policy discussions, ultimately
leading to germane and effective policy. Thus, civil society is indivisible
from democracy.

Democracy can only be sustained through ongoing dialogue that generates commonly accepted rules and norms for society (Cardoso, 2005).
Further, that dialogue requires a public space wherein people can engage.
GCS is an architect of public space. It is the public space, the civic process,
an emergent social order, and the human agency arising from that space. As
architect, GCS creates international public space and facilitates deliberation
among people from around the world via networking, media, and communications technology. As public space, GCS is a realm of autonomous and
free social life wherein people, not states or the market, are sovereign (Barber, 1998; Hall, 2000). As a civic process, GCS debates social issues, articulates the public good, and takes collective action toward shared visions.
As an emergent social order, GCS gives rise to agents that advocate specific causes. These agents include individuals, formal and informal groups,
organizations (e.g., NGOs), and networks of interested parties (e.g., coalitions and social movements).

The World Social Forum exemplifies the multiple manifestations of GCS.
It is a social movement aligned by people's common struggle against neoliberalism. It is an architect of civil society, enabling political action, engaging the media, and consciously developing the movement and its political
space. The movement functions as public space and civic process, encouraging expression, respecting difference, and building common ground. It
is an emergent social order from which rise all forms of human agency
that actively engage in social and political advocacy, both nationally and
internationally.

Civil society and sustainability also are tightly interwoven in a highly
interdependent relationship, illustrating the dual nature of people as agents

and beneficiaries of sustainable practice. Sustainability refers to consciously utilizing the earth's resources to maintain and enhance people's well-being without compromising the ability of future generations to meet their needs. Sustainability has gained international prominence as the paradigm through which to observe, interpret, and make decisions regarding social, economic, and environmental conditions. Social sustainability refers to the sustenance of basic human needs such as nutrition and shelter (Streeten, Burki, Haq, Hicks, and Stewart, 1981); human freedoms, including political rights, economic facilities, social opportunities, transparency guarantees, and protective security (Sen, 1999); and human development, which expands social, economic, cultural, and political choices and leads to equity, sustainability, productivity, and empowerment (Haq, 1999). Civil society and democracy are recognized as essential for sustainable development (Boutros-Ghali, 1996). Living sustainably requires that people continually monitor and improve social, economic, and environmental conditions, and, further, that they make associated decisions regarding policy formulation and implementation. Hence, living sustainably requires access to information, full inclusion, participation, and collaboration. Additionally, it requires government institutions that are open, transparent, accountable, and supportive of community action (United Nations Development Programme, 2005a).

Democracy and GCS are indispensable constituents of sustainability. Democracy provides the structures and mechanisms through which to pursue policies that promote sustainability. Civil society is both the context for and the agent of democracy. Democracy cannot exist absent civil society, and sustainability cannot be maintained without democracy or civil society.

GCS, democracy, and sustainability are intimately and intrinsically connected, hence linking their paths and establishing the necessity of GCS participation in international governance. In fact, in its persistent bid to place the needs of people and the environment on the international policy agenda, GCS has won many achievements. Its efforts, however, are consistently stymied by the extreme democratic deficit in global governance. The international democratic deficit is reflected in interstate relations and reified through international governmental organizations (IGOs). It is further compounded by the contemporary form of economic globalization, which also is regarded as highly undemocratic.

THE DEMOCRATIC DEFICIT IN INTERNATIONAL GOVERNANCE

In the last two decades of the 20th century, 81 countries adopted principles of democratic governance. By 2002, 140 out of 200 countries held multiparty elections (United Nations Development Programme, 2005b). This movement was initiated and demanded by the people, facilitated by the end of the cold war and increasing worldwide interdependencies, informed by international development projects, and promoted by the UN. This third wave of democratization affirmed the universality of democracy as an international value.

However, despite the democratic surge among states, decisions affecting states' vital interests increasingly are relocating to the global arena. This migration is a consequence of globalization, a process wherein the geopolitical boundaries of the Westphalian system of states are dissolved by an increasingly dynamic and global flow of markets, politics, culture, and people (Serrano, 1999; Nye and Donahue, 2000). In this progressively interdependent world, states are no longer the final arbiters of governance, either at the national or international level. Rather, they are enmeshed in various overlapping and highly dynamic policy networks. Actors in the networks have expanded beyond states to include business, civil society, mass media and international governmental organizations, global cities, and regional governance organizations. In these multiple centers of power, regimes complete with systems of rules and operational institutions are negotiated, requiring the relinquishment of state power and sovereignty. Thus, globalization mitigates states' ability to shape their own future (Commission on Global Governance, 1995; Held, 2004).

The state structure reified by the Westphalian system enabled the creation of state governments conducive to democracy and sustainability and accountable to citizens. The weakening of state sovereignty is of concern precisely because decision-making is migrating from states into a highly undemocratic realm populated by international government organizations and markets that undermine the sovereignty of the people to govern the circumstances of their own lives (Cardoso, 2005; Panel of Eminent Persons on UN-Civil Society Relations, 2004).

INTERSTATE RELATIONS AND INTERNATIONAL GOVERNANCE ORGANIZATIONS

Democratic governance is characterized by its participatory, transparent, accountable, and responsive actions (Helsinki Process, 2005). Global governance lacks these characteristics, reinforcing the widespread perception that global governance is not democratic. This democratic deficit is reflected in interstate relations and reified through IGOs. It is further compounded by the contemporary form of economic globalization, which also is regarded as highly undemocratic.

The interstate system reifies the power relations emergent after World War II, permanently locating states within a highly vertical and undemocratic international class system. In this system, the existence or increasing numbers of democratic states do not equate with global democratic practice. Rather, the interstate system creates structural impediments to international democracy and functions on power, not democracy (Falk, 2000; Aksu and Camilleri, 2002). The U.S. invasion and occupation of Iraq is a particularly salient example of undemocratic interstate relations. Despite world opinion expressed through the UN and worldwide antiwar protests, the United States, relying on its international power, made a unilateral decision to attack.

The democratic deficit is further illustrated by decision making regarding the global economy, which rests primarily with the G-7/8 countries (South Centre, 1997). For example, the quota regime utilized by the Bretton Woods organizations (i.e., World Trade Organization, International Monetary Fund, and World Bank) apportions 40% of the vote to just five states (Scholte, 2002). Furthermore, the Bretton Woods organizations are autonomous from the UN, whereas UN functions related to international trade, development finance, and monetary issues have been constrained. These institutional structures have systematically abrogated the right of the word's nations to participate in the world's economic management. Under these highly undemocratic circumstances, the Bretton Woods organizations regularly impose the will of a privileged few on the world's people (Stiglitz, 2002; Oxfam, 2003). The deficit is further illustrated by the UN Security Council, which represents only 8% of the UN member states, one third of whom have never been elected and who retain permanent veto powers. Despite its unrepresentative constitution, the Security Council makes decisions that have extensive effects on countries and people far from its locus of power and to whom it bears no accountability.

Democracy is built on the foundation of the consent of the governed over decisions that influence their lives. However, interstate relations are based on power, not democratic practice, and IGOs are not representative, absent the full range of the worlds' states, the direct voice of the people, and the representative voice of their democratically elected parliaments. So, although matters of vital interest to people's lives have migrated, their ability to affect those interests is being systematically and structurally abrogated (Held, 2004; Panel of Eminent Persons on UN-Civil Society Relations, 2004).

ECONOMIC GLOBALIZATION

Markets require governance to catalyze their valuable potential and to counteract their destructive forces. Markets rely, for example, on widely dispersed property ownership, fair competition, and moral capital, all of which are facilitated through governance. Yet the market untended constricts, transferring property and wealth into the coffers of a few while robbing the capacity for wealth generation from the masses. This constriction leads necessarily to monopolies, unequal competition, and marginalization and exclusion of people from the market (Galbraith, 1998). Markets also require governance to offset inevitable market failures. Markets externalize costs (e.g., pollution), forcing society to rectify the damage and absorb the costs. Markets also fail to provide for public goods (e.g., safety), requiring society to underwrite and ensure those services. Finally, markets do not facilitate justice and equity, but rather appropriate resources from people and countries, systematically depriving them of the ability to compete and, for many, merely to survive. Markets without governance create social, ecological, and economic maladies. Hence, it is only through governance that the benefits of the market are elicited and the self-destructive tendencies are averted (Korten, 1996).

The dangers of ungoverned markets were forewarned. Smith abhorred monopolies, which he condemned for suppression of market forces. His generation witnessed the likes of the British East India Company, notorious for its exploitation and impoverishment of India. In the name of the British crown, the company used force to extract natural resources, dominate ever-increasing lands, maintain monopolies over commodities, fix prices, and abuse labor. In Adam Smith's (1981) mind, monopolies were the antithesis of a free market: "It is to prevent this reduction of price, and consequently of wages and profit, by restraining that free competition which would most certainly occasion it, that all corporations, and the greater part of corporation laws, have been established" (p. 191).

Yet neither his words nor the warnings of his intellectual descendants have stopped the constriction of markets, the damage to human life and the environment, and the restriction of government to direct and guide the market. Korten (1996) states that economists consider an international market to be highly monopolistic when more than half of the market is controlled by five firms. By 1993, economists rated the international market as highly monopolized. Five firms controlled nearly 70% of the entire international market in consumer durables. Five firms controlled more than 50% of the global market in automotive, airline, aerospace, electronic components, electrical and electronics, and steel, and five firms controlled more than 40% of global market in oil, personal computers, and media ("A Survey of Multinationals," 1993). These data do not reflect the continued consolidation within the international market.

The United Nations Development Program (2005) provides recent data on the social side of the economic equation. "The world's richest 500 individuals have a combined income greater than that of the poorest 416 million" (p. 4). Further, 2.5 billion people live on less than $2 a day. While 40% of the world's population share only 5% of global income, a mere 10% retain a full 54% of that income. The report reveals a world of widening inequalities in income and life chances. "In the midst of an increasingly prosperous global economy, 10.7 million children every year do not live to see their fifth birthday, and more than 1 billion people survive in abject poverty on less than $1 a day" (p. 3).

The current form of economic globalization, tied to doctrines of neoliberalism and the Washington Consensus, has systematically eradicated democratic control of the market, both nationally and internationally (Aksu and Camilleri, 2002; Cardoso, 2005). The market is, hence, insulated from political influence (Levine, 1995), effectively checking its accountability to the people for whom it ostensibly works and from the direction and context made available through democratic processes and institutions. Polanyi (2001) presciently stated, "To allow the market mechanism to be sole director of the fate of human beings and their natural environment, indeed, even of the amount or use of purchasing power, would result in the demolition of society" (p. 73).

With 51 of the world's 100 largest economic entities being transnational corporations, most of the world's states have little or no political or economic power (Mokhiber and Weissman, 1999). Even the most powerful—the United States and the European Union—are challenged by the uncompromising force of concentrated globalized capital. It is not surprising then that governments are increasingly held captive to the precepts of neoliberal capitalism and corporate interests (Non-Governmental Liaison Service, 2005). Neoliberal economic globalization is seriously confounding the international democratic deficit. In fact, unrestrained market forces and states' inability to protect their citizenry are now perceived to be the most serious threats to democracy (Aksu and Camilleri, 2002).

THE CALL FOR INTERNATIONAL
DEMOCRATIC GOVERNANCE

Globalization has made indelible changes to the Westphalian system of states (Held, 1995; Nye and Donahue, 2000). It has made permeable the boundaries that demarcated the sovereign rights of states and the social contracts negotiated between citizens and their states. Issues such as environment, population, human rights, and food security have gained global proportions and surpassed the ability of even the richest states to address unilaterally. Neoliberal economic globalization has disarmed states' capacity to ensure economic stability or to provide protection to vulnerable populations. Multiple and dynamic governance systems, some outside the ambit of states, have obligated states to regimes that sometimes have crippling socioeconomic effects. So although states are not passé, they can no longer operate unilaterally or as inimitable actors outside the international system.

Globalization poses a particular challenge to states committed to democratic governance. People are systematically being disenfranchised from sovereign control over their own governments. Further, the locales of international power and decision making that significantly affect people's lives are highly undemocratic. To counter these antidemocratic forces, states need to actively engage in international governance. Moreover, international governance needs be democratized, and markets need to yield to democratic governance (Archibugi, Balduini, and Donati, 2000). Rosenau (1995) defines *governance* as the process whereby a society rules itself through systems of rule born of intersubjective consensus and reified by law. To develop and preserve democracy, we are challenged to apply this basic notion at a global level.

Democratic international governance also is of critical importance to social sustainability (World Bank, 1997; Organization for Economic Cooperation and Development, 2001). Social sustainability concerns the well-being of people and is met through the fulfillment of basic needs, as well as through political, economic, and social freedoms. It requires equity within and between generations, adequate provision of social services, cultural integration, widespread democratic participation, community ownership, self-determination, and political accountability (Harris, 2000). Because people's lives are so affected by global processes, democratic global governance is necessary. Without it, sustainable development is impossible.

Polanyi (2001) asserted that the expansion of capitalism is incompatible with democracy and is a threat to civil society. He predicted that when the market tended toward destruction of society, society would reconstitute itself as an active society to defend itself. Civil society, he astutely asserted, would coalesce internationally and rise up against the socially destructive forces of self-regulated markets.

In fact, globalization has opened new public spaces wherein once geographically separated peoples are discovering common ground, creating communities of interest, and joining forces to make their voices heard. From GCS is emerging what has been called the biggest international social movement in decades. Driven by a common belief that neoliberal economic globalization is the root of many contemporary problems, this disparate collage of the world's people is questioning neoliberal policies, challenging undemocratic multilateral institutions, highlighting the dangers of global capital concentration, standing against socially and environmentally destructive corporate practices, and articulating an alternative vision based on equity, sustainability, democracy, and human rights. Their voices have been heard in Seattle, Cancun, and the remotest locales of the globe (Edwards and Gaventa, 2001; Mertes, 2004). GCS is not, however, merely the voice of growing antipathy toward undemocratic international governance.

GLOBAL CIVIL SOCIETY: CHAMPION OF DEMOCRACY AND SUSTAINABILITY

Civil society, in its national and global forms, is a potent and unrelenting defender of democracy and sustainability. Civil society is rooted in societies bounded by nation-states. Society comprises civil society, the state, and the market all intertwined in highly interdependent, complex, and symbiotic relationships. Civil society is both shaped by and constitutive of the state and market. The dynamic and evolutionary workings of this interdependent society create the social context out of which agents of civil society emerge. They, further, generate the issues to which civil society responds.

Government establishles a country's legal, fiscal, and regulatory framework. That framework dictates the conditions under which civil society can emerge, encourages certain kinds of civic actors, and influences the effect civil society can have on society at large (Mbogori and Chigudu, 1999). Government can give rise to associations that exert significant social and political pressure for the public good (e.g., Amnesty International) or those that threaten the fabric of society (e.g., the Hitler Youth and the Ku Klux Klan; Ehrenberg, 1999). Civil society, however, is not entirely dictated by government. It has the capacity, even in the most oppressive situations, to develop into a formidable force, as illustrated in Central Europe under Soviet occupation, South Africa under Apartheid, and Latin America under autocratic dictatorships (Kaldor, 2003).

Moreover, civil society plays a generative role in the creation and preservation of states. For example, prior to the formal casting of the United States via its constitution, civil society created the public space and produced agents to deliberate and discern the intent and role of the government in relation to its people. The principle "of the people, by the people, for the people" has been fought for throughout the nation's history by citizens intent on shaping the polity toward their image of a democratic republic (e.g., women's suffrage, civil rights movement, environmental movement, peace movement, etc.).

Civil society, similarly, shares a complex relationship with the market. Through the market, people are able to provide for their own sustenance. Moreover, civil society relies on the market to resource its civic actions. In fact, the growth of civil society nationally and internationally has been financed, in part, by the wealth generated through economic growth (e.g., Ford, Mott, and Carnegie; Iriye, 2004). Civil society struggles absent a healthy market (Keane, 2003). Markets, likewise, require civil society for their existence and continued viability. Polanyi wrote that markets are a particular form of socially mediated interaction (cited in Burawoy, 2003). In fact, civil society creates markets, provides the relationships necessary to enable market transactions, and dictates the social norms and rules that guide the market's functioning.

The history of these intricate relationships reveals the inherent proclivity of civil society, the state, and the market to undermine democracy and threaten sustainability. Moreover, it illustrates the unwavering propensity of civil society to counterbalance forces that threaten the sovereignty of people over their own destiny, whether they are anarchical social forces within civil society, oppressive states, or undemocratic globalized markets.

ANARCHICAL SOCIAL FORCES

Civil society includes pockets of incivility within its ambit (Kaldor, Anheier, and Glasius, 2005). Regarding these uncivil forces, Keane (1998) states, "The birth or rebirth of civil society is always riddled with dangers, for it gives freedom to despots and democrats alike" (p. 45). Indeed, some forms of civil society are disingenuous and devious in their self-ascription of the public good. Others commit acts of terror, like the mafia, war criminals, arms traders, and terrorists. Still others discriminate, undermine civility, and erode democracy (e.g., the Ku Klux Clan or the Hitler Youth). Uncivil groups engage in strategies such as blood imagery and violence with the intent and consequence of destroying the bonds between people, as well as between people and their governments. Ehrenberg (1999) provides a chilling reminder that "People bowled, played soccer, and sang in choral groups in Jim Crow Mississippi" (p. 239).

However, although there indeed are pockets of incivility in civil society, Keane (1998) asserts that they are marginalized and opposed within the predominantly nonviolent sector. The norm of civility, characterized by principles of mutual respect, compromise, and physical restraint, distinguish civil society. Civil society, recognizing the danger imposed by these uncivil groups, negotiates social contracts in which people willingly cede part of their independence and authority to socially determined rules of law and the state in return for protection, security, and peace (Kaldor, Anheier, and Glasius, 2003).

THE OPPRESSIVE STATE

Oppressive governments also have roused the antipathy of civil society. In the 18th century, for example, the institution of feudalism gave way to the idea of individual liberty, opportunity, and freedom from age-old oppression. Smith conceived of a brilliant vision based on the presumption that economic wealth leads to freedom. He proposed a radical concept (i.e., that equal access to democracy and economic opportunity could and should be available to all). His vision embraced free choice, a system of equal balances, and voluntary exchange between knowledgeable individuals. Central to his thesis were the requisites that property ownership be widely dispersed, monopolies be avoided, and an environment be created to enable the market's viability. Smith believed that a market thus designed would raise the standard of living for those outside the privileged minority and, hence, expand individual freedom and equality (Muller, 2002). In this iteration of people's quest for self-determination from repressive governments, civil society pursued the promise of the market and differentiated itself from the state.

In the 20th century, civil society again rose against tyrannical states around the world (Kaldor et al. 2003). In Central Europe, civil society fought to create an autonomous space separate from the ubiquitous state wherein people could organize as they wished. In Latin America, civil society arose in reaction to authoritarian military regimes. In South Africa, it rebelled against Apartheid.

UNDEMOCRATIC GLOBAL MARKET

By the 20th century, the market had transformed from a network of community-based businesses to a small constellation of rapidly growing transnational corporations (Korten, 1996). Following the dictates of neoliberalism advocated by the Washington Consensus (Williamson, 1994), the world's states systematically created and institutionalized a world economic regime with the primary objective of freeing the market from constraints imposed by states. As a direct result, states' rights and their ability to govern have been severely undermined. The subsequent collapse of the Soviet Union and advances in computer technology facilitated the liberation of business from the strictures of geographical and political boundaries.

In many significant ways, the global market escaped the social and political forces that would govern its actions and mediate its affects. Global economic forces have become hegemonic in that they operate outside the ability of states and citizens to exert direction and control or to provide vital social contracts and safety nets. Consequently, ever more people have been made permanently superfluous to the world's economy, adding to the growing mass of extremely poor and malnourished. Extreme and concentrated wealth is now accompanied by widespread and abject poverty (Galbraith, 1998; Chomsky, 1999; International Forum on Globalization, 2002).

Civil society, however, also was released from geographical and political constraints in the late 20th century, rendering itself as a GCS. It experienced explosive growth in the form of NGOs, international non-governmental organizations, and expansive networks. These groups regularly join forces to fight the injustices of neoliberal economic policies, for example, the international coalitions inspired by Action Canada Network to oppose the North American Free Trade Agreement (Lujan, 2002), the World Campaign for In-depth Reform of the System of International Institutions,[1] the national workers' movements in Mexico and Canada, and the Living Democracy Movement in India (Piven and Cloward, 1979; Shiva, 2003). By the end of the 20th century, the global anticapitalism movement was born to counter the human and environmental degradation caused by neoliberal economic policies and globalized capital (Krut, Howard, Howard, Gleckman, and Pattison, 2005).

The term *democracy* includes two concepts: *demos* and *kratos*. *Demos* refers to the people within a polity, whereas *kratos* refers to power. These concepts imply, first, that a polity is to be ruled by the people, not an elite, and, second, that all people must have equal access to decision making.

Civil society, in its enduring bid for self-determination, has been a consistent champion of both demos and kratos and, hence, a critical force in democracy within nation states. In its global form, it is relentless in its pursuit of both democratic and sustainability objectives.

The global environment is defined by anarchy, power plays among nation-states, international governance organizations deficient in democratic practices, and the domination of transnational corporations over the global market (Mearsheimer, 2001). GCS wields neither the sword of states, the resources of the market, nor the structures of the bureaucracy, yet its strength and accomplishments as an active agent in international affairs are irrefutable. To understand its efficacy and influence, it is necessary to discern GCS's unique power.

GCS INFLUENCE: BEYOND POWER AND WEALTH

As the world's people come into closer contact via technology and travel, the awareness of difference increases and leads to contention (Barber, 1995). GCS reflects that complexity and diversity. It is populated with a multiplicity of divergent perspectives and opinions. Some claim that the inconsistencies inherent in such diversity corroborate the accusation that GCS cannot present a united front and, hence, is not a legitimate voice in governance (Rooy, 2004). Others, however, state that the diversity is, in fact, a strength of GCS. They contend that democracy is a contested space, that diversity is crucial for democracy, that GCS reflects the pluralism, and that the interactions within GCS create cultural understanding and promote multilateralism (Cardoso, 2005; Kriesberg, 1997).

In fact, a recurrent message has emerged from this diversity and is echoed through GCS's many endeavors. That message concerns justice, equity, democratic governance, peace, human rights, and environmental conservation. These themes have been sustained over time, through wars and across the nations, inspiring the question of how unity is found amid the cacophony and seeming disorder of GCS. The answer lies in civil society's twin propensities to network and generate intersubjective meaning.

GCS NETWORKING

GCS coordinates itself via networks (Hall, 2000). Earthwatch, Association for the Taxation of Financial Transactions for the Aid of Citizens, World Movement for Democracy, Global Call to Action Against Poverty, and Women's Environment & Development Organization are all examples of networks that have championed issues from women's rights to global climate change, debt relief, and anticapitalism. The tendency toward networking in GCS is located within broader global evolutionary trends. First, in the age of interdependence and communication, "Networks constitute the new social morphology of our societies" (Castells, 2000, p. 469). Networking is occurring in all realms, from business to government to civil society. Second, Wallerstein (2004) asserts that the world is in a period of vast change, wherein conventional knowledge is challenged but not yet replaced by new paradigms. In this period of searching and reflection, he states, experimentation, purposeful learning, and ongoing exchange are critical. Networks facilitate that exchange and learning.

A network is a loose, decentered, and informal structure that links independent local actors to each other across time and space and facilitates their cooperation (Hall, 2000). Rajesh Tandon (1991) characterizes GCS networks as open to varied experience and ideas, energized by shared responsibility, and capable of rapid mobilization. The minimal reliance on hierarchies and bureaucratic regulations; the vast linkages across multiple sources of competence, knowledge, and experience; and the access to numerous power centers and resources make networks uniquely suited to the coordination of complex tasks and rapid learning. Through the connections, GCS is finding collective voice amid its immense diversity (Magis, 2007).

GENERATING INTERSUBJECTIVE MEANING

GCS is not vested with power, nor does it have a legally legitimated place in international governance. However, it can claim multiple and significant accomplishments influencing international policy and practice. A portion of its success can be explained by its increasing sophistication as a global political force, its organizational development, and the opportunities created for it within the UN. These explanations, however, do not fully account for GCS' success.

Rather, GCS' puissance is more fully appreciated through the conception of the world as an international society determined by the international distribution of ideas (Klandermans, 1992). Ideas comprise shared interests, values, expectations, and beliefs about appropriate behavior. They create structure, order, and stability in society, and they galvanize evolution of individual societal members and the entire system. Ideas are the basis for norms and regimes, which provide further structure for international society.

Norms are expectations regarding notions of right and wrong, as well as appropriate behavior. Norms can be categorized as regulative (i.e., ordering and constraining behavior), constitutive (i.e., creating new actors, interests, or actions), or prescriptive (i.e., stipulating standards of appropriate behavior). Norms are intersubjective and collective because their meaning is derived through negotiation among members of the community (Finnemore and Sikkink, 1998). Norms proceed through life cycles, from emergence, wherein they are introduced to society, to threshold, wherein a critical mass of society's members accept and assimilate them, to cascade and internalization, wherein they are accorded regulative, constitutive, and prescriptive properties and integrated into legal regimes (Khagram et al., 2002).

International society is created via the iterative construction and institutionalization of norms. States' identities are constructed via the process of defining, acknowledging, accepting, and acting on norms (Finnemore, 1996; Risse, Roppo, and Sikkink, 1999). Further, their identities, interests, and behaviors are continually shaped to align with those of international society. When states endorse a norm, they are formally and publicly endorsing a set of beliefs, thus reifying the states' membership standing within the community. Norms produce social order and stability by encouraging behavioral conformity and constraining choice (Katzenstein, 1996; Kratochwil, 1999). Norms, then, take on the power to make behavioral claims on the states, especially when integrated into international regimes.

Regimes are formally constituted directives around which states' expectations converge. They include principles, norms, rules, and decision-making procedures (Krasner, 1983). State sovereignty is a regime, as are nonproliferation and human rights. Because regimes are institutionalized and accorded legal status, they exert a constitutive force on states, creating identities, informing preferences, and socializing behaviour (Wendt, 1992).

Given the salience of regimes to states' well-being, regimes such as state sovereignty and nonproliferation are understandable. However, states are ratifying and abiding by regimes (e.g., human rights) that fundamentally contradict their interests and undermine their sovereignty. The human rights regime is part of a subset of regimes that promotes neither the economic/political coordination of states nor the stability of states. Rather, it is based on norms that promote human rights, democratic governance, development, peace, and environmental conservation and that fight international corruption (Khagram et al., 2002). Yet despite the detrimental implications for state sovereignty, states continue to voluntarily acquiesce to these norms and regimes.

GCS is an active force behind this apparent incongruity. GCS, locating itself directly at the center of the socialization of international society, generates global public opinion and constructs cosmopolitan norms (i.e., norms regarding international affairs that surpass the claims of states; Held, 2004; Panel, 2004). The Battle for Seattle is one powerful exemplar as traditionally oppositional groups (e.g., environment and labor) stood together against globalized capital and the express interests of powerful states to demand a new world economic order (Broad, 2002).

GCS acts to facilitate and guide the socialization process. It employs persuasion, communication, and moral authority to change international meaning structures and to institutionalize norms. Nevertheless, how does GCS, distinguished by its rich diversity, find common ground much less create international norms? The answer lies in understanding GCS as a process, specifically a transformative and generative process.

The process is that of dialogue, which accommodates and incorporates diversity to generate new and more comprehensive understanding (Ezzat, 2005). Through dialogue, people listen to understand different viewpoints. Their ideas and values are reframed within a larger context, and links are discovered that supersede differences and bond people to a common cause. This new intersubjective meaning then exerts a constitutive force, creating and redefining identities, informing preferences, and socializing behavior (Lipschutz, 1992). The World Social Forum highlights GCS' ability to transcend its multiple particularities, transform and create identities, and create webs of normative meaning and shared understanding.

GCS endeavors are found throughout the norm life cycle, from norm emergence to norm threshold to norms cascade and norm internalization (Finnemore & Sikkink, 1998). Its work does not end with the institutionalization of norms, however. Monitoring state behavior for norm compliance presents an ongoing challenge, as evidenced by the current endeavors of Amnesty International, the International Red Cross, and the Center for Constitutional Rights to hold the Bush administration accountable for alleged human rights abuses and war crimes in Iraq (Amnesty International, 2005).

GCS' active engagement in the international socialization process is the source of its power. Through the socialization process, GCS is building global community and promoting the regimes related to democracy and sustainability that states are ratifying and for which states are volunteering to be held accountable.

GCS: CHALLENGES TO LEGITIMIZATION

GCS is engaged internationally, regarded as an important player in global governance, and vying to further develop its partnership with the IGOs. Yet it faces significant challenges in its bid to institutionalize its legitimate presence in global governance. It is challenged by issues within the IGOs, by a backlash of governments against its growing power, and by its own internal developmental requirements.

UN: A CASE IN POINT

With rare exceptions, GCS does not occupy formal and legitimized places in IGOs. It has enjoyed its most significant influence in the UN. However, GCS is even being challenged within the UN. The UN is questioning the accountability and transparency of NGOs, requiring greater self-discipline, and calling for NGOs to engage in self-regulation. Moreover, since the late 1990s, the UN has curtailed and challenged GCS' access to its quarters. Accreditation is widely perceived to be politicized, with states weighing in on decisions when they perceive civil society groups to be a threat to their interests (United Nations, 2003). Increasingly restrictive and inconsistent security rules, the lack of space for NGOs to congregate, and the application of fees for access to UN documents have exceeded the capacity of many civil society groups to gain access to the UN (Krut et al., 2005). Civil society's access to meetings also has been restricted. The Secretariat is accused of failing to engage civil society even in matters critical to civil society. ESOSOC has considered the restriction of NGOs accredited to particular meetings. The restriction from meetings is particularly significant because the global conferences that catapulted GCS onto the international scene have been discontinued. Issues formerly considered at the conferences have been transferred to the General Assembly and other UN venues, wherein civil society has little to no access (Global Policy Forum, 2003).

The increasing restrictions are explained, in part, by the UN's burgeoning financial crisis. The explosive growth in NGOs, requests for accreditation, and demands for access has overwhelmed the UN's limited capacity. Strategies such as the application of fees to UN services can be explained by the organization's severe resource constraints. The restricted access is, however, far from simply a logistical issue. As if accommodating Newton's third law of motion, the growing force of GCS is being met with an equal and opposing force—that of states.

STATE BACKLASH

GCS claims its place in international society despite the fact that it sits outside the Westphalian polity. Designed by and for states, the Westphalian system designated states as the sole world powers and created the regime of sovereignty to enable their peaceful coexistence. Paramount in the sovereignty regime are the principles of sovereignty, wherein states are accorded full rights to reign over the people and resources within their territories, and nonintervention, wherein states agree to stay out of each other's internal business (Deudney, 1996).

GCS represents a significant threat to the Westphalian system (Clark, 2001). The establishment of internationally accepted human rights, for example, challenges state sovereignty because state actions against their citizens can be contested by actors outside the particular state (Ruggie, 1998). Advancing and protecting human rights is one of GCS' oldest endeavors. In fact, GCS has taken a leading role in monitoring government actions with regard to internationally negotiated regimes, earning for itself the title of the " . . . new world police force" (Spirio, 1995, pp. 45–46). Organizations such as Amnesty International, World Conservation Union, Third World Network, and Transparency International research, disseminate information, and mobilize public opinion to increase government transparency and hold governments accountable. Their reports regularly trigger UN special investigations and focus worldwide attention on offending countries.

The arrest of General Augusto Pinochet in 1998, the Guatemalan truth commissions of 1997, and Suharto's forced abdication in Indonesia in 1998 are indisputable substantiation of the erosion of state sovereignty resulting from application of international human rights principles (Risse et al., 1999). GCS exerts this pressure equally in other policy areas, exposing governments' lack of follow-through on international obligations and pushing for additional extension of government responsibility to humanity. This incursion into state sovereignty is prompting a reactionary force against GCS (Willetts, 1996).

Actions resulting in the separation of GCS from the seat of power within the UN must be considered in light of this reactionary force. Paul asserts that there has been a growing movement within the member states to diminish NGO rights. States are challenging NGO's legitimacy, representativeness, sources of funding, and tactics (Paul, 2005a). For example, global conferences were halted primarily at the behest of the United States, whose representatives claimed they were an unnecessary financial burden and a waste of time. In the same period, environmental NGOs' status was undermined, and funding for women's programs was cut. NGOs were barred from traditional forms of access to the General Assembly and subjected to unprecedented and unpredictable search procedures. Moreover, NGOs' attempts to gain formal access to the General Assembly and the Security Council have been actively prohibited.

DEVELOPMENTAL CHALLENGES

The backlash against GCS, however, is not entirely driven by political antipathy. It also represents a legitimate demand of any actor that claims to speak for the people. GCS is being challenged to justify its new status and influence (Panel, 2004). Furthermore, it must address its own developmental challenges. GCS, as with government or business, cannot be assumed to be democratic (Scholte, 2002). The democratic challenges it faces include its representativeness and its potential to undermine democracy, reinforce structural deficiencies in aid-recipient communities, and reify the disparity in power and voice already extant across GCS.

GCS is challenged with regard to its representativeness. Kaldor et al. (2003) distinguish between mutual benefit and solidarity NGOs. Mutual-benefit NGOs include people who work to improve the conditions of their own lives (e.g., the Macedonian Center for International Cooperation and the Bangladesh Rural Advancement Committee). Solidarity NGOs are comprised of people who may not be affected by the problems they are trying to resolve, but who, nonetheless, are committed to the well-being of others (e.g., Amnesty International and Oxfam). Solidarity NGOs that claim to represent "the people" defy one of the basic tenets of representative democracy (i.e., that of legitimacy gained through popular elections). Such NGOs cannot look to their beneficiary constituency for guidance and, hence, cannot make claims on their behalf without having their legitimacy effectively challenged. Moreover, when different solidarity NGOs make divergent claims on behalf of the same constituency, there is no mechanism to discern which one truly represents the people (Krut et al., 2005).

The relationship between southern and northern NGOs highlights other serious democratic challenges. Northern NGOs dominate internationally, being the primary recipients of donor funding and playing the most prominent political and operational roles. Eight northern NGOs currently receive half the $8 billion funding for NGOs (i.e., CARE, World Vision International, Oxfam, Medecins Sans Frontieres, Save the Children Federation, Cooperation Internationale pour le Developpement et la Solidarite, Coalition of Catholic NGOs, and Association of Protestant Development Organization in Europe and Eurostep).[2] The funding is then channelled to many southern mutual-benefit NGOs, along with dictums regarding mission, required outcomes, and allowable expenditures.

Southern dependence on northern NGOs and donors for resources creates many problems. First, it jeopardizes southern NGOs' ability to respond appropriately to local needs. Southern NGOs tend to organize holistically around a community's needs, addressing issues from the environment to employment and nutrition (Rooy, 2004). In contrast, many northern NGOs are focused on single issues. Hence, directives and purposes of funders and southern NGOs can be ill fit, with funder penchants taking precedence. Further, the method by which aid is delivered can have debilitating effects on the community, its government, and local NGOs. It can create dependencies, supplant government operations, reinforce structural deficiencies, and undermine democratic policy and practice. Finally, the predominance of northern NGOs engaged with IGOs further obscures the voice of southern citizens and reinforces the disparity in power and voice between northern and southern civil society (Hudock, 1999).

While these democratic challenges within civil society remain unresolved, GCS' legitimacy remains vulnerable to question and political subversion. These issues are at the heart of many governments' attacks on GCS. These challenges, however, are not unlike those faced by states or businesses. States, for example, are accorded equal status in the UN regardless of their practices with regard to human rights or democracy. Transnational corporations also are notoriously undemocratic in their operations. They operate outside the authority of the nations in which they do business, making them, in essence, nationless (Multistate Tax Commission, 2005). They are not compelled to abide by the states' laws, regulations, or tax obligations, so they are free to extend their authoritarian rule without constraint. Both states and businesses have undermined people's capacity to sustain themselves, degraded states' ability to govern, obscured people's voice, and reinforced disparities in power.

The democratic challenges faced by GCS are real. However, to impugn GCS and deny it legitimacy in global governance is problematic and suspect when uttered from the mouths of those equally challenged. Rather, the question might be reframed within the context of democratic governance. In a system of democratic governance, laws, institutions, and systems are designed to counter the inherent undemocratic tendencies of organizations and people. These enable the full participation of all members of society, the state, business, and civil society.

CONCLUSION

GCS, although extant for many years, exploded onto the international scene in the 1990s as a powerful force for norms related to democracy and sustainability. It has been a primary architect and champion of virtually all international regimes related to human and environmental protection, and it has promoted democratic governance at all levels. Its agency is formidable, and its achievements are irrefutable.

Yet it has no formal or institutionally protected venue through which to project its voice and parlay its intent into international governance. Rather, it is vulnerable to the vagaries of the international system. While this situation remains, the efforts of GCS to advocate for people will continue to be hindered by hostile and unreceptive political and economic forces that are accorded with legal legitimacy and guaranteed access to international policymaking venues. As a result, the democratic deficit so pervasive in international governance will continue or worsen as one of its natural counterbalances is systematically foiled. GCS makes a unique and important contribution to the world and its people. It serves vital purposes in the development of democracy and sustainability. It needs to be accorded a legally legitimated voice in international governance.

NOTES TO CHAPTER 5

1. A campaign of the World Forum of Civil Society Networks (UBUNTU), www.reformcampaign.net/index.php?pg=81&lg=eng
2. Ibid., 25.

REFERENCES

Aksu, Esref, and Joseph A. Camilleri, eds. 2002. *Democratizing Global Governance*. New York: Palgrave Macmillian.
Amnesty International. 2005. *United States of America Human Dignity Denied: Torture and Accountability in the "War on Terror."* Retrieved November 20,

2004, from http://web.amnesty.org/library/Index/ENGAMR511452004?ope n&of=ENG-USA.

Anheier, Helmut, Marlies Glasius, and Mary Kaldor, eds. 2005. *Global Civil Society 2004/5*. London, UK: Sage.

Archibugi, Daniele, Sveva Balduini, and Marco Donati. 2000. "The United Nations as an Agency of Global Democracy." In *Global Democracy: Key Debates*, edited by B. Holden. London, UK: Routledge.

Barber, Benjamin. 1995. *Jihad vs. McWorld: Terroism's Challenge to Democracy*. New York: Ballantine Books.

———. 1998. *A Place for Us: How to Make Society Civil and Democracy Strong*. New York: Hill & Wang.

Boutros-Ghali, Boutros. 1996. *An Agenda for Democratization*. New York: United Nations.

Broad, Robin. 2002. *Global Backlash: Citizen Initiatives for a Just World Economy*. Lanham, MD: Rowman & Littlefield.

Burawoy, Michael. 2003. "For a Sociological Marxism: The Complimentary Convergence of Antonio Gramsci & Karl Polanyi." *Politics and Society* 31 (2): 193–261.

Cardoso, Fernando. 2005. *High Level Panel on UN-Civil Society: Civil Society and Global Governance*. Available at http://www.un-ngls.org/ ecosoc%20HL%20Panel%20-%20Contextual%20paper%20by%20Mr%20 Cardoso%20Chairman.doc.

Castells, Manuel. 2000. *The Rise of the Network Society*. 2nd ed. Oxford, UK: Blackwell.

Chomsky, Noam. 1999. *Profit Over People: Neoliberalism and Global Order*. New York: Seven Stories Press.

Clark, Ann Marie. 2001. *Diplomacy of Conscience: Amnesty International and Changing Human Rights Norms*. Princeton, NJ: Princeton University Press.

Commission on Global Governance. 1995. *Our Global Neighborhood: The Report of the Commission on Global Governance*. New York: Oxford University Press.

Deudney, Daniel. 1996. "Binding Sovereigns: Authorities, Structures and Geopolitics in Philadephian Systems." In *State Sovereignty as Social Construct*, edited by T. Biersteker & C. Weber. Cambridge University Press, New York, NY.

Edwards, Michael, and John Gaventa. 2001. *Global Civil Action*. Boulder, CO: Lynne Rienner.

———, and Simon Zadek. 2003. "Governing the Provision of Global Public Goods: The Role and Legitimacy of Nonstate Actors." In *Providing Global Public Goods: Managing Globalization*, edited by I. Kaul, P. Conceição, K. Goulven, & R. Mendoza. New York: United Nations Development Program.

Ehrenberg, John. 1999. *Civil Society: The Critical History of an Idea*. New York: New York University Press.

Ezzat, Heba Raouf. 2005. *Beyond Methodological Modernism: Towards a Multicultural Paradigm Shift in the Social Sciences, Global Civil Society 2004/5*, edited by H. Anheier, M. Glasius, & M. Kaldor. London, UK: Sage.

Falk, Richard. 2000. "Global Civil Society and the Democratic Prospect." In *Global Democracy: Key Debates*, edited by B. Holden. London, UK: Routledge.

Finnemore, Martha. 1996, Spring. "Norms, Culture, and World Politics: Insights From Sociology's Institutionalism." *International Organization* 50: 339–347.

———, and Kathryn Sikkink. 1998. "International norm dynamics and political change." *International Organization* 52 (4): 325–347.

Galbraith, John. 1998. *The Affluent Society*.: Houghton Mifflin.

Galtung, Johan. 2000. "Alternative Models for Global Democracy." In *Global Democracy: Key Debates*, edited by B. Holden. London, UK: Routledge.

Global Policy Forum. 2003. *NGOs and the United Nations: Comments for the Report of the Secretary General.* Available at http://www.un-ngls.org/08gpf.pdf.

Hall, Budd. 2000. "Global Civil Society: Theorizing a Changing World." *Convergence* 33 (1–2): 22–32.

Haq, Mahbubul. 1999. *Reflections on Human Development.* Oxford, UK: Oxford University Press.

Harris, Jonathan. 2000. *Basic Principles of Sustainable Development.* Working Paper 00–04. Global Development and Environment Institute, Tufts University.

Held, David. 1995. *Democracy and the Global Order: From the Modern State to Cosmopolitan Governance.* Cambridge, UK: Blackwell.

———. 2004. *Global Covenant: The Social Democratic Alternative to the Washington Consensus.* Cambridge, UK: Polity Press.

Helsinki Process. 2005. *Governing Globalization—Globalizing Governance: New Approaches to Global Problem Solving. Report of the Helsinki Process on Globalization and Democracy.* Available from www.helsinkiprocess.fi/netcomm/ImgLib/24/89/Track1.pdf.

Hudock, Ann. 1999. *NGOs and Civil Society: Democracy by Proxy?* Cambridge, UK: Polity Press.

International Forum on Globalization. 2002. *Alternatives to Economic Globalization: A Better World is Possible.* San Francisco, CA: Berrett-Koehler Publishers.

Iriye, Akira. 2004. *Global Community: The Role of International Organizations in the Making of the Contemporary World.* Berkeley, CA: University of California Press.

Kaldor, Mary. 2003. *Global Civil Society: An Answer to War.* Cambridge, UK: Polity Press.

———, Helmut Anheier, and Marlies Glasius. 2005. "Introduction." In *Global Civil Society 2004/5*, edited by H. Anheier, M. Glasius, & M. Kaldor. London, UK: Sage.

———. Eds. 2003. *Global Civil Society.* Oxford, UK: Oxford University Press.

Katzenstein, Peter. Ed. 1996. *The Culture of National Security: Norms and Identity in World Politics.* New York: Columbia University Press.

Keane, John. 1998. *Civil Society: Old Images, New Visions.* Stanford, CA: Stanford University Press.

———. 2003. *Global Civil Society?* Cambridge, NY: Cambridge University Press.

Khagram, Sanjeev, James Riker, and Kathryn Sikkink. Eds. 2002. *Restructuring World Politics: Transnational Social Movements, Networks, and Norms.* Vol. 14. Minneapolis, MN: University of Minnesota Press.

Klandermans, Bert. 1992. "The Social Construction of Protest and Multi-organizational Fields." In *Frontiers in Social Movement Theory*, edited by A. D. Morris and C. McClurg-Mueller. New Haven, CT: Yale University Press.

Korten, David. 1996. *When Corporations Rule the World.* San Francisco, CA: Berrett-Koehler Publishers.

Krasner, Stephen. 1983. *Structural causes and regime consequences. International Regimes.* Edited by S. Krasner. Ithaca, NY: Cornell University Press.

Kratochwil, Friedrich. 1999. *Rules, Norms, and Decisions.* Cambridge, MA: Cambridge University Press.

Kriesberg, Louis. 1997. "Social Movements and Global Transformation." In *Transnational Social Movements and Global Politics: Solidarity Beyond the*

State, edited by J. Smith, C. Chatfield, and R. Pagnucco. Syracuse, NY: Syracuse University Press.

Krut, Riva, Kristin Howard, Eric Howard, Harris Gleckman, and Pattison Dannielle. 2005. *Globalization and Civil Society: NGO Influence in International Decision-Making.* Available at http://www.rrojasdatabank.org/toc83.htm.

Levine, David. 1995. *Wealth and Freedom: An Introduction to Political Economy.* New York: Cambridge University Press.

Lipschutz, Ronnie. 1992. "Reconstructing World Politics: The Emergence of Global Civil Society. *Millennium: Journal of International Studies* 21 (3): 389–420.

Lujan, Bertha Elena. 2002. "Citizen advocacy Networks and the NAFTA." In *Cross-Border Dialogues: U.S.-Mexican Social Movement Networking*, edited by D. Brooks and J. Fox. San Diego, CA: Center for U.S.–Mexican Studies, University of California.

Magis, Kristen. 2007. *Global Civil Society: Finding Collective Voice in Diversity, Dissertation for Ph.D. in Public Administration and Policy: Portland State University.* Portland, OR: UMI Dissertation Publishing.

Mbogori, Ezra, and Hope Chigudu. 1999. "Civil Society and Government: A Continuum of Possibilities." In *Civil Society at the Millennium*, edited by Civicus. West Hartford, CT: Kumarian Press.

Mearsheimer, John. 2001. *The Tragedy of Great Power politics.* New York: Norton.

Mertes, Thomas. 2004. *A Movement of Movements: Is Another World Really Possible?* New York: Verso.

Mokhiber, Russell, and Robert Weissman. 1999. *Corporate Predators: The Hunt for Mega-Profits and the Attack on Democracy.* Monroe, ME: Common Courage Press.

Muller, Jerry. 2002. *The Mind and the Market: Capitalism in Modern European Thought.* New York: Alfred A. Knopf.

Multistate Tax Commission. 2005. *Corporate Tax Sheltering and the Impact on State Corporate Income Tax Revenue Collections.* Available from www.mtc. gov/TaxShelterRpt.pdf.

Non-Governmental Liaison Service. 2005. *Report of the Consultation with Civil Society on: "The Crisis in Global Governance: Challenges for the United Nations and Global Civil Society."* Available at www.un-ngls/org/publications.htm.

Nye, Joseph, and John D. Donahue. Eds. 2000. *Governance in a Globalizing World.* Washington, DC: Brookings Institution Press.

Organization for Economic Cooperation and Development. 2001. *Sustainable Development: Critical Issues.* Paris, France: Author.

Oxfam. 2003. *Rigged Rules and Double Standards: Make Trade Fair.* Available from http://www.maketradefair.com/stylesheet.

Panel of Eminent Persons on UN-Civil Society Relations. 2004. *We the Peoples: Civil Society, the United Nations and Global Governance.* A report of the Panel of Eminent Persons on UN-Civil Society Relations, United Nations.

Paul, James. 2005a. *NGO Access at the UN.* Available at http://www.globalpolicy. org/ngos/analysis/jap-accs.htm.

———. 2005b. *NGOs and Global Policy-Making.* Available at http://www.global-policy.org/ngos/analysis/ana100.htm.

Piven, Frances, and Richard Cloward. 1979. *Poor People's Movements: Why They Succeed, How They Fail.* New York: Vintage Books.

Polanyi, Karl. 2001. *The Great Transformation: The Political and Economic Origins of Our Lives.* Boston, MA: Beacon Press. Original edition, 1944.

Risse, Thomas, Stephen Roppo, and Kathryn Sikkink, eds. 1999. *The Power of Human Rights: International Norms and Domestic Change.* Cambridge, UK: Cambridge University Press.

Rooy, Allison. 2004. *The Global Legitimacy Game: Civil Society, Globalization, and Protest*. Hampshire, UK: Palgrave Macmillan.

Rosenau, James. 1990. *Turbulence in World Politics: A Theory of Change and Continuity*. Princeton, NJ: Princeton University Press.

———. 1995. Governance in the Twenty-First Century. *Global Governance* 1 (1): 14.

Ruggie, John. 1998, Autumn. What Makes the World Hang Together? Neo-Utilitarianism and the Social Constructivist Challenge. *International Organization* 52 (4): 855–885.

Salamon, Lester, eds. 2004. *Global Civil Society: Dimensions of the Nonprofit Sector*. Vol. II. Bloomfield, CT: Kumarian Press.

Scholte, Jan Aart. 2002. "Civil Society and Democracy in Global Governance." In *Civil Society and Global Finance*, edited by J. A. Scholte and A. Schnabel. New York: Routledge.

Sen, Amartya. 1999. *Development as Freedom*. New York: Knopf.

Serrano, Isagani. 1999. "Coming Apart, Coming Together: Globalization and Civil Society." In *Civil Society at the Millennium*, edited by Civicus. West Harford, CT: Kumarian Press.

Shiva, Vandana. 2003. "The Living Democracy Movement: Alternatives to the Bankruptcy of Globalization." In *Another World Is Possible: Popular Alternatives to Globalization at the World Social Forum*, edited by W. Fisher and T. Ponniah. New York: Zed Books Ltd.

Smith, Adam. 1981. "An Inquiry into the Nature and Causes of the Wealth of Nations." In *The Glasgow Edition of the Works and Coorespondence of Adam Smith*, edited by R. H. Campbell and A. S. Skinner. Indianapolis, IN: Liberty Fund. Original edition, 1776.

South Centre. 1997. *For a Strong and Democratic United Nations: A South Perspective on UN Reform*. New York: Zed Books.

Spirio, Peter. 1995. "New Global Communities: Nongovernmental Organization in International Decision-Making Institutions." *The Washington Quarterly* 18 (1): 45–46.

Stiglitz, Joseph. 2002. *Globalization and Its Discontents*. New York: W.W. Norton.

Streeten, Paul, Shahid Javed Burki, Mahbubul Haq, Norman Hicks, and Frances Stewart. 1981. *First Things First: Meeting Basic Human Needs in the Developing Countries*. New York: Oxford University Press.

"A Survey of Multinationals: Everybody's Favorite Monsters." 1993, March 6. *The Economist* (Special Supplement).

Tandon, Rajesh. 1991. "Civil Society. The State and Roles of NGO" In *IDR Occasional Paper*. Boston, MA.

United Nations. 2003. "UN System and Civil Society—An Inventory and Analysis of Practices." In *Background paper for the Secretary-General's Panel of Eminent Persons on UN Relations and Civil Society*. New York: United Nations.

———. 2005. *World Summit Outcome: Presented to the 2005 World Summit*. Available at http://daccessdds.un.org/doc/UNDOC/GEN/N05/487/60/PDF/N0548760.pdf?OpenElement.

United Nations Development Programme. 2005a. *Human Development Report* Available at www.undp.org/hdr.

———. 2005b. *International Cooperation at a Crossroads: Aid, Trade and Security in an Unequal World. Human Development Report*. Available at http://hdr.undp.org/reports/global/2005/.

Wallerstein, I. 2004. "New Revolts Against the System." In *A Movement of Movements: Is Another World Really Possible?*, edited by T. Mertes. New York: Verso.

Wapner, Paul, and Lester Ruiz. 2000. *Principled World Politics: The Challenge of Normative International Relations.* New York: Rowman & Littlefield.

Weiss, Thomas, and Leon Gordenker. Eds. 1996. *NGOs, the UN, and Global Governance.* Boulder, CO: Lynne Rienner Publishers.

Wendt, Alexander. 1992. "Anarchy Is What States Make of It: The Social Construction of Power Politics." *International Organization* 46 (2): 391–425.

Willetts, Peter. 2000. "From Consultative Arrangements' to 'Partnerships': The Changing Status of NGOs in Diplomacy at the UN." *Global Governance* 6 (2): 191–213.

Williamson, John. Ed. 1994. *The Political Economy of Policy Reform.* Washington, DC: Institute for International Economics.

World Bank. 1997. *World Development Report: The State in a Changing World.* New York: Oxford University Press.

6 In the Absence of Affluence

The Struggle for Social Sustainability in the Third World

Veronica Dujon

Sustainability may be broadly defined as a human quest that seeks to promote human well-being now and in the future, within the context of environmental and economic constraints. Social sustainability is considered to be both a positive condition within societies that supports human well-being and a process within communities that can achieve that condition. Such a broad definition with its worthy goal and holistic orientation seems intuitively coherent, but reveals little of the complicated and difficult nature of the undertaking—a well-documented frustration in the literature.

A commonly accepted practice of categorizing human activity into three spheres (the economic, the environmental, and the social) seemed promising in conceptualizing the key elements of the whole where problems could be identified and solutions sought. Some progress has been made in refining notions and measuring achievements on the economic and environmental fronts. Difficulty in making similar progress on the social front and in the substantive reintegration of the three spheres into a coherent approach in the pursuit of sustainability has been daunting. There are many reasons for this situation.

Deciding on the key factors that promote social sustainability and whether and how limited resources should be used to promote general social well-being is a fundamentally contested process driven by different worldviews, the institutions they give rise to, and the ability of different social groups to harness political power to promote certain outcomes. The quest for social sustainability reflects the particular constraints and opportunities across place, space, and time. For those interested in social sustainability, the task is to identify the processes that generate social health and well-being now and in the future and those social institutions that facilitate environmental and economic sustainability now and for the future.

Concern with sustainability is a fairly recent global phenomenon triggered by global ecological scarcity. It spans both the industrialized and developing worlds. The social and material contexts driving this concern tend to be different across these two worlds, although the underlying principles for social sustainability remain similar. Larsen (Chapter 3) posits that "at the core of the concept of social sustainability is the notion of greater equity in access to resources and the realization of basic human rights for all, across space and time."

We live in a context of increasing ecological scarcity in which human dependence on a finite ecosystem is aggravated by the interacting limits of available resources (Ophuls and Boyan, 1992). Attempting to deal with one problem of scarce resources often leads to a predicament in another. Exploiting nuclear energy to compensate for declining supplies of oil, for example, triggers a toxic waste problem. Using fertilizers to increase food production pollutes water supplies. In such a situation, neoliberal market-oriented policies that promote economic growth as an essentially exclusive guiding principle for social organization have failed to nurture sustainable, healthy, and productive societies for the majority of people in contexts of either affluence or deprivation. Affluent societies buttressed by political and military leverage can command scarce global resources to prolong economic standards, whereas in poor countries, without such power, the threat to survival from ecological scarcity is immediate.

Over the last quarter century or so, the implementation of neoliberal market policies as a prescription for sound economic growth and thriving societies has been aggressively advocated by First World countries under the leadership of the United States. These policies are premised on the argument that private-sector market forms are superior mechanisms for providing for people's needs, and societies are best served by a reduced role of states and communal activity in the economy. In the aftermath of the debt crisis of the mid-1980s, these policies have been implemented relentlessly in Third World countries, with disastrous social and environmental consequences for the majority of poor and working people (Bello et al, 1994).

These hardships have galvanized social movements in the Third World focused on better social outcomes and more sustainable environmental and economic strategies. Recent waves of protest movements in Latin America over the last 10 years or so, beginning with the Zapatista Rebellion in Mexico in 1994, the failed privatization of water in Bolivia in 2003, the containment of the world's most productive gold mine (Yanacocha, Peru) in 2004, and the nationalization of natural gas in Bolivia in 2007, provide convincing evidence that people living in economically and politically oppressive conditions, to some extent, have been able to promote more socially sustainable societies and economies despite the odds. Economic marginalization in the global economy, often coupled with deteriorating environmental conditions, have motivated the search for alternatives to dominant neoliberal prescriptions for development that better respond to social and environmental well-being.

In characterizing these new movements in Latin America, Stahler-Shock, Vanden, and Kuecker (2007) observe that they focus on fundamentally changing the relations of power and holding power brokers accountable to the base. They tend to be autonomous from established political institutions. Some of these movements are not necessarily anticapitalist, but only against neoliberal versions of capitalist policies, nor do they necessarily want to overthrow the state. Economic sustainability is understood as a first phase in a process toward social sustainability, and at the national level these movements expect state governments to ensure that resource extraction is undertaken in a manner that is sensitive to healthy environments and that the benefits are redirected toward more equitable internal economic and social development.

Resource scarcity in developing countries is a consequence of both historic patterns of economic exploitation and more recent neoliberal market policies of structural adjustment that prioritize the generation of economic profits and debt repayment over the health and well-being of ordinary working people.

In developing countries, the concern is over having basic needs for survival: enough to eat, access to clean water, health care, housing, a source of income, or education for one's children are immediate needs. Formal avenues for political expression may exist in constitutions, but they are often discouraged, and protests are violently repressed. In contrast, in affluent countries, standards of living are far higher, in large part, because of the capacity to draw on resources from a global community; political expression is far more freely practiced, and political systems are far more stable. Civil associations abound, and there are more educated and healthy citizens. In such a context of relative socioeconomic comfort, the motivation to pursue change is far less intense. Unless there is a critical mass of awareness of the connection between deteriorating quality of life and the failure of markets to automatically promote environmental and social well-being, it is unlikely that enough political will can be generated to effect change.

The strategies pursued in the two regions reflect this difference and give rise to different trajectories in each of these contexts. It is in situations where people are most deprived, both economically and politically, that they are most highly motivated to effect change. Their social and material conditions provide them with a clearer grasp of the basic requirements needed for social reproduction—what it takes to be healthy, productive, and functioning individuals—and provide the foundation for the next generation to be able to achieve the same. There is a greater consciousness of both the ends sought and various alternatives, political and economic, that might achieve these ends. The ability to direct change successfully is enhanced by the vigor of democratic institutions of civil society and their power to influence the state.

THE ROLE OF CIVIL SOCIETY

In an insightful comparative examination of the works of Antonio Gramsci and Karl Polanyi, Michael Burawoy (2003) makes a convincing argument for the key role of institutions of civil society alongside, but distinct from, the state and the economy in effecting social change in capitalist economies. Burawoy draws parallels between Gramsci's argument that in advanced capitalist societies a combination of the expansion of civil society and state hegemonic activities serve to stabilize class relations that provide the conditions for challenging capitalism, and Polanyi's conclusion that as market expansion threatens society, conditions are created in which society reasserts its (democratic) power via influence on the state to regulate markets and keep them in the service of society.

For Burawoy (2003), these two positions coming from different theoretical angles converge on a focus of the central role that institutions of civil society play in effecting social change. Institutions of civil society are able to articulate the diverse interests of well-being (social, cultural, political) that encompass, but also transcend, economic interests. This diversity in civil society reflects both the material and historical experiences of particular places. Burawoy argues for a less classical Marxism that anticipates revolutionary social change in the most advanced capitalist societies and focuses on a more sociological one that attends to the political economy of a region and the dynamism of its institutions of civil society. This theoretical angle is consistent with arguments that advocate for democracy as a core concept in social sustainability, a process within communities that supports the ability to work toward a positive condition that supports human well-being.

Two observations are relevant here. First, according to Burawoy (2003), it is not necessarily in the most advanced capitalist societies that one should anticipate the creation of a process that supports human well-being. Second, in the context of global resource scarcity, understandings of human well-being will vary in place, space, and time. The fact that people living in the Third World are unlikely (nor should they be encouraged) to achieve the economic standard of living of those in the industrialized world is not as critical as their ability to achieve what Amartya Sen (1999) defines as some basic *freedoms* in the societies where they live.

Sen (1999) argues that the purpose of development is to improve human lives by expanding the range of things that a person could be and do. These freedoms refer to the ability to maintain themselves and to have the power or personal agency to bring about change in the world in which they live. More concretely, these freedoms are achieved via economic facilities (health/health care, education), protective political and civil security, transparency guarantees that enhance trust, and social opportunities. These freedoms are ultimately both a route to and an endpoint of human development.

Burawoy (2003) builds on examples from Gramsci (role of the state as a hegemonic power) and Polanyi (role of society in regulating markets) to illustrate the key role that civil society institutions have played in effecting change in different historical contexts. He then follows that trajectory to identify their pivotal role in more recent social and political changes, among them: the rise and fall of communist orders, the transition from colonialism to postcolonialism, and the development of an emergent transnationalism.

Following from Burawoy (2003), this chapter posits that the recent rise of social movements in Latin America that challenge neoliberal market policies that threaten the basic human well-being of ordinary people illustrates the key role and vigor of institutions of civil society. These movements incorporate both the environmental and economic consciousness of a new era in the struggle for social sustainability. The major push for society to regulate markets is a consequence of disillusionment both with structural adjustment policies that have left huge numbers of people mired in extreme poverty and state governments that seem incapable of responding to their basic needs of survival. The environmentally irresponsible intensification of natural resource extraction of minerals (oil, gold, copper), natural gas, or agricultural products undermines healthy soils, domestic food supplies, subsistence production, clean air, and clean water. The wealth generated is rarely reinvested in the regions where exploitation takes place. Labor standards and compensation are kept low to maximize profits (Kuecker 2007; Rus, Castillo, and Mattiace, 2001).

Harris (2002) notes that the majority of participants in these movements are indigenous people, peasant unions, and rural workers. Although formal structures for democratic participation exist, governments fail to respond to their needs and, in many cases, violently repress civil action (Harris, 2002). In essence, these grassroots movements push for greater democracy along the lines of Sen's (1999) freedoms and, in doing so, re-center the essence of human development as a foundation to build a healthy society.

DIVERGENT PATHS TO SOCIAL SUSTAINABILITY

There are two starting points that are pertinent to illustrate the divergent paths of the First and Third Worlds in the pursuit of social sustainability: the aftermath of the Great Depression for the First World, and the experience with colonialism and postcolonialism for Third World countries. In the First World, the impact of the Great Depression and the failure of the capitalist economy to protect ordinary citizens from the risk of participating in the market would lead to protective guarantees and the development of the welfare state. Across the industrialized world, the institutionalization of social protections for working families in combination with technological prowess would stimulate subsequent waves of economic growth and increasing social and economic well-being.

Three to four decades later, awareness of the limits of available natural resources, rising levels of air and water pollution, and the extinction of species directly correlated to modern forms of industrial production would give rise to a social movement focused on protecting the environment both to promote human health and for preserving it for its own inherent value. The early years of the modern environmental movement would reflect concerns emanating from a First World experience: species extinction, clean air and water, scarcity of natural resources, and overpopulation in developing countries. In wealthy countries that were no longer concerned with basic economic survival, there was enough political will to support the passage of legislation that required some sacrifice of economic gain in the interest of clean air, clean water, and species protection (Kline, 2004).

For developing countries, the devastation experienced under colonialism, the subsequent quest for national economic development, and the impact of the debt crisis of the 1980s with the imposition of structural adjustment programs by international development agencies have created a historical context in which the path to economic and social well-being has been unstable and far more illusive than in the First World.

The majority of Third World states were subject to centuries of colonial forms of exploitation that altered their economic, social, and cultural structures to facilitate the net extraction of primary raw material in the interest of industrial development of the imperial centers. Native populations were systematically oppressed, and natural landscapes were redesigned on a large scale. In the mid-20th century, when many won their independence, these ex-colonies focused on their own national interests. The leading thinkers of anticolonialism—Albert Memmi, Franz Fanon, Julius Nyere, Jean Paul Sartre, Aime Cesaire, among others—would call for the implementation of development models in which the eradication of cultural and racial oppression and promotion of democratic participation in political life were as critical as the pursuit for economic growth.

A series of circumstances would displace this relatively holistic orientation to development in favor of neoliberal and neocolonial models of development that prioritized economic growth. The multilateral international economic development agencies that were established to assist the newly emerging independent nations, such as the World Bank and the International Monetary Fund (IMF), were under the heavy influence of interests of First World nations that sought to prioritize their own domestic interests in their political and economic interactions with the developing countries. Trade and economic agreements were written in a manner that reflected lasting structural disadvantages for Third World countries. Integrated internal development based on ever-increasing industrial growth was discouraged in favor of continued primary resource extraction and agricultural production for export. Newly independent states, anxious to attain the economic achievements and quality of life of the First World, but lacking the funds to pursue any homegrown ideas, were swayed by the growth-based development models emanating from international development agencies and packaged with attractive loans and promises of private foreign investment (McMichael, 2004).

The resulting process of development would be widely critiqued for promoting structural relationships that continued to promote dependence on, and advantage to, industrialized economies, much as colonialism had done, and failing to bring about the expected improvement in quality of life (Prebisch, 1950; Furtado, 1964; Frank, 1967; Rodney, 1972). Admittedly, between the period following the Second World War and the early 1970s, many developing countries experienced overall improvement in economic activity and the delivery of social services (primarily education and health care) when compared with the experience of colonialism. Few countries, however, came close to meeting original expectations. Economic dependence of Third World states made it essentially impossible to overcome structural obstacles that closed off a push to the level of development in the industrialized world.

The expected improvement in quality of life materialized for people only in a handful of countries (the Asian Tigers: Japan, Hong Kong, South Korea, and Taiwan; and Brazil and Mexico in Latin America). These countries experimented with alternative models of state-sponsored development, such as import substitution industrialization, which focused on integrated internal development (McMichael, 2004). These states also tended to support fundamental social services such as education and health care. In general, however, huge gaps remained in the quality of life between the North and South. The majority of people in the South would remain economically marginalized, caught in a global economic structure that trapped them in a peripheral relationship with the more powerful core industrialized countries.

The advent of the debt crisis of the 1970s and 1980s, and the subsequent structural adjustment programs imposed on indebted countries, would not only reverse the gains made in the early decades after independence, but would seriously gut some of the most basic social protections on which people had come to rely. The dominant neoliberal ideology that prioritizes the role of markets as the principal tool for organizing societies has, over the last three decades or so, led to the deterioration of social and environmental wellbeing in the North and South, with extreme consequences in the latter.

Structural adjustment programs (SAPs) are designed to streamline economies along the lines of the neoliberal market models advocated by the U.S. Treasury Department, the World Bank, and the IMF to generate growth. A key objective of these programs was the generation of financial resources for debt repayment, not domestic reinvestment in the interest of citizens. SAPs typically require: (a) the privatization of core social services (health, education, water, and water delivery) that had been typically provided by states; (b) the elimination of consumption subsidies; (c) the increasing extraction of natural resources for export; (d) the intensification of agro-export industries that generally rely on chemical fertilizers, pesticides, and herbicides that find their way in water systems and pollute the soil and the air; (e) the devaluation of currency to improve exports (make them more competitive), which makes imports more expensive; and (f) the elimination of barriers to trade and investment. The resulting massive redirection of resources and scrapping of social programs to pay off debts violates the social and political rights of citizens, leaving huge numbers of people marginalized, unemployed, and destitute. Popular protests against these conditions often met with state repression (Bello et al, 2004).

Extreme deprivation sets into relief the basic needs of a society in its most rudimentary form, creating the potential to question and redefine the path to economic and social development. Concern for social and environmental sustainability in the developing world does not emanate from conditions of affluence, but rather from conditions of structural scarcity. These concerns, although not new, are certainly more critical and urgent than ever before.

CREATING ALTERNATIVE PATHS TO SOCIAL SUSTAINABILITY

The search for more appropriate models of development, beginning as early as the post-World War II period and accelerating after the devastating social and environmental impact of the debt crisis, focused on identifying the basic elements of human well-being as the building blocks of sustainable societies. The United Nations (UN) has played a leading role in this effort. The evolution of key emergent concepts of social sustainability—human well-being, equity, democratic government, and democratic civil society—are principal elements that are required as both imperative preconditions as well as sustained conditions in the pursuit of social sustainability (Harris, Wise, Gallagher, and Goodwin, 2001).

An engaged citizenry or vigorous civil society that has experienced the connections between social and economic deprivation and environmental resource scarcity can be motivated to exercise political power and effect social change. This pursuit is particularly difficult in the increasingly integrated global socioeconomic system largely premised on a dominant neoliberal economic paradigm advocated by powerful international agencies, the countries that support them, and the national governments that implement them.

The ability to effectively participate in decision making is influenced by a combination of the formal and informal institutional mechanisms that structure participation and the ability of individuals to identify and pursue their interests. States that practice democracy in conjunction with civil associations that educate and organize citizens are best poised to reflect citizen interests. In the developing world, where the experience of loss of state-sponsored social supports has been increasingly concurrent with the privatization of basic needs, such as water, health care, and education, marginal groups of people, with few effective formal institutional avenues to democratic forms of participation, have chosen, or have been driven, to respond in ways that challenge the legitimacy of existing procedural structures of democratic participation that fail to effect changing policy at the state level.

On the energy of these grassroots social movements, popular governments have been elected in Venezuela, Brazil, Bolivia, Ecuador, Uruguay, Argentina, and Chile. The majority of these people's movements have linked social justice and democracy, many encouraging horizontal participation in the processes they engage in and some maintaining autonomy from political institutions (Stahler-Sholk et al., 2007). They have focused on fundamentally changing relations of power and holding power brokers accountable to the base (Harris, 2002; Stahler-Sholk et al, 2007; Swords, 2007) and have engaged in consciousness-raising that invigorates civil society and outlasts protests (Kuecker, 2007; Swords, 2007).

In Brazil, the reasonably wealthy cities of Curitiba and Porto Alegre have long represented progressive efforts at sustainable development. The former has been known internationally for its success in urban planning and, in particular, its transportation system. Porto Alegre, in contrast, instituted a participatory budgeting model in 1989 that requires and maintains citizen participation in allocating approximately half the city's budget (De Sousa Santos, 1998). This approach allowed the city to resist the competitive city ideology and reject the construction of a Ford Motor Company plant despite of promises for new employment. The city chose instead to use the anticipated subsidies for other city needs (Goldsmith, 2007). The delegates for the 16 district assemblies and regional councils draw disproportionately from the poor, although participation in the ministerial groups consists of more professionals and technocrats (Goldsmith, 2007).

But more significant, Brazil's push for greater human well-being is better represented by the rise of the Landless Workers' Movement (MST) that would claim and settle millions of hectares of unused land via massive and continuous land occupations under provisions of Brazil's 1964 land law (Martins, 2000). Land reform has been "a key element in unifying Brazilian workers—urban and rural, manual and intellectual—in their struggle for a better society" (Martins, 2000, p. 42). The MST and its successes in consciousness-raising, advocacy of social justice, and actual land occupations have served to strengthen the social foundations for democracy in Brazil and concurrently redefined the relationship among the natural environment, the economy, and the well-being of the people.

The settlement is conceived of as a whole production unit. The MST promotes cooperative relations and forms of production among worker families. Democratic structures of decision making have encouraged the evolution of a variety of property ownership and production arrangements that reflect changing environmental, regional, and social contexts, such as the quality of the soil, the kind of crops, the experience of workers, and the market structure (Martins, 2000). The settlements also are building communal reserves (fundos) from income contributions from individuals to support educational, health, and technical support to families. Martinez (2007) argues that these different kinds of reserves are essentially evidence of an experiment in socialized capital accumulation. The MST enjoys massive unprecedented support across Brazil. Martinez concludes that the movement's pursuit of massive radical land reform is more than an attempt to incorporate small farmers into a capitalist agricultural system, but an attempt by the popular marginalized sectors to shift the production, power, and cultural relations of the entire agrarian structure.

The Water Wars in Cochabamba, Bolivia, at the turn of the 21st century also represented the mobilization of marginalized people in ways that diverged from established patterns and yielded considerable gains. The proposed privatization of water was halted, but, as significant, was the opportunity this different form of mobilization provided to raise the consciousness of the rural and urban poor and working classes and to shift political power relationships in ways that prioritized social reproduction over the implementation of neoliberal market policies.

The experience in Bolivia is very much in line with Polyani's analysis that when markets go against the interest of broad sectors of society, civil society is most motivated to demand that the state regulates market activity in the interest of society. In the aftermath of the debt crisis of the mid-1980s, many factory worker unions had expanded their portfolio of concerns to include broad social issues facing the population. They encouraged cooperation with indigenous coca grower unions, groups sympathetic to environmental issues, and the professional sectors. The convergence between the criticism from middle-class professionals, who were also adversely affected by structural adjustment policies, and that of popular organizations led to the emergence of the COORDINADORA and its capacity to mobilize various sectors of the population (Assies, 2003).

Following repeated mass mobilizations and protests, Law 2029 was finally rewritten to include the establishment of rate structures in consultation with the municipalities and the local units of popular participation. Existing water distribution organizations were officially recognized and protected and given some control over water rate structures. The elimination of the criterion of "financial sufficiency" for water supply agencies to operate opened the way for consideration of social criteria (Assies, 2003).

Upon its victory, however, the members of the COORDINADORA opted not to become a formal organization and seek official recognition. The organization continues to maintain a network that keeps the groups linked and calls open meetings to discuss issues such as the revision of electricity rates and the recovery of privatized state enterprises (Assies, 2003).

In 2006, Evo Morales, Bolivia's first indigenous president, who had been a leader of the indigenous coca farmers' union assumed office with the support of social, indigenous, rural, and worker movements, as well as professional sectors and business people dissatisfied with the failure of the neoliberal economic system. Morales' administration has renegotiated contracts with 10 different gas companies, increasing the share of state ownership to beyond 50%. He has instituted policies to combat illiteracy and health deficits with these newly acquired resources and also has pushed for a "People's Trade Agreement" based on the principles of fair trade, labor and environmental protections, and active state intervention in the economy to promote economic development (Martinez, 2007).

In Venezuela, President Hugo Chavez has followed a similar path of instituting social policies to boost literacy and provide health care and other services to the poor with revenue from the state-owned oil sector. Local economic development through cooperatives also is strongly encouraged. The Venezuelan state, as a result of the efforts of the Global Women's Strike, recognizes work in the home as an economic activity that creates added value and produces social welfare and wealth, and consequently entitles housewives to social security (Fischer-Hoffman, 2006). This policy is particularly significant for its contribution to the sustainable reproduction of society. Feminist economists have long made the case that the omission of significant key services, such as caring and domestic labor in accounting for the social reproduction of human societies, consistently undermines any efforts for socioeconomic sustainability (Waring, 1988; Folbre, 1994; Benería, 2003; Power, 2004).

It is significant to note that even as the Chavez administration has made significant strides towards prosocial economic policies, it has been challenged by environmental and indigenous groups, both within the country and throughout Latin America, over the proposal to build a 5,000-mile gas pipeline from Venezuela to Argentina. This challenge is indicative of the central value that citizens, including marginalized classes, place on a healthy natural environment alongside economic policies.

The manifestation of this consciousness of the fundamental connection between the health of the natural environment and people's physical, social, and economic well-being has generated multiple grassroots protests against irresponsible natural resource extraction across Latin America that have thus far resulted in some success. Indigenous communities in Junin, a region of Intag in northern Ecuador, were able to keep copper mining company Bishi Metals, a subsidiary of Mitsubishi Corporation, out of their forests despite support for these operations by the Ecuadorian state and the World Bank. The marginalized, mostly indigenous people would have suffered the consequences of environmentally irresponsible mining (with state approval) and received minimal economic benefits (Kuecker, 2007).

Prior to the arrival of the company, however, the community had gone through a process of consciousness-raising about the causes of their marginalization under the guidance of the priest, Padre Giovanni Paz, who had introduced the concept of liberation theology and horizontal decision making. That process had already produced some grassroots projects of environmental and economic diversification. A local community organization, Defensa y Conservacion Ecologica de Intag- Ecological Defense and Conservation of Intag (DECOIN), was formed in 1995 in response to the perceived threat that mining operations posed. The organization had the advantage of linking up with national and international environmental NGOs for information gathering and strategic planning. It conducted popular education workshops about the advantages and dangers of mining and included a trip in 1996 to Peru for first-hand observation of the negative ecological and community impact of operating a copper mine (Kuecker, 2007). Repeated government rejections to meet with the community led to protests and the torching of mining camps. DECOIN also challenged the Proyecto de Desarrollo Minero y Control Ambiental—Ecuadorian Mining Development and Environmental Control Technical Assistance Project (PRODEMINCA), which had been funded by the World Bank, for failing to conduct an environmental impact study as required. In 2001, the World Bank ruled in DECOIN's favor. Meeting the new requirements has made mining more expensive than the company is willing to absorb.

In the meantime, the Junin community has undertaken to promote alternative economic activities that are sensitive to environmental sustainability: subsistence farming, shade-grown coffee production, sugar collectives, fish farming, and ecotourism. More recently, however, the price of copper has skyrocketed because of China's consumption, and copper mining in the region has attracted the attention of the Ascendant Exploration mining company. The company has undertaken an aggressive campaign to weaken the resistance of the community by building infrastructure like roads, schools, and health clinics that the state has been unable to provide (Kuecker, 2007).

Community activists continue to fight back, but the outcome of this next assault is not clear. What is clear, however, is that, throughout Latin America, local and indigenous communities are beginning to resist the rising environmental and social costs for mineral extraction and mining. As a result, corporations are being forced, in the words of a *New York Times* article on the Yanacocha gold mine in Peru, to negotiate a "social license" with the affected communities if they want to continue their operations (Perlez and Bergman, 2005).

Although the reduction of adverse environmental impacts often are included on the agenda of these grassroots democracy movements, it is typically from a human health, economic survival perspective, and not from an antigrowth perspective per se—rather, an antigrowth that does not benefit the poor. Economic growth is required for those who lack essentials. According to Alan Durning (1992), what is needed is a moderate level of consumption, together with strong social institutions and a healthy environment. As people with long experiences of economic, social, and political marginalization come to understand the failures of the neoliberal economic systems that organize the production and distribution of resources, they demand the design of social institutions that nurture and reproduce people as a society.

The Zapatista rebellion, conducted by the Ejército Zapatista de Liberación Nacional (Zapatista Liberation National Army [EZLN]) in the southern state of Chiapas, Mexico, in 1994 on the eve of the signing of the North American Free Trade Agreement (NAFTA), heralded perhaps the most unexpected challenge to neoliberal market policies and the persistent poverty of indigenous people in a region endowed with extensive natural resource wealth. There were two fundamental triggers of the rebellion. The first was the government's modification of Article 27 of the constitution as part of the negotiations for joining NAFTA. The modification ended land reform and neutralized the long-standing *ejido* system of communal land ownership and production. The second was the prospect that, under NAFTA, cheaper corn from the United States would be imported into Mexico, posing a significant threat to the subsistence production and traditional way of life of the Mayan peasant farmers who cultivated corn (Gilbreth and Otero, 2001).

The Zapatistas, made up of predominantly Mayan people, have waged a successful consciousness-raising campaign over the last 13 years, exposing the adverse impact of neoliberal market policies on the lives of people and on the environment that sustains them. Key markers of the Zapatistas are the emphases placed on grassroots democracy as a central path to development, the role of a healthy natural environment in sustaining human communities, and their well-recognized policies of promoting gender equity. There has been a remarkable groundswell of civil society mobilization in response to the uprising (Gilbreth and Otero, 2001:17).

Gilbreth and Otero (2001) credit the Zapatistas with being the driving force behind Mexico's democratization, interrupting procedural democracy and 71 years of control by the Partido Revolucionario Institucional

(Institutional Revolutionary Party [PRI]). The EZLN has relied on citizen activism and popular mobilizations to challenge state hegemony and to redirect Mexican society toward a more inclusive democracy that has forced the state to respond to a broad range of social interests (Gilbreth and Otero, 2001). In the process, the authors argue, the movement has won broad domestic and international support. Various groups inside Mexico have organized outside the traditional political channels to protest government military activity in Chiapas, establish peace camps, monitor human rights, and organize health, education, and alternative production projects. The movement also has won international electoral observation (Gilbreth and Otero, 2001).

The EZLN has inspired significant numbers of community-based groups across Mexico sympathetic to its objectives and the path it has identified for achieving these. A growing and diverse neo-Zapatista network of community-based groups has been deepening democracy through local collectives and reembedding political and economic decision making in social values (Swords, 2007). As with the MST in Brazil, the EZLN and the expanded neo-Zapatista networks are challenging the moral and intellectual leadership of the ruling class and, in the process, defining a more socially and environmentally sustainable path to economic viability. Gilbreth and Otero (2001) conclude that,

> The Zapatista movement has criticized the diminishing ability of the nation-state to shape the domestic economy as it becomes increasingly integrated into global capitalism. It has joined the concerns of a transnational movement advocating a reconceptualization of how market forces can be made accountable to principles of social justice to address the harsher effects of neoliberal globalism. (p. 25)

CONCLUSION

Citizens have been motivated to form grassroots associations to find local solutions or make social demands on the state and hold it accountable. They often do so in contexts that many would describe as hopeless. In the cases discussed here, they have been able to hold states accountable for socioeconomic welfare in a global context, in which profits come before people and states abandon protection of citizens' social and political rights.

In the face of the continued socioeconomic hardship that results from the implementation of neoliberal market policies across the developing world, poor and working people have resorted to popular expressions of protest and resistance that transcend the traditional avenues of political expression. In Latin America, movements that have raised consciousness about the connections among economic survival, environmental protection, and social justice have experienced significant successes at regional and state levels in redefining the path to social well-being. It is not clear how enduring or widespread these successes will become, but what is significant in these movements is their particular character when compared with earlier movements: They combine ecological and economic demands, they attempt to democratize the state rather than simply install an old model of a welfare state, and they create new forms of economic participation that focus on the provision of broad social well-being. They express a realization of the need for social sustainability.

REFERENCES

Assies, William. 2003. "David Versus Goliath in Cochabamba: Water Rights, Neoliberalism, and the Revival of Social Protest in Bolivia." *Latin American Perspectives* (30) 3: 14–36.

Bello, Walden, Shea Cunningham, and Bill Rau. 1994. *Dark Victory: The United States, Structural Adjustment and Global Poverty.* Chipping Norten, UK: Pluto Press with Food First.

———. 2004. *Deglobalization: Ideas for a New World Economy.* New York: Zed Books.

Benería, Lourdes. 2003. *Gender, Development, and Globalization Economics as if All People Mattered.* New York: Routledge.

Burawoy, Michael. 2003. "For a Sociological Marxism: The Complementary Convergence of Antonio Gramsci and Karl Polanyi." *Politics and Society* 31 (2): 193–261.

De Sousa Santos, Boaventura. 1998. "Participatory Budgeting in Porto Alegre: Toward a Redistributive Democracy." *Politics & Society* 26 (4): 461–510.

Durning, Alan T. 1992. *How Much is Enough? The Consumer Society and the Future of the Earth.* Washington, DC: Worldwatch Institute.

Fischer-Hoffman, Cory. 2006, February 15. "Venezuela Leads the Way: Welfare Mothers and Grassroots Women Are the Workers for Social Change!" *MRzine.* Available from http://mrzine.monthlyreview.org/cfh150206.html.

Folbre, Nancy. 1994. *Who Pays for the Kids? Gender and the Structures of Constraint.* London: Routledge.

Frank, Andre Gunder. 1967. *Capitalism and Underdevelopment in Latin America.* New York: Monthly Review Press.

Furtado, Celso. 1964. *Development and Underdevelopment* Ricardo W. de Aguiar and Eric Charles Drysdale, Trans.. Berkeley: University of California Press.

Gilbreth, Chris, and Gerado Otero. 2001. "Democratization in Mexico: The Zapatista Uprising and Civil Society." Latin American Perspectives 28 (7): 7–29.

Goldsmith, William W. 2007. *Participatory Budgeting in Brazil.* Available from http://www.pn2007.org/publications/brazil_goldsmith.pd

Harris, Jonathan M., Timothy A. Wise, Kevin P. Gallagher, and Neva R. Goodwin, eds. 2001. *A Survey of Sustainable Development: Social and Economic Dimensions.* Washington, DC: Island Press.

Harris, Richard L. 2002. "Resistance and Alternatives to Globalization in Latin America and the Caribbean." *Latin American Perspectives* 12729 (6): 136–151.

Kline, Benjamin. 2004. *First Along the River: A Brief History of the U.S. Environmental Movement* (2nd ed.). San Francisco, CA: Acada Books.

Kuecker, Glen David. 2007. "Fighting for the Forests: Grassroots Resistance to Mining in Northern Ecuador." *Latin American Perspectives* 34 (2): 94–107

Martinez, Nadia. 2007, Summer. "Democracy Rising." *YES!* Available at http://www.yesmagazine.org/article.asp?ID=1730

Martins, Monica Dias. 2000. "The MST Challenge to Neoliberalism." *Latin American Perspectives* 27 (5): 33–45.

McMichael, Philip. 2004. *Development and Social Change: A Global Perspective* (3rd ed.). Thousand Oaks, CA: Pine Forge.

Ophuls, William, and A. Stephen Boyan, Jr. 1992. *Ecology and the Scarcity of Politics Revisited: The Unraveling of the American Dream.* New York: W.H. Freeman.

Perlez, Jane, and Lowell Bergman. 2005, October 25. "Tangled Strands in the Fight over Peru Gold Mine." *New York Times.* available online: http://www.nytimes.com/2005/10/25/international/americas/25GOLD.html

Power, Marilyn. 2004. "Social Provisioning as a Starting Point for Feminist Economics." *Feminist Economics* 10 (3): 3–19.

Presbisch, Raul. 1950. *The Economic Development of Latin America and its Principal Problems.* New York: United Nations.

Rodney, Walter. 1972. *How Europe Underdeveloped Africa.* London: Bogle-L'Ouverture Publications.

Rus, Jan, Rosalva Aida Hernandez Castillo, and Shannon L. Mattiace. 2001. " Introduction." *Latin American Perspectives* 28 (7): 7–19.

Sen, Amartya Kumar. 1999. *Development as Freedom.* New York: Knopf.

Stahler-Shock, Richard, Harry E. Vanden, and Glen David Kuecker. 2007. "Globalizing Resistance: The New Politics of Social Movements in Latin America." *Latin American Perspectives* 34 (2): 5–16.

Swords, Alicia. 2007. "Neo-Zapatista Network Politics: Transforming Democracy and Development." *Latin American Perspectives* 34 (2): 78–93.

Waring, Marilyn. 1988. *If Women Counted: A New Feminist Economics.* San Francisco: Harper & Row.

7 Child Labor and Improved Common Forest Management in Bolivia

Randall Bluffstone[1]

LITERATURE REVIEW

In rural areas of low-income developing countries, farming systems tend to be household-based and integrated with natural resources, such as forests and pasturelands. Households depend on these natural assets for fuels, animal food, building materials, fruits, and medicines, and they generally access them through "common" ownership and control systems in which resources are not individually owned.

Many of these common resources are important production inputs that also require households to provide "complementary" inputs. For example, villagers may use common forests for fodder and grazing, but exploitation of those resources requires labor. Therefore, the nature and source of those complementary labor inputs becomes an interesting and relevant issue, particularly as forest quality and value increases when management improves.

This chapter examines the relationship between common property forest management and child labor. It raises the possibility that one aspect of social health—or social sustainability—may be affected by policy changes designed to increase environmental and environmental sustainability. Indeed, it may well be in the private interest to increase child labor in response to better community property forest management. Therefore, the private response may collide with what many view as an overriding social interest in reducing the use of child labor and increasing children's educational attainments.

In recent decades, there have been important advances in our understanding of the management of common resources and what is required to increase the direct use values coming from forests on which developing country villagers rely. For example, a large literature has emerged that emphasizes the distinction between open access—where resources are unowned and natural resources tend to become degraded over time—and community ownership where ownership exists, but is in common. The theoretical strand of this literature has largely found that community ownership can provide incentives for high value use of resources similar to private ownership as long as there are incentives for community members to cooperate (e.g., Olson, 1965; Wade, 1988; Ostrom, 1990; Bromley, 1990; Baland and Platteau, 1996, 1999; Sethi and Somanathan, 1996; Dayton-Johnson, 2000).

In response to these research results, many countries policies have been adopted to legislate local-level coordination and therefore improve management of forests and other resources in the interest of efficient resource management. Over time, indeed almost a conventional wisdom advocating the devolution of natural resources primarily from central governments to local groups has emerged. For example, devolution of forests has been underway in Nepal since the early 1980s, and most forest lands were transferred to users in 1993 through the creation of forest user groups (Pradhan and Parks, 1995; Cooke, 2000; Adhikari, 2002). Agrawal (2000, 2001) notes that governments in more than 50 countries are ceding some control over resources to local users.

In addition to devolution, certain policies are now regarded as best management practices when privatization is not appropriate. These policies include institutional characteristics, such as more public participation and democracy, fair allocation of forest resources, and clear criteria for accessing resources. Management tools include clear rules for distributing resources, monitoring by villagers and officials, effective and graduated sanctioning of transgressors, and payments for forest products if appropriate (Ostrom, 1990; Agrawal, 2000, 2001).

Despite the existence of this emerging conventional wisdom, only recently has empirical work emerged that focuses on household responses to common property forest management and evaluates which elements spur behavioral shifts that improve social welfare (Amacher, Hyde, and Kanel, 1996, 1999; Cooke, 2000; Heltberg, Arndt, and Sekhar, 2000; Heltberg, 2001; Adhikari, 2002; Edmonds, 2002; Hegan, Hauer, and Luckert, 2003;Linde-Rahr, 2003). Much of this literature has identified potential problems and complications associated with devolution, and all authors have highlighted the complexity of household responses to changes in local-level property rights.

We know that children are important sources of labor in developing countries; in 1990, it was estimated that 79 million children around the world did regular work (Basu and Van, 1998). Children provide a variety of services to household production systems, including helping in the home, weeding farm plots, grazing animals, and even cutting fuelwood and fodder (Bhalotra and Heady, 2003). A number of these listed activities are complemented by natural resources, such as land, and indeed it has been observed that households with more agricultural land—the most important store of wealth in the developing world—often use more child labor than poorer households (Bhalotra and Heady, 2003). The services provided by children also are widely regarded as important for households subject to labor-intensive production systems. Therefore, it is not altogether clear whether households—or even children—would be better or worse off from, for example, a ban on child labor (Basu and Van, 1998). Because of the importance of child labor in many low-income countries, some have even suggested that household labor requirements at least partially explain high fertility rates (Dasgupta, 2000; Perkins, Radelet, Snodgrass, Gillis, and Roemer, 2001).

The benefits from child labor create tradeoffs for society that can interfere with other goals. One Ethiopian researcher recently noted that, in an attempt to increase the quality of primary education in Ethiopia, the Ministry of Education decided to increase its school day from a half to a full day, but faced strong opposition from village parents who needed their children's labor and was forced to scrap the plan (Ethiopian Development Research Institute, 2006). From a private perspective child labor may make sense, but from a social perspective it is considered a misuse of human resources. Therefore, knowing whether policies affecting natural resources are likely to increase disamenities such as increased child labor in low-income countries is important.

The linkage between child labor and common property forest management is of interest because a variety of effects can be expected as forest quality improves (Fortman, Antinori, and Nabane, 1997; Heltberg et al., 2000; Linde-Rahr, 2003; Kohlin and Amacher, 2005; Jagger, Pender, and Gebremedhin, 2005; Bluffstone, Boscolo, and Molina, 2007; Nepal, Bohara, and Berrens, in press). With the exception of Kohlin and Amacher (2005), for whom child labor is not a central issue, I am aware of no literature that examines the links between common property forest management and child labor.

This chapter is organized as follows. The first section develops a theoretical framework for understanding household level incentives to use child labor and tradeoffs that households face when common forest quality improves due to better management. The second section discusses the data used to analyze the relationship between common property forest management and child labor. The third section presents some preliminary results. The final section concludes the chapter.

THEORETICAL FRAMEWORK

Common property forest management is a class of coordination mechanisms designed to increase the value that villagers obtain from forests. Alternatively, we can think of this notion from the household perspective as a decline in the price of forest products. For example, households may obtain the products they gathered previously more quickly (i.e., the time cost of gathering one unit of fodder, fuel wood, and so on declines).

As is true for all price effects, however, in the jargon of economics, households will experience income and substitution effects. Forests are an important source of capital; when they become more abundant, all else equal households can produce more. Hence, higher incomes can be spent on a variety of goods. More food, candles, cigarettes, and clothes are obvious possibilities, but some goods may be chosen that directly improve the lives of children. For example, households may choose to use some of their higher incomes to improve child nutrition, provide better clothes, or buy schoolbooks. They also may use some income to reduce labor burdens on children—for example, by hiring adults to do their work so children can attend school.

The story can be told another way, however. As forests become more abundant (i.e., as their price falls), forest-based activities become more advantageous vis-à-vis other activities. Therefore, there are incentives to shift household resources out of nonforest activities and into those that rely on forests. This scenario is the substitution effect. Because the most important variable production asset of households is labor, it makes sense that labor could move into forestry activities, such as livestock raising and fuel wood collection. Depending on the household allocation of labor resources, one type of labor to move into the forests could be child labor. For example, children may assist with fuel wood collection (for sale or own use), gathering of fodder, or grazing animals. Alternatively, adult household members may increase their own labor supply to forest-based activities. However, if households have no unemployed labor, children may be called on to increase their participation in activities formerly done by adults.

From a theoretical perspective, therefore, the effect of better common property forest management on child labor is unclear. The income effect suggests that child labor should decrease with better forest management because parents presumably prefer their children to work less. Some of the increased forest value created by better common property forest management may therefore be invested in children. However, as forest quality improves, forest products become cheaper. Thus, households will want to take advantage of those more accessible products, but will need labor to do it. Therefore, children may increase their labor supply, either directly into forest-based activities or in nonforest tasks that previously were done by adults.

DATA AND EMPIRICAL APPROACH

Data to conduct this preliminary analysis of the relationship between child labor and common property forest management come from a year 2000 survey of village level officials and 378 households in 32 communities in the five Bolivian Andes departments of Cochabamba, Chuquisaca, Oruro, Potosi, and La Paz. The sample is stratified to include more villages and households in the more populated departments of Cochabamba, Potosi, and La Paz (about 25% of sample each) and fewer from Oruro and Chuquisaca (about 13%), which are less populous. The survey asked about (a) household characteristics, (b) forest management, (c) consumption, (d) production, and (e) assets and is available upon request.

As is true throughout the developing world, Bolivian communities in mountainous and hilly areas use forests primarily for fuels, construction materials, medicines and fruits, fodder, and grazing. In contrast to the low-land forests of Santa Cruz and Beni Departments, upland forests have rela-tively little commercial value. Therefore, they have largely escaped control by the central government. In the Andes, the average elevation is higher in the north (by about 500 meters), but so are temperature and rainfall, making it more fertile. Spanish colonization was concentrated in the north, which had a culture of private property earlier than other areas (Moscoso and Villanueva, 1997; Castro and Rist, 1999).

There are a variety of institutional regimes that control natural resources in rural Bolivia, but local communities have had substantial control over natural resources since 1952, when a major revolution ushered in an agrar-ian reform. Government reforms in the mid-1990s further decentralized forest control, but these measures mainly affected the lowland forests. In most areas, systems are informal and evolved locally, implying significant and idiosyncratic differences in common property forest management across communities. Indeed, some are indigenous and have evolved over centuries. In our survey of village-level policies, we found that in some villages there was de facto open access, with effectively no management. In the remainder, however, a variety of locally developed structures and officials regulated forests. For example, in some areas, no managers were named, but in meetings villagers agreed on limits to forest use. Other areas had a variety of officials involved, including mayors, deputy mayors, coun-cil members, community directors, general and agricultural secretaries, peasant union presidents, community presidents, forestry officers, forestry directors, and heads of committees for environmental protection. These institutions are locally based, leading to important differences in common property forest management systems that may be related in different ways with levels of child labor.

To analyze the relationship between child labor and forestry, we cre-ate indices for various aspects of forest management, including clarity of access rights to forests, fairness in division of forest products, and pub-lic participation and democracy in decision making. These subindices are then averaged to define the institutional characteristics index. We also define six indices that make up the management tools index. These sub-indices are fixed allotments of forest products to villagers, monitoring by villagers, formal penalties for violating forest rules, social sanctions for violating forest rules, household labor inputs into community forests, and payments for forest products. The management tools and institutional characteristics indices are then averaged to calculate the overall common property forest management index. All these indices range from 0 to 1, with 1 indicating the highest level of the index (i.e., perfectly demonstrat-ing a feature of common property forest management) and 0 not exhibit-ing the characteristic at all.

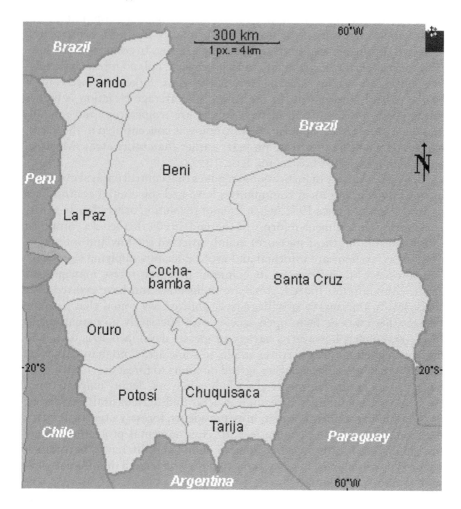

Figure 7.1 Bolivia

It is important to emphasize that our common property forest management indices are based on survey respondent perceptions. Perceptions are used for two reasons. First, in developing countries, on-the-ground management can often correspond poorly with stated policies. Therefore, perceptions have the potential to better reflect reality. Second, developing "objective" measures of common property forest management would require interviews in which village leaders or forest managers provide detailed data on the components of common property forest management they are unlikely to have. We would therefore be unable to analyze the separate effects of different components of common property forest management.

Treating common property forest management in a disaggregated fashion is an important objective of this chapter because it is likely that systems that focus on different aspects of common property forest management have differential implications for child labor. For example, it may be that the use of fees as an instrument to control access and raise revenues for management could cause adults to focus more on wage labor, which might then increase child labor as children substitute for adults on other tasks. For example, they may pick up the slack in grazing and/or home production (e.g., cooking, cleaning, and washing). In contrast, higher levels of fairness and public participation may imply more flexible systems that allow households to arrange their use of forest resources so as to minimize effects on children. Similarly, plausible stories/hypotheses also might be advanced for the other index subcomponents, and one objective of this chapter is to examine whether there might be systematic effects of common property forest management components on children.

If we examine the mean values in Table 7.1, the picture that emerges is one of loose management, which some branches of the literature suggest should lead to limited behavioral effects, presumably including labor reallocations such as those associated with children (e.g., Gibson, Lehoucq, and Williams, 2002). In fact, only 28% say that forest access is at least "somewhat clear." Few respondents reported having fixed allotments for fuel wood (only 8%), and about three quarters thought they would "definitely not" be penalized if they took more forest products than they were allotted.

An important missing institutional element appears to be public participation. Few respondents thought they could influence forest management or that systems were democratic. Yet despite the lack of formal controls and apparent alienation, a substantial minority thought officials and villagers monitored forests. The data also suggest that villagers may be motivated by social pressures. Almost half said other villagers would at least "probably" be unhappy or angry if they took too much fuel wood or fodder. Similar portions would be embarrassed if they took too much, and many thought they could lose some of their forest privileges if they were caught overusing forests.

There are some important differences in common property forest management across departments. Regardless of whether we consider the overall common property forest management, institutional characteristics, and management tools indices, there are some rather strong correlations with opposing signs. For example, the common property forest management index is positively correlated with households being in Cochabamba Department, but strongly negatively correlated with residence in Potosi. Correlation patterns for institutional characteristics are roughly similar to those of the overall common property forest management index. Management tools, however, often have correlations that are exactly the opposite of the overall common property forest management and institutional characteristics indices. For example, the management tools index is positively correlated with households being in La Paz, whereas

Table 7.1 Descriptive Statistics of Community Property Forest Management Components Making up Overall Community Property Forest Management, Institutional Characteristics, and Management Tool Indices. The value 5 means Highest Level of the Index and 1 means Lowest Value of the Index

Overall Common Property Index Average = 0.31

Institutional Characteristics Index Average = 0.45	Management Tools Index Average = 0.17
SUBINDICES	
Clarity of Forest Access Index Average = 0.23	Fixed Allotments to Forest Products Index Average = 0.13
Fairness in Access to Forest Products Index Average = 0.78	Monitoring by Villagers of Forest Product Extractions Index Average = 0.27
Public Participation and Democracy in Decision-Making Index Average = 0.09	Formal Penalties for Violating Forest Rules Index Average = 0.17
	Social Sanctions for Violating Forest Rules Index Average = 0.38
	Labor Inputs into Community Forests Index Average = 0.11
	Payments for Forest Products Index Average = 0.03

there is really no relationship with the institutional characteristics index. Households in Chuquisaca tend to experience higher levels of the institutional characteristics index, but lower levels of the management tools index. This contrast tells us that departments tend to emphasize institutional characteristics or management tools, but not both. Indeed, the institutional characteristics and management tools indices are virtually uncorrelated with each other, suggesting that these components of overall common property forest management operate rather independently of each other in Bolivia.

Table 7.2 presents some key descriptive statistics from the data. Households are generally poor and on average eat meat less than four times per month. Most households have some integration with markets, however, with 73% of respondents having gone to a store during the week before the survey, despite a mean travel time of 2 hours. Borrowing is difficult for households, however, with only 17% of respondents having access to credit from local moneylenders. Mean land holdings are 1.47 hectares (or 3.6 acres) per household. Large animal holdings are relatively limited, with less than half of households reporting cows and 40% reporting pigs; 55% have sheep, with a mean of nine sheep per household.

Village characteristics are taken from our survey of village leaders. As shown in Table 7.2, villages have a mean of 535 households, and most are primarily Quechua. Villages are about evenly split between clustered and disbursed settlement patterns, and virtually all have clear boundaries. About half also have regulations for timber cutting in forests, and a similar proportion allows people to sell their land. Typically, however, custom rather than formal law determines forest management regulations.

RESULTS

Table 7.3 presents key descriptive statistics on household labor allocations across six key activities. We see that, on average, households work quite long hours. With an average of 3.8 members per household and 1.45 of them on average children, covering an average workload of 137 hours per week is likely to be a real challenge. The most labor-intensive activity is agriculture, followed by home production and grazing.

Tables 7.4 and 7.5 break these labor shares down by age group. We note that we do not have data on labor allocations by gender, but only by age. We find that child labor is, on average, an important, but by no means dominant, component of the overall household labor supply. Indeed, 65% of households responding reported using no child labor. Children, on average, supply about 9% of the overall household labor, but do not contribute equally to all activities. Children are especially active in home production (4.2 hours per week or 13% of total input) and grazing (4.3 hours or 16% of the total). Labor input to agriculture is significant (2.5 hours per week on average), but small relative to the input of other age groups. Inputs into fuel and fodder collection, which are fairly small users of household time, absorb virtually no children's time. No children participate in the wage labor market.

In summary, we find that many households use no child labor, but where it exists children tend to participate in household activities that are particularly labor-using. Although by no means concentrated in forest-intensive activities, grazing certainly is one of the most important natural resource-dependent tasks. We also note that, as do Filmer and Pritchett (2002), children tend to be most active in less physically demanding activities. Therefore, there is reason to believe that in the Bolivian case parents tend to allocate to their children tasks that are not too difficult, but that potentially can absorb a lot of time.

Key results also are presented graphically in Figures 7.2 and 7.3. We see in Figure 7.2 that labor input by children is lower than for all other age groups, with the exception of grazing and home production, where children have higher inputs than the elderly. As is true in most societies, the 36- to 65-year-old age group works the hardest, followed by those ages 16 to 35.

Table 7.2 Key Household and Village Data

Variable	Mean	Std. Dev.	N
Household Characteristics			
Number of household members	3.80	2.08	378
Spanish language speaker dummy	0.85	0.36	378
Aymara language speaker	0.25	0.44	378
Years family and ancestors lived in village (1 = <5; 7 = >100	6.10	1.30	376
Average monthly expenditures in Bolivianos/month ($1 = 8B)	13.37	23.71	378
Times to store in past week (0 = none; 4 = 6 to7; 7 = >12)	1.58	1.59	378
Number of males in household	2.00	1.32	378
Number of females	1.79	1.21	378
Number of children	1.45	1.70	378
Electricity dummy	0.026	0.16	378
Farmer occupation dummy	0.87	0.33	378
Highest level of education of any household member (1 = none; 3 = some secondary; 9 = master's/PhD)	3.70	1.82	373
Number of times in previous month ate meat (2 = 1 to 3 times; 3 = 4 to 7 times)	2.25	1.05	378
Number of times in previous month ate eggs (2 = 1 time; 3 = 2 to 3 times)	1.89	0.73	376
Lorena stove dummy	0.47	0.50	378
Tractor plowing dummy	0.063	0.24	378
Credit access dummy	0.17	0.37	365
Land controlled by household (hectares)	1.47	3.49	377
Number of cows	1.42	2.40	378
Number of sheep	9.10	24.59	378
Village Characteristics			
Major ethnic group in village (1 = Quechua; 2 = Aymara; 3 = Other)	1.30	0.52	366
Number of households in village (VIL_HH)	535.24	1065.52	346
Households are clustered rather than disbursed (clustered = 1;0 = disbursed)	0.46	0.50	366
Estimated total village area (hectares) (AREA)	244461	1269936	358

(continued)

Table 7.2 Key Household and Village Data (continued)

Village limits are clear to all inhabitants (1 = clear; 0 = not clear)	0.93	0.26	342
Estimated agricultural area of village (hectares)	1598	4566	346
Estimated village pasture land (hectares)	1914	4608	346
Timber cutting is explicitly regulated (1 = regulated; 0 = not regulated)	0.55	0.50	366
Any regulations on forests are recognized in formal laws (1 = formal laws; 0 = not by laws)	0.33	0.47	366
Any regulations on forests are recognized by custom (1 = custom; 0 = not by custom)	0.78	0.41	366
Villagers can sell their land (1 = can sell; 0 = cannot sell)	0.55	0.50	366

We see in Figure 7.3 important differences in the age distribution of labor input for fuel wood collection and grazing, which are two important natural resource-dependent activities. We see that those people ages 16 to 65 contribute most of the labor to both activities, but fuel wood collection, which is a physically demanding activity, is especially the responsibility of those ages 36 to 65, who are physically mature and often beyond child-bearing years.

We now turn to the relationship between child labor and common property forest management. Using regression analysis, we find that the relationship between total child labor and the overall common property forest

Table 7.3 Household Labor Allocations

Activity	*Mean Hours*	*SD*	*Maximum*	*N*
Home production (e.g., cooking, cleaning)	32.98	22.13	123	304
Agriculture	50.37	30.55	147	329
Felwood collection	9.77	17.43	175	329
Grazing	28.07	31.09	252	329
Fodder collection	10.37	22.23	252	326
Wage labor	5.31	14.46	110	329
Total	136.87			

management index is a positive one, indicating that households which experienced better developed forest management systems had more child labor. When we break the results into management tools and institutional characteristics indices, we find that the positive relationship between child labor and common property forest management is driven not by more use of management tools, but by more highly developed institutional character-istics. Aspects such as fairness, public participation, and clarity are there-fore particularly associated with higher levels of child labor, whereas more stringent management tools are associated with less child labor.

Another way to look at this problem is in terms of correlation coeffi-cients. We find that the overall common property forest management and institutional characteristics indices are positively and rather strongly corre-lated with the total amount of child labor, whether we measure child labor by its existence, by labor hours, or by hours of child labor per household member. Indeed, with the exception of household size, in all three mod-els, the institutional characteristics index was the variable most strongly correlated with child labor. With only a few additional exceptions, the overall common property forest management index also is the variable most correlated with our three measures of child labor. The management tools index is negatively correlated with all measures of child labor, but of a very small magnitude, which suggests that the management tools index is unrelated to child labor.

Edmonds (2005) suggests that income and consumption are likely to be negatively correlated with the use of child labor, and this suggestion

Table 7.4 Labor Input by Age and Activity (Hours)

Total Hours by Activity and Age Group

Age	Home Produc-tion	Agricul-ture	Collecting Fuel	Grazing Animals	Collecting Fodder	Wage Labor	Sum of Means by Age Group
6–15 years	4.2	2.5	0.7	4.3	0.4	0	12.1
16–35 years	10.2	18	3.3	10.1	3.3	2.5	47.4
36–65 years	13.8	23.7	4.3	10.7	4.5	2.2	59.2
65 years	4	6.1	1.5	2.3	2	0.6	16.5
Total	32.2	50.3	9.8	27.4	10.2	5.3	135.2
% Child	13.04%	4.97%	7.14%	15.69%	3.92%	0.00%	8.95%

Table 7.5 Percentage of Labor Input by Age and Activity

Age	Home Production	Agricultural Labor	Fuelwood Collection	Grazing	Fodder Collection	Wage Labor
6–15 years	13.04%	4.97%	7.14%	15.69%	3.92%	0.00%
16–35 years	31.68%	35.79%	33.67%	36.86%	32.35%	47.17%
36–65 years	42.86%	47.12%	43.88%	39.05%	44.12%	41.51%
65 years	12.42%	12.13%	15.31%	8.39%	19.61%	11.32%

is perhaps the conventional wisdom. Wealthier households also may be expected to use less child labor. Why might better management of forests, possibly leading to better quality forests (i.e., more common wealth) in Bolivia, have exactly the opposite pattern? We do not have a conclusive answer to this question, but we note that Edmonds analyzed at the country, rather than the household, level. Most households in the sample (and indeed in Bolivia) are farmers (87%), and wealth tends to be accumulated in terms of land and animals. Both these classes of assets require labor to utilize, and particularly agricultural land is associated with more child labor. This fact is consistent with the findings of Bhalotra and Heady

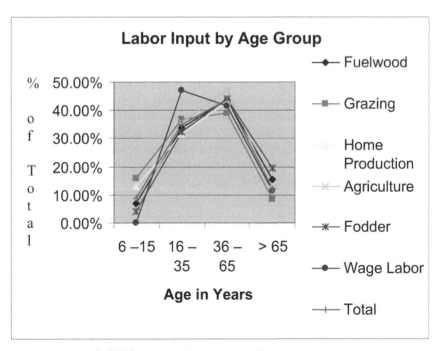

Figure 7.2 Household labor supply by activity and age

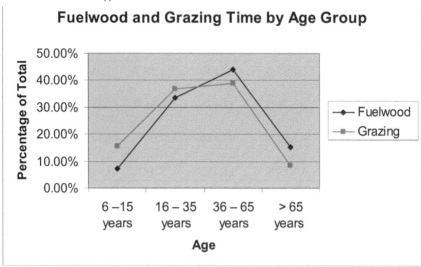

Figure 7.3 Forest dependent activities by age

(2003), who explain their results in terms of labor and credit market imperfections. We do not have terribly good proxies for total household income, but we do note that the amount of meat in household diets in low-income settings is likely to be a good indicator of consumption. This variable is indeed negatively correlated with child labor.

If we examine particular forms of child labor, we find that for home production and grazing, which are the two most important forms of child labor, the results are virtually identical to those for total child labor. For agricultural labor and fuel wood collection, the correlation between the overall community property forestry management index and institutional characteristics index is positive, but of smaller magnitudes. Correlations with fodder collection are small, and there is no relationship with wage labor. Management tools index correlations with specific types of child labor are negative for grazing and home production, but are essentially or actually zero for fodder collection and wage labor.

The question now is why there is such a difference in results between the institutional characteristics and management tools indices. One possibility is that our theoretical framework is correct, and institutional character-istics are more critical to community forestry management performance than management tools. Therefore, background community forestry insti-tutional characteristics may simply be the main drivers of household behav-ioral response. This was the finding, for example, by Bluffstone et al. (2007), who analyze whether better common property management spurs on-farm tree planting. They find that the overall community forestry and institu-tional characteristics indices are highly correlated with more on-farm tree planting, but the management tools index appears to have no effect. They therefore conclude that "it is the overall package of community property forestry management that is most important for behavioral change, such as on-farm tree planting and that important synergies between the individual components preclude identifying the individual effects." Just as in the case of on-farm tree planting, institutional characteristics have the most "power" to influence behavior; perhaps the same also is true for household labor-allocation decisions.

An alternative explanation is suggested by Gibson et al. (2002), who emphasize that successful common property management requires a high level of coordination and some sacrifice by current users in the name of increasing future productivity. They suggest that instruments such as those making up the management tools index are what give community forestry its teeth and therefore determines success. It is therefore possible that high values of the institutional characteristics index really represent excessively loose management that could be characterized as open access. Therefore, the high correlation between it and child labor may not represent a household response to "successful" management, but instead to a substandard situation of highly degraded natural resources brought on by poor management. Under such circumstances, parents not wanting to press their children into increased service may do so simply because natural resources are so scarce. Sometimes this scenario is called the poverty–environment nexus (Dasgupta, 2000).

Unfortunately, with the data we have, we are not able to determine which explanation is correct, although the results using the same data set by Bluffstone et al. (2007) indicate that Gibson et al. (2002) may not be giving institutional characteristics their due weight.

CONCLUSIONS

The analysis suggests that households experiencing what we think of as better community forestry have some important differences in child labor supply from those experiencing open access. Particularly for households working in forests with high levels of the institutional characteristics index (i.e., clarity, fairness, and public participation/democracy), child labor appears to be much higher. Households with higher levels of the management tools index tend to have no child labor and use less of it.

Our theoretical framework suggests that if households prefer to minimize their use of child labor, where forest management is better for some reason they do not do it. One way to think about this result is that the effect of the greater value households obtain from using child labor to exploit better managed forests dominates the impact of greater prosperity that would allow them to reduce the use of child labor. We do not have data on forest values, but if better community forestry practices indeed raise forest productivity, the analysis suggests that households are partly responding to better community forestry management by increasing their labor supply. One consequence of this desire by households to more intensively use forests is that, on balance, child labor participation and total child labor are increasing with community forestry. That is, on net, children increase their labor supply because households want to take advantage of higher quality forests. This finding is consistent with the work of Basu and Van (1998).

To really make constructive empirical statements about the relationship between common property forestry management and child labor, it is necessary to use more sophisticated statistical techniques, such as regression analysis. This step, however, will be left for future work. What is clear is that policies designed to increase environmental and economic sustainability, such as community forestry practices, alter on-farm prices and incentives and may have social impacts that affect social sustainability. If policies create incentives for households to increase their use of child labor and if there are negative spillover effects from private decisions about child labor (e.g., resulting in a less educated youth population), the end result may be a lower level of social sustainability even if incomes increase. Policymakers may want to take note of such possibilities.

NOTES

1. The author would like to thank the AVINA Foundation for financial support with the data collection and Incuestas y Estudios for conducting the household survey. Thanks also are due to the Social Sustainability Workshop at Portland State University for additional financial support. He also is grateful to Ricardo Godoy for his generous and prompt review of our survey instrument and thanks participants in the Portland State University Social Sustainability Workshop seminars for their helpful comments.

REFERENCES

Adhikari, B. 2002, June 24–27. *Property Rights and Natural Resource: Socio-Economic Heterogeneity and Distributional Implications of Common Property Resource Management in Nepal.* Paper presented at the 2nd World Congress of Environmental and Resource Economists, Monterey, CA.

Agrawal, A. 2000. *Sustainability on the commons.* Paper presented at the 8th Biennial Conference of the International Association for the Study of Common Property, Bloomington, IN.

———. 2001. "Commons Property Institutions and Sustainable Governance of Resources." *World Development* 29 (10): 1649–1672.

Amacher G. S., W. F. Hyde, and K. R. Kanel. 1996. "Household Fuelwood Demand and Supply in Nepal's Tarai and Mid-Hills: Choice Between Cash Outlays and Labor Opportunity." *World Development* 24 (11): 1725–1736.

———. 1999. "Nepali Fuelwood Production and Consumption: Regional and Household Distinctions, Substitution and Successful Intervention." *Journal of Development Studies* 35 (4): 138–163.

Baland, Jean-Marie, and Jean-Philippe Platteau. 1996. *Halting Degradation of Natural Resources: Is There a Role for Rural Communities?* Oxford, UK: Clarendon Press.

———. 1999. "The Ambiguous Impact of Inequality on Local Resource Management." *World Development* 27: 773–788.

Basu, K., and P. H. Van. 1998. "The Economics of Child Labor." *American Economic Review* 88 (3): 412–427.

Bhalotra, S., and C. Heady. 2003. "Child Labor: The Wealth Paradox." *World Bank Economic Review* 17 (2): 197–227

Bluffstone R., M. Boscolo, and R. Molina. 2008. "Does Better Common Property Forest Management Promote On-Farm Tree Planting: Evidence from Bolivia." *Environment and Development Economics* 13: 137–170.

Bromley D. W. 1990. *Essays on the Commons*. Madison, WI: University of Wisconsin Press.

Castro J. C. M., and S. Rist. 1999. *Tipos de relaciones bosque-comunidad y normas tradicionales de uso y acceso a la vegetacion boscosa.* (Types of Community Forest Relationships and Traditional Norms for Access to Forests) La Paz: AGRUCO and PROBONA.

Cooke, Priscilla. 1998. "The Effects of Environment Goods Scarcity on Non-Farm Labour Allocation." *Environment and Development Economics* 3: 443–469.

———. 2000, May. "Changes in Intrahousehold Labor Allocation to Environmental Goods Collection: A Case Study from Rural Nepal, 1982 and 1997." IFPRI Discussion Paper no. 87, Washington, DC.

Dasgupta, P. 2000. "Population and Resources: An Explanation of Reproductive and Environmental Externalities." *Population and Development Review* 24 (4): 643–689.

Dayton-Johnson, Jeff. 2000. "Choosing Rules to Govern the Commons: A Model with Evidence from Mexico." *Journal of Economic Behavior & Organization* 42 (1): 19–41.

Edmonds, E. 2005. "Does Child Labor Decline with Improving Economic Status?" *Journal of Human Resources* XL (1): 77–99.

Ethiopian Development Research Institute. 2006, September 22. author presented *Seminar on Economics of Population Growth* Addis Ababa.

Filmer, D., and L. Pritchett. 2002. "Environmental Degradation and the Demand for Children: Searching for the Vicious Circle in Pakistan." *Environment and Development Economics* 7: 123–146.

Fortman, L., C. Antinori, and N. Nabane. 1997. "Fruits of the Labors: Gender, Property Rights and Tree Planting in Two Zimbabwe Villages." *Rural Sociology* 63 (3): 295–314.

Gibson, C, F. Lehoucq, and J. Williams. 2002. "Does Privatization Protect Natural Resources? Property Rights and Forests in Guatemala." *Social Science Quarterly* 83: 206–225.

Hegan, R, G. Hauer, and M. Luckert. 2003. "Is the Tragedy of the Commons Likely? Factors Preventing the Dissipation of Fuelwood Rents in Zimbabwe." *Land Economics* 79 (2): 181–197.

Heltberg, R. 2001. "Determinants and Impacts of Local Institutions for Common Resource Management." *Environment and Development Economics* 6 (2): 183–208.

———., A. Arndt, and N. U. Sekhar. 2000. "Fuelwood Consumption and Forest Degradation: A Household Model for Domestic Energy Consumption in Rural India." *Land Economics* 76 (2): 213–232.

Jagger, P., J. Pender, and B. Gebremedhin. 2005. "Trading off Environmental Sustainability for Empowerment and Income: Woodlot Devolution in Northern Ethiopia." *World Development* 33 (9): 1490–1510.

Kohlin, G., and G. Amacher. 2005. "Welfare Implications of Community Forest Plantations in Developing Countries: The Orissa Social Forestry Project." *American Journal of Agricultural Economics* 87 (4): 855–869.

Linde-Rahr, M. 2003. "Property Rights and Deforestation: The Choice of Fuelwood Source in Rural Viet Nam." *Land Economics* 79: 217–234.

Moscoso R. E., and A. D. I. Villanueva. 1997. Tipos de relaciones bosque-comunidad y normas tradicionales de acceso al bosque. (Types of Community Forest Relationships and Traditional Norms for Access to Forests) La Paz: PROBONA and PRADEM/CICDA.

Nepal, M, A. Bohara, and R. Berrens. 2007. "Investigating the Impact of Social Networks on Household Forest Conservation Effort in Rural Nepal." *Land Economics.*

Olson, M. 1965. *The Logic of Collective Action.* Cambridge, MA: Harvard University Press 83: 171–191.

Ostrom, E. 1990. *Governing the Commons: The Evolution of Institutions for Collective Action.* New York: Cambridge University Press.

Perkins, D., S. Radelet, D. Snodgrass, M. Gillis, and M. Roemer. 2001. *Economics of Development,* 5th ed. New York: W.W. Norton.

Pradhan, A. J., and P. J. Parks. 1995. "Environmental and Socioeconomic Linkages of Deforestation and Forest Land Use Change in the Nepal Himalaya." In *Property Rights in a Social and Ecological Context: Case Studies and Design Applications,* edited by Susan Hanna and Mohan Munasinghe. Stockholm, Sweden: Beijer Institute and the World Bank.

Sethi R., and E. Somanathan. 1996. "The Evolution of Social Norms in Common Property Resource Use" *The American Economic Review* 86 (4): 766–788.

Wade R. 1988. *Village Republics: Economic Conditions for Collective Action in South India.,* Cambridge, UK: Cambridge University Press.

Part III
The Role of Business

8   Social Sustainability
An Organizational-Level Analysis

Jan Bebbington and Jesse Dillard[1]

In advanced capitalist societies, work organizations permeate and shape our lives, be they business organizations, bodies of the state, or nongovernmental organizations (NGOs). Over the last 150 years, however, business organizations, especially corporations,[2] have become increasingly important in shaping choices that citizens face, as well as producing goods and services for society. The material aspect of business organizations' operations has received attention in various national sustainable development (SD) strategies[3] under the label of sustainable production and consumption and often focuses on the environmental impacts of production and consumption activities. However, in addition to the environmental and economic aspects, SD also entails consideration of social aspects of behavior.[4] Here we focus on articulating the issues that arise for business organizations with respect to the social dimensions of SD.[5]

The relative neglect of social aspects of SD in the business/accounting literature arises from four factors. First, the dominant economic aims of business organizations, most commonly expressed as maximizing shareholder wealth,[6] are not always cognizant of the wide-ranging social impact of their behavior and as a result, social impacts have not always been visible. Second, SD has its modern origins in environmental sustainability issues; as a result, social issues have sometimes been seen to be of secondary importance or as relating solely to developing world issues, such as access to water, education, and health care. Third, aspects of social sustainability (e.g., social cohesion, flourishing communities, or the maintenance of human rights) are often seen to fall within the consideration and control of the state and/or civil society, rather than business. Finally, social sustainability appears to present different and more severe challenges in specification, understanding, and communication than environmental sustainability because there is no widely accepted scientific basis for analysis, unlike the ability to debate population ecology, acceptable levels of toxicity, or acceptable concentrations of green house gases in the atmosphere. Nor is there a common unit of measure such as monetary units with the economic dimension of sustainability.

Table 8.1 Social Impacts of Business Activities

Organizational Stakeholder	*Examples of Interactions/Impacts*
Employees (individually and collectively via unions)	• Employment terms and conditions (including job security, pay, fairness of employment practices, and freedom of association) • Union recognition and interactions • Training and job development opportunities • Engagement of employees in management of the firm[8]
Suppliers (via supply chain impact)	• Fair payment and terms of engagement with suppliers • Issues concerning human rights abuses in supply chains, including, for example, slavery and the implications that arise from purchasing goods that may fuel conflict (such as conflict diamonds)[9] • A special case of supply chain issues concerning interactions with host governments (with issues of bribery, corruption, and aiding human rights abuses coming to the fore)[10]
Communities	• Health impacts that arise from living near a production facility • Displacement of communities in order to accommodate activities (the extraction industry is an area where this comes to the fore, as does infrastructure projects that require population movement, such as that in the Three Gorges Dam) • Socioeconomic impacts that arise when an organization leaves a location (taking employment opportunities with it)[11] • Community-based activities (including philanthropy) that an organization undertakes • Where community is defined as a country, relationships with nation-states (in terms of lobbying) also could come within the scope of this category, as do political donations
Consumers	• Product safety • Responsible advertising (especially of products such as tobacco and alcohol)[12] • Collateral damage that arises from consumption of products produced (this notion arises in the context of armaments, violent movies/games, and pornography)

With these challenges in mind, this chapter undertakes a two-track analysis of social sustainability. First, how the actions undertaken by business give rise to social impacts is outlined, and these impacts are, in turn, linked to the SD agenda as it pertains to social issues. The extent to which corporations in North American and Europe disclose these social impacts also is examined as part of this analysis. Second, we expand our understanding of business organizations' actions by considering the context within which social sustainability impacts arise, paying particular attention to societal norms and values that prescribe the parameters for corporate action and that create barriers for change in corporate behavior. We argue that awareness of their implications as they emerge from accounts of their impacts is a necessary but insufficient condition for change. Institutional change also is required (see also Owen, Gray, and Bebbington,, 1997; Larrinaga and Bebbington, 2001, in this context) and the chapter closes by drawing out the possibilities for such change.

SOCIAL SUSTAINABILITY AND BUSINESS

Business organizations have a myriad of social impacts from their interaction with, *inter alia*, employees, suppliers, communities, and consumers. These impacts vary depending on the nature of the organization, its activities, and stakeholder[7] interactions (Table 8.1 summarizes some aspects of social impacts).

For a number of the interactions outlined in Table 8.1, regulation exists that dictates certain standards of behavior (e.g., in product safety legislation, health and safety standards, employment practices, racial/sexual equality legislation, and advertising codes of practice). In line with the arguments presented in Gray et al. (1996), one could anticipate that, where there is a regulatory requirement to act/forebear from acting in a certain manner, organizations may provide accounts of their actions. Indeed, in some countries, there are requirements in various legislation (usually companies' acts or listing requirements) to disclose aspects of performance in some of the areas noted earlier. For example, the UK Companies Acts have long required disclosure of charitable and political donations.

Where there are no formal regulatory requirements for disclosure, it is less likely that there will be disclosure around the items listed in Table 8.1. This is not to say that no disclosure is likely to be forthcoming. Rather, the terms of the disclosure are not formally regulated. The only way in which some of these aspects could be seen to be moderated by society is through the notion of a social contract. In brief, Deegan (2006) maintains that where

society is not satisfied that the organization is operating in an acceptable, or *legitimate* manner, then society will effectively revoke the organization's 'contract' to continue its operations. This might be experienced through, for example, consumers reducing or eliminating the demand for the products of a business, factor suppliers eliminating the supply of labor and financial capital to the business, or constituents lobbying government to increase taxes, fines or laws to prohibit those actions which do not conform with the expectations of the community. (p. 280; for an earlier introduction to this area, see Shocker and Sethi, 1973)[13]

Given the less well-defined (and indeed evolving) nature of the social contract, determining accountability relationships around the social aspects of SD is difficult.

In addition, this problem spills over into the extent to which organizations provide information about their performance on these aspects (noting that accountability and the provisions of accounts go hand in hand; see Meyer, 1986; Hines, 1988; Roberts, 1991; Arrington and Francis, 1993). Having noted the prior challenges, organizations do provide accounts of their social impacts, and there are some studies of these disclosure patterns, albeit that these studies have tended to concentrate on environmental disclosures in recent years (for a small example of this type of work, see Adams, Coutts, and Harte, 1995, Adams, Hill, and Roberts 1998; Gray, Kouhy, and Lavers, 1995; Adams and Harte, 1998; Neu, Warsame, and Pedwell, 1998; Sustainability and United Nations Environment Programme, 2000, 2002, 2004; Kolk, 2003; Milne, Tregida, and Walton, 2003; SustainAbility, United Nations Environment Programme, & Standard & Poor's, 2006). Although these disclosures are generated by organizations, in some instances, stakeholders have sought to hold organizations to account for their (social) impacts directly (see Medawar, 1976; Harte and Owen, 1987; Geddes, 1991; Gray et al., 1996, who discuss the phenomena of external social audits; and Owen, Swift, Bowerman, and Humphreys, 2000, for a critique of more recent attempts to achieve the same ends).

In brief, there is much evidence in the accounting literature that the social impacts of business are, to a greater or lesser extent, regulated by formal or informal norms. In addition, companies often produce accounts of their performance on aspects of social impacts. Over time, these accounts are becoming more formalized. However, as currently formulated and implemented, they are incomplete, and there is large variability between countries/locations as to how these initiatives influence behavior. As a result, using accounting to link corporate action with its social impact and implications is challenging, and this challenge, combined with the relative lack of attention that has been given to social sustainability, means that there has not been much written in this area. Next, we attempt to gain purchase in overcoming this lacuna by more explicitly considering the social dimension of SD and proposing a framework that provides an enabling context, identifying three general levels of analysis, and considering their interrelationships.

SD is a deceptively straightforward concept. It requires that our economic (development) activities to take place within the constraints of ecosystems (in terms of both resource availability and waste assimilation capacity), such that the needs of all alive today as well as those of future generations are met. Just development requires intra- and intergenerational equity. There is ample evidence that these conditions are not met.[14] Little consensus exists with respect to how change can be affected that will deliver a sustainable trajectory or even the amount of time we may have to formulate and implement such change, The social aspects of the SD agenda have focused on intergenerational equity and, thus, have been dominated by the need to consider the living conditions and aspirations of the poorest in society. This notion leads to a focus on specific pressing social issues, such as poverty alleviation, women's emancipation, control of AIDS, education, access to safe drinking water, and sanitation services. At the same time, social concerns within developed countries also are important. The question arises as to how we might address social sustainability at a level sufficiently general to meaningfully address corporate responsibility with respect to social justice, which requires us to connect corporate actions and their social impacts, both positive and negative. Connections between these issues play out in two interactive layers.

First, a connection between corporate actions and SD arises from the social impacts of activities in particular locations or specific industries, much along the lines outlined in Table 8.1. For example, if a company is operating in the developing world, its employment conditions should be fair, focusing attention and opening debate about sweatshop labor for some clothing manufactures, as well as the issue of slavery in supply chains for resources such as coffee, sugar, and cocoa. In addition, where a company is involved in water privatization in developing countries, its actions also may be more closely linked to social sustainability issues by virtue of the type of operations in which they are engaged (see Balkan, 2004, for a critical review of water privatization). Such examples relate to the way in which a particular company has a direct and observable impact on a specific country or group of stakeholders. SD also is concerned with the impact of our current approach to development generally. It is here that corporate activities and social SD links emerge at a systemic level and that the greatest leverage can be gained in understanding and implementing socially sustainable development programs.

Corporate activities are governed by broader societal rules with regard to how economic activity should be conducted and the goals to which such activity are directed. If corporations are focused on maximizing profits for a small set of stakeholders (their shareholders), then, by definition, they will not be concerned with nonshareholders, and they also will seek to externalize any social impacts that arise from their activities. Such actions are not in opposition to a SD agenda if one believes that economic activity will lead to improved social conditions for the poorest (the so-called *trickle-down effect*). There is, however, considerable disagreement that this has or indeed can be expected to happen. For example, Pirages (1990) suggests that it is not at all clear that "a slowly rising tide [of economic growth] will lift all ships. In fact, there is well-founded fear that the tide may be ebbing and leaving them ['developing' countries] behind as litter on the beach" (pp. 2–3; see also Gray et al., 1996). There also is evidence that the effect may actually operate in reverse. That is, certain types of economic development in poor countries will make them less well off as measured by a variety of social indicators (see e.g., Ross, 2001). This situation poses a considerable challenge to the ideology that corporate activity, if left to its market-based, profit-maximizing devices, will lead to SD. Although a full examination of these dynamics is beyond the scope of a single chapter, the next section employs a general framework, wherein we can describe and examines the particular context within which corporate actions are governed and highlights the structural impediments that exist for a corporation that wishes to act in a manner that would be likely to enhance social sustainability as a subset of the SD project.

THE SOCIOPOLITICAL CONTEXT OF SOCIAL SUSTAINABILITY

Organizations operate within a complex web of forces and relationships. Dillard et al. (2004) develop a framework for contextualizing organizational behavior. They propose three levels of analysis: economic-political, organizational field, and the organization. We situate social sustainability reporting within this context. Given the social construction of work organizations, corporations reflect institutional processes that "define what forms they can assume and how they may operate legitimately" (Scott, 1995, p. 136). Social sustainability represents an organizational dimension becoming more recognized as requiring attention by organizational management. As such, we propose that management's actions can be studied as standardized or standardizing social practices. Social accounting represents a reaction to changing social expectations and reflects certain emerging organizational practices. We argue that these activities reflect an attempt to establish societal legitimacy, at least among the organization's primary stakeholders. The legitimacy criteria emerge from a collective perception of what constitutes socially sustainable behavior and the appropriate media for reporting that behavior and its consequences.

We need to consider all three levels of analysis to better understand social sustainable accounting and reporting (organizational representations) and the implicated actions reflected therein. Formalized behavior sets are incorporated into the organization's representations because either they reflect a commitment to a set of norms and values or an attempt to appear to be acting in compliance with the prevailing norms and values.

The political/economic level is made up of societal institutions and imposes societal norms and values. The organizational field level comprises industry groups, professional institutions, geographic collectives, and so on. Individual organizations constitute the third level.

Global market capitalism represents the sociopolitical and economic contexts of most organizations within the Western industrialized societies. As such, economic efficiency[15] is the dominant motivating and legitimating criteria. At least implicitly, a hierarchy of institutional influence prevails, where the economic/political level supplies the context for organizational field structures and expectations, and these structures and expectations provide the basis for organizational processes and behaviors. For example, a societal recognition of the importance for transparency in corporate behavior with respect to social sustainability might materialize in regulatory specification and oversight mandated by legislative action. Constituency groups such as labor unions, professional organizations, community organizations, industrial leaders, trade organizations, and other special interest groups will affect the interpretation and application of these requirements at the organizational field level. Organizational management must then take the social sustainability reporting regulations and the related interpretations and operationalize them. This operationalization includes actions ranging from modifying procedures and processes to conform with the spirit of the requirements and transparently reporting the results to decoupling the regulation requirements from the actual activities of the organization with reports reflecting an adherence to the letter, but not the spirit of the regulations. The latter is not necessarily an irrational strategy. The regulations may be such that by adhering to them the organization's core competencies may be compromised and its ability to survive significantly diminished. Such a situation points up the need for external monitoring and enforcement.

For instance, at the economic/political level, the current securities laws and accounting standards in the United States concern only the financial dimension of the corporation, excluding both the environmental and social dimensions. Further, the extant regulations privilege private property and owner/investor interests. Within the organizational field, these social, economic, and political values are translated into specific expectations and provide the legitimating and regulative grounds for organizational action. Regulators and standard setters develop accounting and reporting requirements for an industry, such as the mining industry, within the economic/political parameters through, for instance, legislation. Following legislative mandates, financial accounting statements must be issued and certified by an independent third party that they conform to the standards. No such legislative mandates address corporate responsibility statements. No reporting standards are in place. Reporting is strictly voluntary, and no certification is required. It appears that some industry sectors (e.g., petroleum and chemicals) have developed certain reporting strategies, but some (e.g.,

Owen et al., 2000) have argued that these tactics tend to be self-serving, providing little of substantive value in accessing and monitoring corporate responsibility. Organizations develop organizational practices in order to comply with expectations set at the organizational field level. These practices may be incorporated into the organization's activities, or they may be decoupled from the actual management or operational procedures. Specific responses are not necessarily the same across organizations (Buhr [1998] looks at one specific example of corporate responses to legislation).

The dualistic nature and the recursive characteristic of the process suggest that actions at the organizational level also may influence expectations and, therefore, processes at the organizational field and economic/political levels. These actions may support the extant practices motivating evolutionary change, or they may be opposed to current practices creating pressures for revolutionary change. New organizational field practices will, in turn, affect the political/economic field by supporting the values and practices articulated by powerful interest groups, modifying them, or eliminating them. As such, resource control may be reinforce or changed. Changes in the extant processes may result as the norms, values, and beliefs are recursively reviewed and possibility revised at each of the three levels.

Before continuing, we present an example illustrating how the process might work with respect to public disclosure of social sustainability information. In the wake of notable corporate debacles and the resulting damage to corporate managements' credibility, as well as loss of faith in the integrity of the capital markets in the early 2000s, demands for action arouse within society for modifications to the current regulatory environment. Legislation ensued that was directed toward increasing transparency in corporate financial disclosures and ensuring more effective corporate responsibility and governance. The Sarbanes–Oxley legislation represents the codification of these efforts.[16] In addition, the extensive social cost incurred, as well as the loss of trust and credibility on the part of corporations, especially large multinationals, provided additional motivation for an expanded scope in corporate disclosure[17] in nontraditional areas, such as environmental and social impact. Reporting procedures were primarily developed at the organizational field level for specific industry segments because of the lack of regulatory involvement (indeed, Kolk [2003], among others, has identified industry-level effects in reporting activity).

It is interesting to compare the actions taken with respect to the financial and social dimensions. In the financial domain, legislation imposed regulatory changes implemented by the Securities and Exchange Commission. Trade organizations and experts within the organizational field developed guidelines and interpretations of the mandated regulatory requirements. Companies developed specific procedures and practices that operationalized the new regulation, and they operated by these new routines. Audit procedures changed, and control systems were fortified. Governance structures required more management accountability and directly assigned responsibility. The dominance of capital and its markets prevails, in that the ownership rights of the shareholders predominate.

Although the pressures for increased environmental and social corporate responsibility emanated from a common logic—a need for increased understanding and transparency—little similarity exists in the outcomes. Legislation and regulations did not mandate stronger responsibility and accountability with respect to social and environmental dimensions.[18] Mandatory standards were not developed. Disclosures were not mandated, and regulatory and verification measures were not strengthened (although the Global Reporting Initiative exists, it has not led to widespread, comparable reporting that is subject to systematic audit/certification). However, organizations did response to the social pressures. Around this time, corporations began to voluntarily publish stand-alone corporate social responsibility statements.[19] For example, from the mid-1990s, there has been a rising trend in report production, albeit it appears that report production has peaked and it has always been subject to significant intercountry differences (see Kolk, 2003). It is interesting to note that, more recently, there is anecdotal evidence to suggest that responsibility for corporate social and environmental issues began to shift from being more operationally oriented (environmental, health, and safety) toward a more public relations orientation. The shift is evidenced by the fact that the reports are usually the responsibility of the legal department (in North America) or the corporate communications department (in Europe), which implies a compliance perspective and "image" orientation (see also Bebbington, Larrinaga-Gonzalez, and Moneva, forthcoming). In the next section, we consider some of the challenges specifically related to the public reporting on social sustainability by comparing its characteristics with those associated with economic and environmental sustainability.

UNDERSTANDING THE DIFFERENCE BETWEEN SOCIAL SUSTAINABILITY AND ECONOMIC AND ENVIRONMENTAL SUSTAINABILITY

In this section, we discuss some of the differences between social sustainability and environmental and economic sustainability relating to public reporting and disclosure. We group the environmental and economic (E&E) together, claiming that, at some level, they are (can be) viewed as having similar characteristics. We do not argue that this is descriptive in every case or along all dimensions, but merely that these perceptions generally weigh heavily in arguments surrounding the measurement and public reporting debates. After we differentiate E&E and social sustainability, we discuss the implications of the distinctions at each of the three levels of analysis discussed earlier as we related the insights to our organizational analysis of sustainable development.

Differentiating Dimensions

Following Dillard et al. (2004), we propose three comparative dimensions, or tensions, useful in understanding social systems, especially private sector work organizations. We label these dimensions representation, rationality, and power. The proposed continua are presented in Figure 8.1.

Representation

The first dimension has to do with the nature of reality and can be classified in terms of the degree of subjectivity or objectivity assumed to make up the representation. We propose that the elements that make up the social dimension tend to be perceived as more subjective than the elements that comprise the E&E dimensions. By *subjective* we mean that the social agents construct the elements as a result of their actions and interactions. By *objective* we mean that the elements are constituted independently of the actors. Subjective representations reflect situations where the legitimating action follows from the interaction between individuals or collectives, and the elements cannot necessarily be represented by concrete, quantitative, measurable outcomes. Evaluation criteria reflect group (social) goals and values. Consistent with the independent nature of the objective representations, legitimating criteria arise from the application of formal logic and scientific calculus, resulting in concrete, measurable elements and outcomes. In contrast to subjective representations of reality, one presumes the correct answer to be legitimated by the appropriate set of norms and values.

Rationality

The second comparative dimension relates to the means by which ideas and practices are deemed legitimate. Rationality, formal and substantive, provides the criteria for evaluation. Formal rationality is value-neutral,

Social Sustainability	Differentiating Dimension	Economic/Environmental Sustainability
Subjective [------------------------ Representation ------------------------]		Objective
Substantive [------------------------ Rationality ------------------------]		Formal
Social Consensus [------------------------ Power Base ------------------------]		Hierarchical Structures

Figure 8.1 Differentiating sustainability dimensions

calculative, and having universal application. The dominant evaluative criterion is efficiency, primarily economic, and is gained by maximizing input–output ratios using formal, logical analysis. As noted previously, the primary criteria for legitimacy resides in the degree to which formal logical reasoning reflects the means by which the conclusion is attained. Substantive rationality relates to ethics and values and the associated needs/ends of the participant social groups. The primary legitimating criteria is the extent to which outcomes are attained within the context of the community's norms and values. We see social sustainability more generally related to substantive rationality and E&E more closely aligned with formal rationality.

Power

Power connotes the ability to control both material and human resources. At the E&E level, control follows from the dominant norms, values, and the associated legitimating processes and can be implemented by either formal hierarchical structures or social consensus. Within a formal hierarchy system, the form of the structures and the duty to obey provide the means for controlling action. Social consensus provides the grounds on which control is legitimized and evaluated, and personal choice and ongoing social interaction provide the legitimating basis for action.

Implications Across the Three Levels

The three dimensions are useful in analyzing and understanding forces acting on organizations and how these forces provide the context within which sustainable actions are considered and implemented. Economic efficiency has become the primary legitimating criterion within Western capitalist societies (Weber, 1958). The domination of one parameter such as economic efficiency at the societal level in effect collapses the distinctions along the three differentiating dimensions. Thus, the attributes of economic efficiency are presumed descriptive and prescriptive. That is, economic efficiency presumes an objective world that can and should be understood and manipulated using formal rationality and that can and should be controlled using hierarchical control structures. The credibility of alternative perspectives is undermined and portrayed as secondary or inferior. Thus, legitimating and evaluative criteria used to undertake and evaluate behavior conform to that of the dominant E&E criteria. For organizational action to manifest contrary to these criteria requires that the organizational structures decouple the action from the external evaluation criteria.

An insurmountable obstacle arises as we are forced to apply the prevailing logic associated with economic efficiency to social sustainability actions, measures, and programs. Social sustainability dimensions adhere more closely to the marginalized characteristics: subjectivity, substantive rationality, and social consensus. When objective measures are required, the social outcomes appear inadequate. When formal logic is applied, the social dimensions are found to be lacking. Social consensus as a means of organizing and controlling resources appears cumbersome and inefficient. By virtue of the underlying dimensional characteristics, social sustainability reporting would be perceived as inherently inadequate and not be taken seriously until the constructs and measures acquire the perceived rigor attributed to the dominant discourse. Thus, within the prevailing context, it is unlikely that routine change will result in any meaningful and acceptable level of social sustainability reporting. A crisis such as major corporate irresponsibility or egregious acts of wanton excess are required for such change to be motivated. However, to date, not even such debacles (e.g., Ford Pinto, Exxon Valdez, Bhopal, Enron) have fostered legislated mandatory corporate responsibility reporting, much less social sustainability reporting.

Imagining Social Sustainability

Assuming our presumptions are correct with respect to the social structures that constitute society, we now develop an ideal type representation of a socially sustainable social system considering all three phases that provides a general template on which to develop authentic social sustainability reporting. It is easy to imagine a society grounded on a belief in objective representation, formal logic, and hierarchical control structures because, at least since the enlightenment, it is the physical world (science) within which we perceive life to unfold. Imagining one in which the social takes precedence over the economic is not so easy.[20] As an illustrative vehicle, we rework a communitarian-oriented[21] example developed in Dillard et al (2004) considering the implications at each of the three organizing levels.

Economic and Political Level

At the economic/political level, laws and regulations follow from and are grounded in subjectively rational, discursively derived, community-based norms and values. The primary debate focuses on wealth redistribution, community property, responsibilities, wage and price controls, currency and trade regulations, and reporting regulations favoring the community constituencies. Action is formulated and evaluated using symbolic representational schemes that subjectively represent, and are predicated on, concepts associated with community well-being. The institutions that control resources include community service agencies, taxing authorities, and local commodity markets and cooperatives. The agent follows a course of action predicated on the collective pursuit of community goals.

Organizational Field Level

The economic and political level provides the context of the organizational field. At the organizational field level, discursively formed norms and values inform industry norms, practices, and regulations directed toward increasing community well-being. Representational structures further community well-being and translate into expectations with respect to social responsibility and sustainable development. Human action is directed toward improving the condition of community stakeholders through resource allocations directed toward community growth and development.

Organizational Level

Operating within the context of the community-oriented organization field, the organization acts within, and is held accountable to, norms and values with respect to social relationships and interpersonal dynamics. Organizations are expected to act in order to provide information about their environmental impact, quality of life contributions, and cultural enhancements. Resources are allocated based on social consensus developed through discussion and debate, and actors are held accountable as members of an ongoing community engaged in community development.

CONCLUSIONS

If the aspirations expressed in national SD strategies for production and consumption to become sustainable are to be realized, corporations will have to be involved in some manner in the SD agenda. Although the SD agenda encompasses a wide array of issues and concerns, this chapter has focused on social sustainability as it pertains to corporate impacts. Although traditional accounting routines and disclosures direct attention to the economic outcomes of corporate activity, there is a substantial array of social impacts that arise in conjunction with that economic activity. These impacts are not usually visible, except to the extent that they are captured in costs and, hence, in financial reports. These impacts, however, are substantive, and developing regulating and reporting mechanisms around these impacts will be an element in companies addressing social aspects of the SD agenda. However, this response is not likely to be sufficient because it does not address the system within which corporate activities take place.

NOTES

1. We wish to acknowledge the support provided by the Center for Professional Integrity and Accountability, School of Business Administration, Portland State University.

2. Given their predominant role, the following discussion is primarily concerned with corporations.
3. For example, see Department of Prime Minister and Cabinet (2003), Department for Environment Food and Rural Affairs (2005), Environment Canada (2006) and Volkery, Swanson, Jacob, and Bregha (2006) for an evaluation of some of these.
4. For example, see the triple bottom line popularized by Elkington (1997).
5. We conceptualize SD to comprise three primary dimensions: environmental, social, and economic. Although we refer to these as separate dimensions, we recognize their interactive nature. See also Gray (1992), Bebbington and Thomson (1996), Gray and Bebbington (2000); Bebbington (2001), and Unerman, Bebbington, and O'Dwyer (2007) for a fuller exploration of the multiple aspects of SD.
6. Maximizing shareholder value is a problematic concept.
7. Stakeholders are usually considered to be those individuals or groups that affect or are affected by an organization (Gray, Owen, and Adams, 1996). This definition creates a large set of potential actors, and considerable effort has been expended within the social accounting literature on refining this notion and exploring which stakeholder at what times are likely to be recognized by organizations (see e.g., Donaldson and Preston, 1995; Friedman and Miles, 2002).
8. Here there are significant differences between North America and Europe (with differences within Europe as well) in terms of the extent to which employees have rights to be involved in management decisions. For example, around 10 million workers across the European Union (EU) have the right to information and consultation on company decisions at European level through their European Works Councils. The Works Council Directive (94/45/EC) applies to an estimated 1,800 companies with 1,000 or more employees, including at least 150 in two or more Member States. Of these, some 640 (36%) have European Works Councils in operation, covering around 60% of workers in the EU.
9. With respect to antislavery activities, see www.antislavery.org. Further, resources on the topic of conflict diamonds can be found at www.stop-blooddiamonds.org and www.conflictdiamonds.com. Often these concerns are manifest in product certification and labeling activities, rather than in accounts of the actions of individual organizations.
10. Organizations such as Transparency International (see www.transparency.org) and the "publish what you pay" campaign (see www.publishwhatyoupay.org) focus on these areas.
11. This area attracted attention in the 1980s in the United Kingdom, where local authorities conducted audits of what the effect would be of plant closures within their boundaries (see Gray et al., 1996, pp. 275–279).
12. These activities may be controlled by state-sponsored advertising standards or industry codes of conduct.
13. One may, of course, question the extent to which these effects have been felt in practice. Bebbington et al., (forthcoming), for example, note that despite incidents such as Bhopal and the Exxon Valdez the corporations behind the generation of these externalities have continued to exist, albeit that their reputations suffered.
14. For example, the United Nations Intergovernmental Panel on Climate Change (2007) set of four reports highlight the extent to which we are not ecologically sustainable in terms of green house gas emissions (see also Stern, 2006, for a description of possible economic consequences of global climate change). In addition, the Millennium Eco-system Report looks more widely at the state

of the environment. With respect to social aspects, the gap between current and desired outcomes is evident in the Millennium Development Goals (see www.un.org/millenniumgoals).

15. This efficiency can take on many forms, such as maximizing shareholder value, return on investment, economic value added, and so on.

16. See Dillard et al. (2004) for an example of the implementation of the financial disclosure issues.

17. The need for additional disclosures has been ongoing at least since the 1960s, and the work on human resource accounting (see Flamholtz, 1999) was renewed in the late 1980s with the social accounting work of Gray and others (see Gray and Bebbington, 2001).

18. Although as discussed previously, the environmental reporting is better developed than is social reporting.

19. These publications take on varied titles, but generally attempt to provide information concerning the entity's response to social and environmental issues.

20. However, theologians, especially those of the Judeo-Christian traditions with which we are familiar, have provided numerous templates, none of which we as a society seem inclined to take seriously. The example we use is, in many respects, grounded in similar conceptualizations of community.

21. We work generally from ideas presented by Etzioni (1993, 1996).

REFERENCES

Adams, C., A. Coutts, and G. Harte.1995. "Corporate Equal Opportunities (Non-) Disclosure." *British Accounting Review* 27 (2): 87–108.

———., and G. Harte. 1998. "The Changing Portrayal of the Employment of Women in British Banks' and Retail Companies' Corporate Annual Reports." *Accounting Organizations and Society* 23 (8): 781–812.

———., W.-Y. Hill, and C. Roberts. 1998. "Corporate Social Reporting Practices in Western Europe: Legitimating Corporate Behaviour?" *British Accounting Review* 30 (1): 1–21.

Arrington, C. E., and J. R. Francis 1993. "Giving Economic Aaccounts: Accounting as Cultural Practice." *Accounting, Organizations and Society* 18 (2/3): 107–124.

Balkan, J. 2004. *The Corporation: The Pathological Pursuit of Profit and Power.* New York: Free Press.

Bebbington, J. 2001. "Sustainable Development: A Review of the International Development, Business and Accounting Literature." *Accounting Forum* 25 (2): 128–157.

———., C. Larrinaga-Gonzalez, and J. Moneva. 2007. "Corporate Social Reporting and Reputation Risk Management." *Accounting, Auditing and Accountability Journal* 20 (3): 333–355.

Bebbington, K. J., and I. Thomson. 1996. *Business Conceptions of Sustainability and the Implications for Accountancy.* London: Association of Chartered Certified Accountants.

Buhr, N. 1998. "Environmental Performance, Legislation and Annual Report Disclosure: The Case of Acid Rain and Falconbridge." *Accounting Auditing and Accountability Journal* 11 (2): 163–190.

Deegan, C. 2006. *Financial Accounting Theory,*2nd ed. Sydney: McGraw-Hill.

Department for Environment, Food, and Rural Affairs. 2005. *One Future—Different Paths: The UK's Shared Framework for Sustainable Development.* London: Author.

Department of Prime Minister and Cabinet. 2003. *Sustainable Development for New Zealand: Programme of Action*. Wellington, New Zealand: Author.

Dillard, J., Rigsby, J. Goodman, C. 2004. "The Making and Remaking of Organization Context: Duality & the Institutionalization Process." Accounting, Auditing and Accountability Journal. 17 (4): 506–542.

Donaldson, T., and L. Preston. 1995. "The Stakeholder Theory of the Corporation: Concepts, Evidence and Implications." *Academy of Management Review* 20 (1): 65–91.

Elkington, J. 1997. *Cannibals with Forks: The Triple Bottom Line of 21st Century Business*. Oxford, UK: Capstone Publishing.

Environment Canada. 2006. *Sustainable Development Strategy: 2007–2009*. Ottawa: Author.

Etzioni, A. 1993. The Spirit of Community: Rights, Responsibilities and the Communication Agenda. New York: Crown Books.

———. 1996. The New Golden Rule: Community and Morality in a Democratic Society. New York: Basic Books.

Flamholtz, E. 1999. *Human Resource Accounting*, 3rd ed. New York: Springer.

Friedman, A., and S. Miles. 2002. "Developing Stakeholder Theory." *Journal of Management Studies* 39 (1): 1–21.

Geddes, M. 1991. "The Social Audit Movement." In *Green Reporting*, edited by D. L. Owen (pp. 215–241).. London: Chapman Hall.

Gray, R. 1992. "Accounting and Environmentalism: An Exploration of the Challenge of Gently Accounting for Accountability, Transparency and Sustainability." *Accounting Organisations and Society* 17 (5): 399–426.

———., and J. Bebbington. 2000. "Environmental Accounting, Managerialism and Sustainability." *Advances in Environmental Accounting and Management* 1: 1–44.

———. 2001. *Accounting for the Environment*, 2nd ed. London: Sage.

———., R. Kouhy, and S. Lavers. 1995. "Corporate Social and Environmental Reporting: A Review of the Literature and a Longitudinal Study of UK Disclosure." *Accounting, Auditing and Accountability Journal* 8 (2): 47–77.

———., D. Owen, and C. Adams. 1996. *Accounting and Accountability: Changes and Challenges in Corporate Social and Environmental Reporting*. London: Prentice-Hall.

Harte, G., and D. Owen. 1987. "Fighting De-industrialisation: The Role of Local Government Social Audits." *Accounting, Organizations and Society* 12 (2): 123–142.

Hines, R. D. 1988. "Financial Accounting: In Communicating Reality, We Construct Reality." *Accounting, Organizations and Society* 13 (3): 251–261.

Kolk, A. 2003. "Trends in Sustainability Reporting by the Fortune Global 250." *Business Strategy and the Environment* 12 (5): 279–291.

Larrinaga, C., and J. Bebbington. 2001. "Environmental Accounting Practices—Organisational Change or Institutional Appropriation." *Critical Perspectives on Accounting* 12 (3): 269–292.

Medawar, C. 1976. "The Social Audit: A Political View." *Accounting, Organizations and Society* 1 (4): 389–394.

Meyer, J. 1986. "Social Environments and Organisational Accounting." *Accounting, Organizations and Society* 11 (4/5): 345–356.

Milne, M., H. Tregida, and S. Walton. 2003. "The Triple-Bottom-Line: Benchmarking New Zealand's Early Reporters." *University of Auckland Business Review* 5 (2).

Neu, D., H. Warsame, and K. Pedwell. 1998. "Managing Public Impressions: Environmental Disclosures in Annual Reports." *Accounting Organizations and Society* 23 (3): 265–282.

Owen D., R. Gray, and J. Bebbington. 1997. "Green Accounting: Cosmetic Irrelevance or Radical Agenda for Change?" *Asia-Pacific Journal of Accounting* 4 (2): 175–198.

————., T. Swift, M. Bowerman, and C. Humphreys. 2000. "The New Social Audits: Accountability, Managerial Capture or the Agenda of Social Champions?" *European Accounting Review* 9 (1): 81–98.

Pirages, Dennis C. 1990. "Technology, Ecology and Transformations in the Global Political Economy." In *Transformations in Global Political Economy*, edited by D. C. Pirages and C. Sylvester. London: Macmillan.

Roberts, J. 1991. "The Possibilities of Accountability." *Accounting, Organizations and Society* 16 (4): 355–370.

Ross, M. 2001. *Extractive Sectors and the Poor.* Boston: Oxfam America.

Shocker, A., and S. Sethi. 1973. "An Approach to Incorporating Societal Preferences in Developing Corporate Action Strategies." *California Management Review* 15 (4) 97–105.

Stern, N. 2006. *The Economics of Climate Change: The Stern Review.* Cambridge, UK: Cambridge University Press.

SustainAbility and United Nations Environment Programme. 2000. *The Global Reporters.* London: Author.

————. 2002. *Trust Us: The Global Reporters 2002 Survey of Corporate Sustainability Reporting.* London: Author.

————. 2004. *Risk and Opportunity: Best Practice in Non-Financial Reporting.* London: Author.

————, and Standard & Poor's. 2006. *Tomorrow's Value: The Global Reporters 2006 Survey of Corporate Sustainability Reporting.* London: Author.

Unerman, J., J. Bebbington, and B. O'Dwyer. Eds. 2007. *Sustainability Accounting and Accountability.* Routledge: London.

United Nations Intergovernmental Panel on Climate Change. 2007. *Impacts, Adaptation and Vulnerability.* Available from http://www.ipcc.ch/

Volkery, A., D. Swanson, K. Jacob, and F. Bregha. 2006. "Coordination, Challenges and Innovations in 19 National Sustainable Development Strategies." *World Development* 34 (12): 2047–2063.

Weber, M. 1958. The Protestant Ethic and The Spirit of Capitalism. New York: Scribner.

9 Social Sustainability
One Company's Story

Jesse Dillard and David Layzell[1]

We describe how one company, Intel Corporation, frames and responds to its perceived social responsibilities. Intel is a Fortune 100 firm, the world's leading manufacturer of microprocessors and has been one of the most profitable business organizations in history. As such, within the normal constraints of global market capitalism, the company has enjoyed substantial latitude and discretion in setting and carrying out socially responsible programs and practices. Our analysis addresses the period surrounding the publication of Intel's 2005 Corporate Responsibility Report (CRR).[2] We look at the historical origins and evolution of Intel's strategy and structure as they relate to social sustainability and the publicly available documents published by the company describing its culture and values. Our purpose is neither to curry favor nor to disparage practices, but to gain insights into how a successful, progressive, well-run business organization operating within the confines of Western democratic capitalism responds to social sustainability issues.

We consider how the company conceptualizes it social responsibility leading to an analysis of the conceptual frames used when referring to related constructs, practices, and procedures. The terms *corporate responsibility* and *sustainability* are used, but the term *social sustainability* is not explicitly part of the formal vernacular. Sustainability originates in manufacturing, has an operational flavor within the company, and is implemented and monitored through input/output ratios. Corporate responsibility resides in public affairs and shareholder relationships and has taken on an external gloss. The two phrases dance around each other, but generally coalesce around the term *corporate responsibility*. The meaning and operationalization of these terms can be explored by following them through their application in the areas of governance, ethics, compliance, risks, and controls.

We analyze the external reports issued by the company, identifying the company's claims with respect to its emergent programs and procedures associated with social responsibility. In addition, we consider the motivation that underlies the corporation's programs and actions related to social sustainability. The motives are, somewhat paradoxically, mutually supportive self-interest and altruism. Four sources of motivation for socially related action (see Figure 9.1) are identified. The first category considers procedures and/or actions that are undertaken because they are forced or encouraged to do so by law or regulation and represent the minimum levels of responsible action necessary in maintaining a license to operate within the boundaries set by the community/society. The second category refers to the expectations of various constituencies. The third option considers procedures and/or actions from an economic perspective and relate to fiscal responsibility. Here we include instrumental expenditures/initiatives/ public relations programs directed toward building community goodwill, with the justification being that such actions/expenditures will ultimately benefit profitability. The fourth category has to do with procedures and/ or actions motivated by noneconomic values and undertaken because the corporate culture sees them as appropriate or necessary in meeting its corporate social responsibility.

As noted earlier, Intel uses corporate responsibility as the collective in referring to issues related to environmental and social responsibility. In this discussion, we consider only those issues/items related to social sustainability. We omit environmental issues, although we recognize the substantial inter-relationships between the two. In fact, we see environmental responsibility as a primary component in being socially responsible. If the environment is destroyed, there is no social sphere for which to be concerned. Alternatively, only through the social can intentional action originate directed toward destruction or construction of the natural system. In discerning Intel's response, we generally presume that, unless specifically stated, corporate responsibility policies, values, and so on relate equally to both environmental and social issues. For example, when the CEO states that corporate responsibility is an important consideration in decision making, we presume that this comment refers to both social and environmental sustainability.

The discussion is organized as follows. Following this introduction, we present a description and a brief history of the company. The third section describes Intel's social sustainable strategy and structures. We discuss both internal dynamics and external influences. Next, Intel's CRR is evaluated and related to social sustainability. In the fifth section, we consider the link between motivational forces associated with corporate responsibility and the associated outcomes. In the concluding section, we attempt to glean from our descriptive rendering of Intel prescriptive insights helpful in moving the social sustainability agenda forward.

DESCRIPTION OF THE FIRM[3]

Demographics

Founded in 1968 by Robert Noyce and Gordon Moore in California, Intel is credited with being one of the premier catalysts for Silicone Valley and the associated technology revolution. Intel is the world's largest semiconductor

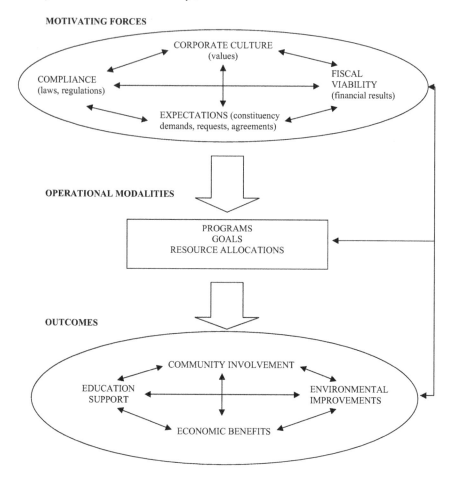

Figure 9.1 Corporate social responsibility.

manufacturer,[4] providing advanced integrated digital technology platforms and components for the computing and communications industries. In 2006, the company reported revenues of $35 billion, a gross margin percentage of approximately 50% based on net income of $5 billion. Assets totaled $48 billion, of which $6.6 billion represents cash or equivalent.

The company's stated goal is to be the "pre-eminent provider of semi-conductor chips and platform solutions to the world wide digital economy" (Intel, 2006, p. 1). Intel's products include microprocessors, chipsets, motherboards, flash memory, wired and wireless connectivity products, communications infrastructure components, and products for network storage. The primary customer groups include original equipment and design manufacturers of computer systems, handheld devices, telecommunications and network communications equipment; PC and network communications products users; and manufacturers of a broad range of industrial and communication equipment.

Intel has facilities worldwide. Six U.S. locations manufacture approximately 70% of the company's wafers, with the rest produced in Ireland and Israel. The majority of assembly and testing is done off shore in Malaysia, the Philippines, China, and Costa Rica. The company states explicitly in its annual report and Securities and Exchange Commission (SEC) filings that it expects its suppliers and subcontractors to meet performance expectations with respect to business integrity, ethics, and environmental, health, and safety compliance regardless of where they are located and to abide by local laws with respect to labor and employment practices. In addition, Intel imposes a minimum age requirement regardless of local law. Expectations for supplier performance are established, communicated, and monitored. Intel currently employs approximately 94,100 individuals, none of whom are covered by collective bargaining agreements.

The products compete primarily on performance, features, quality, brand recognition, price, and availability. Innovative products and worldwide customer support at competitive prices reflect the company's production strategy. In addition, customers require improved energy efficiency, enhanced security, reduced heat output, manageability, and integrated solutions. Due to rapid technological change and product innovations, the product life cycle tends to be short, sometimes less than a year, and success depends on improving products and processes, anticipating customer requirements, and developing new products and platforms at progressively lower costs.

Public Representations

On page 14 of the 2006 10-K form filed with the SEC and published as part of the company's annual report, Intel provides an explicit statement with respect to its compliance with environmental, health, and safety (EHS) regulations. The company states its commitment to achieving high environmental quality and product safety standards, as well as to providing employees, contractors, and communities with safe and health workplaces. The company claims that all of its production facilities meet the International Organization for Standardization 14001 environment management system standard. In addition, an internal EHS auditing program addresses compliance as well as business risk and the integrity of management systems. Intel states its commitment to the protection of human rights and the environment and expects its suppliers throughout the value chain to fully comply with applicable laws and regulations as well as with Intel policies. Specific areas mentioned include nondiscrimination in terms and conditions of employment, child labor, minimum wages, employee benefits, and work hours.

The organizational structure with respect to Corporate Social Responsibility has recently changed, reflecting a shift from its place of origin in operations to the Legal Department, which is located within the corporate headquarters group. During 2006, Intel expanded the role of the legal group to encompass Legal and Corporate Affairs. Corporate Affairs includes Public Affairs, Government Affairs, Education, and Corporate Social Responsibility. The Director of Corporate Responsibility, David Stangis, is the person responsible for issuing the CRR. Being part of legal generally implies more of a regulative, compliance attitude than might be the case if the function were located within a more operationally oriented function. The greater importance that primary external constituencies such as institutional investors are placing on risks associated with social and environmental issues motivated the move. We believe that the restructuring reflects a not uncommon evolution that is motivated by economic and cultural dimensions necessary to respond explicitly and implicitly to compliance requirements and expectations. It remains for the future to say whether the migration of the CSR group will motivate a more compliance driven attitude toward corporate social responsibility, and, if so, whether a more or less socially sustainable corporation will result.

As part of Intel's CRR website, it reports using the Global Reporting Initiative (GRI–2002) format. In addition to economic and environmental performance, the report includes social topics such as labor practices, human rights performance, societal performance, and product responsibility. The GRI report is internet based and generally refers to websites containing the information related to the specific report items, many of which are contained in the company's, CRR and other publicly available filings. The GRI format is a relatively shallow, although inclusive, format gaining wide recognition. However, unlike the financial statements, there is no designated professional or governmental body that promulgates reporting standards or reviews the output, and the results are not subject to independent, third-party verification.

Intel is fairly clear about its own stated motives in all the documents that it presents on its corporate website. Intel thinks of itself as a "What you see is what you get" kind of company that regards transparency as a key business virtue. Their stated mindset is that if information is not proprietary and Intel has a clear position on the topic, then why not state that position? What it publishes and what it chooses to withhold is its choice, and it is possible to call for more transparence, but its corporate website does give some credence to this view. In addition to the CRR, the website contains three documents that explain Intel's business credo: the Values Statement (see Appendix A), the Code of Conduct, and the Corporate Principles for Responsible Business (CPRB) (see Appendix B).

The values have been generally unchanged since they were written down in 1986. At that time, they were meant to be a recording of the values that guided the company, as well as a statement that explained the values on which "Intel culture" was based. During his time as both Chief Operating Officer (COO) and Chief Executive Officer (CEO), the now Chairman of the Board, Craig Barrett, personally adjudicated any changes to the values. All new hires to Intel are introduced to Intel culture and the Values Statements, and all Intel employees are provided with a copy to attach to their ID badge. The values have a convenient calendar on the back, so the incentive to carry the values while at work is increased.

The Code of Conduct was completely rewritten in 2006 and early 2007 and was not in fact posted on the website until May 2007. In its previous incarnation as the Corporate Business Principles, it had been a longer, more rambling document created by a team of authors. The 2006/2007 revision was a conscious effort to draft a simple, clear Code of Conduct that bridged the gap from high-level value statements to day-to-day rules by which the company operated. The intention was to produce a principles-based document with simple guidelines that would be understood throughout the world. Ever practical, the document was intended to serve as the communication vehicle required of public companies for external use and the base document that employees use for their practical business ethics decisions. Inside the company, the code is backed up with more specific guidelines, training, and other learning aids. The themes of compliance, corporate culture, and fiscal responsibility run throughout the code, as does the company's unashamed support of the principle of market capitalism and an affirmation that its first duty is to return value to the shareholders.

Finally, the CPRB statement is a document created as a practical tool for corporate spokespersons to talk to stakeholder interest groups. It draws from the Code of Conduct and the values, but augments them with statements on topics not found in either. Its practical purpose is to have meaningful conversations with external social responsibility lobby groups without the company being drawn into formally signing onto the lobby group. It is intended to be a flexible, changing document that reflects the position that Intel has on leading edge Social Responsibility agendas.

Intel's Corporate Principles for a Responsible Business presents the company's minimum expectations with regard to ethical and legal business practices.[5]

> Intel adheres to strict standards of honesty and conducts business with uncompromising integrity and professionalism. The principles:
> • Reflect a corporate decision on how we perform global activities
> • Are relevant to all Intel employees worldwide
> • Are approved and managed by Intel's Executive Office
> • Are reviewed on a regular basis
> Intel is committed to apply internal management systems and reporting structures to ensure adherence to these principles across our organization. (Intel, 2004b, p. 3)

The CPRBs address: diversity in all aspect of the business; workplace harassment; environmental, health, and safety issues; employment practices;

privacy and security standards; bribes and kickbacks; unreasonable restraint of trade; and complicity with local laws and customs regarding employees. Intel's values provide the backbone for implementing the CPRBs and relate to risk taking, quality, great place to work, discipline, results orientation, and customer orientation. Both the CPRB and the company values provide the formal internal context wherein corporate social responsibility emerges.

INTEL'S SOCIAL SUSTAINABILITY STRATEGY AND STRUCTURE

Strategic Alternatives

In this section, we consider how Intel conceptualizes social sustainability. Three general strategic alternatives can be associated with corporate social responsibility (CSR).[6] The first and least encompassing strategy is to comply with the applicable laws and regulations, as well as, in some cases, powerful stakeholder expectations, such as those of owners/shareholders or labor unions. Meeting the requirements specified in laws and regulations limits a social sustainability strategy to a reactive one that focuses on meeting the minimum requirements necessary to ensure the organization will be able to continue to operate. We refer to this as a legitimation strategy, in that the only reason to address social sustainability issues is to maintain the organization's legitimacy as a viable actor within the socioeconomic context. The second strategy category privileges the long-term economic interest of the firm. If the motivation behind socially responsible actions is long-term economic gain, the decision rule will be to develop the most advantageous economic course of action and to accomplish it in the most socially sustainable way. The third category reflects the motivation to act in the public interest as a good citizen of the community. If the company is motivated by the desire to be socially sustainable, then the primary question asked is: What is the socially sustainable course of action and what is the most economical way of accomplishing that action?

We do not propose that these categories are mutually exclusive and independent. In some cases, one may be a necessary condition for one of the other categories. For example, if a company does not meet regulatory requirements, their right to operate may be terminated, impeding long-term economic success. Also, acting in a socially sustainable manner to enhance the public interest presumes meeting legal and regulatory requirements. Some minimal level of long-term economic success is required for the corporation to engage in socially sustainable actions over an extended period.

Quoting Craig Barrett, president and CEO, the Intel's first report on corporate responsibility[7] suggests an ongoing commitment to social responsibility:

Much like other core operating programs at Intel, our ideas about corporate responsibility are embedded in the way we do business throughout the organization—in human resources; purchasing; quality; investor relations; legal; and environmental, health and safety- in every aspect of our company. Our commitment to doing the right things right runs deep in our corporate culture. We don't view corporate responsibility as a fad or marketing scheme. In fact, much of what we address in this report has been a part of the way we've done business since Intel was founded in 1968. (Intel, 2001, p. 4)

Environmental issues appear to be the first corporate responsibility issues organizationally addressed. As the broad focus of society came onto environmental issues, they coincided with bottom line-driven opportunities to reduce cost by using less and reusing more. To the extent that the environmental messages are reduce, recycle, and reuse, they are embraced willingly by any commercial enterprise. Recycling and recovery of waste was always a high priority for Intel because of the high value of much of its waste. Gold, for instance, was an original wiring component. Environmental responsibility is not a new focus for Intel, but a natural development from its operational pressures and organizational values. Technology and Manufacturing (TMG) led in these efforts because of its size and the nature of its role within the company. Wafer Fabrications Plants use many chemicals, substantial amounts of materials, and large quantities of water. It was sensible, therefore, for the technical knowledge concerning environmental sustainability to be created within the TMG function, where it still resides. Environmental sustainability and its poorer cousin, waste management, initiated a pattern of organizational drift that carries over to the more recent social responsibilities. A pressing need and opportunity arise. The TMG operating group responds with vigor and focus, and then the responsibility moves by osmosis into the other sectors of the organization. TMG, through an extension of new building construction, also manages building services throughout the company so the conduit for ideas generated in the factory is already in place.

Little ambiguity exists as to Intel's top priority. Craig Barrett explains Intel's position in the 2001 Global Citizenship Report:

Over the past several years, expectations have changed. *Making a profit for shareholders is still the top priority.* However, corporations now are also expected to be good citizens. We view corporate citizenship as the relationship forged between Intel, the communities in which we operate and society in general. At Intel, corporate citizenship is firmly anchored in our corporate values. Although this is Intel's first public report focusing on corporate responsibility, it builds on our long-standing efforts to ensure accountability and transparency in our environmental, health and safety reporting—and also on our long-term commitment to being a good neighbor in our communities and a great place to work for our employees. (Intel, 2001, p. 5; italics added)

Intel's position on corporate social responsibility seems to go well beyond meeting society's minimum regulatory and legal standards. The company's social sustainability strategy appears firmly grounded in maximizing shareholder value. This strategy translates as asking first what is the most economically advantageous alternative and then asking what is the most sustainable, or least unsustainable, way of attaining the alternative.

Currently, there are two primary committees addressing what we have called social responsibility: the Ethics and Compliance Oversight Committee and Committee for Corporate Responsibility and Shareholder relations. These two committees reflect the emergent response to the business challenges faced by Intel. The members of the two committees include representatives from operational management, legal, human resources (HR), corporate finance, Audit, Ethics and Compliance, EHS, Information Technology (IT), Security, and Corporate Purchasing, and Corporate Responsibility. Each has its place at these cross-functional forums based on how their functional objectives play into the enterprise-level challenge. The power and relationships are fluid and change both with the challenges facing the business and with the players serving on the forum.

The fluidity stems from a combination of formal roles in the company and the passion and personality of the person holding the job. For example, for a number of years, a driving force on business ethics and compliance was the Purchasing function. The reason was simple. The purchasing function bought almost everything used inside the company and had a front row seat to potential conflicts of interest and actual theft. Purchasing took the lead in driving training, rules, and monitoring to prevent fraud and to create an ethical environment because they were there and because they had a passionate leader in Roger Whittier, the worldwide director of purchasing. Also, Audit has always played a central role, in part, because that is its function in a well-run company. In addition, the group was led by a passionate and energetic manager, Janice Wilkins, who used the independence and reporting responsibilities of the position to exert pressure for a more formal approach to the management of Ethics and Compliance in the company. Alternatively, although no one leader emerged at the enterprise level, EHS has always been a leading influence in the operating units. The risk exposure evidenced by the terrorist attacks of September 11th and the frequency of hacking has recently elevated IT to a position of prominence throughout the company.

Next, we consider the temporal and organizational dynamics that have resulted in the current authority and responsibility relationships. The process yields insights into corporate attitudes and processes associated with corporate social responsibility, providing an understanding of its place within the cornucopia of competing voices attended to in organizational management's decision making and actions.

Organizational Dynamics of Corporate Responsibility

Internal Dynamics

To understand the present, we consider the past, tracing the corporate responsibility function's origins back to the days when Intel first left its roots in the Santa Clara and started to build, mainly factories, in other locations. As the company grew and engaged a wider range of constituencies, it is not surprising that the lead in managing these constituency groups was taken by the division that was most directly interacted with them: site selection and manufacturing. The primary actors include a combination of treasury and tax money people and experienced manufacturing and construction managers. Tax and Treasury were involved because site selection usually involved some level of grant and tax breaks in exchange for the investment and job creation at the selected site. The public, at least in terms of its elected officials, were therefore front and center in the initial contact. Quite often for local tax legislation to pass, the voting public needed to be consulted; to manage the process, Intel recognized the necessity of Public Affairs. It was natural to leave that function reporting to the site manager at the location, who in turn reported to Construction and Factory Management in what became known as the TMG. TMG continued to own the function of Public Affairs for much of the next 40 years. The organizational structure was logical because the company's most visible action in the community was a factory building lasting at least 20 years. This practical dominance of TMG extends across a number of functions directly involved in the rainbow of Social Responsibility. TMG owns EHS and Material Purchasing and Logistics. This dominance stems from the critical role TMG plays in the daily operation of Intel and the importance of Manufacturing to the business model.

To return to Public Affairs, or what Intel would call good community relationships, as a factory is built, there are number of visible factors about which the public cares. First, there is visible change to the landscape in that new factories tend to be built on green field sites. As the site changes, the previous green or sandy field needs to be serviced by infrastructure ranging from water supply to roads. These activities impact the local community. For that local community, the approval of the Intel site was probably obtained on an expectation of job creation. All three of these factors—visible change in the landscape, infrastructure requirements, and employment—involve working with the community, understanding their perceptions and desires, and working together to solve problems. In general, this process is symbiotic because more jobs in the community are seen as desirable. As a result, there is a willingness to work together to remove roadblocks. Intel's public affairs group generally controlled these functions, as well as providing specific technical help where needed. Legal, Human Resources (HR), and knowledgeable engineers played important roles.

HR Management would naturally become a significant player because its expertise was not only necessary in staffing the new operation, but also in running the completed factory in carrying out the traditional roles of HR Management. At the local level, it was not unusual for HR Management to include the supervision of Public Affairs.

It soon became apparent that as you hire a workforce of young people, which tended to be the case for Intel, you acquire the cares of young families such as day care and schooling, Thus, early on, Public Affairs and HR Management meant understanding the local education system from pre-K to college level to help existing workers and to create a pipeline for future hires. Education was on the agenda for Intel as a shared concern with the community from the beginning for mutually beneficial reasons.

Hiring a large, educated, but essentially blue-collar workforce inevitably brought the attention of Unions. Intel held the philosophy that the introduction of a third party between the company and its workers was unhelpful to the efficient and nimble running of the company. Further, they believed that if workers were treated well, there would be no call for a union. Intel characterizes its attitude as not anti-union, but pro good people management. The legwork of such a stand fell to the combination of HR, Public Affairs, and its legal team, which at Intel is separate from the rest of Legal.

From the beginning, Public Affairs had a loose connection to Legal and Government Affairs. The scenario of a new site in a non-U.S. location involved the same conceptual players as a local expansion, but in this case the government players would be national- or supranational-level politicians, development agencies, and the like. At the top of the corporation, informal management committees were created so that Public Affairs, Legal, HR, Finance, and so on could stay linked on the status of "public and government affairs." Over the years, the informal and formal nature of the committees ebbed and flowed in a practical way. Public Affairs remained managed out of the ubiquitous TMG. Government Affairs reported into Legal when it did not report into the Chief Operating Officer.

EHS reflects the traditional, although minimalist, issues associated with social sustainability. Regulatory requirements are in place that, if not met, can result in operations being suspended. Thus, these issues must be attended to. As additional social issues arise, we might expect them to be addressed in ways similar to analogous past issues. For EHS, the pattern of TMG ownership arising from factory needs and then by osmosis into other units continues. Factories have always had a Health and Safety function because the factories contain hazardous substances and dangerous situations where training and technical knowledge is needed to mitigate the attendant risk. Following from extensive regulatory requirements, a large portion of the work is compliance. However, Intel has traditionally taken a more proactive position. For example, the company's programs have focused on formulating and implementing preventative actions, as opposed to only the necessary regulatory response. Similarly, proactive safety initiatives such as benchmarking industrial leaders (e.g., DuPont) have been undertaken to create a safe work environment, instead of only focusing on reducing accidents.

Safety has always been considered an important workplace agent item. Again, it originated within the factories and during the building of factories. From the beginning, Intel saw safety as the key priority during construction; it is not unusual to have a safety stand-down at a building site based on the suspicion that high safety standards were being compromised. A company is serious about safety when it is willing to put the project timeline at risk, rather than compromise safety standards.[8] No group has been as successful in bringing about changes in attitudes and actions, and many functions at Intel attempting to "influence the culture" look to the Safety group model. Another example of the osmosis from factory to office is the role that Safety played at a corporate level in partnership with Security in implementing programs for protecting Intel's property and people around the world. Organizationally, at a senior management level, the head of the EHS function and the head of Public Affairs reports to the head of TMG. Thus, these two players are on the same staff, and there is a natural cross-pollination of ideas at both the operational and strategic levels.

External Influences—Legislation

External influences have been instrumental in the evolution of the current committee structure described previously. In the early 1990s, the Federal Sentencing Guidelines recommended that major corporations have a senior-level committee to review compliance performance. Although Intel's reaction was that this rule was bureaucratic, they complied. The creation of the Compliance Oversight Committee, consisting of mainly director-level involvement with a smattering of vice president-level participation, tightened up some of the linkages between functions responsible for managing compliance. Finance, Legal, HR, and Government Relations at the corporate level and EHS and Public Affairs at the TMG level started to meet more often and more formally. Legal and Audit started to show up as the leader (*primus inter pares*) of this group for the practical reason that they had linkage to the Board, a linkage that followed a recommendation in the Federal Sentencing Guidelines.

The Sarbanes Oxley Act of 2002, which was followed up by a revision of the Federal Sentencing Guideline in 2004, introduced the concept of creating an ethical environment into the compliance mix and strengthened the practical need for the Ethics and Compliance Oversight Committee (ECOC). Over the next few years, the ECOC reviewed its role, tightened its processes, and gradually enriched its composition by including more senior players. The reporting relationship of legal and audit to the Board strengthened their leadership of the committee. However, the committee remained a working group of equals.

External Influences—Corporate Debacles

As an extralegal/regulatory response to the post-Enron/WorldComworld, Intel launched a program to reinforce its commitment to its corporate values. A program called Business Practice Excellence (BPX) was created in 2002, initially reporting to the COO. Through a major training program, it sought to remind the entire Intel population of the company's values. In parallel, the BPX group benchmarked the activities of other companies that had "ethics functions" in search of best practices and good ideas. BPX sought to create a corporate culture based on these values, rather than being driven by any specific compliance activity or objective. In the formulation and development of BPX, we see another example of an evolutionary drift from an attitude or focus on compliance (implementing processes that allow for identifying problems and taking action to correct them) to a focus on prevention (implementing processes that create a context where problems are less likely to arise). Organizationally, BPX was passed to internal audit after its initial creation. The logic for this move was twofold. First, the Audit function reported to the audit committee of the Board, which created governance independence. Second, the audit function already owned a big piece of integrity compliance. The Federal Sentencing Guideline update of 2004 added justification to this move because for the first time it defined what ethics and compliance should look like in a company. Not unrelatedly, Intel published its initial Global Citizen Report covering 2001 activities in 2002. (Also see Intel 2002, 2003)

External Influences—World Events

Around 2002, two functions—Security and Information Technology—started to play a stronger part in the corporate responsibility activities. The motivating factor for both was at least, in part, a reaction to the terrorist attacks of September 11, 2001, which awakened corporate America to the realization that supply lines, information lines, and human beings were at risk from external terrorist activity. A whole industry was spawned under the general heading of Business Continuity. For a while, in its setup phase, business continuity was run as a stand-alone function reporting into the corporate office. Once the base goals were achieved, it was passed through IT to Security. Security reports to the ubiquitous TMG for the same practical reasons as other functions mentioned before (i.e., the first security risk exposures started there).

Security for Intel started as security for product in transit and people in the work environment. There have been times when Intel product has been more valuable per ounce than gold. As Intel manufacturing extended across the world, the risk of losing product or becoming a target of an anti-American terrorist action grew. The response was to create a Security function that spanned the globe and was capable for detecting and protecting

Intel property and people. The security function was staffed, in part, with experienced law enforcement officers and cooperated on a global basis with local law enforcement. Born in the factory, Security continues to work for the TMG organization.

IT also is an enterprise function spanning the globe. The Intel machine has of course become more and more dependent on Information Systems to conduct business. The terrorist attacks and the increase of hacker activity created a need for Information Security as a stand-alone topic with a voice at the ECOC. Information Security does not report to TMG.

Most of the activity described earlier arose from a business need. It was a business need seen in terms of Intel's own self-interest and a respect for people, community, and the environment. In parallel to this, the Corporate Social Responsibility lobby outside of Intel had been watching corporate business and its behavior. The watchers ranged from single-topic lobby groups to broader "best of" measures conducted by the business magazines. Institutional investors also started to play watching and measuring roles. Their motivation was driven, in part, based on what investors were asking for and, in part, from their own shock in the post-Enron world at the paucity of corporate governance. The concatenation of these drives becomes a factor for Intel, and it became Corporate Responsibility's role to understand this new phenomenon and to respond to it. In typical Intel fashion, a responsive approach soon became a proactive approach. The Social Responsibility function within Public Affairs sought out the institutional investors and the lobby groups and learned what they cared about and how their measurements worked. Back inside, these findings were used to evaluate Intel's actions, reach or refine position statements, and to adjust wordings and actions where appropriate. By 2007, this role had become so significant that its connection to Legal was strengthened.

In summary, we provide the following observations from our consideration of Intel's strategy and structure as illustrated in Figure 9.1. There appear to be four interrelated forces motivating and channeling corporate social responsibility: legal and regulatory compliance requirements, expectations of influential constituencies, fiscal viability, and corporate culture. Organizationally, the focal location for corporate social responsibility issues has evolved from operational oriented functions to public relations-oriented groups more oriented toward responding to external constituencies. There has been an evolution in how corporate social responsibility is perceived as the company moved from focusing more on compliance toward an attitude that creates a proactive context that emphasizes and facilitates prevention. These dimensions are not unrelated or linear, and we make no claims as to directionality or causality. Next, we consider how these organizational dynamics are manifest in programs, goals, and resource allocations and associated outcomes by undertaking an analysis of Intel's CRR for 2005.

THE PUBLIC FACE OF CORPORATE RESPONSIBILITY

The four motivating factors of legal and regulatory compliance, external constituency expectations, fiscal viability, and corporate culture are translated into modalities that facilitate their implementation. Programs and procedures are developed, goals are set, and, as a result, resources are allocated, resulting in observable outcomes such as community involvement, support for educational programs, and economic benefits. We look at an explicit public response by Intel to social sustainability issues as reflected in its 2005 CRR to better understand how social responsibility was operationalized and represented during 2005. This snapshot is at best incomplete, but can be useful in articulating the company's inclinations or at least what it wants the perception of those outcomes to be. Also, an evaluation of the outcomes may provide some indication as to the relative influence of the various motivational considerations.

In the Executive Perspective section, Paul Otellini, president and CEO, and Craig Barrett, Chairman of the Board, state that

> 2005 was a year of significant change for Intel. In addition to evolving our business strategy and reinvigorating our brand, we have taken a more focused approach to corporate responsibility. We have worked to more clearly define what corporate responsibility means to Intel, and we met with stakeholders in formal and informal feedback sessions to clarify the key corporate responsibility issues for the company. . . . Corporate responsibility is about good management and a commitment to doing things right. (Intel, 2005, pp. 3–4)

As a result, Intel (2005) now defines *corporate responsibility* as "achieving business success in ways that hone our ethical values and demonstrate respect for people and the planet" (p. 3). This statement reaffirms the primacy of the economic (business) perspective expressed earlier. Three principles guide the company's actions with respect to corporate responsibility: operating with integrity and transparency, strengthening the communities within which the company operates, and improving people's lives through technology. The report identifies the three areas most relevant to the company's corporate responsibility efforts: environment, education, and community. As noted earlier, because our focus is on social sustainability, we consider only the latter two areas. A fourth section of the 2005 report, entitled "Our Business," also is included, and it more explicitly addresses the related fiscal issues and legal compliance issues.

Education[9]

Since its inception in 1968, Intel has invested more than $1 billion worldwide in education programs. The assumption motivating these actions is the belief that education is critical in inspiring and harnessing creativity and innovation. Three stated core objectives include: teaching and learning with technology; advancing mathematics, science, and engineering; and promoting educational development through working with educators, governments, and multilateral organizations (World Bank; United Nations Educational, Scientific, and Cultural Organization; World Economic Forum). Programs include: teacher training programs; after-school programs; and mentoring for, and access to, information technology. The stated objective of these programs is to "accelerate improvement in education for the knowledge economy" (Intel, 2005, p. 20). Toward these programs, the company invests $100 million in 50 different countries. A section in the CRR discusses each of the core objective areas in more detail.

Community[10]

Intel engages with local communities exploring opportunities that "align local needs with our corporate and employee expertise" seeking "positive impacts on education, environmental stewardship and safety, and community development around the globe." The company views "being a community asset as a critical component of our business success"; terms the approach *strategic philanthropy*, which attempts to maximize the payoff of the contributions by selecting opportunities that "align Intel business with the needs of our communities and the expertise of our employees" (Intel, 2005, p. 28); and attempts to engage community stakeholders as part of business practice. Total cash and in-kind 2005 donations by the company, Intel foundation, and employee contributions totaled more than $110 million. The contributions go to programs worldwide and encompass a wide range of activities.

The community activities are outlined in the CRR. Community involvement of Intel employees is summarized in terms of community educational activities, community development, and environmental improvements and is broken down by the country within which the activities took place. Next, the way Intel technology and people come together in meeting community challenges are discussed. Most of these activities relate to the application of, and support for, information technology to underserved constituencies, such as students, farmers, and communities in developing countries, as well as health care applications in the United States. Specific programs such as the Middle East initiative and disaster relief efforts of Intel and its employees also are presented.

Our Business[11]

Interestingly, the next section is entitled "Our Business" and contains information about the restructuring of the company from a microprocessor focus to a platform focus, and it points out their intention to reinvigorate their brand. Next, the CRR presents an organizational profile and a summary of economic performance. It appears that these subsections are included to provide some context for what follows. The next topic is stakeholder engagement, which discusses the company's attempts and methods for engaging its stakeholders and, in some sense, bolsters the legitimacy of the claims made.

One of the areas identified during earlier stakeholder inquiries as needing more transparency was the company's political activities. Two areas are explicitly considered in the 2005 report: government and regulatory stakeholders and political contributions. Both activities exert influence on the political and regulatory processes. Their worldwide policy agenda considers policy topics with the objective of: "fully understanding the various perspectives, and educating legislators about the effects that planned regulations may have on our industry's business processes" and to "contribute constructively to the public policy debate on issues that affect our business, our customers and our employees" (Intel, 2005, p. 51). The specific areas of engagement include: innovation, intellectual property, broadband, workforce, trade policy and market access, legal reform, digital health care, environment, logistics and transportation, and education. Although these issues are laudable, as expected, the company's perspectives reflect a rather traditional neoclassical/free-market view of business–government relationships. Ultimately, the company's actions are attempts to protect and enhance Intel's interests. To conclude that this behavior is acting in a sustainable, or even in a responsible way, in terms of social sustainability, one must accept the assumptions that underlie the utilitarian economic theory.

The first issue considered is innovation. "Continuing innovation and creating the solutions that will improve our lives in the future depends on policies that promote basic, collaborative research and protects intellectual property" (Intel, 2005, p. 51) In addressing this issue, Intel attempts to elevate it in the public debate. The company has been involved in issuing reports and meeting with Vice President Cheney and other top White House staff personnel. Several successful legislative initiatives are cited. Such policies may be beneficial to society, but, at least at some general level, they allow companies like Intel to shift Research and Development costs onto the public sector.

Intellectual property rights are critical to Intel's success in several ways. First, the company as an innovator profits from the exclusive use of the technology. Second, the company wants to facilitate the spread of IT and electronic products that use Intel's products. To this end, the company supports the reduction or elimination in tariffs and levies on such equipment and supports free trade agreements. It could be argued that these perspectives on intellectual property are somewhat at odds. The first allows premium profits though restricted access, thus reducing access to the products. The second argues for reducing levies and restrictions to increase demand. The first relates to, for example, chips produced by Intel. The second relates to products in which Intel's chips are installed. Again, the judgment as to the degree to which society benefits by one or both is debatable.

Several specific issues were addressed. Intel joined with other interested parties in persuading the Federal Trade Commission to adopt broadband "connectivity principles" in the name of spurring the growth of new services and technologies through promoting broadband deployment and limited broadband regulation. To enhance access to a talented workforce, the company advocated the increase in H-1B visas. Free trade through the removal of trade barriers and enhanced market access appear to be general tenets of the Intel's political strategy. Again, opening new markets and continued innovation seem to motivate these actions.

The company supported and lobbied for the passage of the Class Action Reform bill that limited plaintiff's rights in class action suits and has been viewed as beneficial to business to the detriment of other groups. Intel is working for passage of patent reform that would impose rules constraining damages awarded in such suits. Government is called on to take a leadership role in integrating IT into the health care industry. Digital health care is one of Intel's emerging product lines. Addressing the environment, the company works with governments to develop environmental energy policies that are sustainable as well as preserving the ability to innovate and operate. Intel advocates a risk-based approach to cargo security as a way of resolving the trade-off between security and the flow of commerce. The company also has worked with the Department of Education to improve math and science education in the United States.

The next section in the CRR discusses the political contributions made by the company and its employer through the Intel PAC. The evaluation criteria include voting record on Intel's public policy issues, support and concern for Intel's values, and presence and engagement. A total of $176,445 in contributions was distributed. A list of the recipients is provided on the CRR website. Intel responds with respect to corporate contributions as follows: "We will continue to work to collect additional information regarding local U.S. contributions and trade group memberships for future reports" (Intel, 2005, p. 54)

The remaining pages (56–87) address various related topics. Challenges and opportunities include: reputation management in the face of allegations of anticompetitive business practices; workforce representation of females, African Americans, Hispanics, and Native Americans; reducing chemical waste generation; understanding gaps in global medical insurance coverage for HIV/AIDS; implementing of the Electronics Industry Code of Conduct across a complex and vast supply chain; improving communications about political contributions and public policy positions; training their global workforce on regionally relevant ethical expectations; training their global workforce on the restrictions that export controls place on their business activities; and ensuring robust community stakeholder engagement models at new Intel sites. Relatedly, a summary of the 2006 goals are presented under the headings of Environment, Education, Community, and Business/Workplace. Supply-chain responsibility commitment and scope, coupled with assessment procedures and training, addresses such issues as: child and forced labor, freedom of association and collective bargaining, nondiscrimination, working hours and minimum wages, environmental standards, and worker health and safety. In addition, the company's awards and recognitions are included, along with information about workforce diversity, employee training, health and safety, work/life balance, governance and ethics, and active litigation.

Observations

Intel publishes a relatively progressive CRR that seems to cover the accepted areas. The CRR website includes an additional report following the GRI 2002 Sustainability Reporting Guidelines. Both reports are voluntarily prepared and made publicly available. Neither the CRR nor the GRI report is externally verified. Although these reports include problems, they are probably about as good as one would expect from a large, publicly held corporation. As would be expected from voluntary disclosure, the positive overshadows the negative, but goals and actual performance are compared, as well as a brief discussion of areas representing challenges and opportunities.

The report addresses corporate social responsibility, but we find little concerning social sustainability explicitly. As noted earlier, social sustainability is not part of the vocabulary at Intel. It seems that social responsibility is viewed analogous to corporate philanthropy. That is, it is a good thing to do as a good citizen in the global or local community; as long as there are excess resources, the company can make the decision to be socially responsible, at least in the ways they choose to specify it. However, these programs are not generally seen as the organization's primary responsibility, as noted in the quotes by the CEO and the chairman presented earlier. Generally, companies do not have much latitude to act otherwise. Such a position is established by the current legal and regulatory structure, reflecting the extant norms of global market capitalism.

The norms of global market capitalism can be summarized as follows. Free markets fairly distribute resources, in that they provide unbiased measures of value. This perceived unbiased rendering provides the basis for moral legitimacy. Stockholders/owners are the privileged stakeholder group, and, as such, the overriding objective of the organization is to maximize shareholder value. Generally, the dominant discourse within an organization revolves around financial representations, and performance evaluation criteria are generally articulated in terms of financial targets. Meritocracy based on market results represents fair and equitable resource allocations and should provide the basis of organizational rewards. Healthy competition yields ingenuity and dexterity. Informed risk taking is strongly encouraged and is seen as the driving force for progress and innovation. External constraints are to be constrictively overcome, eliminating barriers to progress. Accountability and control are achieved through markets and formal control mechanisms.

Unfortunately, many of the socially sustainable issues are not incorporated into the current market mechanisms. For example, education costs are not incorporated into the cost function of economic organizations. Intel, not solely altruistically, but commendable nonetheless, recognizes the importance of math and science education in innovation, which is central to the success of an organization in a high-tech sector and has initiated programs and allocated resources to advance these objectives. Thus, supporting social institutions are at the discretion of management, and the adequacy of such support is limited by the ability to justify a "legitimate business purpose" to the shareholders.

MOTIVATION TO OUTCOMES

We consider how Intel responds to its conception of corporate social responsibility. As summarized in Figure 9.1, three levels are considered: motivational forces, modalities for operationalizing responses to the forces, and the resulting outcomes. There are four motivational or pressure dimensions. Fiscal viability concerns the economic viability of the enterprise and is primarily motivated by the demands of the financial capital markets. Maximizing shareholder value is the primary driving force, and, generally, return on investment, or some variation thereon, is the primary evaluation criteria. Legal and regulatory requirements are the codified minimum requirements imposed by society for a corporation to be allowed to participate as a part of its economic sector. Within Western democratic capitalism, the citizens through their elected representatives prescribe these parameters of acceptable behavior. External constituencies such as suppliers, customers, workers, and advocacy groups also influence organizational activities. Although not as formal and codified as legal or regulatory requirements, the pressure to act comes through persuasion or leverage along the supply chain. The fourth motivating element is the corporate culture and is grounded in the company's values and norms. It is colloquially referred to in Intel as "doing the right thing right."

These forces are operationalized through programs and procedures developed across the various organizational units, as well as at the central management levels. Goals are established and resources are allocated. These modalities provide the means for implementing values and taking action. For Intel, the outcomes are represented by specific programs that come under the rubric of community involvement and educational support. Environmental issues also are a central part of their publicly reported activities. Economic benefits represent a primary expected outcome from the social programs. The outcomes provide feedback to both the operational modalities and the motivating forces, both of which can be evaluated, reinforced, or changed.

Within Intel, there appears to be an evolutionary progression of corporate responsibility issues that moves from a compliance-motivated start to the creation of a process for identifying problems and risks and taking action to eliminate or prevent them from occurring. This progression also is reflected in the migration of issues through the formal organizational structure. Further, in light of this history and their link to the fiscal viability of the company, it is not surprising to find the three areas defined as the focus of its corporate responsibility efforts to be education, community involvement, and the environment. Good relations with the community have always been seen as both a necessity in doing business and the right thing to do. In the same way, the symbiotic relationship between improving math and science education and the benefit of an educated workforce and customer bases is clear. Caring for the environment, combined with the well-being of the workforce and the surrounding community, have been requirements for economic success that have returned dividends, literally, in terms of economic benefits and, figuratively, in terms of satisfying the company's desire to do the right thing. Not surprisingly, Intel showcases these activities, but that does not negate for the contribution, although constructive criticism is appropriate.

CLOSING COMMENTS

Acting in a socially sustainable manner is acting to enhance the long term well-being of social institutions such as the family, community, education, and government. The moral legitimacy of social sustainability rests on acting in the public interest. Not only does acting in the public interest provide the moral context wherein an action or activity is contemplated and legitimized, it represents the distinguishing characteristic of the social contract by granting rights, privileges, and status in return for the organization acting in the interest of society. Business organizations represent one of the primary societal institutions and should play a central role in ensuring the long-term viability of a democratically governed society grounded in justice, equality, and trust and supported by sustainable natural, social, and economic systems. Organizational management is specifically granted fiduciary responsibility over society's economic resources (human, financial, technical, and natural). Exercising these rights establishes an ethic of accountability, whereby organizational management agrees to being held accountable by society, who grants these rights, and society accepts responsibility for holding organizational management accountable for the use of the resources. To be held accountable, organizational management must provide transparent and understandable information. Accountability requires that actual outcomes be evaluated with respect to some relevant criteria set that reflects the norms and values of the society, not those of powerful special interests.

Intel is a progressive company that is probably at the leading edge in exercising social responsibility, but there is still a long way to go before one might claim social sustainability is attained. To consign the blame solely to the corporation is misplaced. Although it could do better, there are legitimate institutional constraints that prevent a more complete commitment of social sustainability. It is the responsibility of the people within the society and the political system of which they are a part to create an environment that supports, nay demands, socially sustainable actions on the part of all members of the economic sector. If society can grant the right to corporations to act as trustees of its economic resources, then it must exercise the responsibility of specifying the expectations associated with the use of those resources, and it must hold corporations accountable for the extent to which these expectations are met. CRRs such as issued by Intel may represent a nod in the right direction; however, the current regulatory and reporting regime falls woefully short in providing information and understanding necessary to foster and monitor social sustainability within an advanced industrial society.

REFERENCES

Brown, D., J. Dillard, and S. Marshall. 2005. "Incorporating Natural Systems as Part of Accounting's Public Interest Responsibility." *Journal of Information Systems* 19 (2): 79–103.
Intel. 2001. "Vision and Values." *Global Citizenship Report.*
Intel. 2002. "Accountability in Action." *Global Citizenship Report.*
Intel. 2003. "Everything Matters." *Global Citizenship Report.*
Intel. 2004a. "Continuity and Commitment." *Global Citizenship Report.*
Intel. 2004b. *Intel Policy Set.*
Intel. 2005. "Let's Be Clear." *Corporate Responsibility Report.*
Intel. 2006. "It's What's Inside That Counts." *2006 Annual Report.*

APPENDIX A: INTEL'S VALUES
(Source: Intel, 2004b, pp. 5–6)

At Intel, we believe in doing a great job for our customers, employees, and stockholders by being the preeminent building-block supplier to the worldwide Internet economy. Our values are put into practice each day by our employees and govern how we deal with our communities and each of our customers. Our values are at the heart of everything we do.

Risk Taking—We strive to:

- Foster innovation and creative thinking.
- Embrace change and challenge the status quo.

- Listen to all ideas and viewpoints.
- Learn from our successes and mistakes.
- Encourage and reward informed risk taking.

Quality—We strive to:

- Achieve the highest standards of excellence.
- Do the right things right.
- Continuously learn, develop, and improve.
- Take pride in our work.

Great Place to Work—We strive to:

- Be open and direct.
- Promote a challenging work environment that develops our diverse workforce.
- Work as a team with respect and trust for each other.
- Win and have fun.
- Recognize and reward accomplishments.
- Manage performance fairly and firmly.
- Be an asset to our communities worldwide.

Discipline—We strive to:

- Conduct business with uncompromising integrity and professionalism.
- Ensure a safe, clean, and injury-free workplace.
- Make and meet commitments.
- Properly plan, fund, and staff projects.
- Pay attention to detail.

Results Orientation—We strive to:

- Set challenging and competitive goals.
- Focus on output.
- Assume responsibility.
- Constructively confront and solve problems.
- Execute flawlessly.

Customer Orientation—We strive to:

- Listen and respond to our customers, suppliers, and stakeholders.
- Clearly communicate mutual intentions and expectations.
- Deliver innovative and competitive products and services.
- Make it easy to work with us.
- Excel at customer satisfaction.

APPENDIX B: INTEL CORPORATE PRINCIPLES
FOR RESPONSIBLE BUSINESS
(Source: Intel, 2004b, pp. 3–4)

- Intel respects, values, and welcomes diversity in its workforce, its customers, its suppliers, and the global marketplace. Intel will comply with applicable laws and provide equal employment opportunity for all applicants and employees without regard to race, color, religion, sex, national origin, ancestry, age, disability, veteran status, marital status, sexual orientation, or gender identity. This regulation applies to all areas of employment. Intel also provides reasonable accommodation to disabled applicants and employees to enable them to apply for and perform the essential functions of their jobs.
- Intel will provide a workplace free of sexual harassment as well as harassment based on race, color, religion, sex, national origin, ancestry, age, disability, veteran status, marital status, sexual orientation, or gender identity. We will not tolerate such harassment of employees by managers, coworkers, or nonemployees in the workplace.
- Intel is committed to achieving high standards of environmental quality and product safety, and to providing a safe and healthful workplace for our employees, contractors, and communities. We strive to comply with all applicable regulatory requirements as a minimum and implement programs and processes to achieve greater protection, where appropriate. We seek a healthful and safe workplace, free of occupational injury and illness. We strive to conserve natural resources and reduce the environmental burden of waste generation and emissions to the air, water, and land.
- Intel expects its suppliers to comply with applicable laws concerning occupational health, safety, and environmental protection; to strive for a workplace free of occupational injuries and illnesses; and to engage in manufacturing that minimizes impact to the environment and the community. We expect suppliers to maintain progressive employment practices that meet or exceed all applicable laws. These practices include nondiscrimination in employment practices, prohibiting the use of child or forced labor, and providing minimum wages, employees' benefits, and work hours. In the event that local standards do not exist, suppliers shall nonetheless establish progressive employment practices and shall apply U.S. standards where appropriate.
- Intel will not employ anyone under the age of 16 in any position. Intel expects its suppliers to comply with this expectation in placing contingent workers on Intel assignment.
- Intel honors the personal privacy of consumers, customers, and employees. Intel is committed to user privacy in our products and services. We support consumer choice and informed consent.

- Intel will provide a secure business environment for the protection of our employees, product, materials, equipment, systems, and information.
- Intel prohibits bribes and kickbacks. Intel employees may not offer or accept a bribe or a kickback. Bribes and kickbacks are prohibited either directly or through a third party.
- Intel encourages competition, which benefits consumers by prohibiting unreasonable restraints on trade. Intel competes vigorously while adhering to both the letter and spirit of antitrust laws.

Intel is committed to complying with all applicable laws regarding employees in each of the countries in which we operate. This pledge includes laws regarding minimum ages for employment; minimum wages and overtime compensation; benefits; discrimination and affirmative action; employees' right to raise issues and work collectively for their mutual benefit; and health and safety.

NOTES

1. We wish to acknowledge the support provided by the Center for Professional Integrity and Accountability, School of Business Administration, Portland State University.
2. At the time, the second author was the head of Intel's Business Practice Excellence Group and participated in the report's preparation.
3. The information presented in this section was derived from various public sources, Intel's website (www.intel.com), and the 2006 Form 10-K.
4. Based on total annual revenues.
5. Intel Policy Set (www.intel.com) Policy Manual 2004.
6. For a more complete discussion of these ideas related to environmental sustainability, see Brown Dillard, and Marshall (2005).
7. The first four reports (2001–2004) were called Global Citizenship Reports. The name was changed to Corporate Responsibility Report in 2005.
8. During the building of the Fab in Ireland, Intel is credited with changing the entire attitude toward safety in the construction industry of Ireland.
9. Covers pages 20–27 in the CRR.
10. Covers pages 28–42 in the CRR.
11. Covers pages 43–86 in the CRR.

10 Working out Social Sustainability on the Ground

Kathryn Thomsen and Mary C. King

Defining and implementing the social aspect of sustainability is evolving in practice as people commit themselves and their organizations to becoming more sustainable. As remarked on many times in this volume, the social aspect of sustainability has received little attention from researchers or environmental organizations, so practitioners have been left to their own devices in this area. For this chapter, we interviewed small business owners with a reputation for sustainable practices to discover both their conceptions of the social aspect of sustainability and what actions they were taking that we might think of as fostering social sustainability.

What we found was that, although each of the business owners set organizational standards for labor practices and community engagement that were substantially higher than the conventional business model, they were not working with a clear definition of *social sustainability* or of how social goals connect with progress toward environmental sustainability. However, several of their practices—undertaken in the spirit of "doing the right thing" without reference to sustainability—not only fit our working definition of the social aspect of sustainability, but were perceived by the business owners as making good business sense. An analysis and synthesis of their practices may provide the building blocks of a potential code for the social aspect of sustainability, similar to the guidelines for environmental sustainability found in green building standards.

What follows is a short section providing the context in which these interviews were conducted, synopses of each interview, and a concluding discussion. We use pseudonyms for our interviewees and false names for their businesses, although we recognize that people familiar with Portland, Oregon, may well recognize our subjects.

CONTEXT

Portland, Oregon's reputation for sustainability reflects a relatively widespread interest in environmentalism, found in the business community as well as elsewhere. The Natural Step U.S. is based in Portland, where businesses ranging from large transnationals, such as Nike and Hewlett Packard, are participating in the Oregon Natural Step Network, along with a number of small businesses such as the four participating in this study.

Although each of the businesses discussed next are members of the Oregon Natural Step Network, this network appears to provide relatively little guidance on the social aspect of sustainability. One of the Natural Step International's (2007) four "conditions that must be met in order to have a sustainable society" is focused on people, but states only that "people are not subject to conditions that systematically undermine their capacity to meet their needs." It is not clear just what a condition like this might definitively preclude.

We are working with an understanding of social sustainability as elaborated in the definition developed by scholars and students in the graduate sustainability program at Portland State University. It is delineated in two parts as both (a) the processes that generate social health and well-being now and in the future, and (b) those social institutions that facilitate environmental and economic sustainability now and for the future.

This definition guided us in our interviews, conducted in May of 2005, with four successful Portland business owners and their principal employees. The firms are engaged in different kinds of businesses, including fast food, professional consulting, and recycled building materials. The companies range in size from 35 employees to 250, and from gross sales of $3 million to more than $50 million.

These four firms were selected because of their history of implementing environmentally sustainable measures in their daily business practices, for their business success, and for the variety in their size and industry. All of the business owners have, for a number of years, been actively engaged with and influenced by the Oregon Natural Step, a network of Oregon businesses and organizations integrating strategic sustainability decisions into daily operations. Each of them was attracted to working with Natural Step because of prior interests and has independently explored the issue of sustainability.

Most of the business owners also share other common traits. All are active in the community, whether through committees connected to public agencies, membership on the boards of nonprofits, hands-on volunteer work, or environmental education. Most expressed strongly held values of fairness and social justice, as well as commitment to environmentalism.

The business owners were asked to describe their views of social sustainability. None of the respondents had a clear definition of social sustainability, and each looked to the interviewer to provide one. When no definition was forthcoming, respondents were guided into thinking about social sustainability in the context of what social aspects are important for business. Invariably, discussions shifted back to the more familiar ground of the environmentally oriented actions that each interviewee had thought more about and to which they had committed themselves and their organizations to an admirable degree. Therefore, it was within the framework of environmental sustainability that questions of the social aspect of sustainability were posed again and again. The following questions were incorporated through the interview process:

- How do you define social sustainability?
- What social aspects do you think are important for sustainability?
- Do you consciously incorporate these social aspects in business and with your employees?
- Do you use a guide or indicators for social decisions within business?
- Do you think that social standards or codes are important? Which ones?
- Which social aspects do you feel are not your responsibility?
- Do you believe incorporating social sustainability practices is your ethical responsibility? If so, have you always believed that?
- Does practicing social sustainability make your business more profitable?
- Are any of the following social benefits or issues important considerations for your business?
  - A living wage
  - Full medical coverage
  - Day care reimbursement
  - Wage equality
  - Employee turnover rate

INTERVIEW WITH THE OWNER OF THREE PIZZERIAS

"Steve" and his wife own a small chain of three specialty restaurants in Portland, which employ 75 people and bring in annual gross sales of more than $3 million. The company emphasis is on high-quality, fresh and locally grown ingredients. "Eco-Pizza" is not just a "pizza place," but a four-star pizza restaurant. Most everything is made from scratch—from pepperoni to soda to chocolate chip cookies—and most ingredients are locally grown.

Environmental Business Practices

Steve wanted a business that he would be proud to pass on to his children. His interest in sustainability was strongly affected by an Oregon Natural Step presentation about 10 years ago. He was sold on the idea of a personal commitment to sustainability in holistic business practices that aim to do business with reduced environmental impacts. Eco-Pizza follows practices designed to reduce waste, energy use, hormones, and pesticides.

Eco-Pizza minimizes fuel used in transportation (to reduce greenhouse gas emissions) by relying as much as possible on local growers or producers for food, supplies, and services. Free bus passes are provided to employees, and Eco-Pizza is working toward an all-electric delivery fleet.

Eco-Pizza supports a local meatpacking and processing cooperative by entering into guaranteed contracts paying more than the market rate and purchasing whole animals. Without this contractual agreement, a local processing facility could not survive. Further, whenever possible, Eco-Pizza's meat products are free range and hormone-free. Steve's wheat source is Food Alliance-approved, based on a standard that goes beyond the organic certification process to include labor standards and no-till agricultural practices geared toward reducing greenhouse gases.

All packaging is recycled and reduced with reusable and returnable delivery boxes. Eco-Pizza is the first small-scale restaurant participating in a new county effort to encourage on-site composting, virtually eliminating food scraps from the waste stream.

Socially Oriented Business Practices

For Steve, the definition of *social sustainability* begins with the employee, who comes first, but he also thinks that it comes from living and doing business with a sense of local and community responsibility. Employee health and well-being directly impacts the success of the business: "If the employees are healthy and happy, then so is the business."

Some environmentally driven practices have social benefits as side effects. Buying locally supports the local economy and ensures that farmers in the region have the long-term commitment they need, from a significant vendor, to stay in business. An incidental social benefit of supporting organic agriculture is the reduction of potential health risks faced by farmers and field workers. Similarly, the provision of free bus passes benefits restaurant employees as well as the environment.

More socially based business practices at Eco-Pizza include paying wages for foodservice that are high end and atypical. For nonmanagement, nonsalaried foodservice workers Eco-Pizza was paying $10–12 per hour, when the 2005 minimum wage in Oregon was $7.25.

Health care is provided for salaried, management staff only. Steve would like to provide health care benefits for all his employees, but does not think he could stay in business with the small margin that he operates on, coupled with extra costs from environmental practices. However, there is a medical plan that employees can purchase. Steve laments that the burden of health care is unfairly placed on business when it should be the responsibility of the government.

As well as high entry-level wages, Eco-Pizza provides paid vacation time for all employees, an IRA for all employees, flexible work schedules and leaves of absence, a good working environment, free bus passes or bicycle subsidies, employee meals, family lunch, and birthday gift bonuses.

Steve believes that it is important for the company to have a success-ful and close relationship with the community. This philosophy extends to the practice of developing long-term relationships with local suppliers and farmers, even to the extent of sun-drying local tomatoes for use during the winter months.

Eco-Pizza is active in educational efforts. The restaurant sponsors field trips to the restaurant for elementary and middle-school children, during which they make dough, learn the intricacies of making pizza when all the ingredients are made from scratch, and are taught about the impact of food on the environment from energy use to carbon emissions to waste. Steve and his staff volunteer for other educational efforts, such as speaking engagements concerned with food and environmental impact and talking with people at public agencies and universities.

Steve considers himself an activist. He led "Operation Big Stink," work-ing with local representatives to bring pressure on the insurance industry to ensure lightweight vehicles. He and other staff members participate in a number of other community, educational, and charity functions, particu-larly oriented toward food and environmentalism.

Steve believes there is a business case for social sustainability, although a perspective beyond business profits may be necessary to see it. A new defi-nition might take into consideration the social impacts of business.

Steve supports the idea of social codes for business, stating that "the bigger the business, the more important it is to have social codes." He believes that social codes are as important as environmental standards, such as organic certification and standards, and that third-party certifica-tion is critical to their success.

AN INTERVIEW WITH THE OWNER OF AN ENERGY CONSULTING FIRM

"Salim" owns "Enertec," an energy consulting firm that provides analyti-cal and strategic consulting to companies, government, nonprofit agencies, financial services companies, water supply and wastewater utilities, and other businesses requiring advanced analytic services. Thirty-five people work for Enertec, which has gross revenues of more than $5 million annually.

Environmental Business Practices

Enertec has worked toward attaining a level of environmental responsibil-ity over a number of years, and it has won several awards for sustainable practices. These awards were for purchasing green office products, out-standing recycling efforts, and significant steps toward the reduction of transportation-related pollution. Recently Enertec was recognized for the greening of their new office space—an entire floor of a "brown" building downtown. Greening the office space involved using paints with low levels of the volatile organic compounds (VOCs) that can pollute indoor air for years, installing cork flooring, purchasing used furniture, and installing sustainably harvested wood—practices the building owner is now interested in applying to other floors.

The company has supported the employee purchase of low-emission vehicles by offering a $150 monthly subsidy for each employee toward car payments of alternatively fueled vehicles. The transportation subsidy also goes to employees who ride bicycles to work.

Socially Oriented Business Practices

Although Salim is not really sure what a definition of *social sustainability* would be, he believes that he has been programmed with a deep-seated sense of obligation to conduct business in a socially responsible way. He believes that it is our responsibility to take care of the planet because we are "just visiting." Salim has two small children and is concerned that this generation of children is getting a "bum deal" because they are inheriting a tremendous debt. Excessive garbage and fewer resources due to thoughtless squandering of resources will be their legacy if we do not take drastic measures now.

As well as the generous subsidy for alternative transportation, Enertec provides employees with a 401-K matching retirement plan, invested only in "sustainable funds;" full medical coverage for employees (who are largely professional); flex time; paid time off during the week between Christmas and New Year's Day; 3 weeks of personal time per year; and $500 a year for personal development, such as enrolling in classes not related to work.

Although professional salaries "may not be the highest in the industry," because the firm serves many nonprofit and low-income clients, a living wage is important, as well as the staff earnings ratio. The highest paid person does not earn more than four times what the lowest paid employee is paid.

Client and consulting services offered at Enertec focus on environmental and social sustainability, conservation, renewable energy, and issues of equity, welfare, or social justice. The Enertec staff pursues these goals in other ways as well. For instance, after participating in a campaign for a state-wide tax increase to support schools and social services that ultimately failed, Enertec employees calculated how much they would have paid in additional taxes had the measure passed and donated those funds—with an Enertec match—to a local program serving abused children.

Salim believes that there is a business case for socially sustainable business practices. Specifically, Enertec enjoys extremely low employee turnover and a high level of employee commitment to the work, attracts excellent staff, and finds that their sustainable business practices are both attractive to potential clients and give Enertec an edge when bidding for state and city contracts.

Salim advocates a socially sustainable code, starting with a focus on children's programs. As long as environmental and social costs are not born by businesses, it will be hard to convince the general business community to implement sustainable actions. Therefore, voluntary business practices need to be supplemented with regulations requiring higher environmental and social standards of all businesses.

REFURBISHMENT, PRODUCTION, AND SALES OF VINTAGE FURNITURE, HARDWARE, AND FIXTURES

"John" owns "Rehab Inc," which refurbishes, produces, and sells vintage furniture, hardware, and fixtures locally and online. Rehab Inc started in the late 1970s as an architectural salvage retailer and now has annual sales of more than $35 million, employing more than 250 people.

Environmental Business Practices

Rehab Inc has worked with the Oregon Natural Step to reduce the environmental impact of its business practices. The result has been a considerable effort to change their physical processes, including implementing a clear coating system that has reduced VOC output by approximately 75%, implementing a "closed loop" waste and water system for the antiquing process, using an alternative alkaline soap solution for submerging fixture parts, keeping waste water out of the city sewer by evaporating the water and handling the sludge as hazardous waste, shredding used office paper for use in packaging, salvaging material to be refurbished, and calculating their carbon footprint.

Socially Oriented Business Practices

Although John is not clear on a definition of *social sustainability*, he has a strong sense of responsibility to his employees' families. He feels responsible for the improvement of the lives of both his employees and their families.

John asserts that he funds social programs for reasons of enlightened self-interest. The strength of the organization is the employees, who should come first. This viewpoint does not mean that customers come second, but rather the company philosophy is such that if the employee is treated well then he or she will in turn treat customers well. Treating people well reduces the turnover rate.

John is strategic about making decisions about social programs. First and foremost, he wants to improve and stabilize the lives of his employees, who are predominantly immigrants. He also wants to implement socially responsible practices that stabilize the business, reduce training costs, and reduce turnover rates, which are currently about 18% annually.

The key to social programs at Rehab Inc has been finding what works best for the employee population, which is culturally diverse and mostly male. Therefore, the number one concern for John is to "steeply subsidize" full family health care coverage. Although this program is expensive, John feels that, in terms of social programs for his employees, health care provides the "most bang for the buck." Currently, the medical benefit covers 89% of individual employee's costs for the first 2 years of employment; after that, family members are added, so that after 2 years, 70% of the medical costs of employees and their partners are covered, or 63% of the medical expenses of the employee and their entire family.

Other social benefits provided include bus passes for each employee; on-site bicycles for daily use, meetings, or errands around town; subsidies for job-related education; subsidies for fun activities, such as the arts and gym memberships; subsidies for English-language classes; in-house workshops on topics helpful to immigrants, such as how to buy a car or house; and $5,000 in assistance with a down payment on a first house, conceived as an interest-free loan to be forgiven after 5 years of employment. The company also has instituted a"cash-for-kids" program, donating $100 to the classroom of each child of an employee in the Portland public schools.

John feels that it is no longer possible to pay a "living wage," as it was in the 1950s. Competition in his business is too keen; too much can be produced in China at very low cost. He points out that his labor costs are 25 times what they are in China, making it hard to compete. However, although Rehab Inc does have some hardware parts made in China, most of his production is in Portland. He asserts that his business is not about moving production to China so that replications can be made cheaply. His business is about customization, customer service, and the craft of restoration/replications, which must be done locally.

Rehab Inc also leads paid, "volunteer" work parties. Due to cultural differences, John realized that immigrant populations were not comfortable with individual volunteer participation. Therefore, employees volunteer in groups, renovating low-income housing and maintaining hiking trails.

When asked about the business case for sustainable practices, John said that for business stability and employee cost reductions, socially sustainable practices are necessary. Training new employees is costly, and turnover rates can be reduced through successful social programs. Therefore, providing health care and other important benefits saves money in the long run and makes the business more profitable. However, John does not think that customers pay a lot of attention to the issues of social sustainability and social responsibility, so that social practices do not directly increase business or profits due to increased customer support.

John has mixed feelings about the case for standards and codes for social practices in business. On the one hand, minimum standards and regulation might help with environmental damage and lack of health care coverage. On the other hand, regulations can have unintended consequences, benefiting the wrong people and increasing costs.

ARCHITECTURE

"Tom" is a one of seven principals of the "Terra" architectural firm, and "Rick" is an associate and studio leader. Terra employs more than 65 people. Since 1969, Terra has worked to improve the urban core. The company philosophy emphasizes "infill, re-development, and reuse," which implies historical preservation, "adaptive reuse," and preserving culture.

Environmental Business Practices

Terra has been a member of the Natural Step for about 7 years, during which time Terra has actively implemented sustainability practices, including avoiding "green field" projects. Terra recently won an award for the design of their new office space, noting outstanding sustainable design accomplishments in the areas of energy, transportation alternatives, waste reduction/pollution prevention, water efficiency, and sustainable food systems development. They are working on Gold LEED certification for their new space, which has natural and high-efficiency lighting, low-flow water fixtures, certified wood paneling, previously used office furniture, low-VOC finishes, composting for all food waste, reduction of trash by eliminating disposable utensils and encouraging a high level of recycling, and reliance on green power and recycled paper.

Socially Oriented Business Practices

Neither Tom nor Rick was aware of any formal definition of *social sustainability*. However, Tom stated that, from an intuitive perspective, social sustainability has to do with equity, fairness, or social justice, and improving people's lives now and in the future.

Rick believes that social sustainability is a complicated issue depending on one's frame of reference—local or global—and needs to go beyond the typical linear discussion and thinking. For instance, green building is not sustainability, but a step along the way. Likewise, social sustainability is an important step along the way to greater overall sustainability. Social sustainability should include the support of local projects and the local economy and community.

When considering new projects, the company views them through a sustainability filter involving environmental concerns and elements of social obligation to the community. Terra staff has been involved in Oregon Natural Step as well as Northwest Earth Institute educational programs and training, which seek to facilitate cultural transformation within an organization.

Terra's social business practices include providing full medical and dental care to employees, including alternative health care options; an employee stock ownership plan; an employer-matched retirement program; and subsidies for bus and bicycle commuters. Eliminating parking subsidies allowed Terra to provide two additional paid vacation days to each member of the staff.

Additionally, Terra has flattened the management hierarchy of a typical architectural firm by reducing the management layers. There are only principals, associates, and staff. Terra is owned by a trust for employees, and all profits go into building the trust, which creates more transparency of decisions by management.

Terra provides in-kind services to the community, rather than cash donations, including staff and architectural expertise for community events. Terra staff members also donate time for public speaking, and they have given free advice to nonprofit causes. In addition, many staff members serve on advisory committees for public agencies.

Tom believes that there is a business case for social sustainability because demonstrating to the community that the firm is committed to the entire sustainability package helps to create good will and allows Terra to be identified with being "green." The employee stock ownership program is a good business practice because of the tax benefits provided for the company, as well as the way in which the program fosters employees' pride of ownership. Terra's commitment to socially sustainable business practices attracts the best and the brightest, as well as staff members who are committed to sustainable principles.

Rather than social codes, Tom believes that the focus should be on a shift of tax payments, along the lines advocated by Northwest author Alan Durning (and others) to better use our tax system to provide incentives to increase employment while reducing pollution and resource use.

DISCUSSION AND CONCLUSION

Overwhelmingly, the business owners we talked with were more comfortable discussing what they have been doing in the area of environmental rather than social sustainability—and with good reason; each was able to give a long and impressive list of environmentally sustainable measures implemented over a number of years. Throughout the discussion, the small business owners were encouraged to identify and discuss social aspects incorporated in their businesses—with their employees and in the community—that might be considered part of a working definition of socially sustainability. In some cases, connections between the environmental and the social were intentional business strategies in the name of ethical responsibility to the community. In other cases, the social benefit was more incidental.

However, lacking a clear working definition of *social sustainability*, the small business owners were not seeing their actions as social sustainability, but "doing the right thing." In other words, we had the impression that they were committed to environmentalism and to high social standards independently because they were both good, rather than because they were linked as the path to sustainability.

As a result of the questions posed during the interview with the business owners, the makings of a working definition for social sustainability slowly emerged. Their conceptualizations revolved around the employee, in phrases such as, "the employee comes first" or "what is good for the employee is good for the business, or "if the employee is healthy and happy, then so is the business." The business owners we interviewed indicated that the well-being of employees and their families was important to them, as was ensuring that both management and staff play a constructive role in the community. Three interviewees particularly emphasized the role of children and the future in their thinking.

Among the business practices of interviewees can be seen the likely starting points for business standards for social sustainability, including:

a) relatively high compensation for entry-level workers;
b) a commitment to providing safe workspaces and health care benefits, tempered by the recognition that comprehensive health care would be best provided by the government, given the scope of the challenge;
c) the provision of retirement benefits;
d) support for stable housing;
e) support for services for children, whether in their education, health care, or specialty services, and whether as children of employees or as members of the community;
f) support for employees' nonwork activities;
g) conscious use of local products and services to facilitate good livelihoods for local suppliers (e.g., farmers and others); and
h) belief in the necessity of business to collectively support the community through payment of taxes and volunteer work.

This list has a great deal in common with attempts throughout history to obtain human dignity and social health. Certainly labor movements have made several of these demands, and the United Nations' (2007) *Universal Declaration of Human Rights* includes many of them.

Several of the respondents noted the inability of small businesses to accomplish goals such as universal access to health care, affordable housing, or high quality education. Steve stated that health care was the responsibility of the government, and Salim's organization explicitly took steps to assist with the provision of social services in the aftermath of an election that failed to raise taxes.

Although each employer has striven to pay relatively high wages, particularly at lower levels, and to provide health care, small businesses particularly cannot provide a lot more than competitors do and stay in business. Standards need to be raised collectively. As American trade unionists used to say, "Wages need to be taken out of competition." If all businesses have to pay higher minimum wages and whatever taxes would support universal health care, they would compete against each other on grounds such as quality or service, rather than labor costs.

However, small businesses can decide whether to provide support—financial or otherwise—to campaigns to raise or lower tax rates. Indeed, Enertec campaigned for an increase in state income taxes to fund local schools and social services. Certainly the reverse—business support for lower taxes and consequently lower levels of public support for social institutions providing education, health care, and social services cannot be seen as socially sustainable. Further, as noted by Tom and Rick, the U.S. tax code could be better harnessed to provide more incentives for sustainable behavior.

Several of the business owners stressed the importance of supporting the local community, although one noted that it is not clear that we should be thinking about sustainability as a local issue. In some cases, it may be true that working for greater sustainability on a local level will advance the project of sustainabilty internationally. In others, however, more care is needed to ensure that higher local standards are not accomplished at the expense of lower standards elsewhere.

Considered together, we believe that the beginnings of a business code for the pursuit of social sustainability emerge from these interviews. Such a code would include providing living wages and good health care for employees and their families, a safe workplace, retirement benefits, affordable housing, support for high-quality education and other children's services, support for employees in their nonwork lives, reliance on local suppliers where possible, and support for the larger community in the form of tax payments and volunteer work.

ACKNOWLEDGMENTS

Thanks are due to the business owners who generously shared their time and thoughts with us, as well as to Clifford Lehman, Barbara Dudley, and Jesse Dillard for critical reflections.

REFERENCES

Natural Step International. 2007. *What Is Sustainability?* Accessed on August 21, 2007, from http://www.naturalstep.org/com/What%5Fis%5Fsustainability/
United Nations. 2007. *Universal Declaration of Human Rights*. Accessed on September 27, 2007, from http://www.un.org/Overview/rights.html

11 Triple Bottom Line
A Business Metaphor for a Social Construct

Darrell Brown, Jesse Dillard,
and Scott Marshall[1]

Organizational management is specifically granted fiduciary responsibility over society's economic resources, which consist of natural and human resources. Because of their privileged status, organizational management and the associated business professions play a central role in the long-term viability of a democratically governed society grounded in justice, equality, and trust. Acting in the public interest requires consideration of natural, social, and economic systems. Natural systems provide the context and sustenance for social systems and, therefore, must be respected, nurtured, and sustained. Social systems provide the context and purpose of economic systems. Business professionals, such as accounting and other information providers, analysts, and monitors; and regulatory agencies, such as the Securities and Exchange Commission (SEC),[2] Environmental Protection Agency, and Food and Drug Administration, facilitate and scrutinize organizational management in carrying out their fiduciary responsibility.

By accepting the right to control society's economic resources, organizational management accepts the responsibility to be held accountable for their use of these assets. Upon exercising the right to grant organizational management control over its economic resources, society accepts the responsibility to hold organizational management accountable for their use of these assets. Corporate accountability[3] represents the lynch pin for motivating responsible behavior. Throughout the world, publicly held corporations control and transform natural and social resources into economic goods and services. Publicly available information is a necessary, although not sufficient, prerequisite for responsible resource stewardship and management. Thus, the relevance and integrity of information contained in and made available by measurement and accountability systems holds a place of central importance in our ability to hold accountable those granted the responsibility for society's resources.

The triple bottom line is emerging as a popular conceptualization and reporting vehicle for articulating corporate social, environmental, and economic performance and is receiving significant attention in connection with its efficacy and sufficiency as a means for reporting the extent to which an organization meets its societal responsibilities. By preparing and disseminating triple bottom line statements, an organization conveys an image of concern and sensitivity to the three dimensions of societal responsibility: economic, environmental, and social. However, as currently conceived and operationalized, we question whether the triple bottom line reports actually provide information relevant to accessing corporate responsibility and enforcing accountability, particularly social sustainability. In addition, we discuss the efficacy of using the bottom line as a metaphor to help determine the metrics and measures relevant to social sustainability. Our conclusion is that triple bottom line reporting, although a step toward increasing the awareness of multiple, competing, simultaneous objectives for organizations, is an inadequate, and perhaps detrimental, representation of organizational sustainability. Although our primary concern is social sustainability, the associated issues cannot be adequately addressed without considering the natural and economic systems. This work is part of an ongoing program of research concerned with developing an enabling accounting.[4]

In the following discussion, we explicitly consider the concept of the triple bottom line report that has been generally set forth in the accounting and reporting literature as a significant step forward in the quest for enhanced social and environmental corporate responsibility. The triple bottom line statement purports to render corporate actions more understandable and transparent in areas not covered under current reporting conventions. Within a democratically governed society, information provides the basis on which citizens and their representatives stipulate and regulate the parameters within which organizations are required to operate. If managers are held accountable for the social and environmental impacts of their decisions through the external reporting of results in these areas, they will of necessity more fully incorporate them into their decision processes.

Following this introduction, we consider the origins of the triple bottom line report. The third section explains the meaning of the metaphorical bottom line. In the next section, we consider whether the triple bottom line can sustain social sustainability. Brief closing comments conclude our discussion.

THE ORIGINS OF THE TRIPLE BOTTOM LINE

Whence the triple bottom line? The term *triple bottom line* is often attributed to John Elkington, a cofounder and chair of SustainAbility, a sustainable business consultancy (Elkington, 2004). Elkington explicitly chose the language to resonate with business managers. As it evolved, triple bottom line reporting has been employed by organizations for a plethora of purposes. Some argue that the primary application is no more than a means for enhancing the organization's public image (Schilizzi, 2002). Others (Cheney, 2004) argue that it is a method for the organization to show its engaging in legitimate environmentally and socially responsible activities. A third application is an acknowledgment and representation of trade-offs made among the three components (Centre for Innovation in Corporate Responsibility, 2004). The reporting formats range from providing a "dashboard" of measures (Epstein and Weiser, 2001) to attempts to monetize all three perspectives (Richardson, 2004). Schilizzi (2002) points out the difficulties in attempting to quantify the environmental and social dimensions of organizational performance and, as an example of one possible solution, recommends "real options" valuation techniques.

Numerous consultancies, organizations, and researchers are working to develop metrics that can, in some way, capture the relevant values of the components of the triple bottom line in a way that can allow users of reports to "understand the full, blended value" of the organization (Emerson, 2003; Lingane and Olsen, 2004). For example, Howes (2004) presents a statement of "environmentally sustainable adjusted profit." Although the final determination of what the triple bottom line may look like is not yet completed, Richardson (2004) notes the most commonly held conception presumes that each of the three components can be calculated in monetary terms.

Advocates of the triple bottom line argue that, because an organization's long-term viability is dependent on sustaining profitability over all three dimensions, they should be measured, reported, and assessed on a periodic basis in a manner conceptually similar to the current financial reporting model. Further, stakeholder groups, such as socially responsible investors, nongovernmental organizations, green consumers, and governmental regulators and agencies, are increasingly calling for information related to the social and environmental dimensions. Responding to the increasing desire for both financial and nonfinancial information related to a broader conceptualization of corporate responsibilities, all of the major accounting consultancy firms, along with a host of others, offer dedicated services to assist companies in developing triple bottom line reporting tools (Tschopp, 2003). The proponents allege that these tools assist in enhancing the organization's reputation, as well as reducing the risk profile and aligning managerial and stakeholder needs (Group of 100, 2003). Next, we consider how the measures of the triple bottom line report developed and how they relate to social sustainability.

The Road to Social Sustainability

In the 1960s and 1970s, there was a widespread, although by no means dominant, recognition that human activities, including corporate activities, had great and potentially disastrous impacts on the natural environment. Although the root of the world's sustainability problems may well be cultural and political (Hart, 1997), corporations and their activities have a significant impact on the environment. As society began to demand cleaner water, cleaner air, fewer toxins, and the other benefits of environmentally thoughtful stewardship, corporations, however reluctantly, initiated improvements in their environmental behavior (Hoffman, 2000). As we moved into the 1990s, leading thinkers in the environmental movement as regards corporations began to talk about environmental sustainability. Without addressing the reality or sincerity of the sustainability initiatives undertaken by corporations, it is significant that many corporations began to acknowledge at least the notion of environmental sustainability.

However, in the early and mid-1990s, it became increasingly apparent to a variety of thinkers and organizations that environmental sustainability was unlikely to be achievable without addressing issues of social sustainability as well. For example, The Natural Step introduced social awareness as an integral component, identifying four system conditions required to achieve a sustainable society: (a) nature must not be subjected to systematically increasing concentrations of substances extracted from the Earth's crust, (b) nature must not be subjected to systematically increasing concentrations of substances produced by society, (c) nature must not be subjected to systematically increasing degradation by physical means, and (d) the ability of humans to meet their needs worldwide must not be systematically undermined (Robèrt, 2003). A casual reading of the four conditions presents a picture of three rigorously conceived (although not necessarily rigorously implementable) environmentally related conditions and one vague condition relating to social issues. The first three conditions state that "nature must not be subjected to . . . ," followed by specific, if complex, requirements. It is possible, from the conditions, to determine whether an action, if sufficiently understood, violates the condition. The fourth condition, dealing with social systems, states that the object of the condition is not impaired without any real reference to what that may mean. To know whether an action violates the condition, we must not only understand the action, but we also must come to some common agreement about what it means to impair the ability of humans to "meet their needs." The concern then is whether social sustainability is either weakly conceived or has been attached to the framework as an afterthought. Alternatively, perhaps the social systems are so fundamentally different from environmental systems that we cannot create social system conditions analogous to the environmental system conditions.

The centrality of the corporation's public interest responsibility is reflected in the legitimating arguments for their initial chartering (Bakan, 2004). In the 18th and 19th centuries, corporations were chartered to undertake public works projects such as building bridges, roads, and canals and had an explicit duty to operate in and for the public's interest (Champlin and Knoedler, 2003). As corporations grew and as absentee owners (shareholders) became the primary corporate stakeholders, the public interest dimension became subordinate to the goal of maximizing shareholder (owner) wealth. Ultimately, in most capitalist societies, not only did the corporations abdicate any pretext of acting in the broader public's interest, but also their responsibility to shareholders has been effectively outsourced to regulators and auditors, not the least of which were Certified and Chartered Accountants. This explicit assignment of protection of the public (at least protection of shareholders) to entities completely outside the organization represents the nadir of corporate social responsibility. It might be argued that any organization that relies on regulations and verifiers/enforcers of the public interest cannot be thought of as a socially responsible business.[5]

Updating this conversation within the current vernacular, social sustainability represents the social dimension of the public interest. For businesses, the idea of social sustainability, if recognized at all, is narrowly and conveniently conceived and likely to be interpreted as the ability to continue to stay in business through good relations with supply-chain partners, employees, and unions, an interpretation that is rather limited and possibly destructive. Rather than expanding the scope of their public interest responsibilities, managers focus on reducing social resources to monetary terms, measuring, and maximizing it. Hawkens, Lovins, and Lovins (1999) attempt to broaden this perspective they refer to as human or social capital by including it as one of four primary types of capital: natural, manufactured, financial, and human. When the stocks and flows of these objectified concepts are managed effectively, organizations become sustainable. Social capital, by implication at least, represents another factor of production and a profit generator for the organization.

Elkington (2004) accurately, and in some respects prophetically, articulates the subordinate position of the social dimension in his initial conceptualization of the triple bottom line: "We felt that the social and economic dimensions of the (environmental) agenda . . . would have to be addressed in a more integral way if real environmental progress was to be made" (p. 1). The interesting issue here is that the social (and economic[6]) issues are subordinate to the environmental agenda. Not surprisingly, researchers find that issues relating to reporting social aspects of corporate responsibility generally lag behind the reporting of environmental issues in terms of both timing and quality (Adams, 2002; KPMG, 2002; Kolk, 2003).

Thus, one might conclude that the road to social sustainability reflects more of a meandering and awkward afterthought (e.g., the Natural Step Framework), an objectification through mechanistic management (e.g., social capital), and a subordinated and imprecise objective within an enhanced reporting initiative (e.g., triple bottom line). We now consider more explicitly how the accounting and reporting dimensions of social sustainability have culminated in the current rendering of the triple bottom line.

The Road to Accounting for Social Sustainability

Using the history of accounting as a guide,[7] we can see that as business organizations were conceived, developed, and matured, they required and created new ways to address the issues of concern to their stakeholders.

Initially, accounting was developed to meet the needs of business owners and managers to address the day-to-day concerns of running a business by making the processes and their effects more transparent. As the owners delegated the tasks of managing to others, accounting methods were developed to communicate the important business characteristics, predominantly the effects of operations and the status of the business, to the owners. Although the scope of concern, and the concerned, has changed, the process continues to evolve along the same trajectory. The needs of affected constituencies needs to continually develop and change, and accounting methods, rules, and regulations must evolve to meet these ever-changing information needs.

Information needs regarding organizations' environmental and social impacts are an example of the expanding scope of concern. Unlike the efforts associated with the conception of triple bottom line reporting described earlier, relatively early on, accounting recognized the importance of human capital and attempted to measure and report its attributes previous to and separate from environmental capital. Social accounting arose in the 1970s, but never gained purchase partly due to the inability of relevant stakeholders to agree on an acceptable method for quantifying and reporting the relevant attributes. Social accounting, to most businesses, was an attempt to capitalize the value of the employees, management skills, and business acumen that generated wealth for shareholders. For some social activists, social accounting was an attempt to expand the recognized benefits and costs that businesses created for society. The significant measurement problems, coupled with the financial community's skepticism, thwarted the attempt to recognize the previously ignored (unrecorded) social and human capital. Insufficient political will and waning public demand thwarted the move toward enhanced social impact reporting by corporations. At the time, acceptable measurement systems were not available to companies for achieving their goals of recognizing unrecorded assets, and there was insufficient public demand for reporting the social impacts of companies. Thus, the concept of social accounting faded away (Gray, 2001), only to be resurrected in the waning of the 1990s. Next, we consider this resurrection as it has culminated in the metaphorical bottom line manifested in triple bottom line reporting.

THE METAPHORICAL BOTTOM LINE

The *bottom line* is a metaphor arising from within the business lexicon that confers the ability to capture in a unique representation (a number) the effect of a multitude of separate actions (transactions) by systematically representing these actions using a common metric and summing the contributions (benefits) and detriments (costs). The quintessential symbol of the bottom line is the net income (earnings) reported on the financial statements of publicly held corporations. Net income is the difference between the revenues of a period generated by selling the products or services, capturing the organization and the costs of producing, and selling those products or services and purportedly captures the organization's inflows and outflows in a single figure.[8] As a metaphor, the bottom line (net income) represents information capture of a collection of activities enabling the synthesizing of the effects in a concise representation. The requisite unit of measure is presumed to be compensatory, additive, inclusive, and, to be useful, relevant. The triple bottom line is a reporting technique that applies the bottom line metaphor to the social and environmental aspects of a business organization. The legitimacy of such an application depends on the extent to which the characteristics of the application domain (social and environmental) conform to those of the initiating domain (economics/accounting).

Representation

Figure 11.1 illustrates the resource and information flows associated with a business organization. The organization occupies the center of the diagram. The circle on the left represents the social system, and the circle to the right represents the natural system. The top portion of the figure shows actual resource flows into and out of a business organization. Both natural and social systems provide resource inputs to the organization, and both are impacted by its resource outputs. These inputs from the natural and social worlds inform the "organization action space," the behaviors and activities of the business. In turn, the behaviors and activities of the business impact the natural and social worlds. The lower portion of Figure 11.1 shows information flows. The organization's information systems and measurements identify, filter, and measure inputs from the organization's actions, the natural system, and the social system. These inputs are then used to create, among other communications, triple bottom line reports.

The information flows between the organization and the social and natural systems, as well as throughout the organization. The accounting systems inform the organizational strategies that ultimately motivate changes in the organizational action space. So, ultimately, the process that produces organizational reports relies on information systems that collect information designed for, and are controlled by, the organization that takes a predominately economic perspective in collecting and analyzing information related to the natural and social systems. Next, we consider the basic characteristics that underlie each of the three dimensions of organizational activity.

Economic Systems

Exchange of (markets for) scarce resources provides the operational model on which economics and accounting is predicated. The transaction represents the instantiating atomic unit. Measurement and accumulation

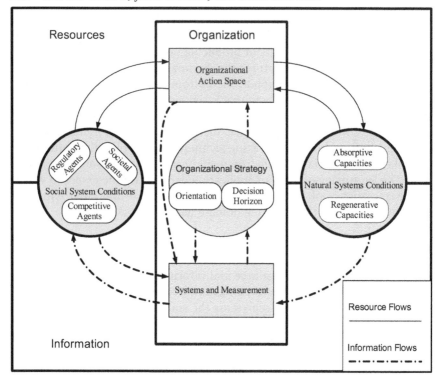

Figure 11.1 Resource and information flows among the economic, social, and natural systems.

systems reflect resource flows associated with exchange transactions consummated. It might be argued that the offsetting debit and credit system as currently articulated in U.S. accounting presupposes an ends-oriented perspective and implies a cost–benefit decision frame arising from a utilitarian foundation. That is, extant accounting systems are based on neoclassical economic theory. Neoclassical economic theory is philosophically based on utilitarianism. Utilitarianism is a teleological philosophy that assumes benefits and costs can be specified measured and aggregated. The greatest good for the greatest number is presumed to be represented by the alternative that maximizes the net benefit.[9] The bottom line metaphor embodies this utilitarian base. We now must consider whether this metaphor is appropriate when considering the natural and social systems.

Natural Systems

Ecosystems make up the environmental system. Ecosystems are interrelated natural systems that are in constant and symbiotic interaction. These complex, self-organizing systems are studied and monitored by scientists and engineers using formal representations (equations/models) of the eco-systems. The elemental concept underlying natural systems is balance in the effective and efficient use of biomass, energy, resources, and so on within the context of the system boundaries. Balance, not maximization, represents the controlling decision rule. The means, or in this case the for-mula, is preeminent, not the outcome, which is the consequence. The inputs and the rules determine the outcome. The scientific method structures the fundamental decision framework. Representations of the natural system are predicated on and attained through the application of the scientifically specified relationships.

The underlying logic of the natural system is, generally, the natural laws that are perceived to underlie the physical world. The laws of physics rep-resent the dynamics of the universe; the laws of thermodynamics represent the flow of heat or energy within an ecosystem. The accounting system for the environment is implemented by scientist and varies with the components being considered. For example, energy use is measured based on the laws of thermodynamics. The accounting systems such as electricity metering or heat loss calculations are application-specific, with mechanical or chemical measuring devices calibrated in the appropriate units of measure such as kilowatt hours or degrees centigrade. The underlying philosophy reflects the cause-and-effect logic of science, and the process is one of observation and experimentation.

Natural resources can be classified into the following three types:

- Critical resources—resources without which the biosphere could not sustain life and must not be violated (ozone layer, critical biomass, etc.).
- Sustainable, substitutable, or renewable resources—resources that are renewable or that substitutes can reasonably be expected to be found (fossil fuels).
- Artificial resources—resources created through the transformation of natural resources that are no longer in harmony with the natural eco-systems (machines, roads, products, waste). (Gray and Bebbington, 2001, pp. 307–308)

These categories cannot be combined or aggregated, nor can they be eval-uated using a cost–benefit calculus because of their diversity and inter-relatedness. The philosophical grounding tends to direct effort toward identifying and specifying the physical models that reflect the behavior of the individual system components as well as their interrelationships (e.g., see Gunderson and Holling, 2002). The classical scientific con-structs associated with cause and effect underlie the undertakings and representations.

Environmental systems are less amenable to maximization because there are considerable difficulties arriving at a currency that is fungible, agreed on, and can be aggregated.[10] For example, consider the environmental objective of achieving biological diversity, a commonly stated indicator of environmental health, stability, and resilience. *Biological diversity* refers to the possible ecological niches that must be occupied to achieve maximum energy captured and to support living organisms over long time periods. The system achieves biodiversity when no more renewable inputs are available. At that point, it is impossible to add to the biological store. In the environmental world, *biodiversity* can be defined as:

> The sum total of all the plants, animals (including humans), fungi and microorganisms, along with their individual variations and the interactions between them. It is the set of living organisms and their genetic basis that make up the fabric of the planet earth and allow it to function as it does, by capturing energy from the sun and using it to drive all of life's processes. (Rutgers University Biodiversity Initiative, http://aesop.rutgers.edu/~biodiversity/whatis2.htm#DEFINE)

Here we see that the input is the sun's energy and the output is life's processes. Any addition to the ability to capture the sun's energy and any increase in the genetic pool are increases in biodiversity. However, as opposed to maximizing an objective function, the system prospers only if a balance is maintained that incorporates a sufficient, that is, enough but not too much, amount of all the requisite component factors in the system. Balance arises as the objective. At the core, the actionable objective functions relate to achieving objective functions that represent a dynamic range of possible values, none of which are maximized or minimized.

There may be instances where subobjectives may lead to maximizing or minimizing objective functions, but these are not the ultimate goal of the natural system, just a recognition that certain impacts have an absolute benefit or detriment to the natural system. For example, consider the emission of greenhouse gasses from the production of human-useable energy from fossil fuels. A reasonable case can be made to absolutely minimize these emissions. At a broader level, we may be able to convert environmental measures to one currency. The concept of *ecological footprint*, relating the impact of an individual human to the consumption of naturally renewable resources, is proposed (Pearce and Barbier, 2000; Lenzen, Lundie, Bransgrove, Charet, and Sack, 2003). Attempts to arrive at a single measure or index to allow maximization or minimization of one factor have not yet achieved universal or even common support.

Social Systems

Social systems are the "patterning of social relationships across 'time and space' understood as reproduced practices" (Giddens, 1984, p. 377). These systems are highly variable in these representational patterns relative to the internal structural unity of biological systems. The elements of social systems are human relationships and interactions. The underlying logic of these systems is grounded in social integration and reflects generally a communitarian logic. Measurement systems are grounded in political, social, and psychological models[11] of social relationships and characteristics of human populations. The models are developed by sociologists, psychologists, and political scientists. The accounting system reflects the social structures as articulated by these particular models based on underlying social theory.

In a broad sense, social systems differ dramatically from systems that can be maximized (or minimized). Social sustainability attributes do not fit a scarcity (conservation/natural capital/limits to growth) mindset in that at least some of them will increase the more they are employed. For example, the quality of daily life is an attribute of social sustainability that many people could agree is important. Creation of a feeling of community might well be one of the components of quality of life.[12] It seems likely that as a feeling of community increases, the ability to create a feeling of community increases. Some psychologists argue that feelings of self and community are recursive and that they can enhance each other, creating reinforcing loops that, conceptually, have no limit (Stein and Edwards, 1998).

MacGillivray (2004) conceptualizes social capital as "creative trust" and represents the "stock of networks, stakeholder relationships and shared rules that help organizations and their surrounding communities work more effectively" (p. 121). Creative trust, unlike economic or natural capital, is not inherently depleted when used. Using economic capital leads to a depletion of these assets. Using nonrenewable natural resources means that the natural system is permanently diminished. Using social resources, however, may often increase their stock. For example, showing and using trust in relationships results in more trust, not in the depletion thereof. Exchanging knowledge is more likely to result in additional sources and stocks of knowledge.

In economic systems, maximizing wealth may be appropriate. In natural systems, maximizing (or minimizing) biological diversity (or greenhouse gas emissions) may be desirable, but does it really make sense to either maximize or minimize in the realm of social sustainability? However, when we talk of social diversity, we talk of increasing the range of racial, gender, sexual preference, national heritage, religious affiliation, age, and ethnicity diversity in a given community.[13] What is the input to a community that can be renewably consumed? How do we measure the diversity—by the gene pool? Do we really want to have the greatest possible amount of biomass exist in a particular volume of space when we are talking about humans and human social sustainability?

The core nature of the triple bottom line dimensions emerge from fundamentally different domains. The environmental system tends more toward an objective function that attempts to achieve interactive balance. The social system, we argue, tends to an objective function that values quality of ongoing integration and interaction. The fundamental differences in the attributes of social, economic, and environmental sustainability illustrate the inappropriateness of measuring, reporting, and conceiving of these three facets in the same ways.[14] Next we directly address the concept of the triple bottom line using the ideas developed earlier.

THE TRIPLE BOTTOM LINE: CAN IT
SUSTAIN SOCIAL SUSTAINABILITY?

Metaphor is a figure of speech used to describe one concept with attributes normally associated with another. Lakoff and Johnson (1998) identify metaphors as the primary medium by which humans gain an understanding and through which they communicate this understanding to others. Metaphorical structures are both enabling and constraining with respect to the ability to understand and communicate. As discussed earlier, the bottom line represents a simple and widely understood metaphor grounded in the cost–benefit calculus of neoclassical economics, conveying a facility to sum a vast array of (potentially disparate) attributes into a single, commoditized value, and excludes any representation of social (and environmental) well-being beyond a crude materialism. This is the metaphorical representation on which we are to represent, communicate, and evaluate the social and environmental stewardship of business organizations using triple bottom line reporting. We consider the enabling and constraining capabilities of triple bottom line reporting with respect to measuring, reporting, and evaluating social sustainability.

The initial legitimating argument for triple bottom line reporting was to direct management's attention to the social dimension of overall sustainability. Drawing attention to economic sustainability was not a concern at this point, and the issues of environmental sustainability were being recognized, at least at the level of internalized costs and benefits. The bottom line metaphor provided a representation that resonates with business owners and managers, who see it as real, meaningful, and relevant; therefore, using this terminology increases the likelihood of awareness and action by the target audience. Although certainly not universally accepted, the triple bottom line and its various derivatives, such as Triple-E (economy, environment, equity) or 3P (people, planet, profit), are penetrating the traditional language of business.

Triple bottom line reporting represents an application of the bottom line metaphor to facilitate a more complete and transparent representation and, therefore, more prudent management of the actual stocks and flows affected by business operations. For example, in supporting the concept, MacGillivray (2004) states that the "economic, environmental and social balance sheets must all be in the black for a business to be sustainable" (p.

121). Wright et al. (2002) touts its inclusively and exhorts decision makers to look to the "triple bottom line from which tradeoffs can be more clearly defined and simultaneous social, economic, and ecological benefits can be achieved and maintained over time" (p. x). As illustrated in such directives, the metaphorical frame conveys an impression of compensatory relationships among the three dimensions, implying a common currency and additivity. However, as discussed previously, the lack of the requisite attributes is particularly apparent in the social sustainability domain.

Use of the bottom line as a common metaphor for these sustainability systems constrains our ability to see them as both different and interrelated and, therefore, inhibits the development of different approaches for representing, measuring, and understanding them. First, we consider the problem of specifying the systems as different when, in fact, they are interrelated, which is implied by the triple bottom line format. Second, we consider the problem of assuming the systems are interrelated, or at least compatible, by applying a common economic-based metaphor to all three systems. Third, we consider the current weaknesses in how the reporting is being described and carried out.

Perhaps the greatest disservice in applying triple bottom line reporting is the implication that there are three separate, assessable measures (or sets of measures). Returning to Figure 11.1, we see that there are multiple relationships among and within the three facets of the sustainability triad. It is important to note, however, the relationships among the systems. The organization affects and is affected by both the social and natural systems. The systems have different goals, objectives, and performance criteria; however, changes in one system impact the others. Even such careful observers as the Global Reporting Initiative (GRI) explicitly devise sets of indicators that conceptualize and measure each factor separately (Global Reporting Initiative, 2002). As such, the interactions among the components yield synergies and new complex relationships that would not be recognized, therefore restricting the representations' validity. Masking the interrelational complexity at best leads to misrepresentation and misunderstanding, culminating naive responses on the part of managers, regulations, and stakeholders. These distortions go beyond merely not knowing what to measure, how to measure, or even how to define attributes. Implying that the attributes are separate conveys a dangerous illusion of noncompensatory precision.

The concept of triple bottom line, in fact, often turns out to be a "good old-fashioned single bottom line plus vague commitments to social and environmental concerns" (Norman and MacDonald, 2004, p. 256). Privileging the economic dimension not only obfuscates the interrelations among the factors at another level, but also adds unwarranted legitimacy and perceived accuracy to the resulting triple bottom line portrait. As previously discussed, the attributes of economic and environmental sustainability are functionally and fundamentally different from the attributes of social sustainability. The economic bottom line, as the dominant bottom line frame, can project attributes of measurability and aggregation on to these systems that they do not possess. In this case, implying that the attributes are similar conveys an illusion of compensatory precision and validity.

The triple bottom line report purports to provide information about the status and progress on each of the three sustainability dimensions. However, most counsel associated with triple bottom line reporting in the professional literature represents little more than platitudes. Statements such as "implementing (the triple bottom line) would not be as demanding as one would think" (Tschopp, 2003, p. 11) are intermingled with statements that the triple bottom line helps "investors distinguish companies that are efficient now and well-positioned to protect their market competitiveness" (Cheney, 2004, p. 14). Companies that prepare sustainability reports, include (and exclude) a variety of social, environmental, and economic issues in them. By and large, the economic issues are related to traditional accounting and finance concepts that are, in general, comparable among companies and over time. However, as described in SustainAbility's 2004 report, even the top 50 corporate sustainability reporters provide a mixed bag regarding environmental and social reporting. GRI standards, currently the most developed standards for sustainability reporting, are rarely adhered to, and even the few companies reporting in accordance with GRI standards produce only minimally comparable information. As yet, there are no generally accepted accounting or auditing standards, no public or regulatory requirements, and no uniform reporting format, rending comparability across organizations and over time difficult, if not impossible.

The bottom line is a disconnected and misconstrued metaphor when it is applied within the guise of triple bottom line reporting and provides little, if any, utility for organizations or their stakeholders. As argued, the application of the bottom line metaphor, as currently construed, represents a limited and conceptually flawed application. It then follows that the resulting triple bottom line reporting also would be flawed as a portrait of the three categories of sustainability. The categorical reporting moves from the traditional economics-based business-related concept of bottom line to broader, more ill-defined, and nonrigorous concepts of the environment and the social systems. The triple bottom line report gathers together the three legs of sustainability, but provides no focus and fails to address, even at a high level, the need to arrive at some salient point, some essential value. The bottom line is a disconnected and misconstrued metaphor, with no real utility for organizations or their external stakeholders when operationalized within the triple bottom line statement.

CLOSING COMMENTS

An organization's bottom line is perceived as the ultimate measure of its performance for many managers, owners, investors, creditors, and other various constituencies. The bottom line carries a patina of finality, summary, and importance, and it is traditionally formulated in wholly economic terms. In the previous discussion, we explore whether the bottom line provides a suitable metaphor measure for representing sustainability, generally, and social sustainability specifically. To do so, we discuss the elemental properties of a bottom line. We argue that, although strongly interrelated, the elemental dimensions for each of the sustainability systems are fundamentally different.

The triple bottom line report was developed to meet the needs of businesses engaged or interested in sustainable development. Adams, Frost, and Webber (2004) call the triple bottom line "an inspiring metaphor that challenges contemporary corporations" (p. 17) to meet economic, environmental, and social goals simultaneously. The idea of sustainable development addresses some businesses' desire to see the opportunity to engage and embrace environmental and social issues without giving up the desire to be economically prosperous. The triple bottom line report uses the bottom line metaphor from financial reporting as a template for the reporting of economic, social, and environmental sustainability.

We conclude that the bottom line as a metaphor for measuring and reporting business' contribution to social sustainability is fatally flawed. The metaphor's application through current triple bottom line reporting protocols allows businesses to ignore critical sustainability concerns for several reasons. First, businesses attempting to legitimate themselves without actually addressing sustainability can use the reporting exercise to coopt the external pressure for true sustainability. Due to the lack of mandatory standards, businesses freely pick and choose which characteristics they measure, derive their own metrics and standards for these characteristics, and produce a report that reveals precisely what they wish to disclose. The bottom line metaphor implies rigor and objectivity that fail to exist in these situations. Second, businesses that start with a genuine commitment to enhancing their sustainability efforts can be distracted as the interrelationships among the dimensions are masked by the apparent independence of the three bottom lines. There is neither demand to analyze interrelationships nor pressure to consider how the impacts from one dimension affect the others. The focus is an atomistic one, a (relatively) easy and uninformed perspective for addressing sustainability objectives. Third, the fundamental differences among the three the triple bottom line elements make using a single framework problematic. The major differences are in the ability to identify, quantify, and measure these central constructs; the applicability of being metaphorically designated as capital; and the metaphorical representations and conceptual approaches to understand, quantify, and report the dimensions.

Our conclusions reflect the complexity and richness of the character of sustainability. To give credit, however, the triple bottom line metaphor does provide notice that sustainability includes social issues. This seemingly intuitive insight became real for most companies now embracing social sustainability only after the bottom line terminology became prominent in reporting discourses. The triple bottom line did yeoman's work in this arena. But it is time to move on to better, more thoughtful, and more useful notions to drive sustainability. It is time to find a new metaphor for imaging sustainability. As a start, we propose the following: Accounting is the language of business. Triple bottom line reporting attempts to frame social sustainability in the language of business. Why can we not articulate business in the language of social sustainability? This should be our next metaphorical quest.

NOTES

1. Support is acknowledged from the Center of Professional Integrity and Accountability, School of Business Administration, Portland State University.
2. In the United States.
3. We consider this term to be inclusive of the economic, environmental, and social responsibilities of organizations.
4. See Dillard, Brown, and Marshall (2005), Brown, Dillard, and Marshall (2005), and Broadbent, Ciancanelli, Gallhofer, and Haslam (1997).
5. There is less than a little irony in the fact that, in 2002, as a result of the Sarbanes–Oxley Act, the primary guardian for third-party interests, the accounting profession, in the United States, lost the right of professional self-monitoring and regulation with respect to its public interest responsibilities to the SEC as a result of the widespread misconduct and conflicts of interests that took place during the late 1990s and early 2000s that culminated in historic corporate failures.
6. Given their current overwhelming dominance, it is difficult to conceive of the economic well being subordinate.
7. The history of accounting is well detailed in books and articles galore. See Johnson and Kaplan (1987), Chandler (1977), and Previts and Merino (1998).
8. We realize, of course, that *net income* is a technical accounting term that includes many complex and sometimes convoluted ideas and activities. For purposes of this chapter, we choose to provide a more intuitive and understandable description of net income. We feel the more simple description avoids unnecessary detail that will be more likely to obfuscate than illuminate. In addition, the metaphor of the *bottom line*, which is the focus of this chapter, is not burdened with the additional detail. The bottom line metaphor is a relatively simple metaphor addressed sufficiently by our description.
9. If a choice is required among alternatives, all of which evidence costs greater than the benefits, then the alternative with the lowest net costs would minimize the detriment.
10. The mixed-unit problem.
11. We recognize the influence that these models have on the specification of the economic domain. An adequate critique of the perceived neutrality of neoclassical economic theory is beyond the scope of this discussion. For a

discussion of its influence on accounting, see Tinker, Merino, and Neimark (1982) and Dillard (1991).

12. To further probe the meaning of *feeling of community*, see a set of quotes relating to this concept at http://ourworld.compuserve.com/homepages/hstein/qu-comm.h (accessed on November 13, 2004).
13. Here *community* is a term that implies a coherent, bounded group of people joined in this bounded group by some social institution.
14. Note, we are not saying that all social systems constructs are nondiminishing. For example, a good reputation can be destroyed by behaviors in opposition to the reputation; a culture of trust can be lost by changing the leaders of an organization. Alternatively, cultural variability may impact the effects on social sustainability attributes.

REFERENCES

Adams, C. A. 2002. "Factors Influencing Corporate Social and Ethical Reporting: Moving on From Extant Theories." *Accounting, Auditing & Accountability Journal* 15 (2): 223–250.

———., G. Frost, and W. Webber. 2004. "Triple Bottom Line: A Review of the Literature."In *The Triple Bottom Line: Does It All Add Up*, edited by Adrian Henriques and Julie Richardson. London: EarthScan.

Bakan, J. 2004. *The Corporation*. New York: The Free Press.

Broadbent, J., P. Ciancanelli, S. Gallhofer, and J. Haslam. 1997. "Enabling Accounting: The Way Forward?" *Accounting, Auditing, and Accountability Journal* 10 (3): 265–275.

Brown, D., J. Dillard, and S. Marshall. 2005. "Incorporating Natural Systems as Part of Accounting's Public Interest Responsibility." *Journal of Information Systems* 19 (2): 79–104.

Centre for Innovation in Corporate Responsibility. 2004. "The Triple Bottom Line." Accessed on November 13, 2004, from http://www.cicr.net/tblbasics.htm.

Champlin, D. P., and J. T. Knoedler. 2003. "Corporations, Workers, and the Public Interest." *Journal of Economic Issues* 37 (2): 305–313.

Chandler, A. 1977. *The Visible Hand*. Cambridge, UK: Belknap.

Cheney, G. 2004, July 12. "The Corporate Conscience and the Triple Bottom Line." *Accounting Today* 18 (12): 12–14.

Dillard, J. 1991. "Accounting as a Critical Social Science." *Accounting, Auditing and Accountability Journal* 4 (1): 8–28.

———., D. Brown, and S. Marshall. 2005. "An Environmentally Enlightened Accounting." *Accounting Forum* 29: 77–101.

Elkington, J. 2004. "Enter the Triple Bottom Line." In *The Triple Bottom Line: Does It All Add Up*, edited by Adrian Henriques and Julie Richardson. London: EarthScan.

Emerson, J. 2003. "The Blended Value Proposition: Integrating Social and Financial Returns." *California Management Review* 45 (4): 35–51.

Epstein, M., and P. Wisner. 2001, May/June. "Good Neighbors: Implementing Social and Environmental Strategies with the BSC." *Balanced Scorecard Report*, p. 4.

Giddens, A. 1984. *The Constitution of Society*. Berkeley: University of California Press.

Global Reporting Initiative. 2002. *Sustainability Reporting Guidelines*. Boston, MA: Author.

Gray, R. 2001. "Thirty Years of Social Accounting, Reporting and Auditing: What (If Anything) Have We Learnt?" *Business Ethics: A European Review* 10 (1): 9–15.

———., and J. Bebbington. 2001. *Accounting for the Environment.* 2nd ed. London: Sage.

Group of 100. 2003. *Sustainability: A Guide to Triple Bottom Line Reporting.* Melbourne, Australia: Author.

Gunderson, L., and C. Holling, eds. 2002. *Panarchy: Understanding Transformations in Systems of Humans and Nature.* Washington, DC: Island Press.

Hart, S. J. 1997. "Beyond Greening: Strategies for a Sustainable World." *Harvard Business Review* 75 (1): 66–77.

Hawken, P., A. Lovins, and L. H. Lovins. 1999. *Natural Capitalism.* Boston, MA: Little, Brown.

Hoffman, A. J. 2000. *Competitive Environmental Strategy.* Washington, DC: Island Press.

Howes, R. 2004. "Environmental Cost Accounting: Coming of Age? Tracking Organizational Performance Towards Environmental Sustainability." In*The Triple Bottom Line: Does It All Add Up,* edited by Adrian Henriques and Julie Richardson. London: EarthScan.

Johnson, H., and R. Kaplan. 1987. *Relevance Lost.* Cambridge, MA: Harvard Business School Press.

Kolk, A. 2003. "Trends in Sustainability Reporting by the Fortune Global 250." *Business Strategy and the Environment* 12: 279–291.

KPMG. 2002. *Beyond Numbers: How Leading Organizations Link Values With Value to Gain Competitive Advantage.* KPMG LLP White paper.

Lakoff, G., and M. Johnson. 1998. *Philosophy in the Flesh.* New York: Basic Books.

Lenzen, M., S. Lundie, G. Bransgrove, L. Charet, and F. Sack. 2003. "Assessing the Ecological Footprint of a Large Metropolitan Water Supplier: Lessons for Water Management and Planning Towards Sustainability." *Journal of Environmental Planning and Management* 46 (1): 113–141.

Lingane, A., and S. Olsen. 2004. "Guidelines for Social Return on Investment." *California Management Review* 46 (3): 116–135.

MacGillivary, A. 2004. *The Triple Bottom Line: Does It All Add Up,* edited by Adrian Henriques and Julie Richardson. London: EarthScan: 121–130.

Norman, W., and C. MacDonald. 2004. "Getting to the Bottom of the 'Triple Bottom Line.' " *Business Ethics Quarterly* 14 (2): 243–262.

Pearce, D., and E. Barbier. 2000. *Blueprint for a Sustainable Economy.* London: Earthscan.

Previts, G., and B. Merino. 1998. *A History of Accountancy in the United States.* Columbus: Ohio State University Press.

Richardson, J. 2004. "Accounting for Sustainability." In*The Triple Bottom Line: Does It All Add Up,* edited by Adrian Henriques and Julie Richardson. London: EarthScan: 34–44.

Robèrt, K. H. 2003. "Integrating Sustainability into Business Strategy and Operations: Applying the Natural Step Approach and Framework and Backcasting From Principles of Sustainability." In *Ants, Galileo, & Gandhi: Designing the Future of Business Through Nature, Genius, and Compassion,* edited by Sissel Waage.Sheffield, UK: Greenleaf.

Schilizzi, S. 2002. "Triple Bottom Line Accounting: How Serious Is It?" *Connections.* Accessed on November 13, 2004, from http://www.agrifood.info/10pub_conn_Win2002.htm

SustainAbility. 2004. *Risk and Opportunity: Best Practice in Non-Financial Reporting.* London: Author.

Tinker, A. M., B. Merino, and M. D. Neimark. 1982. "The Normative Origins of Positive Theories: Ideology and Accounting Thought." *Accounting, Organizations and Society* 7 (2): 167–200.

Tschopp, D. 2003. "It's Time for Triple Bottom Line Accounting." *The CPA Journal* 73 (12): 11.

Wright, P. A., G. Alward, J. L. Colby, T. W. Hoekstra, B. Tegler, and M. Turner. 2002. *USDA Forest Service. Monitoring for Forest Management Unit Scale Sustainability: The Local Unit Criteria and Indicators Development (LUCID) Test (management edition).* Fort Collins, CO: USDA Forest Service Inventory and Monitoring Report No. 5:54.

Part IV
Local Applications

12 Exploring Common Ground
Community Food Systems
and Social Sustainability

Leslie McBride

Can a community's food system serve as an indicator of social sustainability for that region? Are there initiatives and programs within the community food system movement that contribute in essential ways to social sustainability? If so, and if we examine the nature of their contributions, will we increase our understanding of how social sustainability is developed and strengthened? This chapter attempts a response to these questions.

The chapter begins by providing background on community food system concepts. Then it takes a closer look at three emblematic expressions of community food system work: farmers markets, community gardens, and food policy councils, highlighting their basic contributions (e.g., building relationships and strengthening community ties). This discussion sets the stage for the introduction of social sustainability using definitions and indicators proposed by McKenzie (2004). The chapter's concluding discussion explores common ground, summarizing and making explicit how the development of a community's food system enhances social sustainability by considering McKenzie's indicators in light of farmers markets, community gardens, and food policy councils.

A SYSTEMS APPROACH TO FOOD

The concept of a community food system is derived from an ecological, systems-based orientation to food and farming. With slightly different emphases reflecting their disciplinary origins, community food systems, sustainable food systems, regional (or local) food systems, fully integrated food systems, and civic agriculture share this orientation and its original agricultural, civic, and environmental foundations. As it gained both recognition and advocates, this systems-based orientation evolved into what is referred to increasingly as a *movement*—attracting the attention of professionals working in community development, urban planning, education, nutrition, and public health. In general, it focuses on educating about local agriculture, improving economic vitality within communities, addressing food security, and strengthening relationships among area residents (Feenstra,

1997). Additional background on three of these concepts—community food systems, fully integrated food systems, and civic agriculture—helps to illustrate their original intent and provides information that will be helpful when exploring common ground with social sustainability.

The Sustainable Agriculture Research and Education Program at the University of California, Davis, describes a community food system as

[A] collaborative effort to promote sustainable food production, processing, distribution and consumption . . . to enhance the environmental, economic, and social health of a particular place. Farmers, consumers, and communities partner to create more locally based, self-reliant food economies. (Sustainable Agriculture Research and Education Program, 2005)

Six intended outcomes of a community food system, which address environmental, economic, and social aspects of sustainability, are listed on the program's Web site. They are:

1. Improving access[1] to an adequate diet that is both affordable and nutritious;
2. Improving living and working conditions for farm and food system labor;
3. Strengthening direct marketing and processing links between farmers and consumers;
4. Creating jobs and recirculating financial capital within the community;
5. Creating food and agriculture policies that promote local or sustainable food production, processing and consumption; and
6. Establishing a stable base of family farms that uses less chemical and energy-intensive production practices and emphasizes local inputs.

Access to a healthy diet and better living and working conditions for farm and food system labor are outcomes that ensure basic needs are met for members within a community. Direct marketing and processing links between farmers and consumers depend on establishing and maintaining personal relationships, thereby promoting aspects of interconnectedness. Job creation and a more stable family farm base enhance equity and quality of life. As is discussed later, these are outcomes held in common with social sustainability.

Similar to community food systems, fully integrated food systems (Spector, 2002) emphasize the importance of strong, direct connections between farms and their local communities. Farmers who sell directly to consumers earn a higher percentage of the food dollar, whereas consumers buying from them receive fresher produce and have the opportunity to learn how their food was grown and about the land on which it was grown. The resulting relationships lie at the heart of fully integrated food systems. Spector claims they may facilitate a shift away from a lifestyle characterized by alienation, thereby helping to put "the culture back in agriculture" (p. 294).

Civic agriculture (Lyson, 2004) also emphasizes the direct relationship between consumers and producers, embedding local agriculture and food production within the community. Civic agriculture embodies "[A] commitment to developing and strengthening an economically, environmentally, and socially sustainable system of agriculture and food production that relies on local resources and serves local markets and consumers" (Lyson, 2004, p. 63). Enterprises that make up and support civic agriculture constitute part of a community's problem-solving capacity, relying on cooperative, mutually supportive social relationships.

Considered together, these descriptions provide a basic outline of potential goals held in common between community food systems and social sustainability. An examination of farmers markets, community gardens, and food policy councils provides further definition. Farmers markets and community gardens have long histories within local food systems; food policy councils are more recent developments. All three originated in response to food access issues. General background is given for each, with emphasis given to their respective contributions to social sustainability (e.g., enhancing equity, interconnectedness, and quality of life).

THREE FOOD SYSTEM PROGRAMS

Farmers Markets

Farmers markets are a form of direct marketing, an approach that includes community-supported agriculture and farm-to-table initiatives[2] and attempts to link local farmers directly to community members, institutions, and businesses. Farmers markets were originally organized to bring fresh fruits and vegetables to communities where access to nutritious food was limited. For example, the Interfaith Hunger Coalition of the Southern California Ecumenical Council sponsored development of the area's first five farmers markets in 1980 to improve food access for the poor after supermarkets fled the inner city (Parsons, 2006). These early markets were organized to address not only food access for the urban poor, but also the plight of small farmers who were being driven out of business by commercial agriculture (Parsons, 2006). According to Vance Corum, one of the original market organizers, for every retail dollar spent on what they grew, farmers earned 30 to 35 cents. Considered appallingly unfair in 1980, today that figure stands at approximately 19 cents per retail dollar. Farmers selling directly to consumers at farmers markets, in contrast, realize the full value of what they grow and are paid in cash at the time of sale, rather than waiting weeks to receive payment (Parsons, 2006).

No doubt these factors explain, at least partially, the phenomenal growth of farmers markets in the United States. According to the National Farmers Market Directory (U.S. Department of Agriculture, 2005), the 3,700 markets operating in 2004 constituted a 111% increase in 10 years, clearly indicating that farmers markets benefit small- to medium-size farm operations. Consumers benefit as well. They enjoy access to locally grown, farm-fresh produce and personal interaction with the farmers who grow it.

Unlike grocery stores and supermarkets, farmers markets are events, and they tend to have a festive air about them. Local musicians often perform at markets. Area organizations may be present at information booths or with volunteers to help publicize and distribute information important to local residents. Perhaps this is why people attending farmers markets interact more with each other. It has been estimated that people attending farmers markets engage in 10 times the number of conversations they engage in at supermarkets (Halweil, 2004). Shopping at farmers markets helps remind people that food has always been a primary means for enhancing community (Feenstra, 1997). Another important expression of community enhancement is the support that farmers markets provide to food security concerns.

Over 50% of farmers markets participate in Women, Infants, and Children (WIC) coupon, food stamp, and local and/or state nutrition programs; 25% participate in gleaning programs (U.S. Department of Agriculture, 2005). The U.S. Department of Agriculture's (USDA's) Seniors Farmers Market Nutrition Program (U.S. Department of Agriculture, 2005), established to help low-income seniors access farmers markets, provides help in three ways. First, the program provides seniors with coupons that they can exchange for food at the markets. Second, it encourages senior centers to provide transportation to the markets. Third, it helps local growers deliver their produce directly to senior housing facilities. In 2003, some 2,000 farmers markets participated in this program.

Strengthening the relationships between producers and consumers may play an essential role in social sustainability. Norberg-Hodge (1998) has observed that, through direct connections, people remember their dependence on one another. Area farmers who know the local people buying their produce are less likely to use toxic chemicals on their crops. Consumers who know and have an investment in the farmers growing their food are more likely to offer them assistance. Norberg-Hodge tells of a farmer in Kentucky whose crops were saved from an early frost when local residents, who were members of the farmer's CSA, pitched in to help with the harvest. His neighbors, who sold to agribusinesses, lost their crops to the bad weather.

Community Gardens

Recently described as "exceptional" for their ability to address an array of public health and livability issues (Twiss et al., 2003) and as "environmental tipping points" for their ability to jumpstart profound changes throughout an ecosocial system (Marten, Brooks, and Suutari, 2005), community gardens actually began in response to food shortages during the two World Wars (Twiss et al., 2003). Community gardens are open spaces managed and operated by members of the local community for a variety of purposes (Holland, 2004), including access to fresh foods, physical activity, and enjoyment of nature (Armstrong, 2000). When limited financial and community resources or inconvenient transportation systems make it difficult to access nutritious food from grocery stores and retail outlets, people can access these gardens. Additionally, participating gardeners can extend their garden's reach by donating portions of their harvest to neighbors, area soup kitchens, food banks, senior centers, and community centers (Sneed; cited in Williamson, 2002). Research shows that community gardens also serve education and training functions. Participants learn about gardening methods—including permaculture, composting, and other organic practices—cooking techniques, and nutrition (Holland, 2004).

While working together in community gardens, people learn about other cultures and generations. Gardeners preserve aspects of their culture through using native seeds (e.g., heirloom tomatoes) or growing foods that they cannot find in stores (Williamson, 2002). This feature makes community gardens particularly appealing to newly arrived immigrants, who can grow the foods of their homeland (Twiss et al., 2003). Continuing to grow, prepare, and consume these foods helps immigrants preserve important cultural and ethnic traditions. Sharing information in the garden about foods grown and eaten by different cultures can progress to sharing recipes, food, and organizing community dinners. As a result, social networks develop that span ethnoracial divisions (Hancock, 2001). Similarly, community gardens encourage intergenerational interaction because they provide ideal settings for combining elders' knowledge and experience with the physical energy and strength of youth (Williamson, 2002). Sharing between generations and across cultures creates ideal conditions for the development of new perspectives. A sense of belonging can develop that also may include a sense of place in the world (Williamson, 2002).

People report getting involved in community gardens because they want to socialize with other gardeners, neighbors, family members, and friends (Lertzman, 2004). Participation and involvement are particularly strong features of community gardens because they require a cohesive social network for their organization and management (Hancock, 2001). Armstrong (2000) found that the organizing processes facilitated through development and maintenance of community gardens helped residents in low-income neighborhoods address other issues. To create the Little Puerto Rico garden in New York City, for example, neighbors had to organize to drive out the drug dealers operating in the area. The garden they created functioned like an outdoor community center where people cooked meals together, celebrated birthdays, and held weddings (Marten et al., 2005).

In Cleveland, Ohio, the Juvenile Court, juvenile offenders, and local groups developed a garden-based partnership that converted vacant lots into productive, attractive gardens. The teens involved experienced a sense of accomplishment when their work was recognized and appreciated, and the court was acknowledged for its involvement in an effort symbolizing hard work and positive change (Williamson, 2002). Interactions among neighbors at community gardens can lead to the formation of neighborhood watch groups. In Philadelphia, one neighborhood experienced a drop from 40 burglary and theft incidents per month to 4. Similarly, a garden developed in the Mission District of San Francisco was associated with a 28% drop in crime after its first year (Williamson, 2002).

These kinds of changes led Marten et al. (2005) to refer to community gardens as environmental tipping points for their ability to reverse cycles of urban decay. Once constructive cycles begin repeating themselves, nurturing development of community pride and stronger ties among neighbors, they inspire more gardens and the resources necessary for their maintenance. Although there may be no better model for the implementation of social (as well as economic and environmental) policies at the local level than the model provided by the community garden movement, lack of data supporting their positive impact hinders attempts to argue persuasively for them when resources (e.g., funding, land, water) are at stake (Holland, 2004).

Food Policy Councils

The State and Local Food Policy Project, initiated by the Agricultural Law Center at Drake University, defines a Food Policy Council (FPC) as convening

> citizens and government officials for the purpose of providing a comprehensive examination of a state or local food system. This unique, non-partisan form of civic engagement brings together a diverse array of food system stakeholders to develop food and agriculture policy recommendations. (Agricultural Law Center, 2006)

A defining characteristic of FPCs is their comprehensive approach to analyzing food issues, which allows for recognition of interrelationships within the food system and development of coordinated, integrated actions. The usual focus on agriculture and food production is broadened, providing the opportunity to pose questions about issues that frequently go unasked. FPCs begin with the assumption that governments and community groups should take active roles in planning for and ensuring food security (Allen, 1994). Although limited in comparison to government involvement in planning, housing, and education, the opportunity that FPCs provide to examine food issues and recommend policy changes in a coordinated fashion raises public awareness of their significance, which can, in turn, create considerable momentum for change. The frequently unasked questions that FPCs are likely to examine include: What are the causes of hunger in our area and how effectively do our food assistance programs respond to them? How food-secure is our state or city? How much of the food consumed in our state or region was grown locally? Do area schools (or hospitals or prisons) buy any locally produced food (Agricultural Law Center, 2006)? The process of answering these questions and developing appropriate solutions builds local capacity, improving control over local and nonlocal challenges to food needs (Bellows and Hamm, 2001) and enhancing the social sustainability of a community or region.

A systems approach to examining food issues involves interested parties throughout the system, ranging from farmers to consumers. Ideally, FPC membership should reflect this range and include food processing and distribution representatives, chefs and restaurant owners, food access and antihunger advocates, faith community and diversity representatives, educators, and community gardeners. Officials from state agencies also should participate so that state and stakeholder interests, involving not only agriculture and transportation, but also public health and cultural affairs, are represented.

State and local FPCs have been founded and officially recognized in a variety of ways (Hamilton, 2002). Connecticut created the first FPC at the state level in 1997 by enacting legislation for this purpose. In 2000, the governor of Iowa created the Iowa Food Policy Council through executive order. Efforts by commissioners of agriculture in North Carolina and Utah were instrumental in the development of their state FPCs. North American counties including Marin and Knox Counties; cities including Toronto, Berkeley, Hartford, and Knoxville; and even county/city combinations, such as Oregon's Portland/Multnomah County collaboration, have recognized the need for local FPCs.

Although they may serve as catalysts for projects, the main focus of a FPC's work is on changing policy to positively influence food and agriculture (Food Security Learning Center, 2006). To illustrate the types of contributions that FPCs have made to the vitality and security of their food systems and, thereby, to social sustainability, this section concludes with examples of FPC work at state and local levels. Unless otherwise cited, this information is summarized from program profiles described on the Food Security Learning Center Web site.

The City of Hartford's Advisory Commission on Food Policy helped establish a new bus route that connected the city's low-income residents to affordable food stores, cutting in half the 90 minutes previously required for the roundtrip. The Hartford FPC recommended changes to improve performance of the city's WIC program, hosted workshops for teachers and administrators on the school breakfast program, and monitored meal quality and participation rates in the summer food service program. At the state level, Connecticut's FPC promoted a single application format for assistance programs, including food stamps, WIC, reduced price lunch, and health care for uninsured children and youth that saved time and reduced paperwork. The state FPC also helped sponsor a public hearing on barriers to food access in Connecticut. Testimony at the hearings resulted in legislation proposed to support supermarket development in low-income areas.

Iowa's FPC developed the following four principles on which to guide its work: "Ensure access to nutritious food for all Iowans; manage Iowa's resources sustainably; promote diversity in Iowa's food, culture, and people; and support prosperous, independent farm and food businesses in Iowa" (Food Security Learning Center, 2006). Based on these principles, it developed recommendations for strengthening Iowa's food system through increasing food security, consumer awareness, and opportunities to increase farm to institution marketing. The FPC also helped to evaluate Iowa's Senior Farmers Market Nutrition Program and to create its coupon program.

Lack of federal and provincial leadership around food security concerns led to the Toronto, Ontario, FPC's initiation in 1991. Working toward its stated aim of "A food system that fosters equitable food access, nutrition, community development and environmental health" (Toronto Food Policy Council, 2004), its remarkable accomplishments are presented on its Web site within the following seven categories: food and hunger action; health; agricultural land preservation and urban planning; economic development; urban agriculture and food waste recovery; community gardens; and communications, capacity building, and public education. Because descriptions of progress made within four of these categories provide particularly fine illustrations of how strengthening a community's food system also enhances social sustainability, they are summarized here.

1. Food and Hunger Action—The Toronto FPC produced a series of 15 discussion papers linking hunger to food systems policy and conducted a feasibility study of a not-for-profit health food delivery system for the city's low-income citizens. These papers laid the groundwork for a "Field-to-Table" program that has made available nourishing, regionally sourced food to 15,000 people each month.

2. Health—Acknowledging the significant long-term costs that a public health care system incurs when large numbers of the people it serves are hungry, poorly nourished, or eating unsafe foods, the FPC collaborated with Toronto's Student Nutrition Coalition to increase the number of school food programs in the city from 53 to 350 and participated in a campaign promoting nutritious homemade baby food. The FPC also participated in a successful advocacy campaign preventing licensure of Bovine Growth Hormone for use in Canadian dairy operations.

3. Community Gardens—Supporting this movement's success at growing not only food, but also neighborhoods, skills, fitness, and leadership, the FPC led expansion efforts that more than doubled the number of community gardens in 10 years. Additionally, the FPC completed a manual on guidelines for school gardens and composting and conducted 25 workshops for parents and teachers on the topic.

4. Communications, capacity building, and public education—Working to develop community capacity for food security, members of the Toronto FPC have delivered hundreds of lectures and slide show presentations on community food security, sustainable food systems, and urban agriculture. It has given these presentations at colleges and universities, to community groups, and to organizations focused on environmental and sustainability issues.

This overview of farmers markets, community gardens, and FPCs, and of their positive influence within communities, provides the first of two starting points for exploring common ground with social sustainability. The second is a definition of *social sustainability* and a set of indicators for its assessment. The following section considers a definition and related indicators developed by McKenzie (2004) that are particularly useful to exploring common ground in that they consider social sustainability as both a condition and a process.

SOCIAL SUSTAINABILITY AND ITS INDICATORS

Widespread adoption of the Brundtland definition[3] of sustainable development as a general definition of sustainability "presupposes the necessity of *development* rather than focusing on strategies for the maintenance of current conditions . . . " (McKenzie, 2004, p. 2; italics added). Furthermore, because sustainable development is aligned more closely with environmental and economic aspects, social aspects have been more likely to fall off the sustainability agenda (Barron and Gauntlett, 2002), and research aimed at understanding what sustains and promotes an equitable and just society is rare (McKenzie, 2004). This reasoning may explain, in part, why community food system literature has been incorporated more extensively into discussions on environmental and economic aspects of sustainability.

In a working paper developed to explore current thinking around social sustainability and to provide a helpful framework in developing a common research agenda, McKenzie (2004) defines *social sustainability* as "a positive, life-enhancing condition within communities, and a process within communities that can achieve that condition" (p. 12). The equal emphasis given to *condition* and *process* addresses a tendency in the literature to focus on social sustainability as a current condition or future goal while overlooking the processes and actions involved in its establishment and maintenance. Before considering McKenzie's indicators, it is useful to bear in mind the conclusion that Hilderink (2004) drew following an extensive review of indicators for sustainable *development*[4]: There are no ultimate indicators. Hilderink warned that this fact may be true for the human and social domain of sustainable development in particular: "Processes in the human and social domain tend to be multi-causal, and usually only associative relations can be distinguished" (p. 53). Still, after issuing this caveat, Hilderink advocates for their use, observing that, despite their inherent problems, the need for indicators remains strong. The indicators that McKenzie (2004) proposes may address these concerns, in that they attend to " . . . aspects of the condition [of social sustainability] but can also readily be seen as parts of the process a community could undergo in order to move towards the ideal" (p. 23). The indicators are all interrelated and "may be measured, or cross-referenced with one another to look for patterns of cause and effect" (p. 23). The indicators are:

1. Equity of access to key services (including health, education, transport, housing, and recreation);
2. Equity between generations, meaning that future generations will not be disadvantaged by the activities of the current generation;
3. A system of cultural relations in which the positive aspects of disparate cultures are valued and protected, and in which cultural integration is supported and promoted when it is desired by individuals and groups;
4. Widespread political participation of citizens not only in electoral procedures, but also in other areas of political activity, particularly at a local level;
5. A system for transmitting awareness of social sustainability from one generation to the next;
6. A sense of community responsibility for maintaining that system of transmission;
7. Mechanisms for a community to collectively identify its strengths and needs;
8. Mechanisms for a community to fulfill its own needs where possible through community action; and
9. Mechanisms for political advocacy to meet needs that cannot be met by community action. (p. 23)

With the addition of the process aspects of these indicators, consideration of the range and depth of contributions that farmers markets, community gardens, and food policy councils make to social sustainability increases significantly. A clearer understanding of common ground between social sustainability and community food systems results, making it possible to appreciate the extent to which a vibrant community food system contributes to social sustainability within a region.

CONCLUSION: EXPLORING COMMON GROUND

This chapter concludes by reviewing the descriptions of farmers markets, community gardens, and FPCs provided earlier and considering their relationship to each of McKenzie's indicators. In this concluding discussion, common ground is explored and initial responses to the questions posed within the chapter's opening overview are developed.

1. *Equity of access to key services* (including health, education, transport, housing, and recreation). Although McKenzie does not include access to nutritious, affordable food among the examples provided—or does so indirectly via health—farmers markets, community gardens, and FPCs all originated in response to food access issues. Farmers markets bring fresh fruits and vegetables to communities where access to nutritious food is limited based on socioeconomic level, age, and other factors. When limited financial and community resources or inconvenient transportation systems make accessing grocery stores and retail outlets difficult, residents can develop and then access community gardens. FPCs have improved access to food in many ways, not the least of which has been the improvement of transportation routes. They also have worked to ensure that food programs for infants, children, and adolescents contain the most nutritious food possible (e.g., monitoring school meal quality, promoting nutritious homemade baby food). The importance of food access to the work of FPCs is illustrated by the State of Iowa's FPC, which places improved access first among its four guiding principles.

This indicator's condition and process aspects are well illustrated via community gardens and FPCs. A community garden's initial development and continued maintenance constitute process aspects of food access; the actual presence of a garden within a community and the fresh food it produces constitute condition aspects of food access. The process aspects of an FPC include steps taken toward its development and implementation, as well as activities and processes entailed in the development and implementation of policy. The condition aspects include the actual existence of the FPC, the policy it develops, and the results from that policy (e.g., a new bus route).

2. *Equity between generations* (meaning that future generations will not be disadvantaged by activities of the current generation). An essential issue related to this indicator is the protection of fertile farmland from urban sprawl and unnecessary or unplanned development. FPCs have played an important role in this regard, raising awareness of the importance of farmland preservation, particularly in and near urban areas. Farmers markets also have played a role, helping area farmers maintain the financial stability necessary to

continue farming, thereby preventing the sale of fertile land to developers and protecting its use in food production for future generations.

Farmers markets constitute a condition aspect of this indicator, as does the presence of farmland around and within urban areas. The indicator's process aspects include the planning, organizing, policy development, and relationship-building required to maintain farmers markets and preserve local farmland.

3. *A system of cultural relations* (in which the positive aspects of disparate cultures are valued and protected and in which cultural integration is supported and promoted as desired). Community gardens address this indicator directly and comprehensively. Cultivating, preserving, preparing, and consuming the foods of a culture are essential means for valuing and protecting its positive aspects. Cultural integration is supported and promoted through community gardens when members of different cultures share information about the foods they are growing, when they exchange traditional recipes and dishes, and when they participate in community dinners.

The condition aspects of this indicator include the community garden and the foods, representing the culinary and dietary traditions of different cultures grown within it. Other condition aspects include dinners and events resulting from garden participation, as well as the network of relationships established through garden cultivation and maintenance. The subtle distinctions between condition and process aspects of McKenzie's indicators are evident here because a network of relationships can be regarded from two perspectives—as a resulting condition *and* as a process on which the condition depends.

4. *Widespread political participation of citizens* (not only in electoral procedures, but also in other areas of political activity, particularly at a local level). FPCs are an excellent expression of this indicator. The basic assumption of FPCs is that community groups should be actively involved in food security issues, and FPCs seek participation from representatives throughout the local food system. Although farmers markets do so less directly, they also encourage political participation of citizens, as organizations advocating for issues important to food and to the local area are typical features of farmers markets.

The condition aspects of this indicator include policy created and enacted, increased public awareness, and an engaged citizenry; process aspects include participation in the FPC process and the series of steps taken as FPC members inquire into food access issues within their community.

5. *A system for transmitting awareness of social sustainability from one generation to the next.*

6. *A sense of community responsibility for maintaining that system of transmission.* As community food systems innovations, farmers markets, community gardens, and FPCs display their coherence with social sustainability through their participatory nature: All three invite citizens to get actively involved in their food systems. Their involvement develops awareness of conditions and processes essential to social sustainability and carries these skills forward to future generations through continued cycles of participation and awareness building. Community responsibility for maintaining this system of transmission is supported by the same process.

Here, the condition aspects of the indicator are the system that is developed, the awareness of social sustainability, and the sense of responsibility for its maintenance. The process aspects are involved in both the transmission of awareness between generations and the maintenance of this transmission.

7. *A way for a community to collectively identify its strengths and needs.*
8. *A way for a community to fulfill its own needs where possible through community action.*
9. *A way for political advocacy to meet needs that cannot be met by community action.* Described as a nonpartisan form of civic engagement, FPCs were initially created to enable community representatives to identify strengths and needs related to food security and antihunger issues. FPCs assume community groups will take active roles in food system planning. They provide the essential mechanism at state and local levels for comprehensively examining food system issues and developing appropriate policy to address those issues. Finally, they recognize the interconnectedness within all aspects of the food system, as well as the coordination and integration required if policy goals are to be achieved[5] (Hamilton, 2002).

NOTES

1. Programs developed to enhance food security are an important aspect of improved access. These programs include traditional approaches, such as food banks and pantries, soup and community kitchens, and elderly feeding programs, as well as newer initiatives, such as Community Supported Agriculture's low-income share options and special purchasing programs at local farmers' markets (Winne, 2004, 2005).
2. Farm-to-table initiatives include, for example, farm-to-school, farm-to-hospital, and farm-to-prison programs.
3. "Sustainable development is development that meets the needs of the present without compromising the ability of future generations to meet their own needs" (World Commission on Environment and Development; cited in McKenzie, 2004, p. 2).

4. Emphasis is added here to highlight the conflation of terms as per McKenzie's point.

REFERENCES

Agricultural Law Center. 2006. "Food Policy Council Questions and Answers." Drake University. Accessed on August 31, 2006, from http:www.statefoodpolicy.org/sfpcqanda.htm.

Allen, P. 1994. "The Human Face of Sustainable Agriculture: Adding People to the Environmental Agenda." Sustainability in the Balance Series, Issue Paper No. 4. Center for Agroecology and Sustainable Food Systems, University of California, Santa Cruz.

Armstrong, D. 2000. "A Survey of Community Gardens in Upstate New York: Implications for Health Promotion and Community Ddevelopment." *Health & Place* 6 (4): 319–327.

Barron, L., and E. Gauntlett. 2002. "Stage 1 Report–Model of Social Sustainability." Housing and Sustainable Communities Indicators Project. Accessed on August 31, 2006, from http://wacoss.org.au/images/assets/SP_Sustainability/HSCIP%20Stage%201%20Report.pdf.

Bellows, A. C., and M. W. Hamm. 2001. "Local Autonomy and Sustainable Development: Testing Import Substitution in Localizing Food Systems." *Agriculture and Human Values* 18: 271–284.

Feenstra, G. W. 1997. "Local Food Systems and Sustainable Communities." *American Journal of Alternative Agriculture* 12 (1): 28–36.

Food Security Learning Center. 2006. "Food Policy Councils: FAQs." Accessed on August 31, 2006, from www.worldhungeryear.org/fslc/faqs/ria_093.asp?section=8&click=3.

Halweil, B. 2004. *Eat Here: Reclaiming Homegrown Pleasures in a Global Supermarket*. New York: Norton.

Hamilton, N. 2002. "Putting a Face on Our Food: How State and Local Food Policies Can Promote the New Agriculture." *Drake Journal of Agricultural Law* 7: 407–443.

Hancock, T. 2001. "People, Partnerships and Human Progress: Building Community Capital." *Health Promotion International* 16 (3): 275–280.

Hilderink, H. B. M. 2004. "Towards Human and Social Sustainability Indicators: A Multidimensional Approach." RIVM Report No. 550012002/2004. The National Institute for Public Health and the Environment. Accessed on May 1, 2007, from http://www.rivm.nl/bibliotheek/rapporten/550012002.pdf.

Holland, L. 2004. "Diversity and Connections in Community Gardens: A Contribution to Local Sustainability." *Local Environment* 9 (3): 285–305.

Lertzman, R. 2004, September/October. "Common Interests." *Hope*, pp. 39–41, 46.

Lyson, T. A. 2004. *Civic Agriculture: Reconnecting Farm, Food, and Community*. Medford, MA: Tufts University Press.

Marten, G., S. Brooks, and A. Suutari. 2005. "Environmental Tipping Points: A New Slant on Strategic Environmentalism." *World Watch* 18 (6): 10–14.

McKenzie, S. 2004. "Social Sustainability: Towards Some Definitions." Working Paper Series No. 27. Hawke Research Institute. Accessed on January 15, 2005, from http://www.unisa.edu.au/hawkeinstitute/documents/wp27.pdf.

Norberg- Hodge, H. 1998. "Think Global–Eat Local! Delicious Ways to Counter Globalization." *The Ecologist* 28 (4): 208–212.

Parsons, R. 2006, May 24. "The Idea That Shook the World: Straight From Farmer With No Middleman? That Was a Radical Notion 27 Years Ago. *Los Angeles Times.* Accessed on May 25, 2006, from http://www.latimes.com/features/food/la-fo-farmer24may24,1,4457723.story.

Spector, R. 2002. "Fully Integrated Food Systems: Regaining Connections Between Farmers and Consumers. *The Fatal Harvest Reader: The Tragedy of Industrial Agriculture* (pp. 288–294). A. Kimbrell, ed. Sausalito, CA: Foundation for Deep Ecology.

Sustainable Agriculture Research and Education Program. 2005. "What Is a Community Food System?" University of California, Davis. Accessed on December 28, 2005, from http://sarep.ucdavis.edu/cdpp/cfsoverview.htm.

Toronto Food Policy Council. 2004. "Food Policy." City of Toronto. Accessed on April 10, 2004, from http://www.city.toronto.on.cahealth/tfpc_index.htm.

Twiss, J., J. Dickinson, S. Duma, T. Kleinman, H. Paulsen, and L. Riveria. 2003. "Community Gardens: Lessons Learned From California Health Cities and Communities." *American Journal of Public Health* 93 (9): 1435–1438.

U.S. Department of Agriculture. 2005. "AMS Farmers Markets–Facts." Accessed on December 28, 2005, from http://www.ams.usda. gov/farmersmarkets/facts. htm.

Williamson, E. 2002. *A Deeper Ecology: Community Gardens in the Urban Environment.* Unpublished master's thesis, University of Delaware.

Winne, M. 2004, Winter. "Food System Planning: Setting the Community's Table." *Progressive Planning: The Magazine of Planners Network* Accessed on February 29, 2006, from http://www.plannersnetwork.org/publications/2004_winter/winne.htm

———. 2005. "The Food Gap." *Orion* 24 (5): 60–67.

13 Social Capital and Community
University Partnerships

W. Barry Messer and Kevin Kecskes

Advocates of sustainability focus on measurable outcomes as well as processes involved in achieving desirable states. This is the case in considering social sustainability. Stephen McKenzie (2004) defines *social sustainability* as a "life-enhancing condition within communities, and a *process* with that can achieve that condition" (http://www.unisa.edu.au/hawkeinstitute/publications/downloads/wp27.pdf; italics added). This perspective of social sustainability provides a valuable conceptual and practical basis for framing our understanding of desirable social activity. But how useful is this construct to framing action? In other words, how does one operationalize social sustainability to inform policy aimed at addressing important challenges facing communities today? This chapter examines this question and looks at how the concept of social sustainability can be conceived as a useful tool and construct for shaping policy direction for higher education. Specifically, this paper examines the larger effects and mutual benefits that are realized through efforts made to establish community–university partnerships that are informed by concepts and principles of social sustainability to offer a better understanding and appreciation of the value of this construct in policy.

CONCEPTS AND CONSTRUCTS

The Construct of Social Sustainability

One of the most complete efforts to define *social sustainability* and construct a model that covers potential factors associated with the concept has been documented by Stephen McKenzie (2004) in covering the work developed by Western Australian Council of Social Service (WACOSS). Starting with the definition:

> Social sustainability occurs when the formal and informal processes, systems, structures, and relationship actively support the capacity of current and future generations to create healthy and livable communities. Socially sustainable communities are equitable, diverse, connected, and democratic and provide a good quality of life. (McKenzie, 2004, p. 21)

The model then offers a set of "aspirational and visionary statements" or principles, characteristic of socially sustainable communities by which this condition may be achieved (McKenzie, 2004).

The key principles for social sustainability include (a) "equity," which highlights community provision of equitable opportunities and outcomes for all its members, particularly the poorest and most vulnerable; (b) diversity; (c) interconnectedness—systems and structures that connect within and outside the community at the formal, informal, and institutional levels; (d) quality of life—community ensures basic needs are met and fosters a good quality of life for all; and (e) democracy and governance—open and accountable governance structures.

Each principle in this model is followed by a series of characteristics and statements addressing each principle. The model is an important and valuable synthesis and articulation of what has been otherwise an elusive concept. McKenzie acknowledges that sustainability is inherently a contested concept and offers the work of the WACOSS as a construct for guiding a collective understanding of the concept of social sustainability and cohesive research. As such, this model is an important contribution to the field.

But as useful as the model is, it is still largely descriptive and leaves many questions as to *how* a community pursues social sustainability as a course of action. To explore how one may potentially use the construct of social sustainability as an "actionable" concept, it is useful to explore the related concept of social capital.

The Construct of Social Capital

Social capital has been the focus of much attention by community researchers and the community of development professionals. Although much has been made of the potential usefulness of social capital in better understanding key elements of healthy functioning communities, it remains a contested concept (Rohe, 2004). Nevertheless, there are some commonly held perspectives among those that have focused attention on this concept.

Social capital is commonly understood to be composed of norms of reciprocity and mutual trust. As such, it inheres in the structures of relations between and among actors (Coleman, 1988). Putnam (1993) further develops the conceptualization of social capital as "features of social organization that facilitate coordination and cooperation for mutual benefit. Social capital enhances the benefits of investment in physical and human capital" (pp. 35–36). In both of these characterizations, social capital is conceived as the currency of social organization that, through processes of coordination and trust, results in achievable products or goods for those in the organization and community. Social capital is an expression of shared expectations that lead to cooperative behavior that produces mutual benefits.

The process and outcome elements of social capital are further elaborated by the work of community development researchers who have focused on the two different but related sets of elements that are included within the constructs of social capital: understanding social capital as "capital" and understanding social capital as "social" (Drishna and Uphoff, 2002). The concept and constructs of social capital share both a process and an outcome focus similar to the construct of social sustainability.

Although many have contributed to the literature and research with different perspectives and assessments of social capital as an essential feature of community processes, there are some key elements that are common among these different offerings. Social capital is a way of considering processes and interactions within communities built on trust and reciprocity. This process of building trust and reciprocal exchanges is the basis for producing desired social outcomes for those who participate in the community. These outcomes are the "goods" of social organization and result in (a) more efficient achievement of shared purposes, and (b) lowering transaction costs. Thus, social capital formation leads to more efficient and effective achievement of commonly pursued interests of those within the community.

The elements of social capital can be seen to provide a framework for action required in the process to achieve outcomes and, as such, provide a potentially useful way of approaching socially sustainable action. Table 13.1 represents how we can map the principles of social sustainability to the essential elements of social capital.

Gittell and Vidal (1998) further the operationalization of a social capital construct by focusing on community capacity in relation to increasing social capital. Building from the inherent notion of social capital that involves a process of building trust and reciprocity is a function of (a) bonding—expansion of strong ties within communities; and (b) bridging—the strengthening of weak ties across communities, Gittell and Vidal focus on the building blocks of a community: individuals who relate to one another in families and through informal associations and organizations (public, nonprofit, and private).

Given these building blocks, Rohe (2004) suggests four broad strategies, or *levers*, for strengthening community capacity through actions to build social capital:

Table 13.1 Mapping the Principles of Social Sustainability to Actionable Constructs of Social Capital

Social Sustainability "Principles"	Social Capital Elements
Equity	Mutual interest
Diversity	Inclusive participation
Interconnectedness	Building and sustaining relationships
Quality of life	Embedded shared purposes
Open and accountable governance	Reciprocity through trust

1. enhancing the abilities of the individuals (education, leadership development),
2. making the organizations stronger (capacity development),
3. building links among individuals (community organizing) and,
4. building links among organizations (through collaborations, partnerships, etc.).

These levers for social capital formation provide a foundation for how a policy directed toward increasing community capacity and addressing the principles of social sustainability can be approached.

AN AGENDA FOR SOCIAL SUSTAINABILITY: COMMUNITY–UNIVERSITY PARTNERSHIPS

There is an important role for higher education in the global society, but the exact nature of that engagement is contested. Higher education's failure and best self can be found by engaging community partners in mutually transformative work that allows us to re-imagine, in ways both creative and practical, sustainable communities. Our choice of partners and our visions of what may be accomplished together create opportunities for us to become members of communities and of a world of which we would like to be part. (Enos and Morton, 2003, p. 40)

Each day, members of the academy have a choice to make. They can continue to support a half-century-old agenda of increasing specialization and silo-like disciplinary focus or take inspiration from the moral roots of American higher education and build on the emerging educational trend to partner with communities in the "mutually transformative work" that Enos and Morton envision. The choice is critical and makes a daily difference for three important constituencies. For students, at stake is the opportunity to explore and test their civic sensibilities and skills as they apply new learning and grow into effective leaders. For communities, at stake is the prospect of partnering with higher education to teach, learn, and act cooperatively on important community-based projects and create informed research agendas that will make a palpable difference in people's lives. For the academy, a historical opportunity is at hand to either respond positively and creatively to society's increasing call for relevance or retreat into the ivory tower.

Building Social Capital for Three Centuries . . . Almost

American higher education institutions have a rich history of service; the contemporary expression of this history in the form of community–university partnerships directly relates to the building of social capital and the further-ing of a social sustainability agenda.

Academic civic engagement is not a new concept. For over 30 years, with the care of trained historians, Lee Benson and Ira Harkavy of the University of Pennsylvania have been documenting the democratic history of American higher education. They remind us that in the 17th century, the colonial col-leges (most of today's Ivy League schools) were founded on Christian values with service as a central aim (Benson, et al, 2005). They recall that in 1862, the Morrill Act established America's land-grant institutions to spread edu-cation, advance democracy, and improve the mechanical, agricultural, and military sciences. This act continued to anchor higher education to its original purpose of service to society. Research institutions followed soon afterward.

Indeed, at the turn of the 20th century, higher education had an abid-ing belief in the democratic purposes of higher education. However, in the middle of the 20th century, coinciding with the outset of the cold war, a new trend in higher education emerged: commodification (Benson, et al, 2005). This market-driven trend in the Academy would not be seriously challenged for four decades. Benson and Harkavy (2002) characterize this time in American history as the beginning of the big science, cold war, entrepreneurial, commodified, American research university system.

A troublesome aspect of this trend toward higher education commer-cialization is the effect it has had on college students' values and ambitions. When students witness universities acting in ways akin to competitive, profit-making corporations, it legitimizes a career-only, credential-focused approach to education. A predictable precipitate of this shift is a decrease in student engagement, youth voting, and so on (Benson, et al, 2005). This concern is well established (Colby, et al, 2003; Ehrlich, 2000).

In America and internationally, higher education is attempting to reclaim the civic purposes of its mission—affirming and implementing the institu-tion's civic responsibility whether public or private. This movement to refo-cus American higher education to reclaim its public purposes began in the early 1980s. As Saltmarsh and Gelmon (2006) assert, Newman's 1985 book *Higher Education and the American Resurgence* captured the early stirrings of the "movement" to revitalize the civic mission of higher education. Many others, including Ernest Boyer (1990, 1997) and former Harvard President Derek Bok (2003), in *Universities in the Marketplace*, condemn the com-mercialization of higher education. They call for a renewed commitment to what Stanford's John Gardner often called the compact between freedom and service. In short, for the past decade and a half, public higher education intellectuals and leaders have called on their institutions to return to their his-torical roots and recommit to the social compact that informed their found-ing. Today, nearly 1,000 colleges and universities have publicly vowed to take this concern seriously by signing National Campus Compact's *Presidents' Declaration on the Civic Responsibility of Higher Education* (1999). Several years prior to the *Declaration*, Portland State University helped devise and test an innovative institutional response based in large part by intentionally building reciprocal community–university partnerships and bringing them to life by infusing service learning into the curriculum.

Commitment to Social Responsibility: A Decade of Innovation at Portland State University

Since the early 1990s, service learning and a broader focus on civic engagement have challenged and helped change the culture of the academy. What started as a student movement in the 1970s and 1980s, inspired by a desire for greater social justice, morphed into a course-connected pedagogical initiative. Service learning initially attracted some faculty partly because of the social resonance it shared with educators trained in the 1960s. Surprising traditionalists, service learning expanded quickly due in part to its proven positive impact on student learning (Astin and Sax, 1998). As five straight years of top rankings in *U.S. News and World Report* attest (http://www.pdx.edu/cae/rankings.html) and as Portland State University's (PSU's) Partnership Map (www.partner.pdx.ed) publicly displays, PSU has more than 8,200 students annually working in community settings, learning how to apply new knowledge and learning about their role in building sustainable, democratic communities.

This institutional transformation began over a decade ago when a historic agenda of comprehensive reform was set forth to align the curriculum, undergraduate and graduate academic programs, scholarship and research with community outreach, and partnership development. On a sky bridge at the university, students embossed PSU's motto, *Let Knowledge Serve the City* (Kecskes, et al, 2006). PSU's location downtown enhances its possibilities to be *in* and *of* the city and the metropolitan region and symbolically captures its commitment to the communities of which PSU is a part. In the early 1990s, PSU's undergraduate program—University Studies—emerged as a model for integration of student learning with service in the community (Colby, Ehrlich, Beaumont, and Stephens, 2003; Ehrlich, 2000; Williams and Bernstine, 2002). The University Studies program has four primary goals that are explicitly integrated into the curriculum during the four years of undergraduate experience: inquiry and critical thinking, communication, the variety of human experience, and ethical issues and social responsibility (see www.ous.pdx.edu). In their final undergraduate year, PSU students must take a six-credit Senior Capstone, which is designed to integrate each of the four goals, with particular emphasis on social responsibility. In 1995, there were five Capstone courses. In the 2005–2006 academic year, there are more than 220 Capstone course offerings. Each Capstone is interdisciplinary and team- and community-based. Although some Capstones change each year, many, based on sustaining strong community–university partnerships, have continued now for over a decade. One of these "transformational partnerships" (Enos and Morton, 2003)—the Community Watershed Stewardships Program (CWSP)—is the subject of the next section. The CWSP provides empirical evidence in direct support of the claim that well-conceived and executed community–university partnerships are "actionable" examples of how one can both teach about, as well as bring to life, an active social sustainability agenda.

CWSP

The CWSP is a joint venture by the City of Portland Bureau of Environmental Services (BES) and PSU. The partnership began in 1994. Since that time, it has provided an essential mechanism for the partners to focus on furthering their primary institutional roles, as well as jointly participating in an innovative effort to increase community capacity.

The primary goals for the CWSP are (a) to encourage citizens to establish activities that form partnerships in the community, and (b) use volunteers to affect change and improve watershed conditions within the neighborhoods. Other goals for the CWSP are to improve the quality of water in Portland's watersheds (in keeping with BES' directive) and to provide a platform for education and research for students and faculty while addressing important community challenges (consistent with PSU's mission of "let knowledge serve the city"). These goals in no way conflict with each other. In fact, they are mutually supportive. The challenge that exists for the CWSP is to keep the different goals in perspective, supporting and complementing each aspect, while neither elevating nor diminishing the significance of either one. As such, the CWSP provides a useful case study of the challenges of a partnership, as well as the possibilities for how this form of collaboration can be an essential mechanism for building institutional and community capacity through social capital formation.

Community Stewardship

As the name implies, the CWSP is concerned with promoting two broad goals among its participants: community and stewardship.

Stewardship is based on the idea that if people take an active role in improving the health of the environment, they will be more invested in the long-term results, will get involved in other avenues, and will be more involved in their community in general. Citizen members gain an understanding of environmental issues and, in turn, pass their knowledge on to other members of their community. The result is a cumulative effect of education and information dissemination over time and across generations.

Much of the drive toward stewardship stems from the human need for a sense of place within the natural environment (Howell, 1997). To economists, this feeling is often recorded as the notion of existence value. Individuals' lives no longer depend on a close relationship with the land. In many cases, people have distanced themselves from any deep interaction with the environment, and in its place is a latent desire to feel connected. Many Americans hold a romantic notion of going back to "simpler" days, when the environment was pristine, and the most important activities of the day brought us into contact with the earth. By taking part in steward-ship actions, community members can begin to reestablish the connection between their actions and the health of the environment. They become propelled by the notion that individuals have a responsibility to future gen-erations or the notion that people, as a collective, need to protect the envi-ronment for their grandchildren's grandchildren and further down the line. Stewardship can be a legacy for the future and a way to teach our children valuable lessons about the importance of environmental issues. It also is a bridge across race, culture, and gender because the state of the environment affects everyone living in a proximate area.

The term *community* has been traditionally difficult to define because it has the capacity to take on many roles depending on the context in which it is used. At the simplest level, it is a collection of people who share simi-lar interests and involves the strength of attachment. Community can be defined geographically, such as a neighborhood or watershed, or it can be defined socially, such as interactions through religious or academic institu-tions or in a service club. Size is irrelevant. Communities can be as large as 100,000 or as small as three. The unifying factor is a shared interest to work for similar purposes to achieve common goals (Cochrun, 1994).

Community involvement in public activities and planning initiatives is desirable if only for the fact that no one knows better than community members what the local, day-to-day problems are and who will be affected by them. Those people who live in the community have a personal stake in the future of the neighborhood and are likely to be more passionate about the success of a program than an outside agent. Involvement increases the chances that decisions will reflect the desires of the community (Cochrun, 1994). If residents involve themselves in the planning process from the ini-tial concept stages, they retain the ability to affect the outcome and shape the community to meet their needs.

Involving the community in a project transforms it from being a techni-cal and impersonal activity to one of establishing relationships that will influence the way the local government acts. Local associations can act as mediating bodies between small groups and larger institutional entities. The balance of power is shared, and people experience greater satisfac-tion in their neighborhood and increased social bonding (Cochrun, 1994). Empowerment and recognition are gained from the experience of partici-pation and belonging.

A connection with the environment is important to establish a sense of community. People who use public spaces reinforce their identification with a neighborhood and strengthen the sense of community by interacting in that space (Cochrun, 1994). Public parks, interpretive trails, and tree plantings are examples of opportunities that encourage people to interact with each other in their surroundings. By taking an interest in their natural surroundings, community members develop a sense of responsibility and a shared purpose in protecting something that is incapable of defending itself.

Elements of the Partnership

The PSU/BES Partnership has worked as a team to build social sustainability via community ownership of watershed stewardship. This work involves the following activities carried out through the mechanism of the partnership:

1. Faculty and graduate students participate with program managers in BES to discuss BES watershed priorities and PSU educational and research interests in order to weave community involvement opportunities into the developing CWSP plans each year.
2. Students at every level of education are provided with community-based learning opportunities in general and specific research or projects in their area of study. This study occurs through work study, internships, the community-based learning program, and undergraduate curricula, including Senior Capstones.
3. The community is given access to the knowledge and resources of the University through a number of accessory programs.
4. Graduate students are provided an opportunity to work in the community so that they might offer organizational and technical assistance to community groups interested in implementing their own watershed education or water quality improvement projects.
5. A working plan establishes the foundation for continuing to develop stronger connections between PSU faculty and graduate students, community watershed leaders, BES watershed managers, public involvement professionals, and community organizations.

The beginning of the partnership was spent defining the work program, understanding the roles each organization would play, and implementing how the two could work together as a team. The scope of work for PSU was defined theoretically and in broad terms, which provided both the opportunity to be creative and the challenge to define it. The most challenging part of the partnership is and will likely continue to be a difference in cultures. University culture is set up around four terms and midterms, finals, and vacations, with deadlines based on each. Curricula must be established months in advance. However, government work does not cease for the summer months, and the faster pace of project implementation and external deadlines makes it difficult to incorporate academic pursuits. For example, professors need to plan their classwork over the course of the summer months; during this window of opportunity, the program is operating with only one or two graduate students. The CWSP acted as a broker for agreements and relationships between community groups and

PSU faculty and students. Students are provided the opportunity to make their work meaningful and useful while providing a service or information to the community.

The real strength of the partnership is that it is possible for PSU, BES, and several community partners to share their goals and bring resources to the partnership that would otherwise be inaccessible. PSU provides credibility and a willing group of volunteers and students; graduate student input provides a fresh perspective and a solid knowledge base. BES provides technical expertise and resources. Community members create a holistic community integration of programs. The end product is an amalgamation of ideas, responsibilities, resources, shared visions, and an agreement to work collectively for a common goal. Together these groups can achieve more than if they worked alone and, in so doing, build social capital that directly enhances social sustainability.

This method of establishing goals for the program encourages unity among community members and helps people define their own roles within the larger intent of the partnership. This unity then becomes infused into other sectors of community involvement and improvement. The process of relationship building promotes stewardship of watersheds and understanding of larger issues of human impact on the environment, such as water quality, erosion, and native species reintroduction. Many projects target children in service projects by planning and implementing hands-on educational activities. The foundation for future lessons for the children is established. Thus, from an early age, their respect for the environment is shaped. Through these avenues, the entire community can be involved, including youth, adults, and professionals alike.

A Catalyst for Change

A key element of the CWSP is a small grants program to community members who seek seed money to help get their education, monitoring, and restoration projects initiated. Grantees are given up to $5,000 to spend on materials and project coordination. Over the past ten years, more than 100 grants have been given to community organizations.

Desirable projects are ones that demonstrate stewardship and long-term community involvement and provide resources to empower the community to improve Portland's watersheds. Although the amount of funds for any given community project is small, the grants supply an important catalyst for community involvement and partnership. In addition, the grants provide an essential tool for capacity building. Community groups are invited to apply for the grants each year through a request for proposal issued by the BES. PSU graduate student program assistants work with the potential grantees in helping to frame the project idea initiated by the community group. This group effort provides a mechanism for students and community partners to collaborate and identify important work elements for the envisioned projects, as well as opportunities for other forms of community and student involvement. As a result of this collaboration, important resource areas are identified within the community, the university, and in the BES. Interconnecting resources and people builds social capital and increases the capacity of the grantee to leverage the grant amounts into considerable additional resources. As such, the grants become a catalyst for building groups and engaging numerous entities and resource systems that otherwise would be missing from the envisioned projects.

The success of any organization is ultimately based on its ability to mobilize financial and other necessary resources to forward its own purposes. Connections, knowledge, time, and skills, among other intangible and tangible resources, also are key to the ultimate success of organizations, particularly grassroots associations that invariably have few, if any, institutional resources on which to operate. For grassroots associations, effectiveness often depends on their ability to leverage a variety of resources situated within themselves—that is, among their membership and outsiders whom they can convince to support their cause (Chaskin, Brown, Venkatesh and Vidal, 2001).

From the City's perspective, the involvement of citizens in the production of a public service, otherwise known as coproduction (Glover, Parry and Shinew, 2005), is a mechanism for filling in gaps between what the institution can achieve and what is needed within the community (see Backman, Wicks and Silverberg, 1997). Coproduction is a means for BES to deliver services and is especially appropriate in the area of confronting the health of urban watersheds. Many of the problems experienced with the degradation of water quality and watershed health in general emanate from the community as nonpoint sources of pollution (Adler, 1995). Thus, to effectively address these problems, it is essential to directly engage the community at its closest source to these problems— namely, the individual residents and businesses within the neighborhoods. The PSU–BES partnership grants' initiative facilitates access to and encourages participation from residents that are closest to the source. What has resulted from these initiatives is more than 100 community projects sponsored by neighborhood schools, civic organizations, churches, and neighborhood groups. These projects have leveraged thousands of volunteers and scores of additional neighborhood-based organizations, public agencies, and businesses to address neighborhood-scale projects of watershed and water quality improvement

From the university perspectives, mechanisms are needed within the community that provide opportunities for educational work that addresses real problems with real community organizations. The CWSP provides such a mechanism for university students and faculty to engage in meaningful educational and research projects that directly increase community livability, thus adding to the community's social sustainability.

Soft Infrastructure

*Constructing an action model of social sustainability—
the soft infrastructure of community*

The systems and processes that we put in place to increase community capacity to address important challenges can be thought of as the soft infrastructure of the community. *Soft infrastructure* is a term used by Len Duhl, Professor of Public Health and Professor of Urban Planning at the University of California at Berkeley, to describe those elements of the community that contribute to social well-being. This soft infrastructure includes formal human services (health, education, social services, recreation, and culture, etc.), as well as the community's informal structure—the web of voluntary organizations and social relationships that comprise community.

The CWSP framework adds to the soft infrastructure by providing diverse and numerous opportunities for the institutions to find common ground and opportunity within the community to explore and expand the involvement of an increasingly wide array of volunteers, organizations, and associations. Through the initiatives supported in the PSU–CWSP partnerships, a mechanism has been provided by which the soft infrastructure within the community continues to be constructed and capacities are built to address commonly shared goals among the collaborators and community partners. The building of this infrastructure has been a key success factor contributing to an increase in the level of involvement of community organizations, volunteers, and residents, as well as of the city and university partners. These gains can be summarized as follows:

- *Impact on students*: The CWSP provides an opportunity to directly engage students in community-based learning activities. Over the course of the partnership, more than twenty Senior Capstone courses and twelve other undergraduate courses involving more than 600 undergraduate students completing projects working alongside community volunteers have been offered. The CWSP has provided the organizational mechanism for these courses to be offered. The effectiveness of these courses has been greatly enhanced by having access to an organizational structure that has continued. Students in these courses were afforded the opportunity to build off the work and relationships with community partners built by the CWSP.
- *Impact on community organizations*: The partnership has strengthened community organizations and their capacity to be direct participants and contributors to public policy initiatives. The CWSP has provided the mechanism by which community groups are given direct access to both the technical assistance to address conditions resulting from nonpoint source pollution, as well as access to a means of increasing their workforces to address these issues. In addition to the undergraduate students who supported the work of community partners, more

than twenty graduate students have been engaged in providing technical assistance to organizations developing and implementing projects
within their neighborhoods. This assistance has been invaluable in
providing the bridge between the nearly 100 community organizations that have partnered with the CWSP and the City's Bureau of
Environmental Services to become involved in the production of critical improvements to watershed conditions city-wide.

- *The multiplier effect*: The mechanism for collaboration has resulted
  in numerous links among individuals and organizations within community through the opportunities for participation provided and supported by the partnership. Neighborhood schools and both formal
  and informal community associations have been given direct access to
  structures for participation in neighborhood work connected to similar
  associations doing like work throughout the City. Many of the community organizations that have partnered with the CWSP have benefited
  from each other's participation. Each year a growing number of new
  organizations have participated in the CWSP as a result of connections
  among the participants. The increasing awareness of the different neighborhood projects has had a multiplier effect in terms of disseminating
  information about the opportunities to become involved and the work
  that benefits the neighborhoods and watersheds. This multiplier effect
  is demonstrated by the more than 800 organizations, schools, and businesses that have worked to contribute support to the community organizations that have partnered with CWSP.

- *Impact on the main partners–the City and the University*: The mechanism for collaboration has resulted in increased capacities for both
  the City and University partners. By having a continued mechanism
  for engaging work with volunteers and organizations at the community and neighborhood levels, numerous emergent opportunities and
  innovations have been experienced. Individuals within the community working alongside of students in designing and implementing
  approaches to improving watershed conditions in the neighborhood
  have developed unique and effective ways to address the challenges
  faced within an urban area. Such applications have greatly contributed to the richness of learning experienced by the students. Also,
  effective approaches to urban watershed challenges have been developed that neither the University nor the city would have had access to
  without the mechanism provided by the CWSP.

- *Impact on the physical environment*: In addition to the structures for
  partnership, the mechanism for collaboration has directly produced
  physical improvements to neighborhoods and watersheds. The CWSP
  has been the mechanism through which community organizations have
  conducted projects that resulted in extensive measurable outcomes. In
  the twelve years of the CWSP program, more than 27,000 volunteers
  have contributed nearly 150,000 total hours to plant 76,000 native

plants and restore more than two million square feet of upland/riparian areas in watersheds throughout the City. Over that time, the City made nearly 100 small grants totally $436,000 that have generated matching contributions of nearly $2 million. Without the mechanism to connect community residents and organizations, these results would not have been possible.

CONCLUSION: COMMUNITY–UNIVERSITY PARTNERSHIPS ENHANCE SOCIAL SUSTAINABILITY

The diverse outcomes of the CWSP are indicative of the benefits that can accrue from systematic efforts to build and maintain mechanisms for supporting partnerships between institutions that engage at the community level. Such mechanisms become success indicators when we intentionally set out to build the soft infrastructure of the community. This soft infrastructure adds capacity and energizes the mission of public institutions as well as organizations and individuals within the community. As the CWSP case indicates, building this infrastructure can enhance the capacity of groups and individuals involved. It also can lead to hard, cost-effective results. Quantitatively, less than a half-million dollars of hard resource investment has generated five times that amount in soft match. One primary community–university partnership, the CWSP, has impacted thirty-two courses, providing more than 600 students over the past dozen years with opportunities to learn critically important soft life skills—personal agency, collaboration, communicating with diverse groups, public problem solving, and so on—skills often undervalued in the hardened walls of the Cold War Academy. That same primary partnership—between Portland's city government and its public University—has increased the bridging capital of more than 80 community-based organizations working on the common cause of nonpoint source water management. More than 27,000—twenty-seven thousand!—volunteers have strategically placed more than 76,000 native plants into the ground to restabilize the soil, enhance wetlands, and augment the city's watershed management plan. These significant results are incentivized by pennies on the dollar when one compares the size of most cities' hard infrastructure investment budgets.

However, what remains to be quantified (and what is the focus of our next study) are outcomes much more challenging to measure, but perhaps more important in the medium and long term: the increases in social capital and the associated social sustainability generated in the community. What quantifiable differences might be documented in some of those 100 community-based organizations that partnered with the CWSP or in even 100 of the 27,000 volunteers that felt a sense of civic agency when planting trees and restoring wetlands, or in graduate students that helped facilitate creative solutions in neighborhood communities? How many of those 100 organizations have since continued to partner with each other, in new and dynamic ways, to address other compelling community-level issues at no cost to the taxpayer? How many of those 600 undergraduate students now work in the nonprofit sector or in social or political advocacy groups and so on?

When the academy of higher education began to reawaken and return to its moral roots in the 1980s, service learning was officially born. Over the past quarter century, the growth of community–university partnerships has been substantial. What the literature suggests and the experience of the CWSP confirms is that when university faculty design and deliver high-quality community–university partnerships, everyone wins. Perhaps one day in the not too distant future the lines between the hard content outcomes of traditional courses and the soft learning outcome—such as effective communication, coalition building, a strong sense of social responsibility, and so on—will blur and maybe even disappear. In similar measure, city planners, community organizations, civil engineers, and neighborhood citizens may soon choose to evaluate infrastructural outcomes with more equanimity between the hard, tangible results and the less visible, soft infrastructure that is built among us all. Higher education can and must continue to play a role. Building and sustaining effective community–university partnerships can build social sustainability in our communities, help address entrenched public issues, and be a powerful response to legislators and taxpayers clamoring for a sense of higher education's relevance as the 21st century continues to dawn.

REFERENCES

Adler, R. W. 1995. "Addressing Barriers to Watershed Protection." *Environmental Law* 25: 973–1106.

Astin, A. W., and L. J. Sax. 1998. "How Undergraduates Are Affected by Service Participation." *Journal of College Student Development* 39 (3): 251–263.

Backman, K. F., B. Wicks, and K. Siverberg. 1997. "Coproduction of Recreation Services." *Journal of Park and Recreation Administration* 15 (3): 58–75.

Benson, L., and I. Harkavy. 2002. "Saving the Soul of the University: What Is to Be Done?" In *The Virtual University? Information, Markets, and Management*, edited by K. Robins and F. Webster (pp. 169–209). Oxford, UK: Oxford University Press.

———, I. Harkavy, and M. Hartley. 2005. "Higher Education for the Public Good: Integrating a Commitment to the Public Good into the Institutional Fabric." In Higher Education for the Public Good: Emerging Voices from a National Movement, edited by A. Kezar, T. Chambers, and J. Burkhardt. (pp. 185–216). San Francisco: Jossey-Bass.

Bok, D. 2003. *Universities in the Marketplace: The Commercialization of Higher Education.* Princeton, NJ: Princeton University Press.

Boyer, E. L. 1990. *Scholarship Reconsidered: Priorities of the Professoriate.* Princeton, NJ: Carnegie Foundation for the Advancement of Teaching.

———. 1997. "The Scholarship of Engagement." *Journal of Public Service and Outreach* 1 (1): 11–20.

Chaskin, R., P. Brown, S. Venkatesh, and A.Vidal. 2001. *Building Community Capacity*. Hathorne, NY: Aldine D Gruyter.

Cochrun, Steven Edward. 1994. "Understanding and Enhancing Neighborhood Sense of Community." *Journal of Planning Literature* 9: 92–99.

Colby, A., T. Ehrlich, E. Beaumont, and J. Stephens. 2003. *Educating Citizens: Preparing America's Undergraduates for Lives of Moral and Civic Responsibility*. San Francisco: Jossey-Bass.

Coleman, J. (1988). "Social Capital in the Creation of Human Capital." *American Journal of Sociology* 94 (Supplement: Organizations and Institutions: Sociological Economic Approaches to the Analysis of Social Structure): 95–120.

Drishna, A., and N. Uphoff. 2002. "Mapping and Measuring Social Capital Through Assessment of Collective Action to Conserve and Develop Watershed in Rajasthan, India." In *The Role of Social Capital in Development: An Empirical Assessment*, edited by Christiaan Grootaert and Thierry Van Bastelaer. Cambridge, MA: Cambridge University Press.

Ehrlich, T. 2000. *Civic Responsibility and Higher Education*. Phoenix, AZ: Oryx Press.

Enos, S., and K. Morton. 2003. "Developing a Theory and Practice of Campus-Community Partnerships." In *Building Partnerships for Service-Learning*, edited by B. Jacoby (pp. 20–41). San Francisco: Jossey-Bass.

Gittell, R. J., and A. Vidal. (1998). *Community Organizing: Building Social Capital as a Development Strategy*. Thousand Oaks, CA: Sage.

Glover, T. D., D. C. Parry, and K. J. Shinew. 2005. "Building Relationships, Accessing Resources: Mobilizing Social Capital in Community Garden Contexts." *Journal of Leisure Research* 37 (4).

Howell, D. 1997. *Environmental Stewardship*. South Hadley, MA: Bergin and Garvey.

Kecskes, K., S. Kerrigan, and J. Patton. 2006. "The Heart of the Matter: Aligning Curriculum, Pedagogy and Engagement in Higher Education." *Metropolitan Universities: Indicators of Engagement* 17 (1): 51–61.

McKenzie, Stephen. 2004. *Social Sustainability: Towards Some Definitions*. Working Paper 27, Hawke Research Institute, Magill, South Australia.

Newman, F., L. Couturier, and J. Scurry. 2004. *The Future of Higher Education: Rhetoric, Reality, and the Risks of the Market*. San Francisco: Jossey-Bass.

Presidents' Declaration on the Civic Responsibility of Higher Education. 1999. Campus Compact. http://www.compact.org/resources.

Putnam, R. (1993). *Making Democracy Work*. Princeton, NJ: Princeton University Press.

Rohe, William M. 2004. "Using Social Capital to Help Integrate Planning Theory, Research and Practice." *Journal of American Planning Association* 70: 2.

Saltmarsh, J., and S. B. Gelmon. 2006. "Characteristics of an Engaged Department: Design and Assessment." In *Engaging Departments: Moving Faculty Culture from Private to Public, Individual to Collective Focus for the Common Good*, edited by K. Kecskes (pp. 27–44). Bolton, MA: Anker.

Williams, D. R., and D. O. Bernstine. 2002. "Building Capacity for Civic Engagement at Portland State University: A Comprehensive Approach." In *Learning to Serve: Promoting Civil Society through Service Learning*, edited by L. A. K. Simon, M. Kenny, K. Brabeck, and R. M. Lerner (pp. 257–276). Norwell, MA: Kluwer Press.

14 Advancing Social Sustainability
An Intervention Approach

Jan C. Semenza

Social sustainability is a cultural value and, as such, is grounded in the richness of social interactions; thus, isolation is socially unsustainable. Isolation disrupts communities and results in societal decay. Civic engagement is the cornerstone of building sustainable communities; however, it has proved difficult to encourage public participation in the civic decision-making process (Portney, 2005). Here I describe a field-tested and evaluated strategy, developed in Portland, Oregon, USA, to advance social sustainability. The strategy is based on the theory of social capital and employs a broad participatory process required to transform communities and push back unsustainable social, environmental, political, or business practices (Semenza and Maty, 2007). The motivation behind sustainable communities is the need to address the deleterious impact of social inequality, environmental degradation, political exclusion, and unrestrained economic growth (Semenza, 2007).

One manifestation of such development is the vast expansion of suburban subdivisions and the coincident decline of inner cities in America. The human dimension is missing from many urban layouts, which leads to a decline of the urban core, manifest in the numerous abandoned American downtowns that lack economic and social vitality. Many of these American cities suffer from dilapidated physical environments and degraded infrastructures, which have been linked to alienation and social ills, which in turn can negatively impact the mental and physical health of their residents. The majority of Americans live in metropolitan areas, where the social cement that holds people together is declining. Poorly designed urban layouts can stifle physical activity, degrade the environment, and curb spontaneous social interactions (Jackson, 2003).

Public squares are vital nodes for community life where residents can gather and socialize; however, American cities tend to lack such squares. The rectangular network of streets has been the geometric form of choice for many American cities (Fig. 14.1) (Semenza, 2005). Cities laid out on such a grid have high connectivity, meaning that there are many different pathways that connect two random points on the grid. High connectivity is advantageous for the efficient movement of goods and services within the city because it diversifies the transportation options and routes. Grid cities also tend to have high densities of people and amenities, as well as a mix of uses, bringing together residential and commercial activities and maximizing infrastructure. Taken together, the grid has many functional advantages.

The orthogonal grid has its historic roots in Mesopotamia, where the Assyrians and Babylonians used it for military camps and cities around 3,000 B.C. (Kostof, 1985). As one of the greatest cities of the antiquity, Babylon was built on a rectangular grid where streets, paved with bricks, intersected at right angles. The Greeks also applied the grid as early as 479 B.C. to urban planning, when Miletus, on the western coast of Anatolia, was rebuilt by Hippodamus, a Greek town planner. However, the grid was predominantly the layout of choice for the colonial outposts and fortifications for both the Greeks and Romans. For example, the Roman military defensive positions (*castrum*) was laid out according to the grid, with two main perpendicular streets, called the *cardo* and the *decumanus*, intersecting in the center and extending through the gates of the fortified camp. Such a street plan gave the city administration, located at the center, total control over the movement of people and goods throughout the city.

The grid layout was adapted in America in 1785 by the Continental Congress as part of the National Land Ordinance and was applied to the land during the westward expansion; it also was applied to cities and towns (Fig. 14.1). Despite its functional advantages, a strict grid tends to favor transportation over human interaction, and in contemporary America, community life succumbs to a steady stream of through-traffic. The lack of public gathering places can diminish spontaneous socializing, and thus adversely affect interpersonal networks. Loss of opportunities for people to interact with each other in urban neighborhoods can deteriorate mutual understanding and reciprocity; a weakening of communal ties and relationships and alienation from collective norms and shared values are leading to the progressive erosion of social capital (Bourdieu, 1986; Coleman, 1988; Putnam, 1995). Indeed, empirical data indicate that membership in associations, interpersonal trust, informal interactions, and other social capital indicators have been in steady decline in the United States (Putnam, 1995).

Social capital manifests itself through two complementary components: structural and cognitive social capital. The former is inherent in the social organization of communities and can be described through social networks. These social networks are societal measures of communal health. Social capital relies on such networks for collaboration between residents of decaying urban environments to initiate collective problem solving (Ziersch, Baum, Macdougall, and Putland, 2005). It can be seen as a consequence of social relationships that promote community participation and mutual cooperation and are therefore not a characteristic of one particular individual, but rather a collective characteristic. In contrast, cognitive social capital includes norms, values, attitudes, and beliefs that emerge during community meetings, and it is defined as people's perception of level of interpersonal trust, sharing, and reciprocity.

Social capital is a two-dimensional construct and also can be portrayed as bonding (localized) and bridging/linking social capital (Hawe and Shiell, 2000; Szreter, 2002). Localized (bonding) social capital refers to the value assigned to social networks between homogenous groups of people and is inherent in existing social or religious groups; it is essential, but not sufficient, for neighborhood problem solving because it may produce redundant information not applicable to improving inner-city neighborhoods. Bridging social capital, in contrast, connects different organizations and individuals and can reveal new information for problem solving and the creation of new opportunities. Linking social capital, an extension of bridging social capital, can connect parties unequal in power and access, such as residents with city officials (Szreter, 2002).

The concept of social capital is the theoretical underpinning of the interventions presented here. By retrofitting the urban grid with public gathering places, this process culturally reactivates urban communities for the collective benefit. Civic engagement, as presented in these case studies, is an example of how to advance social sustainability in urban settings by building social capital.

THE INTERVENTION

Uninspiring urban environments can be detrimental to community life and can result in alienation and isolation. To reverse this trend and to advance social sustainability in Portland, Oregon, a city laid out on a grid blueprint, The City Repair Project was founded in 1996 as a nonprofit (501 c3) organization. The organization focuses on education and activism for community building. The mission statement reads, "The City Repair Project is group of citizen activists creating public gathering places and helping others to creatively transform the places where they live." The organization is driven almost entirely by volunteers, while a Board of Directors oversees the long-term vision and financial responsibility and a Council the daily operations. However, the organizational structure is nonhierarchical and adheres strictly to a consensus decision-making process. The Board of Directors and Council meet on a monthly basis to discuss project activities related to localization and placemaking, a process of creating public gathering places that will attract people because they are pleasurable or interesting.

The City Repair Project created a number of other creative interventions that are listed in Table 14.1. One such strategy, intersection repair, aimed at restoring public gathering places by retrofitting the rectangular street layout with public squares (Semenza, 2003). The major project goal of intersection repair is to engage residents in neighborhood revitalization by retrofitting the urban setting with a network of public gathering places throughout the city that foster social interactions. Through a participatory process, the City Repair Project assisted communities in developing a shared vision for their urban environments (Semenza and Krishnasamy, 2007). The underlying values of this approach included honoring the community as the expert, creating an accessible and inclusive participatory process, and integrating local community values, history, and geography. In this process of personal and community empowerment, multiple voices and perspectives were incorporated in shaping a public square.

The goal of this strategy was to revitalize urban neighborhoods through community-initiated designs, with public gathering places in the right of way. By building these places with the participation of residents, the City Repair Project hoped to transform the car-dominated grid layout of the city into a human-scale environment for pedestrians. The intersection repair strategy is described step by step and illustrated schematically in Figure 14.2.

Structural Social Capital

City Repair Project staff members and volunteers engaged in community outreach as part of the intersection repair strategy of advancing social sustainability. They reached out to a number of different neighborhoods in Portland, Oregon, and documented structural social capital (or lack thereof) among residents and stakeholders, but also the existing bonds among neighborhood associations, churches, community leaders, and other groups (Green and Kreuter, 2005). In the process of corroborating stores of structural social capital among these groups, urban stressors in these neighborhoods were revealed as well, including crime rates, drug use, desolate urban landscapes, debris, graffiti, abandoned properties, or a general state of disrepair. Taken together, this assessment was instrumental in determining whether and how to proceed with an intersection repair intervention: if multiple residents expressed a strong interest to address urban blight issues collectively, the City Repair Project initiated the next step in the process.

Social Networks

Interested parties came together in community meetings to talk about challenges to their communities and allowed residents to express their concerns and opinions. New connections and social ties were built, and existing social networks were expanded. By fostering these social relationships, social nodes emerged both for individuals and organizations. These social networks were essential for social capital and played a critical role in determining the way problems were solved.

Cognitive Social Capital

Through these large community meetings, smaller neighborhood-specific groups of interested residents emerged in certain areas of the city. Members of these neighborhood groups shared similar norms, values, attitudes, and beliefs, a manifestation of mutual cognitive social capital. This group reached out to a wider range of residents and organizations within their neighborhood with an informal community survey about other assets in the neighborhood. Asset-mapping appraised skills and indigenous resources (primary building blocks, such as residents' talents, experience, and expertise) had the potential to promotinge community development (McKnight and Kretzmann, 2005; Green and Kreuter, 2005). The goal of this process was to determine not only the level of interpersonal trust, sharing, and reciprocity, but also organizational resources, professions, and expertise as well as individual capacities and abilities within the neighborhood relevant for the intersection repair project. These resources were spatially charted on residential maps.

Civic Engagement

During the community meetings, urban blight issues were discussed, including how they could be ameliorated with structural improvements in the urban landscape. The first step was the development of a base map with significant landscape features and architectural structures. The City Repair Project provided technical assistance if no capacity was available in the individual neighborhoods. The core groups of residents became the driving force for this civic engagement process, which lies at the core of the intersection repair process. These groups helped to develop the knowledge, skills, and motivation to tackle the neighborhood problems and to come up with potential design solutions.

Bridging Social Capital

Designs for the public place were a reflection of the local culture and public art. These solutions could include large street murals, garden features, traffic-calming devices, interactive art, seating areas, lighting, signage, paths, water fountains, or information centers/kiosks. The design workshops involved a series of steps with feedback loops, where ideas and suggestions were transformed into designs, moving from the general to the specific. Architects and design professionals worked on the construction plans collaboratively with the residents. This interaction between design professionals and residents was an opportunity to cultivate bridging social capital, which is a measure for interactions between groups with different levels of expertise. The neighborhood core group disseminated the design concepts and ideas as part of the outreach activities, and feedback was incorporated into architectural drawings for the purpose of obtaining construction permits. The group ensured that all voices were heard by having open discussions as well as anonymous ranking of design plans.

Linking Social Capital

The completed construction plans had to be submitted to the city for permitting. This step of the process was designed to increase linking social capital by connecting residents with city officials through the permitting processes for their construction projects. The neighborhood core group and staff from the City Repair Project presented the proposal to City traffic engineers for approval and permitting. This process provided an opportunity for residents to interact with city officials as a manifestation of linking social capital, which is defined as networks among groups unequal in the governmental hierarchy.

Mobilize Stakeholders

Community members, under the guidance of expert natural/ecologic builders, implemented projects during a 1-week construction workshop called the Village Building Convergence. This workshop attracted volunteers and stakeholders, both from out of town and locally. Construction was executed with natural and recycled materials such as cob (a mixture of sand, straw, clay, and water) to promote principles of sustainability.

Civic Capacity

Promoting interactions among residents for the purpose of solving problems of urban blight benefits the political decision-making process. Creating parks, gardens, and other amenities increases social interactions, a prerequisite for social sustainability. Completing the projects is a manifestation of civic capacity.

Localized (Bonding) Social Capital

The completion of the community project was grounds for celebration and an opportunity to expand friendship ties to a larger circle of residents. The relational dimension of these events focused on the connection between individuals and existing groups of the same neighborhood. Thus, the inclination from such events was to boost localized (bonding) social capital and to continue the investment in the common good.

Evaluation

To assess the social acceptability of the intersection repair projects, a convenience sample of written and oral comments were collected onsite from bypassers and participants during the installation of the intersection projects. Such feedback was important to accommodate potential concerns and to respond to negative outcomes.

THE EVIDENCE

In 2003, three communities were selected from a number of candidate sites according to the key principles of community-based participatory research that support successful research partnerships (Israel, Schulz, Parker, and Becker, 1998). The inclusion criteria for the site selection specified: low-to moderate-income neighborhoods, a core group of committed residents, strengths and resources within the community, collaborative equitable involvement of all partners in all phases of the research, a cyclical and iterative process, and mutual benefit of all partners through an empowering process. Sites that did not meet these inclusion criteria were engaged in physical revitalization of the neighborhood, but not evaluated as part of this research project.

In February 2003, design concepts were developed during community workshops, organized by trained facilitators and design professionals (Fig. 14.2). In collaboration with City officials, structural engineers, and architects, community members from the three different sites finalized their plans according to City building codes. Construction plans were submitted to the Portland Department of Transportation and Bureau of Planning for approval and permitting. To support the three communities with sufficient expertise in ecological and sustainable building techniques, experienced site coordinators and workshop team leaders were assigned to the three sites.

A workshop, "The Village Building Convergence," was held May 9-18, 2003, with hands-on construction directed by national and international ecological builders. More than 1,000 residents and community members participated in a variety of community-building activities. At site 1, community organizing and public engagement resulted in the painting of a large street mural and the construction of several interactive art structures; the community raised three wooden trellises and a large metal dome sculpture at each corner of the intersection and installed planters on the street corners (Figs. 14.3 and 14.4). The two other sites created unique ecological constructions, including a cob kiosk, cob benches, a street mural, a lawn chessboard, a light clay sauna, and a walking labyrinth.

Study Design and Data Collection

A prospective longitudinal study with two consecutive cross-sectional surveys was conducted from April through July 2003. The sampling frame was defined by a comprehensive line listing of all residences within a two-block radius of the three sites. Residents within this sampling frame were required by city ordinance to approve the design concept prior to construction. Portland State University undergraduate students, trained in interviewing techniques, systematically sampled all residences by going from door to door. At least four attempts were made to enroll an adult (over 21 years of age) head of household for each household in the areas; in rare instances, two subjects per household were interviewed (7%). Data collection for the first round (time 1) was initiated on April 16 and completed before the start date of the workshop (May 9). Attempts were made to blind subjects to the purpose of the study, and no reference was made to the upcoming workshop to prevent the Hawthorne effect. The follow-up survey was initiated on May 19, immediately after the end of the workshop and completed in July (time 2).

The survey instrument (Table 14.2) included topics proposed by community members and were derived from validated instruments pertaining to depression (CESD-11), well-being (SF-36), social capital, and community capacity (Radloff, 1977; Ware and Snow, 1993). These questions were evaluated by subjects using multiple-point rating scales. Demographic and general health information as well as personal identifiers for the follow-up survey were recorded.

Study Sample

Two surveys were conducted with 265 subjects before and after the intervention at three sites. Of the respondents, 55% were women, the majority (83%) was under 50 years of age, and 58% were renters. Property owners of their residence in the sample were similar to the distribution in each neighborhood overall.

Quantitative Results

Using the measures obtained for each subject on each of the scales, a repeated measure *t*-test was conducted to ascertain whether the subjects' responses had changed after the intersection repair intervention (Semenza, March, and Bontempo, 2007). The sample for these analyses included the 265 respondents who were surveyed before and after the intervention. Subjects who were interviewed at both times 1 and 2 experienced an improvement across all measures of social capital and well-being, although not all variables displayed a statistically significant change. After the intervention, multivariate results revealed statistically significant improvements in mental health, increased sense of community, and an overall expansion of social capital. Social interactions improved, although it was not statistically significant, nor was perceived neighborhood control nor neighborhood participation.

Qualitative Results

One month after project completion in June/July 2003, all households within a two-block radius of the three intervention sites were contacted (Semenza and March, 2008). Using an open-ended questionnaire, the effects of the improvements to the neighborhood on the respondents' lives were assessed, as well as whether respondents had participated in the design and/or construction of the art. Based on a content analysis, categories were created and comments were assembled into groups. Of 560 eligible households, 359 (64%) household members agreed to be interviewed. Without probing by the interviewers, 60 respondents spontaneously reported having gained more friends as conversations and friendships had emerged during the painting of intersections, landscaping of parking strips, and construction projects: "I feel better about the neighborhood and coming together as a community, meeting people who I hadn't before" or "Great opportunity to meet more neighbors [and] learn more lessons about human nature: we are challenged to share different opinions." Through these communal events and working toward a common goal, residents were able to overcome their differences while building civic capacity and augmenting bonding social capital.

In all, 27 respondents mentioned that their sense of place had been altered as a result of the intervention in their neighborhood. The sense of place was described as follows:

> It is a wonderful and great community builder because it gives people the sense of ownership of their neighborhood; I feel it is a creative and positive way to have people do something for the neighborhood; I think it definitely adds to the sense of community; I highly agree with [the] neighborhood getting together. It creates a nice environment.

These expressions reflect cognitive social capital with norms and values among the residents that can be translated into interpersonal trust, sharing, and reciprocity.

Besides social network density, structural social capital also can be assessed by indicators of civic engagement. Of those who knew about the workshops (201 individuals), 87 study participants mentioned neighborhood participation. Project completion per se is a manifestation of existing social capital in the neighborhood.

However, not all residents agreed with these activities: 13 study participants expressed concern about aesthetic aspects of the project, and 7 participants voiced process limitations. Four individuals reported concerns about the projects: "I walked by and felt very discouraged by the attitude from the participants"; "[the project] really set people against each other in a way I had never seen before"; and "It will raise our taxes." These conflicts were an opportunity to draw on community capacity and advance bridging social capital to overcome these differences.

These quantitative and qualitative data indicate positive steps toward social sustainability. They vindicate the merits of public participation in urban design. Residents are considered the experts in an accessible and inclusive participatory process, which integrates local community, economy, and ecology for the direct benefit of the common good. In this process of personal and community empowerment, multiple voices and perspectives are incorporated in shaping a public square. This method ensures that the final construction plan will be a well-designed, functional place of which the community takes true ownership. Navigating the field of social conventions and norms of isolation, apathy and top–down bureaucracy can be inherently challenging and requires significant trade-offs, but every success produces multiple benefits. Similarly, obstacles can turn into opportunities by mobilizing community support for these projects. Current urban land-use and transportation infrastructures are based on the rectangular grid system in which streets are designed for efficient transport and intersections are merely overlapping or colliding corridors. The human dimension is missing from this urban layout, which can lead to a decline of the urban core. The goal is to create human-scale urban landscapes that are more conducive to walking and biking by placing community art in the public realm. Such aesthetic improvements encourage residents to stroll and engage in conversations. The long-term project goal of Intersection Repair is to establish a network of public gathering places in the urban environment that foster social interactions.

CONCLUSION

The intersection repair method has been applied to a range of different settings with diverse demographic, socioeconomic, race/ethnic, and cultural compositions. Today, there are intersection repair projects in several U.S. and Canadian cities, including Asheville, North Carolina; Eugene, Oregon; Ithaca, New York; Ottawa, Ontario; Minneapolis, Minnesota; Seattle and Olympia, Washington; and State College, Pennsylvania. The City Repair Project in Portland, Oregon, also helped design, permit, and build "Dignity Village," a self-help ecological urban village for the homeless, free of drugs, alcohol, and violence, that supports recovery and reintegration into society. Initially composed of a collection of tents, "Dignity Village" illegally occupied unused public land near downtown Portland. In 2001, the Portland City Council allocated an unused parcel of land, 7 miles from downtown, to "Dignity Village," where more substantial structures were built using principles of eco-friendly green construction such as light clay straw housing. It has since become a role model for a better future for the disenfranchised in American cities, as a self-governing, city-recognized campground as defined by city code.

Intersection repair not only improves cities physically, but, more important, engaged residents in a process of conceiving, developing, permitting, and constructing interactive urban features while advancing both localized and bridging/linking social capital. Through collaboration and cooperation between residents and City officials, the democratic process has been revived on a local level and has led to social transformation. The stunning success of such a creative approach manifests itself in the civic engagement of the residents and has caught the attention and support of local politicians. As a result, these activities continue to occur throughout Portland on a yearly basis and engage large numbers of volunteers and residents in new and existing projects.

The City Repair Project has developed a new and innovative approach to urban place-making, where urban form directly impacts and uplifts the quality of life in the city. Furthermore, this strategy was successful at augmenting collective efficacy and engaging residents in direct action for the common good. Cooperation and participation in democracy advances common goals, and the benefits of public participation extend to the individual as documented previously. A sense of control over the world around us confers significant benefits (Kelly, Hertzman, and Daniels, 1997; Wilkinson, 2005), whereas social isolation can have detrimental consequences (Semenza et al., 1996). Thus, advancing social sustainability through grassroots movements and cultural initiatives has benefits for both for the collective as well as the individual.

ACKNOWLEDGMENTS

I would like to thank members of the City Repair Project for their dedication to advance social sustainability in Portland and beyond. City Repair is in debt to the Larson Legacy Foundation (Oregon) for their generous and continuous support to advance the physical and social fabric of communities. Funding for these projects was obtained, in part, from the Meyer Memorial Trust in Portland, Oregon; the Community Initiatives Small Grant Program from the Bureau of Housing and Community Development at the City of Portland; a faculty enhancement award from Portland State University; and scholarly and creative activity grants for undergraduates (to Andrea Thompson, Eva Rippetau, and Troy Hayes) from Portland State University, Portland, Oregon.

Figure 14.1 The urban grid layout in Portland, Oregon, where public squares for social gatherings have been omitted.
Source: City of Portland, reproduced with permission.

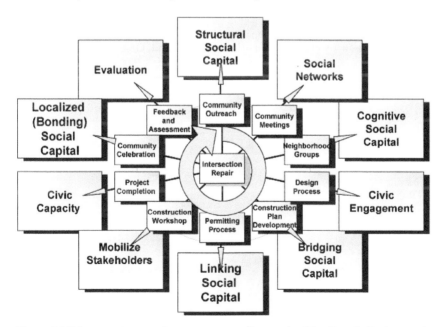

Figure 14.2 Intersection repair process according to the City Repair Project at the center, with social sustainability indicators in the outer wheel. Follow the process in a clockwise manner and see text for details.

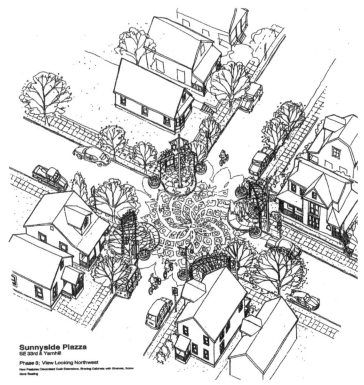

Sunnyside Piazza
SE 33rd & Yamhill

Phase 3; View Looking Northwest

New Features: Decorated Curb Extensions, Sharing Cabinets with Shelves, Some
More Seating

Figure 14.3 Plan for intersection repair project with large street mural, trellises for hanging gardens, art wall, and planter boxes in Portland, Oregon.

Figure 14.4 Inauguration of street mural in 2003, Portland, Oregon.

Table 14.1 Examples of Social Sustainability Interventions by the City Repair Project, Portland, Oregon

Sellwood Moonday T-Hows (1996). A neighborhood gathering place on a street corner in Portland serving hot tea and pie free of charge on a weekly basis by the community for the community. The structure was built with recycled materials without any permanent fixtures.

T-Horse Mobile Neighborhood Public Square (1996–present). A mobile tea house on a truck travels to different Portland neighborhoods, providing a comfortable, creative atmosphere where people can meet their neighbors and expand their social networks.

Intersection Repair (1996–present). A community-driven transformation of street intersections into neighborhood public squares. Through civic engagement, a neighborhood group designs new features in the public right of way and implements the projects after obtaining city approval for construction.

Hands Around Portland (1997–2000). A city-scale human circle of approximately 7,000 people, around the city center as a gesture of hope, community, and human interconnectedness.

Earth Day Celebration of Localization (2000–present). An annual festival of local music, arts, and crafts planned and realized by community members without corporate sponsorship. Principles of sustainability are demonstrated through waste reduction, recycling, and onsite energy production.

Village Building Convergence (2002–present). An annual 10-day event that reclaims urban spaces and transforms them into community places. Daytime hands-on workshops and evening events teach, inspire, and connect thousands of people to celebrate our local communities.

Table 14.2. Selected Survey Questions Administered To Residents At Intersection Repair Sites, Portland 2003.

Neighborhood
How would you rate your present neighborhood as a place to live?
How would you rate the safety of your neighborhood in regard to crime?
How would you rate the safety of your neighborhood in regard to traffic?
How long have you lived in your present neighborhood?
Sense of Community
My neighborhood is a good place for kids to grow up.
I feel part of this neighborhood.
I think my neighborhood is a good place for me to live.

(continued)

Table 14.2. Selected Survey Questions Administered To Residents At Intersection Repair Sites, Portland 2003 *(continued)*.

It is very important to me to live in this particular neighborhood.

I feel at home in this neighborhood.

People in my neighborhood share the same values.

Neighborhood Social Interaction:

Gone out for an evening with one of your neighbors to a movie, a sports event, for a drink, or some other activity?

Asked one of your neighbors over to your house or gone over to their house for a meal, to play cards, to watch TV, or just to socialize?

Asked one of your neighbors for help?

Talked to one of your neighbors about personal problems you were having or they were having?

Perceived Control at the Neighborhood Level

I can influence decisions that affect my neighborhood.

I am satisfied with the amount of influence I have over decisions that affect my neighborhood.

By working together with others in my neighborhood, I can influence decisions that affect the neighborhood.

My neighborhood has influence over things that affect my life.

By working together, people in my neighborhood can influence decisions that affect the neighborhood.

Neighborhood Participation

Most people in the neighborhood are active in groups outside of the local area.

People in this neighborhood have connections to people who can influence what happens in the neighborhood.

People in my neighborhood work together to influence decisions at the city, state, or national level.

When it comes to getting things done to improve your neighborhood, who takes part?

REFERENCES

Bourdieu, Pierre. 1986."The Forms of Capital." In *Handbook of Theory and Research for the Sociology of Education*, edited by J. Richardson. New York: Macmillan.

Coleman, James S. 1988. "Social Capital in the Creation of Human Capital." *American Journal of Sociology*, 94 (Suppl.): S95–S120.

Eng, Parker E. 1994. "Measuring Community Competence in the Mississippi Delta: The Interface Between Program Evaluation and Empowerment." *Health Ed Quarterly* 21: 199–220.

Green, Lawrence W., and Marshall W. Kreuter. 2005. "Applications in Communities." In *Health Program Planning, an Educational and Ecological Approach* (4th ed., pp. 255–316). New York: McGraw-Hill.

Hawe, Penelope, and Alan Shiell. 2000. "Social Capital and Health Promotion: A Review." *Social Science & Medicine* 51 (6): 871–885.

Israel, Barbara A., Amy J. Schulz, Edith E. Parker, and Adam B. Becker. 1998. "Review of Community-Based Research: Assessing Partnership Approaches to Improve Public Health." *Annual Review of Public Health* 19: 173–202

Jackson, Richard J. 2003. "The Impact of the Built Environment on Health: An Emerging Field." *American Journal of Public Health* 93 (9): 1382–1383.

Kelly Shona, Clyde Hertzman, and Mark Daniels. 1997. "Searching for the Biological Pathways Between Stress and Health." *Annual Review of Public Health* 18: 437–462.

Kostof, Spiro. 1985. *A History of Architecture, Settings, and Rituals*. Oxford: Oxford University Press.

Maholy-Nagy, Sibyl. 1968. *Matrix of Man: An Illustrated History of Urban Environment*. Pall Mall Publishers (London).

McKnight, John L. ., & John P. Kretzmann, 2005. "Mapping Community Capacity." In *Community Organizing and Community Building for Health*, edited by M. Minkler (pp. 158–172). New Brunswick, NJ: Rutgers University Press.

Portney, Kent. 2005. "Civic Engagement and Sustainable Cities in the United States." *Public Administration Review* 65 (5): 579–591.

Putnam, Robert. 1995. "Bowling Alone: America's Declining Social Capital." *Journal of Democracy* 6: 65–78.

Radloff, Lenore S. 1977. "The CESD: A Self-Report Depression Scale for Research on the General Population." *Applied Psychological Measurement* (1) 385–401.

Semenza, Jan C. 2003. "The Intersection of Urban Planning, Art, and Public Health: The Sunnyside Piazza." *American Journal of Public Health* 93 (9): 1439–1441.

———. 2005. "Building Healthy Cities: A Focus on Interventions." In *Handbook of Urban Health: Populations, Methods, and Practice*, edited by D. Vlahov and S. Galea (pp. 459–478). New York: Springer Science and Business Media.

———. 2007. "Case Studies: Improving the Macrosocial Environment." In *Macrosocial Determinants of Population Health*, edited by Sandro Galea (pp. 463–484). New York: Springer Media Publishing.

———, and Prassana V. Krishnasamy 2007. "Design of a Health-Promoting Neighborhood Intervention." *Health Promotion Practice*; 8 (3):243–56. *Epub* 2006 Jun 30. PMID: 16816029.

———, and Tanya L. March. 2008. *An Urban Community-Based Intervention to Advance Social Interactions. Environment and Behavior*; 0:0013916507311136v1 (in press).

Semenza, Jan. C., Tanya L. Marsh, and Brian D. Bontempo. 2007. "Community-Initiated Urban Development: An Ecological Intervention." *Journal of Urban Health* 84 (1): 8–20.

———., and Siobhan C. Maty. 2007. "Acting upon the Macrosocial Environment to Improve Health: A Framework for Intervention." In *Macrosocial Determinants of Population Health*, edited by Sandro Galea (pp. 443–461). New York: Springer Media Publishing.

Semenza, Jan C., H. Carol Rubin, Ken.H. Falter, Joel D. Selanikio, Dana W. Flanders, and John L. Wilhelm. 1996. "Risk Factors for Heat-Related Mortality During the July 1995 Heat Wave in Chicago." *New England Journal of Medicine* 335 (2): 84–90.

Szreter, Simon. 2002 "The State of Social Capital: Bringing Back in Power, Politics and History." *Theory and Society* 31: 573–621.

Ware, John E., and Ken K. Snow.1993. *SF-36 Health Survey: Manual and Interpretation Guide.* Boston, MA: New England Medical Center.

Wilkinson, Richard G. 2005. *The Impact of Inequality: How to Make Sick Societies Healthier.* New York: New Press.

Ziersch, Anna M., Fran E. Baum, Collin Macdougall, and Christine Collin.2005. "Neighborhood Life and Social Capital: The Implications for Health." *Social Science & Medicine* 60 (1): 71–86.

Part V

Integration and Conclusion

15 Reflection and Directions for the Future

Jesse Dillard, Veronica Dujon, and Mary C. King

To pull together the contributions made in this volume, we start with Gary Larsen's (Chapter 3) observation that, although they generally appear in discussions of sustainability either as threats to the natural environment or as subsumed in their economic roles, "people are the very *raison d' etre* of the quest for sustainability in the first place." Larsen's aim was "to *give voice to* and *place people in* the very center of their own development as agents and as beneficiaries." As Kristen Magis and Craig Shinn (Chapter 2) point out, "Principle 1 of the 1992 Rio Declaration on Environment and Development places people directly at the center of sustainable development," while noting that, "in the pursuit of human development, the environment must be protected and sustained."

As a group of scholars working on the social aspect of sustainability, our collective aim has been similar—to focus on the place of people, social goals, and social processes in the context of what Larsen has called the "quest" for sustainability that is occurring at many different organizational and geographical levels.

Despite the complex mix of individuals, constituencies, and organizations engaged in defining and working for greater social sustainability, Kristen Magis and Craig Shinn glean from the multiple discourses "four universal principles [that] emerge—human well-being, equity, democratic government, and democratic civil society." These themes are still emergent because, as Mary King has demonstrated for the field of economics, even within the boundaries of a discipline, progress on the thinking about one aspect of sustainability is still too often occurring without regard for the need to integrate key advances in others.

Clearly, the scholarship on the social aspect of sustainability, and sustainability more generally, is not yet integrated or comprehensive. As Larsen says, the science of sustainability is young, so key principles are only starting to coalesce. The field is so nascent that participants do not yet have a clear view of each other. Randy Bluffstone's chapter (Chapter 7) shows that our awareness of the issues critical to the achievement of sustainability needs to be much expanded so that, as in the case he presents, policymakers concerned with environmental outcomes such as deforestation also think about social impacts, such as incentives for the use of child labor. Working collectively as scholars on this volume, we have not set out to provide a comprehensive view of the social aspect of sustainability, but to add our efforts to illuminate those aspects we are each best fitted to investigate. An integrated science of the social aspect of sustainability is still in the future, although we believe this volume represents a step down that path.

Key elements are, however, increasingly clear. As Kristen Magis and Gary Larsen have both noted, civil society is providing the impetus for greater social sustainability. Veronica Dujon (Chapter 6) demonstrates that this notion is true even where we might least expect it: poor people in poor countries, organized in social movements, are effectively demanding socially and environmentally sustainable policies from their governments and, in the process, successfully confronting large global forces and powerful transnational corporations.

Nongovernmental organizations and social movements are pressing interests not well represented even in many countries with formally democratic electoral processes. Non-governmental organizations (NGOs) and social movements are presented as playing a crucial role as countervailing powers to business interests and to governments that have been captured by business elites. However, NGOs are not inherently democratically representative. Certainly in the United States, we have seen the political influence of concentrated wealth exercised in the domestic policy arena through nonprofit think tanks.

An aspect of the quest for social sustainability—for full human development—may be the demand for more effective democracy, as well as an energetic civil society. It has become clear that formally democratic institutions in many nations cannot avoid excessive influence by monied interests. Also, some countries may simply be too diverse (geographically, culturally, ethnically, etc.) for effective representation of people in different circumstances and regions. Evolving systems of governance that currently appear facilitative of a more effective democracy include the systems of solidarity and local empowerment along the lines implemented in the European Union, the decentralized planning taking place in Kerala, India, and the participatory budgeting programs in Brazil. A strong effective local voice may be necessary not only for a truly democratic process, but also to ensure that decisions reflect local knowledge and concerns. As demonstrated in Randy Bluffstone's chapter, a national-level policy codifying communal property rights regimes may have unintended consequences in particular settings—in this case, increased reliance on child labor.

Empowering local groups will not adequately meet the clearly emerging need for sustainability-oriented regulation by the state. As Jan Bebbington and Jesse Dillard (Chapter 8) have clarified, the impacts of large corporations on social sustainability may be quite far flung, affecting not only employees and shareholders, but also consumers, suppliers, and the communities surrounding any site of related activity. As demonstrated by

Jesse Dillard and David Layzell (Chapter 9), the standards for social sustainability to which even a progressive and profitable corporation will hold itself will tend to be low and utilitarian, with an eye toward public relations, rather than as directed by the needs of the community. In contexts of self-regulation, no wider democratic process will inform the allocation of corporate resources toward social ends.

Small businesses cannot hope to compete if they take on social obligations substantially larger than those shouldered by their competitors, as was expressed clearly in the interviews conducted by Kathryn Thomsen and Mary King (Chapter 10). Only regulation will effectively "take sustainability standards out of competition," to paraphrase the wisdom of the U.S. labor movement arguing for industry-wide wage norms. That the current rage for "triple-bottom line accounting" cannot be expected to substitute for regulation is the message of Darrell Brown, Jesse Dillard, and Scott Marshall (Chapter 11).

When confronted with the challenge of strong interests, especially those pursuing economic gain, that directly oppose efforts for greater sustainability, regulation may often be required. In other situations, behavior might be changed by widespread implementation of codes that encapsulate standards. Clearly, the standards developed for green buildings have had substantial impact, supported by market interest in environmental options.

In other situations, what is required may be a change in "habits," as Veblen characterized entrenched institutions. Barry Messer and Kevin Kecskes (Chapter 13) demonstrate how a public university can orient itself toward education for the community in a way that develops social capital, or the "soft infrastructure" that constitutes community capacity. In the case of the Community Watershed Stewardship Program they showcase, Portland State University faculty and students are implementing "soft" solutions to divert waste water from the river, which could obviate the need for a large, expensive "hard" technological fix while also building skills and relationships. Their findings are echoed by Jan Semenza's (Chapter 14) contribution, demonstrating the ability of social efforts to overcome the negative impact of an urban landscape designed for efficiency rather than community development.

Leslie McBride (Chapter 12) has shown that local policy efforts can facilitate the development of sustainable community food systems that not only meet the environmental and economic sustainability benchmarks they were designed to achieve, but also contribute to social sustainability, as defined in a specific, multifaceted, and comprehensive way. Concrete policy actions can pave the way for a flourishing system of farmers markets and community gardens that provide fresh, local food and social centers, while supporting local farmers.

Each of the implementation efforts showcased in this section of the book concentrates on local projects that are geographically contained. Nevertheless, we recognize that many of the most difficult challenges to sustainability engage dynamics that are now global in scope. These require coordinated international action, building on the institutional infrastructure of the United Nations, the International Labour Organisation, the World Bank, international treaties on trade and other issues, as well as environmental accords, and nongovernmental organizations.

Achieving socially sustainable societies is an iterative project that simultaneously requires defining what the concept means, conditions necessary for pursuing social sustainability, ways we might measure the outcomes of policy and action directed toward that end so that progress can be assessed and adjustments made. The chapters in this anthology reflect an initial, but ambitious, effort to introduce and engage some of the key concerns in understanding the social aspects of sustainability from a multidisciplinary perspective. At this point in the effort, given the areas of the authors' substantive interests, we can comment on some fundamental realizations and point the way for future deliberation and research. Undoubtedly this is a modest beginning—a considerable amount of work remains to be done.

We would like to close with several observations based on an attempt at understanding the social aspect of sustainability. To adequately address social sustainability requires a significant interdisciplinary effort that includes expertise from such social science fields as anthropology, sociology and cultural studies, public administration, political science, social work and public health, economics, and business, as well as architecture, environmental studies, and engineering. We see this collection of studies as a first step.

We began this anthology by identifying eight interrelated issues that framed our conversation. The research reported herein confirms the relevance of these issues, as well as the necessity and potential for further work in these areas. The essential overarching question is the place of government as an extension of civil society and the role of democracy in forming, facilitating, and monitoring social sustainability. Within the current sociopolitical context, the core issue relates to government's responsibilities as compared with the private sector. Within the context of Western, democratic capitalism, the central debate concerns the compatibility of a market-driven economy with the pursuit of social sustainability. The resolution primarily depends on assessing the value of codification and government regulation, as opposed to voluntary compliance in motivating socially responsible behavior. Within a society, we must articulate the diverse roles that different institutions and entities might play in attaining and sustaining social sustainability. We also must consider the differences in rights and responsibilities of developed compared with developing countries and the need for local, global, and integrative strategies. Finally, there is a need to identify and develop useful measures of social sustainability, whereby we could motivate and gauge progress in all these areas. The work reported herein has provided rudimentary theoretical and empirical inclinations for moving the agenda forward.

We have presented no clear and measurable specification of social sustainability as an end state, and we have come to believe that it is inappropriate to do so. Several chapters reiterated the analytical value of conceptualizing social sustainability as a process by which the pursuit of better living conditions reflects the collective actions of community members. Human development premised on social health, equity, and democratic society is a superior path to socially sustainable societies than economic development models that focus on raising Gross Domestic Product per capita that exclude nonmarket areas of self-provisioning by households and communities. Market-oriented approaches that presume that the stimulation of market forces is sufficient to correct imbalances between social consumption and the limits of natural resources once they become known also fall short of making reliable progress toward social sustainability.

Powerful players in the market concentrate on maximizing shareholder wealth and will compromise that objective in the interest of environmental and social well-being only when regulations require it. Large businesses that use the triple bottom line notion as a metric and measure to promote practices that enhance social sustainability experience severe challenges in specification and measurement of social goods such as social cohesion, flourishing communities, or human rights protections.

The evidence collected suggests that states do have a valuable role to play in holding markets accountable to the needs of society by regulating market behavior particularly at the local and national levels. In the context of active, healthy, and multiple economic actors, voluntary compliance in the form of corporate social responsibility is unable to produce the fundamental adjustments needed within businesses for effective change because of the constraints of the wider economic structure that favor growth and wealth accumulation for specific economic actors over general social health. In other contexts, predominantly in the developing world, where the number of effective economic actors is few and the excluded many, states have a responsibility to intervene to enhance general social health and human well-being by facilitating investment in people-centered development. States do not automatically accept that responsibility, however. People, as democratic actors, can make them.

Perhaps the single most significant conclusion of the chapters in this volume, sometimes explicit and sometimes not, is the central role of people as social, economic, and political actors to demand and create environments and institutions that support human well-being. Magis and Shinn give primacy to democratic society as one of the four primary dimensions of social sustainability. From a Third World perspective, Dujon examines the political power of excluded economic actors to hold states accountable by mobilizing their civil society associations. In the First World, and at a more local level, Semenza, McBride, Messer, and Kecskes examine community-level actions that range from small neighborhoods to city and county policy development to community and university partnerships.

As we look forward, it is clear that a great deal of work remains to be done in all areas to better understand the impetus to greater social sustainability, the emerging conditions that foster social sustainability, the strategies that will promote greater social sustainability, and the measures that will guide our progress. Building an expanded library of examples and case studies will be critical. Empirical work, based on measures such as the Human Development Index, the Human Well-Being Index, child poverty rates, the goals of the U.N. Universal Declaration of Human rights and others, will allow us to assess the impact of regulatory and voluntary strategies.

We expect that, even as we gain analytical clarity on the dimensions of the social aspect of sustainability, our understanding of what that means in different places and times will evolve, as will our measures and strategies. In reaching for social sustainability, we are engaged in a social process, rather than working toward a clear and unchanging goal.

Contributors

Jan Bebbington is Professor of Accounting and Sustainable Development in the School of Management at the University of St. Andrews and the Director of the St. Andrews Sustainability Institute. She is also Vice-Chair (Scotland) of the Sustainable Development Commission. Jan has extensive experience of educating for sustainable development, both within her discipline of social and environmental accounting as well as in interdisciplinary settings. Jan's own research interests focus around the dual themes of corporate social reporting on sustainable development and full-cost accounting and modeling. In the area of full-cost accounting, Professor Bebbington has worked with many organizations that are seeking to model their sustainable development impacts, and especially their externalities, in the context of project appraisal processes.

Randall Bluffstone is Associate Professor of Economics at Portland State University. His research and teaching interests focus on various aspects of environmental and resource economics, including pollution policies in developing and transition economies, environmental liability and privatization, deforestation in low-income countries, and the economics of suburban sprawl. Prior to September 1999, Dr. Bluffstone was deputy director of the International Environment Program at the Harvard Institute for International Development (HIID) at Harvard University. Dr. Bluffstone received his PhD in economics from Boston University in 1993, and from 1983 to 1985, he was a Peace Corps volunteer in Nepal.

Darrell Brown teaches and researches at Portland State University, where he started in the fall of 1994. His primary teaching responsibilities are accounting information systems and managerial accounting. Darrell's current research interests relate to the decision-usefulness of corporate environmental reports and the use of environmental metrics to inform stakeholders of corporate behaviors. He teaches several interdisciplinary sustainability courses centering on metrics.

Jesse Dillard currently holds the Retzlaff Chair in Accounting, is Director of the Center for Professional Integrity and Accountability in the School of Business at Portland State University, and holds an honorary appointment in the University of Sheffield's Management School. He is the founding editor of *Accounting and the Public Interest* and has published widely in the accounting and business literature. His current interests relate to the ethical and public interest applications of administrative and information technology particularly as they affect social and environmental accountability.

Veronica Dujon is Associate Professor and Chair of the Department of Sociology at Portland State University, where she coteaches a graduate course on Social Sustainability with Barbara Dudley and Mary C. King. She also teaches courses on environmental sociology and the sociology of globalization. She received her BA in History and Spanish from the University of the West-Indies, Cave Hill Campus, and a PhD in Land Resources/Environmental Sociology at the University of Wisconsin–Madison.

Kevin Kecskes is the Director for Community–University Partnerships at Portland State University. He has spent a dozen years in the developing world in various capacities and formally studied at Boston College, Harvard University, and Portland State University. Kevin has numerous peer-reviewed journal articles and book chapters. He recently edited *Engaging Departments: Moving Faculty Culture from Private to Public, Individual to Collective Focus for the Common Good* (2006, Anker Publications).

Mary C. King is Professor of Economics at Portland State University, where she coteaches a graduate course on Social Sustainability with Veronica Dujon and Barbara Dudley. Her research focuses on the dynamics of sex and race in the economy, labor markets, and sustainability. She received a BA in Economics from Stanford University, studied at Oxford University as a Rhodes Scholar and earned a PhD in Economics from the University of California at Berkeley.

Gary L. Larsen, Forest Supervisor of the Mt. Hood National Forest for 12 years, was Senior Natural Resource Policy Advisor for President Clinton's Council on Sustainable Development and lead U.S. negotiator for forestry and natural resource issues for the UN Earth Summit in Rio de Janeiro in 1992. He has been the International Agreements Officer and head of strategic planning for U.S Forest Service International Forestry Deputy Area. Prior to becoming Forest Supervisor, he was Chief of Staff for the Undersecretary for Natural Resources and Environment, U.S. Department of Agriculture. He is currently working on his PhD in Public Administration and Policy at Portland State University.

David Layzell is a Fellow of the Institute of Chartered Accountants in England and Wales. He recently retired after 26 years at Intel Corporation where he held a number of senior finance positions and most recently ran the Corporation's Business Ethics function. He is currently Associate Director of the Centre for Professional Integrity and Accountability at Portland State University and teaches Accounting and Ethics at the University. His interest is in the Philosophy of Corporations in Modern Capitalism and hopes to save Western Democratic Capitalism by encouraging conversation between business and the academy.

Kristen Magis is owner of the Leadership Institute in Silverton, Oregon, and research fellow at the Hatfield School of Government at Portland State University, Portland, Oregon. She received a Masters in Management from Brandeis University and a Doctor of Philosophy in Public Administration and Policy from Portland State University. Her research agenda includes social justice, sustainability, global civil society and democratic governance. Her recent work includes; research on Global Civil Society coalitions' proclivity to find collective voice in diversity, and consultation with the U.S. Roundtable on Sustainable Forests to develop a measurement protocol for Community Resilience, a social indicator new to the Montreal Process Criteria and Indicators.

Scott Marshall is the SBA Corporate Partners Professor and Director of the Center for Design and Innovation for Business & Sustainability at the School of Business, Portland State University. His research focuses on environmental strategies, certification systems, and corporate reporting. He has published a number of articles in leading academic journals, including *California Management Review, Journal of International Business Studies, Business Strategy & the Environment, Organization & Environment*, and *Journal of Information Systems*.

Leslie McBride is Associate Professor of Community Health at Portland State University. Since 2003, she has been exploring the role of community food systems in developing social sustainability and civic capacity, including case study work examining the role of regional and sustainable food systems in public health and higher education.

W. Barry Messer is Assistant Professor of Urban Studies and Planning at Portland State University. His professional experience includes nearly 20 years in public service as a community development director for an NGO and as a chief administrative officer for county government. As a faculty member, teaching and research experience has included numerous sponsored research activities, publications, and projects involving community-based environmental management initiatives and community–university partnerships.

Jan C. Semenza is a senior expert at the European Centre for Disease Prevention and Control (ECDC), a new public health agency in Europe founded in the aftermath of the SARS pandemic and at the dawn of the recurrent avian influenza outbreaks. He also is a faculty member at Oregon Health and Science University and at Portland State University, teaching in the Oregon Master's of Public Health Program. He has conducted extensive research in the biomedical and public health field and was awarded a Certificate of Commendation from the City of Chicago in 1995, when he led the CDC response to the heat wave that killed more than 700 people. He identified social isolation as a major risk factor for heat-related mortality and has since developed intervention strategies to advance social sustainability.

Craig Shinn is Associate Professor of Public Administration and Associate Director of Executive Leadership Institute in the Hatfield School of Government at Portland State University, where he coordinates the concentration in environmental and natural resource policy. His research interests center on questions of environmental governance, including administrative aspects of adaptive management, social aspects of sustainability, civic capacity building, and interjurisdictional administration of natural resources.

Kathryn Thomsen is a climate change mitigation consultant for EcoSecurities in Portland, Oregon. Previously a small business owner, she completed a master's degree in 2006 from Portland State University, where she focused on energy, environmental, and sustainable economics.

Index

For Product Safety Concerns and Information please contact our EU
representative GPSR@taylorandfrancis.com Taylor & Francis Verlag GmbH,
Kaufingerstraße 24, 80331 München, Germany

Printed and bound by CPI Group (UK) Ltd, Croydon, CR0 4YY
08/05/2025
01864511-0002